WITHDRAWN

Slavery in South Africa

Slavery in South Africa

Captive Labor on the Dutch Frontier

EDITED BY

Elizabeth A. Eldredge
and Fred Morton

Westview Press

BOULDER • SAN FRANCISCO • OXFORD

University of Natal Press

PIETERMARITZBURG

This book is included in Westview's African Modernization and Development Series (Paul Lovejoy, Series Editor).

Published in 1994 in the United States of America by Westview Press, Inc., 5500 Central Avenue, Boulder, Colorado 80301-2877, and in the United Kingdom by Westview Press, 36 Lonsdale Road, Summertown, Oxford OX2 7EW

Published in 1994 in South Africa by The University of Natal Press, P.O. Box 375, Pietermaritzburg 3200

Library of Congress Cataloging-in-Publication Data
Slavery in South Africa : captive labor on the Dutch Frontier / edited
    by Elizabeth A. Eldredge and Fred Morton.
        p.   cm. — ([African modernization and development])
    Includes bibliographical references and index.
    ISBN 0-8133-8473-7
        1. Slavery—South Africa—History—18th century.   2. Slavery—
South Africa—History—19th century.   3. Blacks—South Africa—
History—18th century.   4. Blacks—South Africa—History—19th
century.   I. Eldredge, Elizabeth A.   II. Morton, Fred, 1939–   .
III. Series: African modernization and development series.
HT1394.S6S57   1994
306.3'62'0968—dc20   94-20527
                                                                                         CIP

ISBN 0-86980-907-5 (S. Africa)

Printed and bound in the United States of America

The paper used in this publication meets the requirements
of the American National Standard for Permanence of Paper
for Printed Library Materials Z39.48-1984.

10   9   8   7   6   5   4   3   2   1

Dedicated to our parents,

Glenna B. and M. Byron Morton
and
Charlotte M. and Donald H. Eldredge

Contents

Illustrations

Acknowledgments

Among the many who contributed in one way or another to the appearance of this volume, the editors wish to thank in particular Dr. Robert C. -H. Shell, for his contributions to the bibliography and for drawing our attention to the Bell sketches; The Brenthurst Library, Johannesburg, for permission to reproduce a sketch from the Charles Davidson Bell collection; Jan C.A. Boeyens, for obtaining photographs of the Struben sketches; Mrs. R. Krause, for permission to reproduce the Alexander Struben sketch of the attack on the VhaVenda; the Transvaal Archives Depot, Pretoria, for permission to reproduce Alexander Struben's sketch of Schoemansdal; Barry Morton, for alerting us to Thomas Baines's watercolor; and the editors of *South African Historical Journal* and *African Economic History*, for permission to publish in chapters 3, 7, and 8 the revised versions of articles appearing previously in their journals.

We are also grateful for the generous support of the Department of History and the Vice President of Academic Affairs, Loras College, who aided this project with funds for mailing, photocopying, faxing, graphics, and copyediting. Diane Neumeister and other members of the Wahlert Memorial Library at Loras College have provided much valuable and cheerful service. Thanks also to the Department of History, Michigan State University, for its financial help with photocopies and postage.

Especially fond gratitude is reserved for Sue Morton and David Plank, whose support and patience made it possible for us to produce this volume.

Elizabeth A. Eldredge
Fred Morton

Abbreviations

AR	Algemene Rijksarchief
BN	*Bechuanaland News* (Vryburg)
BNA	Botswana National Archives
C.	Command Paper, Parliamentary Papers
CAD	Cape Archives Depot
CJ	Court of Justice
CO	Colonial Office records
COCP	Colonial Office Confidential Prints
CWMA	Council for World Missions Archives (London Missionary Society)
DO	Deeds Office
DRC	Dutch Reformed Church
DRCA	Dutch Reformed Church Archives, Cape Town
DSAB	*Dictionary of South African Biography*
EVR	*Argief van die Sekretaris van die Eerste Volksraad van die ZAR*
GJ	*Graham's town Journal* (Grahamstown)
HC	High Commissioner
HCS	H.C. Stiemens Collection, Transvaal Archives Depot
IUATM	Indiana University Archives of Traditional Music
LL	Landdrost Lyndenburg
LM	(H.C.V.) Liebbrandt's Manuscripts
LMS	London Missionary Society
LMS-SOAS	London Missionary Society Archives, School of Oriental and African Studies (London)
MAB	*Mahoko A Becwana* (Kuruman)
MN	(*Wesleyan*) *Missionary Notices* (London)
MOOC	Master of Orphan Chamber
NM	*Natal Mercury* (Durban)
OFS	Orange Free State
PEMS	Paris Evangelical Missionary Society
PRO	Public Record Office, Kew Gardens
R	Inkomende Stukke
RCC	*Records of the Cape Colony*
Rds	(*Rijksdaalders*) Rixdollars

RH	Rhodes House (Oxford)
RLR	Receiver of Land Revenue
RPS	Report of the Protector of Slaves
SAR Tvl	South African Archival Records, *Notule van die Volksraad van die Suid-Afrikaanse Republiek (Volledig met Alle Bylae Daarby), Transvaal*
SM	Special magistrate
SS	Argief van die Staatsekretaris (Archives of the State Secretary)
STB	Stellenbosch Records (indexed in the Cape Archives as 1/STB)
Supl	Supplementêre stukke
TA	*Transvaal Argus* (Pretoria)
TAD	Transvaal Archives Depot
UCT	University of Cape Town
Uitv	*Uitvoerende* [Raad] (Executive Council of the SAR)
URB	*Uitvoerende Raadsbesluit* (Resolution of the Executive Council)
VC	Verbatim Copy, Governor's Journal
VOC	Verenigde Oostindische Compagnie (Dutch East India Company)
WP	Willoughby Papers, Selly Oak College, Birmingham
ZA	*De Zuid-Afrikaan*
ZAR	Zuid Afrikaansche Republiek (South African Republic)
ZNA	Zimbabwe National Archives (Harare)

Glossary

agterryers	African auxiliaries
amabutho	military regiments (among Nguni-speakers)
assagai	wooden spear, often tipped with a metal blade
balata	servile groups (among BaTswana)
batlhanka	slaves, servants (among BaTswana), sing. motlhanka
bijwoner	client, sharecropper
biltong	dried game meat, venison
botlhanka	indigenous servitude (among BaTswana)
burgher	a white, Dutch-speaking land owner
commando	armed, mounted party
complot	plot, conspiracy
dienstoende	labor service
difaqane	SeSotho term, an equivalent of mfecane, q.v.
dikgosana	headmen
drift	ford
droster	deserter, escapee
field-cornet	district police officer, military officer
heemrad(en)	district councillor(s)
inboekeling(e)	indentured servant (s), slave(s)
inboeksel	certificate of indenture
inboekstelsel	indenture system
inkosi	ruler, king
inkosi enkhulu	king
kaptein	chief
kaross	a rug or blanket made from dressed furs
kgosi	ruler, king, pl. dikgosi
kgotla	public square, assembly, court (among BaTswana)
kloof	cliff, perch
knecht	VOC servant, sometimes hired out
(knob)kierie	wooden club with a knotted end
kraal	homestead, usually associated with stock keepers
landdrost	district magistrate, military commander
legplaatsen	pastures

mafisa	loan-cattle system
mandoor	slave overseer
Mantatee	SeSotho-, SeTswana-speaking refugees (1830s)
mfecane	a period of conflict in southern Africa in the late eighteenth, early nineteenth centuries (IsiZulu term)
molata	slaves, servants pl. lelata
motlhanka	see batlhanka
Mozbiekers	slaves imported to the Cape from Mozambique
opgaaf	tribute, tax (Transvaal)
smousen	itinerant traders
trekboer	European (usually Dutch) Cape frontier pastoralist
veldkos	wild, gathered food
veldwagtmeester	field-cornet (q.v.) in VOC-controlled Cape
Wagmeester	Also veldwagtmeester/field-cornet

Terms and Designations

"South Africa" refers to the Union and Republic, whereas "south Africa" refers to the area prior to 1910.

Khoisan, Bantu, or Dutch (Afrikaans) terms used in the volume may be found in the glossary. Terms that are seldom encountered in south African historical literature are italicized. Khoisan-, Bantu-, and Dutch-speaking persons, groups, and polities are designated as far as possible by the names preferred at the time by those to whom the names refer.

Khoisan-speaking persons (i.e., speakers of the so-called "click" languages) are the most difficult to represent because no eighteenth- and nineteenth-century recorder appears to have learned their languages or understood their societies, almost all of which have since disappeared. The generic and usually derisory terms for Khoisan people (e.g., Hottentot, Bushmen, etc.) appear throughout the literature and are unsatisfactory on a number of counts, but usually only such references survive. Thus, writers in this volume either enclose in quotation marks a designation used by an observer, italicize a designation that assumed some consistency of meaning (even if derisory) in a given time and place, or ascribe the more neutral and somewhat more precise Khoikhoi or San. Derisory terms for groups originating from among Khoisan speakers, such as the Bastaards or the BaSarwa, are used without emphasis when they have been adopted by the persons concerned.

Bantu-speaking persons (i.e., speakers *inter alia* of Nguni languages [AmaZulu, AmaXhosa, etc.], Northern and Southern Sotho [BaSotho, Ba-Pedi, etc.], and Western and Eastern Tswana [BaKgatla, BaTawana, etc.]) are designated with the proper prefixes rather than with the root term (e.g., Zulu, Tswana, etc.), because prefixes are uniformly standard in these modern southern African languages, in both written and spoken form. Prefixes may denote a group (e.g., AmaSwati), a person (e.g., MoKwena), or a language or custom (e.g., IsiNdebele).

Dutch-speaking persons (i.e., speakers of eighteenth- and nineteenth-century Dutch and its south African offshoots, such as Afrikaans) include persons of diverse European and African origin. Difficulties arise when using terms that are both descriptive (e.g., *boere*, farmers) and ascriptive (e.g., Boers). As a rule, individual and group names in this volume are capitalized (e.g., Boer, Griqua, Voortrekker), whereas terms referring to social or economic categories within European societies are either italicized or, if commonly known, rendered in lowercase (e.g., *trekboers*, burghers).

About the Contributors

Jan C. A. Boeyens is Senior Lecturer in the Department of Anthropology & Indigenous Law at the University of South Africa. His master's thesis, "Die Konflik tussen die Venda en die Blankes in Transvaal, 1864–1869," was published in the *Archives Year Book for South African History* (1990). He is the author of several articles on the history of Zoutpansberg and is writing his doctoral thesis on the later prehistory and early history of the Marico.

Elizabeth A. Eldredge is Associate Professor of History at Michigan State University. She is the author of *A South African Kingdom: The Pursuit of Security in Nineteenth Century Lesotho* (1993) and co-author with Robert Edgar of *The Historical Dictionary of Lesotho*, new edition (forthcoming).

John Edwin Mason is Assistant Professor in the Department of History and Center for African Studies, University of Florida, and in 1993–1994 Senior Fellow at the Carter G. Woodson Institute for Afro-American and African Studies, University of Virginia. He is the author of *"Fit for Freedom": Slavery and Emancipation in South Africa* (forthcoming) and several articles on the emancipation period in the Cape colony.

Barry Morton is a Ph.D. candidate at Indiana University and a Fulbright-Hays Fellow researching the colonial history of Ngamiland. He is the author of *Pre-Colonial Botswana: An Annotated Bibliography and Guide to the Sources* (1994), co-author with Jeff Ramsay of *The Historical Dictionary of Botswana*, revised edition (forthcoming) and *The Making of a President: Sir Ketumile Masire's Early Years* (forthcoming), and co-author with Jeff Ramsay and Temba Mgadla of *A History of Botswana to 1910* (forthcoming).

Fred Morton is Professor of History at Loras College. He is the author of *Children of Ham: Freed Slaves and Fugitive Slaves on the Kenya Coast, 1873 to 1907* (1990), co-author with Andrew Murray and Jeff Ramsay of *The Historical Dictionary of Botswana*, new edition (1989), and co-editor with Jeff Ramsay of *The Birth of Botswana: A History of the Bechuanaland Protectorate from 1910 to 1966* (1987).

Nigel Penn is Lecturer in the Department of History at the University of Cape Town. He is the author of several articles on northern Cape frontier history and is writing his doctoral thesis, "The Northern Cape Frontier Zone, 1700–1815," for the University of Cape Town.

Robert C.-H. Shell is Assistant Professor of History and Director of African Studies at Princeton University. He is the author of *Children of Bondage: A Social and Economic History of Slavery in the Cape of Good Hope, 1652–1838* (1994) and many articles on Cape history.

1

Slavery and South African Historiography

Fred Morton

Though attention to south African slavery began more than a half century ago with the appearance of Isobel Edwards' *Towards Emancipation: a Study of South African Slavery*, scholars have yet to determine the extent to which the institution was practiced. By and large, the study of slavery has been restricted to the western Cape, where in the seventeenth and eighteenth centuries the Dutch East India Company imported slaves from other parts of Africa, Madagascar, and the East Indies to work for company employees and private grain and wine estate owners. The most recent, and substantial, published studies of south African slavery are concerned with slaves imported into the Cape under Dutch rule and conclude with the abolition of legal slavery (1834) under British rule.[1] The possibility that slavery existed outside the western Cape on any significant scale, or that south Africans themselves were systematically enslaved, has not been entertained until recently.[2] Yet, the studies in this volume demonstrate that thousands in the interior were indeed captured, traded, or held as chattel. On the expanding "Dutch frontier,"[3] slave raiding was part of a process of dispossessing indigenes of their cattle and land for commercial gain. Frontier slaving began at least a century before legal abolition and continued decades after. As early as the 1730s, commandos captured Khoisan on the western Cape frontier and bound them to servitude; and as late as the 1870s on the fringes of the Transvaal, slave raids on SeTswana-, SeSotho-, and Nguni-speaking peoples were conducted. Along the moving horizon of the "Great Trek," peoples living in the eastern and northern Cape, Orange Free State, and Natal were attacked and seized. Most of the slave raiders were Boers aided by African allies, and most of the Africans they captured were children. Young captive laborers, often bound to Boer households and

raised to adulthood without parents or kin, helped to sustain and consolidate the advancing Dutch frontier. They served as herders, hunters,
artisans, farmers, drivers, domestics, messengers, and in some cases even as
raiders themselves. The neglect of their history deserves comment in its
own right, especially given that information about slavery on the frontier
has long been available in published sources.

A volume such as this is overdue in part because the literature on slavery
has limited itself in comparing the Cape only with other European colonies.
Since the 1950s a growing literature on comparative slavery has described
how slaves, especially as plantation laborers, were integrated into the
mercantile system.[4] Once Cape slavery itself began to receive systematic
scrutiny with the appearance of studies by Greenstein (1973), Böeseken
(1977), and Armstrong (1979), discussion emphasized the Cape's similari-
ties with the southern United States, where plantation slave labor made
possible the development of an expanding frontier of white settlement.[5]
Cape slavery seemingly lacked a parallel in Africa, notwithstanding a few
articles to the contrary by Shell, and attention to the growing literature on
African slavery was thus averted.[6] In certain respects, Cape slavery *was* like
slavery in other contemporary European colonies and unlike slavery in
other parts of the African continent. For example, plantation slaves were
imported there by water rather than by land, and slaves were rarely brought
from the interior for plantation work or for export. Yet, though slavery in
the environs of Cape Town resembled plantation slavery elsewhere, slavery
on the Cape frontier did not. For, as will become apparent, the Cape's
Dutch-speaking frontiersmen and settlers captured and traded indigenes,
rather than imported slaves from overseas. And, in contrast to the Western
Hemisphere, where *conquistadores*, planters, and mine developers readily
enslaved or drove off Amerindians as they seized their territories, south
Africa's frontier was entered initially by Dutch-speaking hunters, traders,
and pastoralists, who moved and settled often amidst equally, if not more,
powerful African communities. In order to satisfy their demand for slave
labor, they promoted conflicts among Africans and cultivated African allies
rather than depended on a strategy of outright conquest. Behind the settled
western Cape, slavery expanded along the frontier as an African institution.

Three generations of frontier historians have passed over the slavery
question, combing as they were the eighteenth and nineteenth centuries for
incipient forces that ultimately shaped modern South Africa. Europeaniza-
tion, race and ethnicity, liberalism, Afrikaner nationalism, African resistance, capitalism, and class formation have in rough sequence claimed
priority, all without noting the causes, patterns, and extent of frontier
enslavement.[7] Throughout the literature on preindustrial south Africa,
neglect of this important dimension of frontier history is revealed in the
eerie consistency with which captive laborers are referred to as "appren-

tices" and "servants," even by such disparate and eminent scholars as Macmillan, Marais, Marks, and Elphick.[8] Discomfort in accounting for a sizable coerced element in frontier societies has been present at least since Legassick's monumental study of Transorangia began italicizing these terms.[9] Nowadays, in the wake of the neo-Marxist debate, captive laborers are also referred to as "serfs," "dependents," or "unfree servants," but apart from indicating what position in a given class structure they occupied, their presence in frontier societies generally remains at best only partially accounted for. Typically, Legassick's own evolving interpretation of nineteenth- and twentieth-century south Africa reflects in his terminology a persistent ambivalence about captive laborers on the frontier, drifting as it does from "apprentices" to "proletarians" to "dependents," terms he sometimes uses interchangeably.[10] And Legassick, as with others who note their common presence on the frontier, can state with reference to Khoisan "dependents" that such persons were "[seized] as captives...subordinated...or distributed or sold...," that "obtaining [arms and powder] generally meant selling cattle, or selling 'apprentices,'" and that "it seems reasonable to suppose that the 'normal' position of the Khoi was seen as slavery [by persons living in the Cape]."[11]

Historians who acknowledge that "virtual slavery," at least, existed on the frontier have for some time argued nevertheless that it resulted from "individual acts of violence and brigandage" rather than from what this volume shows was part of a process of expansion and consolidation.[12] At first glance, Giliomee appears to have defined this process. "The trekboers of the eighteenth century," he comments, "brought to the interior the cultural tradition of slavery and were gradually able to transform free indigenous peoples into unfree laborers."[13] But for Giliomee the "cultural tradition of slavery" did not result in the extension of slavery into the interior, and Giliomee does not mean by "unfree laborers" that Africans were as a rule captured, bonded, and sold. He refers instead to individual Africans and African groups who in varying degrees were coerced into providing labor, up to and including the establishment of mining labor compounds. Giliomee distinguishes between what he terms the "open" frontier, the scene of "local coercion" of labor, and the "closing" frontier, "where the state and the market played a growing part in providing labor." Only in the former were raiding and indentureship "resorted to" by frontiersmen, who because of a "lack of market opportunities...did not make a concerted effort to find long term solutions to their labor problems," whereas in the "closing" frontier the "central government...sought to harness the labor of Africans more effectively...[in response to] commercial opportunities." Thus "local coercion" (indenturing children) gave way to "institutional coercion" (taxation, tenancy, and pass laws).[14]

Yet, at least insofar as captive labor was concerned, the distinction between open and closing frontiers was in practice indiscernible. For, in areas controlled by a Boer central government, just as in areas contested by Boer frontiersmen and indigenous African polities, captive laborers remained in demand. Raids for captives were commanded by elected state officials as often as they were by local frontiersmen. State builders and frontiersmen alike raided for slaves *because* captive labor was needed in order to take advantage of market and commercial opportunities. As Etherington notes, commodity production was "prominent on the agenda of the Trekkers," no less than of their successors, and recognizing this fact affords a needed corrective to the established image of the Voortrekkers as "precapitalist, eighteenth-century white nomads in flight from modernizing British rule."[15] Ross makes a similar point with reference to the Griqua, among the earliest Dutch-speaking communities to occupy the frontier, and who, as noted by Eldredge, were engaged in slave raiding.[16] Rather than simply a "cultural tradition" that influenced Boer attitudes toward African labor, slavery was commonly practiced on the frontier, and not exclusively by Boers, as a proved means to economic ends.

Recent recognition that slavery became part of the Dutch frontier may be seen in the work of Nigel Penn. In his study of labor relations between colonists and Khoisan in the western Cape during the eighteenth century, Penn noted a trend away from attracting Khoikhoi labor and stock onto *trekboer* farms through cooperative arrangements, to exercising "paternalistic protection" of the same, and toward confiscating the same through commando raids.[17] The commando system, revealing as it did the "expansionist nature of the Trekboers' pastoralist economy," developed especially after 1770 as a means of crushing Khoikhoi resistance and generating women and children captive laborers. It functioned as an official military arm of the colony, conscripted Khoisan of mixed descent (the so-called "Bastaard-Hottentots") into its ranks, and reflected the declining status of Khoisan within the Cape colony. Alongside the capture of women and children there emerged a new category of *Ingeboekte Bastard Hottentoten* (apprenticed persons of mixed descent), who were liable for bonding to their masters until the age of twenty-five. Apprenticed Khoikhoi children were treated like "Bastaard-Hottentots," and Penn concluded that after 1770 the "status of both free and captive Khoisan differed little from each other, or indeed, from the status of slaves."[18] Penn and other Cape historians, such as Nicholas Southey, have begun to realize that Cape slavery should be viewed alongside indigenous, including apprenticed, labor systems and within the broader context of south African historiography.[19]

This volume's reinterpretation of slavery, and its upward revision of the extent to which slavery was practiced in south Africa, was occasioned by Cobbing's challenge to the AmaZulu-oriented historiography of the *mfecane* (or *difaqane*).[20] Cobbing asserted that the widespread upheavals in the interior, rather than caused by the rise of a militarized AmaZulu state under Shaka, were the result of slave raiding and slave trading by British missionaries and Griqua in the interior and by Portuguese and British traders on the eastern coast. Generations of European historians, he argued, have concealed these crimes by perpetuating the myth of Shaka, the AmaZulu tyrant. Cobbing undermined his slave-trading case, however, by misusing his evidence, and he overlooked that slave raiding was conducted in the interior by Dutch-speaking frontiersmen.[21] Cobbing succeeded, nevertheless, in exposing the literature's fixation on the AmaZulu and its neglect of slavery and slave raiding in the interior. One noteworthy consequence was an open debate of Cobbing's thesis at the University of Witwatersrand in September 1991.[22] Another was the advent of communication among scholars already engaged in studying slavery in different parts of south Africa.[23] Collaboration led to *Slavery in South Africa: Captive Labor on the Dutch Frontier*.

This volume is intended to demonstrate that slavery is of central importance to south African history. Rather than an institution limited to the coastal Cape periphery, slavery spread throughout south Africa, was adapted to fluctuating human and physical environments, and deeply affected the human landscape. It was beyond question an established feature of Boer society. As will also become apparent in this work, slavery remains an underresearched topic. Of the studies to follow, those pertaining to areas outside the Cape have been written by scholars for whom slavery is a recent, secondary research interest. This collection is offered also to suggest the *potential* for systematic archival and oral field research into areas outside the western Cape. *Slavery in South Africa* represents the initial volume in what is hoped will be many to address south African slavery in its broadest context, contributing thereby to the reinterpretation of nineteenth-century south African history and to the comparative study of slavery systems in Africa and in other parts of the globe.

Robert Shell (ch. 2) offers the first statistical overview of the ocean-going slave trade into the Cape (1658-1808) and details the provenance of the Cape's unique, polyglot, Afro-Asian, Dutch-speaking population, which included Khoikhoi captured on the frontier. His study of creolization bridges the divide, so commonly encountered in the literature, between "slaves and Khoikhoi." He demonstrates, *inter alia*, that the Cape's domestic slave culture developed the proto-Afrikaans patois later adopted by slave masters. White domination, much less Dutch cultural hegemony, was by no means absolute, nor is it a coincidence that Afrikaans, the one indigenous language understood by most South Africans and which proved so useful to the Boers in resisting the British, was forged by mainly female slaves of mixed cultural background and free slave-owning women for the purpose of communicating across lines that divided them and resisting those who exploited them.

Nigel Penn (ch. 3) recreates an episode involving *drosters* (runaways) on the eighteenth century northern Cape frontier that illustrates how Khoikhoi, Bastaards, San, and legally defined slaves shared a single status. *Drosters* hailed from all enslaved groups. Fugitive Khoikhoi, Bastaard, and San were chased down, as were legally owned slaves, because they were supposed to be bound to their masters. Penn's study demonstrates that whether imported as slaves or enslaved as indigenes, those bonded on the frontier lived under severe constraints. The northern Cape frontier was brutal, in that much of it was uninhabitable. *Drosters* were desperate, distrustful, and violent. Though united in the desire to escape, competition for scarce resources bound them in conflict. The dilemma faced by the few women who fled their masters was more extreme; they experienced violence meted out by the men with whom they fled, and they were unable to protect their own children. The violence of *drosters* reflected, rather than magnified, the life they had escaped; theirs was an "inhumanity honed by a lifetime of enslavement."

As John Mason demonstrates (in ch. 4), in the eastern Cape in the early nineteenth century the status of slaves resembled closely that of legally free laborers on Boer farms. By the 1830s when slavery was abolished and ex-slaves were regarded under the law as "apprentices," owners had already created in previous decades a system of rewards for their slaves that accorded them more favorable conditions and greater personal autonomy than is customary in slave systems. Slave owners were forced to do so; they had realized that slaves who owned property and raised families were less likely to run away. Such were the "fortunate slaves" described by Mason. Slaves and legally free laborers experienced similar conditions of labor and remained subject to threats and acts of violence from farmers. Their existence remained precarious, but less so than that of the *drosters*, and therefore dependent on the protection of their owners. Slave owners favored abolition of legal slavery, because they had other means with which to control their laborers. In the aftermath of legal slavery, ex-slaves remained with their ex-owners, including those who migrated into the interior as part of the "Great Trek."

Elizabeth Eldredge (ch. 5) reveals the pattern of violent procurement that originated in the Cape and accompanied Griqua, Kora, and Boer expansion onto the highveld. She chronicles slave raiding on the northern Cape frontier between 1790 and 1860 and provides a replete and substantiated survey of slave raiding in Transorangia, much of it unmentioned or glossed over by Legassick, Ross, and Cobbing. She demonstrates that the upheavals of the 1820s and 1830s commonly associated with the so-called *mfecane*, rather than generated by Shaka's AmaZulu or Mzilikazi's AmaNdebele, were caused by drought, competition for food resources, and most importantly by raids for cattle and slaves.

Elizabeth Eldredge then examines (ch. 6) the allegations that the export slave trade from Delagoa bay was a major contributing cause to AmaZulu militarism. She concludes that Delagoa bay, southern Africa's only port involved in the slave export trade, became important in this respect after 1823, by which time Shaka's AmaZulu were well established, and that no evidence is available even to suggest that even then Africans in the interior were engaged in supplying slaves to Delagoa bay, apart from several small groups located near to the Portuguese fort. For reasons of currents and prevailing commercial routes used by European vessels, Delagoa bay remained largely out of reach for the European slave traders, who preferred Madagascar and the more accessible and commercially developed northern Mozambique and Swahili coastal towns. The only slave traders known to have operated in the interior and to have maintained connections with Delagoa bay emerged in the 1840s following the arrival of the Voortrekkers in the eastern and northern Transvaal.

The consequences of slavery's extension into the interior from the Cape are then examined in three distinct settings. Fred Morton (ch. 7) details the system of slave raiding that functioned in the two decades following the Sand River Convention (1852) mainly in the western Transvaal under the leadership of ranking Zuid Afrikaansche Republiek (ZAR) officials. Commando raids were assisted by auxiliaries drawn from resident African groups, the leaders of which amassed followers and personal wealth. The process by which some of the Boers' ex-slaves were assimilated into these African societies is also discussed. Jan Boeyens (ch. 8) describes the captive trade in children and the institution of "apprenticeship" in Zoutpansberg, operated by the northernmost trekkers with support from ZAR officials. Children were taken in outright raids, claimed as tribute, and in some cases obtained through barter with the AmaSwati from among their war prisoners. Of the hundreds "apprenticed" annually before 1870, many were exported for sale in the Boer republics. As far away as the Cape, Zoutpansberg was known as a major source of "black ivory." Barry Morton (ch. 9) explores the long-distance potential of slave trading between Boers and independent African communities, in this case between Marico district Boer traders and the BaTawana of northwestern Botswana, near Angola. Morton as well provides a detailed survey of coerced herding and domestic labor among the BaTswana of the Kalahari before, during, and after the era of slave trading, and reopens discussion of the one area used for comparing slavery in southern Africa with other parts of Africa.

Fred Morton (ch. 10) concludes by attempting in a preliminary way to quantify slave raiding in south Africa in the eighteenth and nineteenth centuries and by developing the themes, arising from the case studies, that are significant for south African historiography and comparative slavery literature. He notes the preponderance of children captives, the relationship between legal apprenticeship and domestic slavery in stock-keeping societies, and the highly adaptive nature of *inboekstelsel* as it was introduced into the highveld from the Cape. He regards apprentices as slaves attached to Boer farmers also using other, less reliable, more costly types of labor. Parallels between Africans bound to Boer farms and herders permanently attached to BaTswana stock owners in the Kalahari demonstrate the importance of further research into pastoral and agricultural labor systems throughout southern Africa before, and since, the mineral revolution.

Notes

1. Ross (1983), Worden (1985), Armstrong and Worden (1988), Watson (1990), and Bank (1991).

2. Newton-King (1981a) showed that on the eastern Cape frontier the Khoisan were victims of slave raiding in the eighteenth and early nineteenth centuries, but the significance of her findings has since languished. Moreover, Phil Bonner on the AmaSwati and Delius, Trapido, and Wagner on the eastern and northern Transvaal uncovered much evidence of slave raiding and slave trading involving the Boers with a variety of African groups but concluded that slavery as an institution did not exist among the Transvaal Boers. Bonner (1983), Delius and Trapido (1983), Wagner (1980). Slavery in the eastern Cape is the subject of Crais (1990), Mason (1991a), and Mason (1992).

3. By "Dutch" is meant "Dutch-speaking," as distinct from Dutch in origin, and includes primarily the *trekboers*, *voortrekkers*, *boers*, and *burghers* of Dutch, French, German, and English origin, together with a much smaller number of Dutch- (and Afrikaans-) speaking groups of mixed origin such as the Griqua, Bastaards, Oorlam, and "Coloured," who were responsible for extending the frontier beyond the western Cape.

4. For a recent summary, see Curtin (1990).

5. See especially Frederickson (1981), ch. 2, and Worden (1985), ch. 1.

6. Lovejoy's comprehensive 1982 study of African slavery, in which he concludes that slavery was practiced systematically in the South African interior by Dutch-speaking frontiersmen, has met with no response from South African scholars, even from those on whose published work Lovejoy inferred his argument. Lovejoy (1982), 232-4.

7. For a detailed overview of trends in south African historiography, see Smith (1988), which however along with earlier surveys of the historical literature ignores the vast anthropological and ethnographical literature, itself laden with historiographical importance.

8. Macmillan (1927), 148, 164 and passim; Marais (1939), 18-9 and passim; Marks (1972); Elphick (1979), 28-30; and Elphick and Malherbe (1989), 24-8.

9. Legassick (1969), 353 and passim.

10. Ibid; Legassick (1977), 176; Legassick (1980), 60-1; Legassick (1989), 368.

11. Legassick (1989), 360, 376, and 372. Crais (1990 & 1992) acknowledges that Boers raided systematically for children on the eastern Cape frontier but includes these youngsters for purposes of analysis in groups labeled as "serf-like tenants," "debt peons," and "unfree dependents" of Boer masters. See also Ross (1986) for a discussion of the "forcible incorporation" of Khoikhoi "proletarians" outside the southwest Cape.

12. The phrase is from Marks and Atmore (1980), 8. See also Crais (1992), 97.

13. Giliomee (1981), 93.

14. Ibid, 86-7. See also Marks and Atmore (1980), 18.

15. Etherington (1991), 16, 19.

16. Ross (1976), 10; ch. 5 by Eldredge in this volume.

17. Penn (1989).

18. Ibid, 17-8.

19. Southey (1992).

20. Cobbing (1988).

21. Eldredge (1992). See below, as well as Eldredge's ch. 5 in this volume.

22. "The 'Mfecane' Aftermath: Towards a New Paradigm." For a summary of this conference, see *South African Historical Journal*, 14 (1991): 3-30. The published proceedings, edited by Carolyn Hamilton, are in press with the University of Witwatersrand Press/University of Natal Press.

23. CAAS York: "Slavery in South Africa: New Issues," chaired by Jan Hogendorn, with papers presented by Eldredge (1991a) and Morton (1991a). ASA St. Louis: "Slavery and Slave Procurement in the South African Cape and Cape Frontier, 1770-1870," chaired by Richard Elphick, discussed by James Armstrong and Paul Lovejoy, with papers presented by Shell (1991), Mason (1991b), Eldredge (1991b), and Morton (1991b).

2

The Tower of Babel:
The Slave Trade and Creolization
at the Cape, 1652–1834

Robert C.-H. Shell

In modern South Africa, the emphasis on ethnicity and race disguises the fact that most of today's descendants of the premodern, immigrant South African population do not know from whence they came. If anything, ignorance of geographical roots has been a primary incentive to classify, legally and socially, all persons in South Africa according to origin and to construct a plethora of odd and exotic identities. Some were legally imposed, such as the "Coloured," others evolved, such as the "Malay." Distorting group origins in South Africa, though, is hardly a modern predilection. From the early years of settlement at the Cape, concocting identities has violated history as certainly as it has advanced the interests of those in power. South Africa's most potent identity, that of the "Afrikaner," has served persons claiming descent from Dutch, English, French, German, and also "free black" origins. Yet the Afrikaner identity, or at least its soul, the Afrikaans language, can be shown to have originated from the richly textured, syncretistic, domestic creole culture of the Cape's slave population and in particular from the crucible of colonial identities—the kitchen.

The complexity of early Cape culture was in part the result of a constantly changing oceanic slave trade to the Cape. Slaves were drawn from a multitude of starkly different geographic and cultural origins, constituting easily the most diverse population of any recorded slave society. Their diversity was apparent in the confusion of languages spoken in Cape households and reemphasized over the years by an unparalleled palette of stereotypes, based on origin. These attitudes were developed, adumbrated, and elaborated by the slave-holding community to rationalize constantly changing labor hierarchies imposed on enslaved people.

Slave creolization undermined the assumptions built into these stereotypes and helped slaves and others overcome the absence of a shared culture at the Cape. Creole languages developed by slaves made it possible for Cape dwellers in general to communicate. The emergence of pidgin and patois languages, a creole culture, and ultimately a lingua franca was the result of slaves' and owners' attempts to forge a medium of communication with each other. This "mighty language," as the Afrikaans poet I.D. du Plessis termed it , the owners would later adopt and call their own. Thus, a changing slave trade, which imported many languages and cultures into the Cape, set in motion a complicated demographic and cultural creolization process that transformed the whole colony.

Slave Origins

Between 1652 and 1808, approximately 63,000 slaves were imported into the Cape from the Indonesian archipelago, India, Madagascar, the Mascarenes, and Africa. Geographically diverse origins within the Cape's slave population were the result of mercantile rivalries, changing shipping patterns, fluctuating trading company fortunes, and shifting commercial alliances between urban slave traders and transient maritime personnel. The ever-changing trade to the Cape is represented in Figure 2.1.[1]

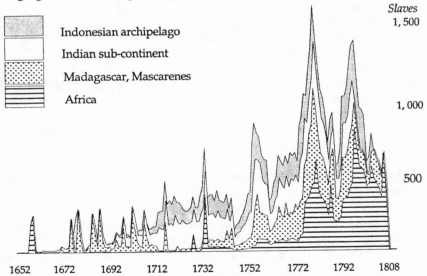

FIGURE 2.1 Origins of 62,964 Slaves Imported to the Cape, 1652 to 1808. *Sources:* based on AR VOC Opgaafs, VOC ships registers, DO Scheepenkennis en Transporten, Samuel Hudson, Journal, Freund (1971), and Boucher (1974).

Until 1792 the basic vectors of the Cape slave trade were determined by rivalry between the Dutch West India Company and Dutch East India Company (VOC). The West India Company, which held a monopoly over west Africa, denied the VOC permission to import slaves from west Africa and early on demanded the award of the Cape colony itself, arguing that Cape Town was technically on the west coast of Africa. The Dutch Estates General rejected this claim, but the West India Company remained hostile to the VOC and turned down its requests, made as late as 1704, to traffic in slaves, even in Angola.[2] Nevertheless, a small number of slaves were smuggled into the Cape from west and west central Africa. One secret expedition to Dahomey in 1658 returned with a few slaves. In the same year, 174 slaves were landed at the Cape from among 500 Angolans seized by a Dutch ship from a captured Portuguese slaver bound for Brazil.[3] Thereafter, only a handful of slaves were imported from West India Company territory, mainly by VOC ships that took slaves on board clandestinely at Cape Verde on outward-bound voyages. Imports from west Africa were sufficient to boost the African component of the slave population during the first period (1658-1671), when few slaves were held at the Cape, but west Africans or their descendants were present at the Cape for the entire period of legal slavery.

In the first 130 years of occupation, however, the Cape turned east for most of its slaves. They were drawn from the Indian Ocean basin—from the east coast of Africa to the outer reaches of Borneo and the shores of China. Slaves as far removed from one another as Abyssinia, Arabia, Bengal, Borneo, Burma, China, Iran, Japan, and Sri Lanka were registered as part of the slave population at the Cape.[4] Until the mid-eighteenth century, slaving on the east coast of Africa proved unreliable and dangerous, and by 1731 slaves from the eastern possessions of the VOC outnumbered all other slaves imported into the Cape and remained in the majority until the collapse of VOC shipping in 1780.

Officially, Cape commerce faced east until the Commissioners' General statute of 21 November 1792 permitted Cape colonists to trade on their own account on the west coast of Africa and in all of the VOC's former eastern possessions.[5] The mercantile phase of the slave trade was over. But with the rise of international maritime commerce around the Cape after 1784, the east African mainland and Madagascar became the prime sources of slave importation. Just as they had been the first slaves to be imported into the Cape, so Africans became the last. And perhaps more significantly, the years from 1784 until the overseas trade was abolished in 1808 mark the period when most of the Cape's slaves were imported.

Shipping Patterns

The decline of the VOC and Dutch shipping in the second half of the eighteenth century also altered the cultural composition of imported slaves. During this period the number of fleets from Sri Lanka, together with the number of ships within fleets out of Sri Lanka and India, suffered a downturn.[6] The proportion of slaves imported from the Indian subcontinent correspondingly declined from nearly 80 percent of all slaves imported in the first decades to around 15 percent in the last decades of the legal overseas slave trade. The proportion would have been lower still without the steady Tranquebar-to-Cape slave trade carried on by the Danes.[7] As ships based in American, Austrian, French, Hanseatic, Portuguese, Prussian, and Russian ports arrived in large numbers, Cape Town's slave traders broadened their sources of supply. Carrying a range of products and some carrying slaves, the new shipping trade quite overshadowed the VOC's shipping of the previous 125 years and enabled all Cape slave owners to break the slave-trading monopoly of the port's patriciate and VOC skippers.

The Fourth Anglo-Dutch War of 1780-84 proved to be the true watershed for changes in shipping patterns and the origins of Cape slaves. The war, which destroyed most VOC shipping, thereby opened the Cape to French traders, later to English control, and to new, larger, and entirely African sources of slaves. During this war, the VOC aligned itself militarily with the French and invited the French to garrison their troops at the Cape. The purchasing power of these huge garrisons ushered in a period of unparalleled prosperity at the Cape, increased investment in slaves, and stimulated competition in the slave marketplace at the port. Rural gentry and urban patricians competed for east African slave cargoes brought in by private French traders and French ships. At the time French interests were participating in the aggressive build-up of a sugar plantation complex in the Mascarenes by developing slave trading in the southeastern Atlantic. In the process, the old VOC patriciate monopoly on slave trading was broken, and Cape burgher slave owners for the first time traded for slaves directly. The French connection resulted in slaves arriving at the Cape from mainland eastern Africa, especially Mozambique, and from Madagascar and the Mascarenes.[8] During the war, too, the VOC suffered crippling shipping losses. With the treaty of May 1784, the English obtained freedom of navigation in and around the Indonesian Archipelago. Prior to the war, the bulk of slaves had formerly arrived in Dutch bottoms from Dutch Indonesian possessions. After the treaty, few Dutch ships brought slaves to the Cape. As Figure 2.2 represents, other shipping nations not only took up the slack in, but acquired by default , the Cape's expanding slave market. Before the war, VOC shipping round the Cape was in relative decline; after the war, the decline became absolute, with Dutch maritime trade past the Cape plunging precipitously.

After the British occupied the Cape for the first time in 1795 and broke French contacts with the Cape, Portuguese slavers en route to Brazil moved in and made the east coast of Africa the Cape's major source of slaves. Mozambique was the most important source of slave labor from the 1792 proclamation of the free trade statutes to the end of the licensed slave trade of the first British occupation (1795–1803). Cape slave owners called these slaves *Mozbiekers*. After the French revolution, French shipping resumed old contacts, and in 1803 the Batavian commissioner at the Cape, J. de Mist, remarked that "slaves are...brought in large numbers from Madagascar [and] Mozambique by the French for purposes of trade."[9] The Africanization of the slave force under the post-1795 administrations is dramatically illustrated by William Freund, who shows that, of the 1,039 slaves who arrived in Cape Town alone during the three-year Batavian period, at least 790 came from Mozambique.[10] In 1806 one local English settler noted that the "slaves at the Cape principally consist of Mosambiques, Malays and Bouganeese. Some few from the other countries, but these compose the general mass."[11] In the wake of the VOC collapse,

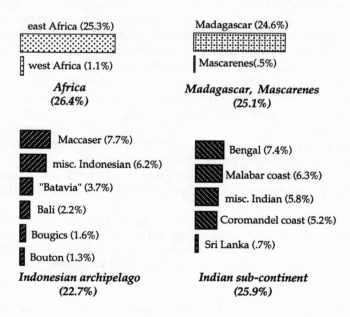

east Africa (25.3%)

west Africa (1.1%)

Africa
(26.4%)

Madagascar (24.6%)

Mascarenes(.5%)

Madagascar, Mascarenes
(25.1%)

Maccaser (7.7%)

misc. Indonesian (6.2%)

"Batavia" (3.7%)

Bali (2.2%)

Bougics (1.6%)

Bouton (1.3%)

Indonesian archipelago
(22.7%)

Bengal (7.4%)

Malabar coast (6.3%)

misc. Indian (5.8%)

Coromandel coast (5.2%)

Sri Lanka (.7%)

Indian sub-continent
(25.9%)

FIGURE 2.2   Geographic Origins of Imported Cape Slaves, 1652–1808. *Sources*: *Transporten en Scheepenkennis, CAD Court of Justice; MOOC; Vendu Rolls.* Bradlow and Cairns (1978), Bommaert (1938), Shell (1986), Mentzel (1921-1944), Worden (1985), Davids (1985), de Kock (1950), Armstrong (1979), Freund (1971), Barrow(1806), and Pedersson (1954). Total number imported= 62,964, including lodge.

Mozambique comprised the single main source of Cape slaves (and, after 1808, "prize slaves"). Mozambique's late preeminence in the Cape slave trade corresponds, however, to its brief role as a voluminous supplier in the Atlantic and Indian Ocean slave trades. Curtin estimates that in the same period approximately 40 percent of all slaves imported to Brazil came from the same source.[12] Measured by such comparisons, the Cape's role in Mozambique was small alongside other importing nations and colonies. What distinguishes the Cape's slave trade, apart from the relatively high volume of slaves imported in the closing decades of the legal overseas trade, is the diversity of the slave population it created. Figure 2.2, showing the origins of all slaves imported from 1652 to 1808, constitutes a palette of origins much broader than any recorded slave population anywhere else in the world.

Creolization

Cape slaves were also among the few slave populations to reproduce themselves prior to abolition of the legal oceanic trade. Generally, 1808 is regarded as the date around which slave populations in the English-speaking colonial world started to creolize.[13] The presumption is that slave owners favored natural increase and "slave breeding" only after they became conscious of a shortfall in supply. Such might have been true elsewhere, but not so at the Cape. As Figure 2.3 shows, long before 1808 the Cape slave population had several "moments of creolization" (i.e., when more than 50 percent of the slave population was locally born). What accounts for an apparent lack of sustained creolization after 1770–89 was the renewed surge in slave importation rather than any decline in slave fertility. By the last quarter of the eighteenth century, the slave population was reproducing itself but not fast enough to satisfy the demands of the expanding population of slave owners.

The first hint at significant creole origins of the Cape slaves appears in the late eighteenth-century account of Otto Mentzel, referring to the 1740s:

> On the farms there is always room for more slaves. It therefore pays farmers to keep an equal number of male and female slaves and by their natural increase to cope with the growing needs of the farm and avoid the necessity of buying additional slaves....The majority of privately owned slaves have been born in the [colony].[14]

Mentzel's observations underline what in the 1740s and 1750s represented a jump in the percentage of locally born slaves, as illustrated in Figure 2.3.[15] His reference to privately owned slaves also confirms data gleaned from probate records, which indicate that most of the slaves belonging to noncompany owners were creole by 1770. In contrast, VOC-owned lodge slaves suffered high mortality, leaving but few to propagate a generation of locally born slaves.

Low creolization rates also characterize the lodge after 1808. Even in 1826, the lodge held more imported than creole slaves. In spite of the increase of creoles among privately held slaves, their proportion receded following the arrival of French garrisons. The surge in slave imports was so massive as to outweigh the number of slaves who were born at the Cape in the following decade.

Greater importation had nevertheless an exponentially positive effect on creolization rates in the long run, because the post-1770 trade imported higher proportions of younger and female slave cargoes than had been the case before 1770. When these slaves reached maturity after 1800, the entire slave population (imported and creole) was younger and had many more women than before. As a result, the Cape slave population creolized at an increasing pace when the legal slave trade was abolished in 1808. Though slave breeding may have played a part, increased creolization rates were more likely the result of favorable age and sex population composition after 1770 (see Figure 2.4). Although African cargoes had more women and children than the earlier Asian male slave cargoes (eight males to one female), they still had twice as many men as women. Such cargoes, while lowering the excessively high sex ratios of the past, could never on their own normalize the slave population. While the slave trade worked in erratic waves, creolization worked in a steady linear fashion, which explains why creolization could supersede the slave trade *at several moments* before 1808.

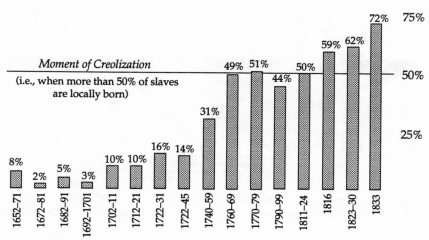

FIGURE 2.3 Percentage of Cape Slave Population Who Were Locally Born, 1658–1833. *Sources:* Estate inventories, MOOC, Vendu lists, SO 17/1; PRO CO 53/57; Bradlow and Cairns (1978), Tables; Worden (1985), Table 4.1.

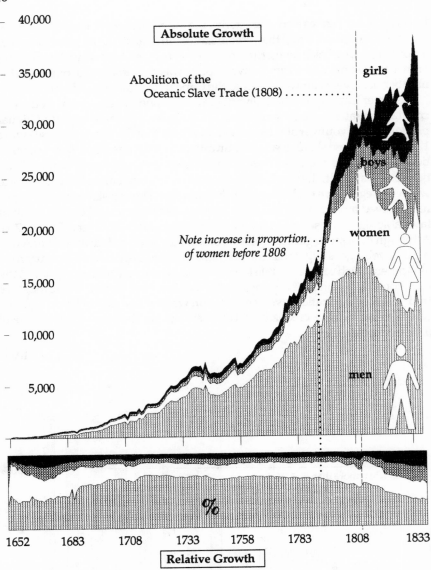

FIGURE 2.4 Age and Sex Composition of the Slave Population, 1652–1833. *Sources: VOC Opgaafs*, Beyers (1929), Ross and van Duin (1987), Blue Books, Theal (1897-1905).

Because Cape slaves had such broadly diverse origins, however, a common slave culture had to wait on substantial creolization. Of all the slaves imported to the Cape, only the slaves who originally belonged to the VOC can be said to have shared a common, in this case Malagasy, culture.[16] Only they derived from the same language group, religious background, geographical areas, and, in some cases, kin network. For a time, or at least until 1744, after which the lodge was supplemented by slaves and "convicts" from China, Bengal, Sri Lanka, and Zanzibar, a slave culture emanated from the lodge. Evidence of this culture may be glimpsed in a ca. 1713 play about a ravished Cape slave woman, which was "regularly performed at night by firelight in the lodge."[17] Religious meetings led by a Muslim slave overseer were also first reported in the lodge in the 1740s.[18] Thereafter, the constantly changing slaving areas of the company altered this large household of 500 slaves into a potpourri of imported subcultures. The same process occurred among the bulk of the slave force, but from the start, slaves living in individual burgher households were much more culturally heterogeneous and more isolated than was the case in the lodge.

Stereotyping by Origin

Just as cultural heterogeneity and geographic dispersal among burgher households delayed the creation of a common slave culture, individual slave owners' awareness of broad differences in the origin of their slaves occasioned the wholesale construction of slave stereotypes by origin. Such stereotypes, arising at the household level, may best be seen in the varying auction prices of slaves from different origins. Premiums based on origin were not unique to the Cape, as was recognized at the time.[19] Philip Curtin and other scholars have also noted that stereotyping by origin characterized all New World slave societies:

> Slave buyers distinguished between African cultures following a set of stereo-typed "national characters" highlighting traits that seemed important to slave-owners—industry, proneness to rebellion, faithfulness, honesty, or physical suitability for fieldwork. Such stereotypes differed through time and from one colony to another, but they could have a marked influence on the price offered in particular American markets.[20]

Curtin's italics around "national character" show that geographic origin, rather than national character, was the prime source of stereotypes, though it is apparent how one could become the other. The same stereotyping process occurred in the Cape, though here, where the slave population was more heterogeneous than in any other slave society, stereotyping rose to unprecedented, even fantastic, levels.

To some extent, stereotyping was a consequence of a system of slave premiums based on either creole status or geographic origins. A creole slave was the most valuable (43 percent premium) and also the least likely to appear on the market. Below the creole level, the hierarachy was based on origin. For instance, a male slave originating from Indonesia fetched on average a 7.2 percent premium, the highest premium based on origin, confirming the stereotype of the skilled "Malay" or "Asian" craftsperson. The most conservative statistical tests of the Cape data reveal that all influences being equal, including age, sex, and distance to the market, a clear hierarchy of slave prices existed at the Cape in which creole slaves were on the top tier, followed by slaves from the eastern possessions, with Malagasy slaves on the bottom tier (see Figure 2.5). Yet, price differentiation may be explained also by several noncultural variables. For example, expectations of high mortality for certain types of slaves may account for the lower prices of African and Malagasy slaves. Shortages of slaves from one area also led to a complicated arbitrage, or system of price substitution.

Slave owners fostered stereotypes that reinforced cultural and linguistic differences among slaves in their households. Owning slaves of various origins who spoke mutually unintelligible languages certainly posed problems of communication for owners and slaves alike, but this domestic Babylon had other advantages—such as security. Too many slaves of the same origin in one holding increased the risk of flight or rebellion. As an analysis of runaway slaves at the Cape illustrates, newly arrived slaves tended to run away in groups to reach "home" together. For newly arrived slaves, geography posed few obstacles to escape.[21] *Baaren* ("greenhorns"), especially at the lodge, were the most likely to run away.[22] Much less likely to escape were newly imported

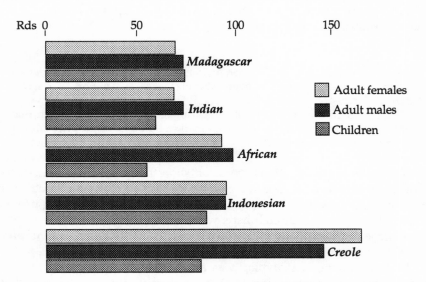

FIGURE 2.5 Price Differentiation by Origin, Sex, and Age. *Source:* DO, *Transporten en Scheepenkennis*, CJ, MOOC, Vendu Rolls (1658-1731, 1767-8, 1783). N=4,122 slaves, 566 slave sales, or 13.7 percent, had missing values.

slaves who joined a household in which other slaves had been acculturated or who were creole. Language barriers, though an irritant for owners in communicating with their polyglot household of slaves, prevented slaves from sharing a culture. The Greek slave holders' maxim, "Mix the nationalities of the slaves, both within the individual holding and within the city," echoed with real meaning in the Cape.[23] The cultural mix undermined slave solidarity and reduced rebellion at the Cape to predominantly individual acts. Arson and "running amok" (frenzied violence against all, including other slaves), the most widely feared forms of slave rebellion in the Cape, were nearly always carried out by imported slaves acting alone.[24] Owners who mixed their slaves by origin and undermined their sense of community also expected their trusted slaves to hunt down runaway slaves and inform on one another for comparatively minor crimes. Slave conspiracies were often revealed to the owner by a fellow slave.[25]

Settlers' and officials' perceptions, subject to a variety of influences, appear to have been the most decisive factor in stereotyping slaves and assigning slaves' occupations. Otto Mentzel, for instance, noted: "Female slaves from Bengal or the coast of Coromandel, from Surat and Macassar, are in great demand, because they have a reputation as skillful needlewomen."[26] Imported women slaves from these areas were set to needle craft within the house rather than used in agricultural work. This set a pattern: Their skills in fact earned all other slave women the right to stay out of agriculture. The first sight visitors encountered upon entering a typical eighteenth century Cape house was "a long, broad gallery where four or six slave women sat on small wooden benches, sewing or knitting."[27] Initial stereotypical notions of eastern women slaves in the western Cape had important long-term consequences for the role of *all* slave women in later Cape households. Even African women imported as slaves in the late eighteenth and early nineteenth centuries were likewise employed within the Cape household (see Figure 2.6). With respect to the influence of stereotypes on gender roles, the Cape also stands in striking contrast to the New World, where African slave women, *from the outset of colonization*, were immediately placed to work in the field.[28]

Over the eighteenth century, stereotypes of origin became more pronounced. Even insignificant skills became attributed to origins. For example, even a scientifically trained observer such as Anders Sparrman asserted in the 1770s that Malagasy slaves "had a particular knack at finding wild bees and honey."[29] Though skills in a slave's place of origin may have lent some validity to such notions, stereotyping by geographic origin prevailed throughout the eighteenth century and reached its apogee, significantly, just before the abolition of the oceanic slave trade. In other words, it had become the entrenched way of classifying slaves at the Cape. By 1806, an elaborate set of attitudes of group attribution had been developed by Cape householders. Samuel Hudson, a slave owner of some eight years standing, provides a typical example:

The Mosambiques are mild, peaceable and patient under this slavery. It seldom happens that they are guilty of those crimes so frequent among the Malays and Bouganeese. These [Mozambique] slaves are therefore more useful in the colony for hard labour and all agricultural concerns. Some of them are very ingenious and make excellent workmen. They are capable of conveying heavy burthens which they do without murmuring [and they] are affectionate and faithful to those who treat them well..... Each slave is put to a particular employment: the Mosambiques carry water, fetch wood, serve as masons, labourers, coolies and indeed, are generally set to the common drudgery of outdoor work though many of them are extremely serviceable. I have seen good carpenters, masons, markers at billiard tables, cooks, stable boys, in short, every kind of tradesmen from this race of poor despised patient beings. Prejudice has stamped them a dull, stupid link in the great chain and 'tis hard to do away [with] these errors which long custom has rendered sacred. Was I permitted to make choice of slaves for a continuance in the colony, I would certainly make choice of Mosambiques for fidelity and a mild disposition. The Malays certainly are much superior in all kinds of works where a ready imagination and genius is required, but they are a treacherous, shrewd, deceitful race. Scarce one but what has his *crese* [a long, twisted dagger] and his drugs, and woe betide the man who offends them. They may pass over an injury for a time, but let years roll on, it lives in their remembrance and they will watch the unguarded moment to revenge it. Punishment deters them not: they are fearless of danger, regardless of the consequences, and many of them look upon death as a release from misery and the immediate passport to their own...country....Such are the Malay slaves....[For] this readyness in all kinds of business they are preferred by the Dutch inhabitants to all others. They bring very great prices when exposed to sale: two, and sometimes three, thousand Rix Dollars has been given for these slaves. The Bouganese are likewise a treacherous set of slaves. These are by no means numerous. They are employed by the butchers and for the most disagreeable offices of slavery.[30]

Hudson describes a division of labor at the Cape based entirely on perceived attributes of origin. It is doubtful that such geographical/ethnic stereotypes approached reality, given that societies other than the Cape developed different stereotypes for the same people. And once started, these stereotypes were constantly updated within each host society, each stereotype having an arbitrary history of its own. By the nineteenth century, Cape householders considered it "natural" that Malagasy and African slaves worked in the fields, that Indonesian slaves were the artisans, and that Indian slaves were the service workers of the colony.

The manner of classifying slaves at the Cape changed after the abolition of the slave trade. In official slave transfers recorded in the 1820s, slave origins went increasingly unmentioned. Whether the new practice of omission was the result of post-revolutionary thought, the British occupation, or the greater proportion of creole slaves, or whether it simply reflected the cessation of all sectors of the slave trade is not clear. What is certain is that the old system of stereotyping by individual origin gave way to a new one based on descent and race. Descent consciousness had always been present at the Cape, but by the 1820s it was in the foreground. The writing of W.W. Bird, a British colonial official, reveals the change:

> The Negro, who is the least valuable, was brought from Madagascar and Mozambique. These slaves are chiefly hewers and carriers of wood, and drawers of water, coolies, or public porters for hire, and also employed by the boers and others as the hardiest labourers of the field....The Malay slaves are coachmen, tailors, painters, shoemakers, carpenters, and fishermen. In fact, they are usually engaged in everything where what is called cleverness is required. [31]

In a fashion becoming typical of new immigrant settlers, Bird combined his racial construction with biblical embellishments that reinforced notions of descent. Furthermore, his sense of slaves' geographical origins (i.e., Malagasy and Mozambique) is collapsed into the appellation, "Negro." Bird's was a Eurocentric, hierarchical classification and attribution scheme that was attractive to colonial immigrants dealing with a new and uncertain social universe.[32]

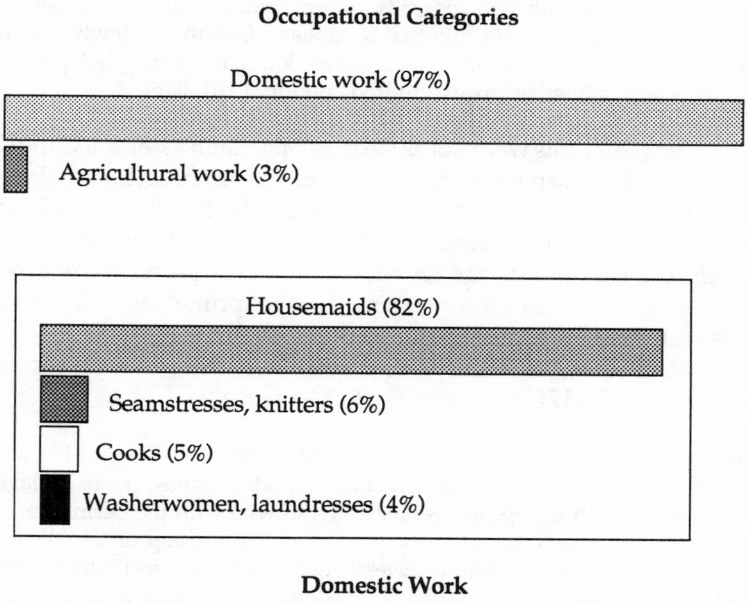

Occupational Categories

Domestic work (97%)

Agricultural work (3%)

Housemaids (82%)

Seamstresses, knitters (6%)

Cooks (5%)

Washerwomen, laundresses (4%)

Domestic Work

FIGURE 2.6 Cape Slave Women's Occupations, 1823–1830. *Sources:* CAD Slave Office, 17/1, Compensation Lists. N=268.

Bird was, in fact, writing for such a readership. Under the British, new identities were imposed on Cape slaves that accommodated the household construction of hierarchies based on origin and ethnicity, but that erased the erstwhile primacy of geographic origin. In the process, the identity of all persons not from Europe was greatly diminished. During this period, "coloured" entered the South African vocabulary. The older and elaborate system of stereotyping by origin was being modified, in other words, to fit a predominantly locally born slave population into a simplified classification system based on descent and race. This new way of thinking at the Cape was more pronounced than anywhere in the New World. "Ideology" is too grand a term for this development; it may best be characterized as a naïve household anthropology.

Creole Slaves and the Household

In the Cape slave owners' view, creole slaves formed the elite of the Cape slave population. They were considered both the most valuable and the most "trustworthy." As Anders Sparrman noted in the 1770s, they were often entrusted with the supervisory duties on a plantation and priced accordingly.

> [A] slave born in the country...who can drive a wagon well and who can be trusted to inspect the other slaves, or is looked upon as a clever and faithful servant, bears the price of five hundred Rixdollars. One that is newly bought from Madagascar, or is in other respects not so skilful, nor so much depended upon, costs from a hundred to an hundred and fifty Rixdollars.[33]

Though creole premiums were not as steep as Sparrman asserts, a Cape slave purchaser was willing to pay on average a 43 percent premium for a male creole slave (i.e., almost half as much again as the mean price for all slaves sold at the Cape). Moreover, among slaves sold on the Cape market the creoles as a group were much younger (the average age was below eleven years) and well below what the purchasers of other slaves regarded as the "prime" age of 25–30 years, which also reflected the highest point on the price curve.

Mulatto (half-slave/half-European) creole slave children were especially prized as early as the 1740s. According to Mentzel, they

> are found useful at a very tender age and cost little to bring up. They are likewise better mannered and better educated than imported slaves. Female slaves sometimes live with Europeans as husband and wife with the permission of their masters who benefit in two ways: the cost of upkeep of the slave is reduced through the presents she receives from the man, and her children are the property of her master since children of female slaves are themselves slaves.[34]

When George Barrington, the Superintendent of Convicts, visited the Cape in 1791, creoles remained "the most esteemed [among slaves] at the Cape, and whom Bird also termed "creole," was the most valuable class of slaves. And by Bird's time, "creole" was synonymous with "mulatto":

> The last and most valuable class of the slaves is the African born slave,—the produce [sic] of an European, or of a Cape Dutchman, and of a slave girl. So many years have passed away since the Cape has been in the uninterrupted possession of the Dutch or English, that from black, this class has graduated into brown or yellow, not much darker than a southern European and many have progressed nearly to white. Of this race, both male and female, are the slaves preferred by the inhabitants. The men are active and subtle in mind, slender and of good appearance in body. The females are rather under the middle size, with a bust inclined to fullness.... Both sexes have much of the character of the Creole. These slaves are engaged in the domestic and most confidential services of the house, and frequently in a store or warehouse where goods are sold.[36]

Five attributes suggest why creoles were the most expensive and most preferred of all slaves. First, for epidemiological reasons they lived longer than imported slaves. All imported slaves suffered higher mortality than creole slaves. Second, they included the specially favored mulatto slaves, or slaves of half-European descent, whose high values pushed up all other creole prices.[37] Third, the creole slaves' first language tended to be the patois.[38] The creole slaves made natural overseers. Fourth, the crime records of accused slaves in the early period reveal that creole slaves were the least likely to run away, commit crimes, or rebel.[39] And fifth, the owners of a creole slave had to bear the comparatively high cost of child rearing for creole slaves. In other words, Cape slave owners were willing to pay a substantial, 7 percent premium based on origin for a slave, regardless of age, transportation costs, or any other known price influence, but they were willing to pay as high as 43 percent for a locally born slave of possible European descent.[40] After 1808, the value of creole slaves was magnified, too, by the abolition of the legal overseas slave trade, which crushed expectations of an increasing slave force through importation.

Thus creolization at the Cape, which accelerated in the 1780s with the coincidental Africanization of the slave trade and the lowering of sex ratios and age composition of household slaves, also reflected intensifying household labor demands, which became acute after 1808. Such were the pressures that also induced slave owners (and younger, would-be owners) to turn to autochthonous sources of labor. The population pyramid in Figure 2.7 represents the effect of all these factors related to the slave trade on the slave population.[41] As such the pyramid encapsulates both the history of the slave trade and the progress of creolization at the Cape. Though Cape slave-holding households had imported many slaves, by 1833 of all slaves in Cape households many more had been born into slavery than had been imported.

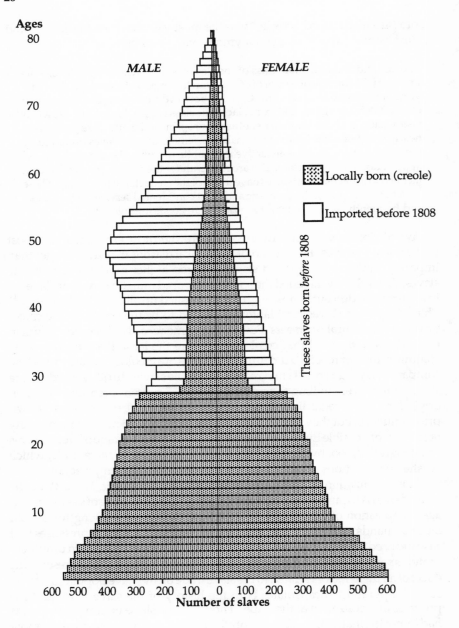

FIGURE 2.7 Population Pyramid of Cape Slaves Showing Creole Status in 1833. *Sources:* based on PRO CO 53/57 (31 Aug. 1833). Thanks to John Mason for this reference.

Creole Language in the "Tower of Babel"

The diversity of geographic origins was of immediate practical significance for the slaves' adjustment and acculturation in their—for want of a better word—"home." Arriving in the typically small, often quite isolated, Cape slave-holding homestead, the uprooted slave was rudely thrust into the foreign domestic milieu of the new owner, and hence unlikely to encounter persons who spoke the same language, ate recognizable food, or even looked similar. Chances that any kinfolk were waiting to provide a buffer of sympathy were negligible. These minor consolations, which some African slaves found in the larger Brazilian, Caribbean, and North American African slave populations, were virtually absent at the Cape. Newly imported slaves arrived into households which were entirely alien places. Urban Cape households and rural plantations were inhabited by somatic and linguistic strangers.

The more diverse the origins of slaves within each holding, the more difficult it must have been for incoming slaves to converse with other slaves and for their new owners to talk with them. Illustrating the possible confusion of languages was the slave holding of Pieter van der Bijl, a farmer in the Drakenstein district in the 1690s. Van der Bijl bought individual slaves from Macassar, Bengal, Malabar, Ternate, and Malacca.[42] The local Khoikhoi, who provided seasonal labor around van der Bijl's farm, added a further ingredient to the linguistic variety. During this period the Khoikhoi had been obliged to learn to speak French.[43] The result of hearing Dutch, French, Hindi, Khoikhoi, Malay, and Portuguese inspired van der Bijl, a pious man who built a church on his farm, to name his property *Babijlonsche Tooren* ("the Tower of Babel").[44]

That confusion of languages was a major problem in Cape households is confirmed by the crime records. For example, when all the slaves on the Klapmuts farm of Daniel Pheijl, a settler councilor, were interrogated in 1726, their depositions were given to interpreters as follows: Hercules van Bougies and Cupido van Padang (both from the Indonesian archipelago) spoke Malay, Scipio of Bengal spoke Portuguese, and only one slave, Jacob of Cochin, gave his evidence in Dutch.[45] Slave owners could have understood their slaves only partially, because a battery of court interpreters had to be called as a matter of course to deal with slaves' depositions in the event of any crime. For reasons of juridical efficiency and accuracy, the Cape courts took testimony in the interpretable language with which the slave felt most comfortable. Thanks to this courtesy, a clear idea of the linguistic diversity of the early Cape slaves may be obtained. The most common court languages of imported slaves were Buginese, Chinese, Dutch, Javanese, Malagasy, Malay, and Portuguese. Prior to 1731, and most likely later, no purely African languages of slaves were translated in Cape courts.[46]

The multilingual and well-travelled François Valentijn, a minister writing in 1728, was struck by the variety of people and languages at the Cape:

> [A]ll nations [*Natien*] are found here, Dutch, English, French, Germans from all parts, Savoyards, Italians, Hungarians, Malays, Malabaris, Sinhalese, Macassar-folk, Banians, Amboinese, Badanese, Buginese, Chinese, men of Madagascar, Angolese, inhabitants of Guinea and the salt islands [Cape Verde], with whom one can get along in Dutch, Malay and Portuguese.[47]

Just how poor communication was in some Cape households as late as the 1760s is indicated by one observer who claimed that it was not uncommon for slaves to communicate solely in sign language and "peculiar noises."[48] The persistence of languages of origin and the failure of any "official" language to gain acceptance among slaves at the Cape is attested in one case by a letter written by a slave in the Buginese alphabet when communicating with Cape authorities (Figure 2.8).[49]

Although a slave lingua franca emerged early in the Cape, research into its genesis and extent has been limited by the reluctance of Afrikaans-speaking linguists to confront squarely the issue of the creolization of the Dutch language, the forerunner of Afrikaans. Other Dutch colonial slave societies developed creole languages, such as "Neger Hollands" or *Papiamento* in

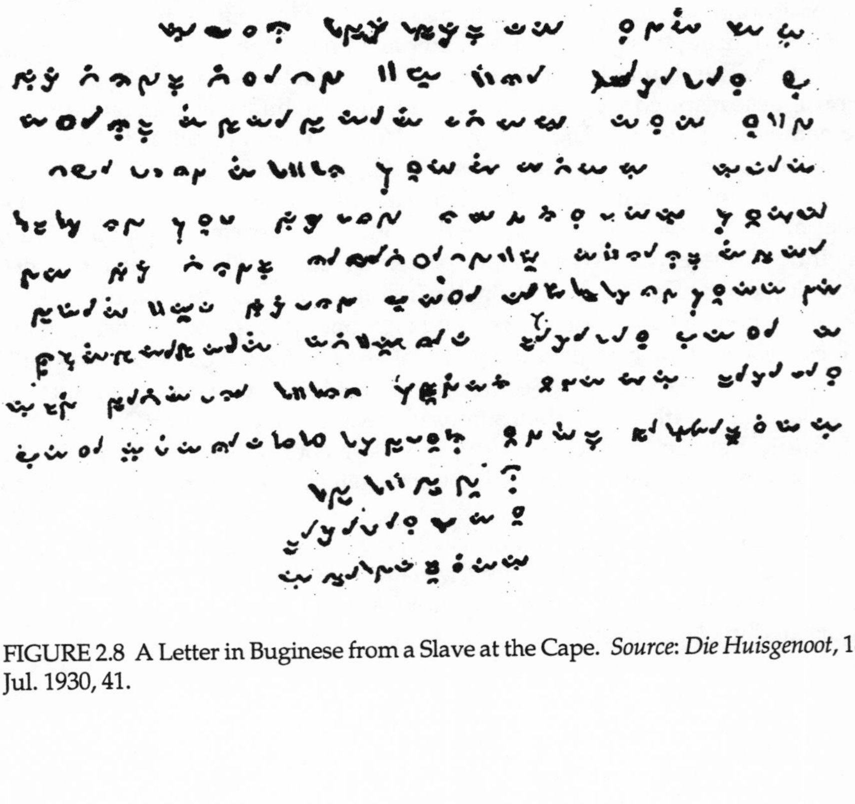

FIGURE 2.8 A Letter in Buginese from a Slave at the Cape. *Source: Die Huisgenoot*, 18 Jul. 1930, 41.

Curaçao, and such was the case in the Cape. The simplification and creolization of Dutch in early South Africa resulted, not from the spontaneous development of Dutch dialects, as early Afrikaans-speaking scholars have fondly argued, but from the domestic interaction among imported, creole, and autochthonous slaves and servants, and their owners. Slaves fashioned their own language (i.e., the primary instrument of a new culture) in order to overcome the conglomeration of highly diverse cultures at the household level. Creole language developed in two overlapping stages, the first being the Malayo-Portuguese "pidgin" phase (1652+), and the second, which began in the late eighteenth century, resulting in a true creole sometimes referred to as "kitchen Dutch." Malayo-Portuguese, which may be regarded as the forerunner of Ur-Afrikaans, was characterized by a large number of loan words and new grammatical intrusions. It emerged when the Cape slave population had a high proportion of imported slaves. An example of this language appears in the first published words of a Cape slave in 1731: *Dios, mio Pay* ("God, my father").[50] This was a pure slave language not clearly understood by the master class. As an English visitor discovered in 1765, owners were obliged to learn the slaves' lingua franca, not the other way around:

> What seems extraordinary is that the slaves do not learn to talk Dutch, but the Dutch people learn their dialect, which is called Portuguese, and is a corruption of that language, some of them are called Malays, brought from the country of Malacca and the islands to the eastward of India.[51]

By the 1770s Khoisan peoples used Malayo-Portuguese to bar communication with Europeans:

> We found [wrote Anders Sparrman] the farm inhabited only by some hottentots who were left there by a colonist in order to look after it. They were so ill-disposed as not to answer either in Dutch or Portuguese Mr. Immelman's enquiries about the road, although he promised to give them some money, and though, as we were afterwards assured, they perfectly understood both these languages; but they jabbered a great deal to us in their own language, of which, however we could not comprehend a syllable. I do not know whether this behavior proceeded from a wicked disposition, the foundation of which is to be sought for in the general depravity, as it is called, of human nature, or whether it might not rather be considered, as a well-founded grudge harboured in the breasts of these people against the Christian colonists. We since heard of many instances, in which the same thing had happened elsewhere to other Christians, who by way of putting a trick on these poor fellows, pretended to be ignorant of the hottentot language; and by this means heard unsuspected the answers of the hottentots, consisting in mere impertinence and scoffing jests, which they threw out against the Christians with the highest glee, and as they thought with impunity, till the latter pulled off the mask in order to avenge themselves.[52]

As the slave trade continued, and new languages were added to the mix, this emerging Cape lingua franca acquired additional linguistic borrowings, a process that was as chaotic as it was dynamic. Mirzu Abu Taleb Khan, a Persian visitor to Cape in the late eighteenth century, wrote that "besides the Dutch, there are to be found at the Cape people of many other nations, and at least seven or eight languages are spoken here."[53] In words that echo from the Drakenstein farm of van der Bijl nearly a century before, Sparrman provided in 1770 perhaps the most fitting description of what the slave trade continued to imply for communication in a Cape household.

> At mealtimes, various European dialects, together with the languages used in commerce with the Indians, viz. the Malay, and a very bad kind of Portuguese, were spoken at one time, so that the confusion was almost equal to that of the tower of Babel.[54]

Eventually, Malayo-Portuguese was transformed into a purified Malay as it became the religious language for Cape Muslim slaves. That assumption at any rate was made by the Anglican clergy who launched a pamphlet war to convert the Cape Muslims in the early nineteenth century. By then, however, Malay was dying out under the massive pressures of creolization, but it left trace elements in many Afrikaans words and constructions. Malay was last heard in Cape Town in 1923.

The second and more profound phase of the formation of a creole language started with both the biological creolization of the Cape slaves and the increasing, forcible incorporation of the Khoikhoi as domestic laborers. A new creole language was being fashioned as early as the 1740s.

> It was no easy task to instruct the Madagascar slaves, for they spoke no language but their own. East Indian officers brought slaves from Java, Mallebar, Bengal, Banda and many other islands and sold them to the inhabitants of the Cape. They [the eastern slaves] introduced a common slave language, or *lingua franca*, which they had acquired from the Portuguese and which could easily be picked up. This language has now been spoken for many years by slaves, Christian inhabitants and even by half-breed hottentots.[55]

This second language was intelligible to all in the household and accessible to all in the colony. The new language was the result of a wholly different process than was present at the emergence of Malayo-Portuguese. Creolization of this language was associated with the creolization of the slave population. More-over, this second phase was a strongly gendered process. Women, slave and free, were the creators of this language. It emerged clearly from the household, and from a special place within the home. This accounts for the derogatory, nineteenth-century phrase for Afrikaans: "Kitchen Dutch." More compelling is the otherwise inexplicably large number of Malay and Indian words in the

"Afrikaans" culinary lexicon of 1992. "The most potent influence [on the Cape cuisine itself]," wrote C. Louis Leipoldt, Afrikaans poet and chef, "has been the methods, tastes and culinary customs of the Malay cooks brought directly from Java in the early eighteenth century." The exotic cuisine of the imported slave quite overshadowed all the European culinary traditions.[56] From the food came the kitchen language.

Only much later did men acquire the creole language and introduce it to the public sphere. The first book in Afrikaans was written in the 1850s by an *imam* (Muslim prayer leader), of slave descent.[57] Decades later, in the 1860s, patriotic male European colonists took up the language for themselves. Men were the last to use the Afrikaans language. Some, such as Jan Christiaan Smuts, disdained Afrikaans throughout their lives. The Afrikaans poet, Breyten Breytenbach, explained, from his own perspective, why Afrikaners avoid admitting the creole origins of the language. "We are a bastard people with a bastard language. And like all bastards, we have begun to cling to the concept of purity."[58]

Bonded Autochthonous Labor

Creolization was a process that from the onset involved the Cape's indigenous Khoisan population. Beginning in the early eighteenth century autochthonous people had been bonded to households with official knowledge, and at two subsequent points, additional legal forms of binding Khoikhoi and San to Cape households were devised. Originally the colonists turned their attention to autochthonous women. Khoikhoi women were the first to appear, as Elphick has noted in an 1696 reference, "in their own huts on a white farms." Ostensibly, Khoikhoi men did not want to work the colonists' ground.[59] In 1721 eight of the wealthiest farmers in the interior districts of Stellenbosch and Drakenstein made the following request:

> we would like to mention how by the present conjuncture [*conjuncture*] of time, which has resulted in the Hottentots, in securing their own sustenance, have come to seek shelter among the free burghers. It transpired that some of the slave men belonging to the undersigned mixed in with the women of this nation, and have bred children from these unions. The costs of the consequent child-rearing have been born by us...so that we ask if you could decree that a certain number of years may be stipulated during which these offspring might be bonded [*verbonden*] to serve their foster bosses [*voetserbasen*] otherwise we would have no further recompense for our trouble and expense.[60]

Böeseken and Cairns, and Malherbe, have asserted that this matter was "left in abeyance for fifty years," yet the Council of Policy with obvious approval passed the request on to the jurisdiction of the local heemraden and landdrosten of Stellenbosch and Drakenstein.[61] One of the signatories to the request himself worked in the Stellenbosch landdrost's office, and two others, Hermanus van Brakel and Matthijs Krugel served as heemraden of Stellenbosch and Drankenstein, respectively.[62] Elphick, writing of a slighty earlier period, has noted that the Company studiously avoided all disputes over local labor contracts.[63] And, within several years of the above request, it is clear that an informal *inboekstelsel* (i.e., registration of autochthonous bonded labor) had been inaugurated. As Mentzel wrote of the period 1732 to 1741:

> Hottentot women, in the service of the colonists do not dislike the slaves, and easily let themselves be persuaded to live with them. Children, born of such a union are always free, although their father is a slave, but they have to stay for 25 years with their mother's employer, unless the mother immediately returns to her kraal with her new born child.[64]

Though legal *inboekstelsel* began in 1775, the date historians have used to mark the beginning of the bonding system, the above evidence makes clear that after 1721 local magistrates oversaw the bonding of Khoikhoi laborers *without* registration.[65] This new system of procuring labor was a specific form of bondage. De facto rights over a person's bonded labor period could be inherited or transferred along with the property on which people resided. *Inboekstelsel* originated, in other words, as a form of cadastral slavery or, more properly, serfdom.

Very early, *inboekstelsel* acquired features more akin to slavery. Descent of bonded labor of the Khoikhoi followed the descent rules of Cape slavery. Both were based on what Orlando Patterson calls "uterine descent."[66] Children born to bonded women or slave women were respectively bonded or enslaved.[67] For Khoikhoi, the bonded labor period was from twelve years to twenty-five years. Children born to such "bonded" women were also attached. Some children of Khoikhoi mothers/slave fathers were possibly registered as part of the census "slave" population. Certifying that any Khoikhoi were so incorporated into the legal slave population may be impossible, because the Khoikhoi population remained unenumerated throughout the VOC period. But significantly, in every year after 1721 the Stellenbosch regional censuses reported higher slave child/slave women ratios than the Cape district closest to town.[68] Such figures may reflect, of course, that raiding for female and children slaves was underway. Nigel Penn has found that in 1731 a Khoikhoi woman and her three children were captured by commandos and placed in bondage in another part of the colony. The governor instructed the perpetrators that they should "not write about such incidents, but report them in person."[69] In 1767 Gunjeman Khoikhoi around Cape Town were alleged to "furnish slaves for the service of the Honorable Company or for private citizens."[70] And before the legal *inboekstelsel* was instituted in 1775, reports of "runaway Khoi women" were being reported. In 1772, a plantation owned by one European who had become "simple in the head," was the "happy resort of Hottentot women who have run away from their masters, and who already form a considerable number, remaining there, in spite of everyone."[71]

As of 1785 an Englishman sent to the Cape to spy in the event of a British invasion could confidently report that:

> At most of the Farm houses in the province there resides from 10 to 20 Hottentots. The Dutch have made slaves of them all, and they understand a little of the Dutch language. *They are called free because the master cannot sell them, as they do the negroes,* but the Hottentot cannot go from one master to another and is obliged to work *without payment* [. T]he Dutch farmers give some of the most faithful and intelligent a cloth coat once in two years which is to them a most magnificent present....[I]f a British Army Acts in that country they should make them presents of clothing according to their services, and feed them with meats which attracts them, as they seldom get anything from their masters but Bread, Milk, Roots, and Vegetables [emphasis added].[72]

Wages for autochthonous labor had all but stopped in the frontier region, where outright coercion was occurring.[73] In 1795 the "revolutionary" patriarchs of hinterland Swellendam district presented ten "articles of demand" to the Cape authorities, one of which called for permanent, legalized, captive enslavement.

> *Articul 5* that any bushmen or Hottentot women caught singly or on commando either previously or now, shall henceforth be the *property* of the farmer employing them, and *serve him for life*. Should they run away, their master shall be entitled to pursue them and punish them *na merites*....[74]

Honoratus Christiaan Maynier, landdrost of Graaff-Reinet, confirmed that such activities were being perpetrated against the San:

> I was also made acquainted with the most horrible atrocities committed on those occasions [slave raids] such as ordering the Hottentots to dash out against the rocks the brains of infants (*too young to be carried by the farmers for the purpose to use them as bondsmen*), in order to save powder and shot [emphasis added].[75]

The process of capturing and bonding Khoisan continued under British rule, but it became most apparent after the abolition of the slave trade in 1808, a period of intense missionary activity and nervous imperial scrutiny. Lord Caledon's proclamation to regularize and, in a certain qualified measure, to protect Khoisan laborers in the future contains two clauses that reveal how they had been victimized in the past:

10. That the master shall in no case be allowed to detain, or prevent from departing, the wife or children of any hottentot that has been in his service, after the expiration of the term of contract of their husband or father, under pretence of a security for what may be indebted to him...and not be allowed by his own authority to attempt the repayment of himself, by the personal services of these natives.

11. That likewise in the case of the Hottentot's dying, through which the effect of his personal contract of hire ceases, the wife and children shall be at liberty to depart....[76]

LMS missionary John Philip believed that the abolition of the oceanic slave trade had resulted in an *increased* bondage of Khoisan, because rising slave prices put slave purchases out of the reach of farmers and the growing European population at the Cape. "To supply that population with substitutes for the slaves, double the number is wanted; slaves cannot be got and the Hottentots are seized and reduced to a state of slavery." After he drove ten Khoikhoi off a mission station, a farmer living in the Zuurbrak area told Philip:

These children are my treasure, they will cultivate my farm, they will serve me instead of slaves, I shall have them all bound to me, until they are twenty five, and perhaps until they are twenty nine years of age.[77]

In 1823 the incorruptible utilitarian royal commissioner, John Thomas Bigge, and Thomas Colebroke informed the colonial secretary that Khoisan women and children were being "enslaved" in the new frontier districts on the pretext of being the by-product of retaliatory raids.[78]

Thus, by the time of the Ordinance 50, passed in 1828, what had begun more than a century earlier as a form of enserfment had become one of enslavement. The local name for Ordinance 50, which helped to give rise to settler grievances leading to the Voortrekker movement of the 1830s, was the "Emancipation of the Hottentots." The term *emancipation* was well chosen, for by that time, the Khoisan bondservants of Cape households, too, were slaves.

Notes

1. For a printed discussion of the methodology used to arrive at the figures, contact the author.

2. Armstrong and Worden (1989), 77; De Kock (1950), 30-1.

3. Armstrong and Worden (1989), 111.

4. The first commandant of Cape colony, Jan van Riebeeck, owned two "Arabian slave girls from Abyssinia," Cornelia (10 yrs.) and Lijsbeth (12). Blommaert (1938), 6. For Ackmat van Arabia, see *Cape Town Street Directory, 1824* (Cape Town, 1824). Deeds Office (DO), "Transporten en Scheepenkennis" (hereafter "Transporten"):

"Fabia from Brazil (8 Mar. 1712), "Soutanji from Burma" (24 Jun. 1706), and "David Casta from China" (15 Mar. 1685). "Anthony, Moor van Japan" was owned by Jan Dirckz de Beer on "Ecklenberg" farm: see Master of Orphan Chamber (MOOC), 8/1/ 63 (1 Mar. 1701). [Cf. Böeseken (1977), 93, 95-6, 101. Anthony was probably first owned by the Nagasaki station Dutch commandant, who brought him to the Cape and sold him before retiring. Four Japanese were classified as "free blacks" in the nineteenth century (Anthony Whyte, personal communication)]. See "Werf van Persien" in Court of Justice (CJ) 3047 (11 Feb. 1767), 23-4; "Lacqui van Persie" in Leibbrandt (1790), 2: 726 [The VOC had a post in Gamron in Persia. Liebbrandt (1702), 46]; "Leonara van Siam" in Liebbrandt (1790), 1: 191; "Achilles van Siam" in ibid, 2: 1086; "Silvia van Borneo" in ibid, 1: 266.

5. De Mist (1920), 247.

6. Based on the count of departure ports of "homeward voyages" of Indiamen between 1652 and 1795 in Bruijn (1979), 1: 60-573.

7. Since 1825, the literature on the Cape slave trade has emphasized 1767 as a watershed, because Batavian officials resolved that year that no males slaves would in future be brought from the east to the Cape on Dutch ships. Armstrong and Worden, for example, attribute the ban to the Dutch fear of "violent crimes [committed] by Indonesian slaves [at the Cape]," and assume the ban was more or less enforced (1989), 117. See also du Plessis (1972), 3, quoting "Realia," Landsarchief, Batavia, 28 Sep. 1867. A stronger line of argument, however, would attribute the decline in imported slaves from the east to the precipitous decline in VOC shipping past the Cape, as represented in Figure 2.2. The ineffectiveness of statutes cited by Armstrong and Worden is apparent in the continuous sequence of Batavian legislation from the seventeenth through the eighteenth century to stop homeward-bound captains from transporting eastern male slaves to the Cape free of charge. See van der Chijs (1885), 1: 600, 4: 37, 69, 80, 84; 5: 3; 7: 291; 10: 592, 692[sic], 726; 11: 629; 13: 618; 15: 1053; 16: 181 and passim. The slave trade carried on by Dutch officers in the East was probably responsible for this outpouring of legislation. Similar laws forbade Dutch officers from taking eastern slaves on board to Sir Lanka. Ibid., 8: 673. Evasion of these laws is certain. The 1767 statute was reissued in 1784 and 1787, indicating that clandestine importation of eastern male slaves continued. Jeffreys and Naude (1944-1949), 3: 164. Only one slaving skipper was ever arrested for importing eastern male slaves, and only two slaves returned to Batavia, the confiscations executed under Fiscal Boers, a man hardly representative of VOC officialdom. Armstrong and Worden (1989), 171 n. 42.

8. Ross (1988), 209-19.

9. De Mist (1920), 252.

10. Freund (1971), Table IV ("Imports of Slaves Documented for the Batavian Period"), 249. Freund's figures are based on tallies of advertisements of individual imported slaves.

11. Shell (1984), 46f.

12. Curtin (1969), 229-30. For the Delagoa bay slave trade, see ch. 6 in this volume.

13. Bank (1991), 6.

14. Mentzel (1921-44), 2: 90, 126.

15. Figure 2.4 is based on a tabulation of domestic slaves between 1823 and 1830, a population pyramid from 1833, which British officials tabulated from the slave population of August of that year, and records of individual slaves as found in Slave

Registration Office, lodge censuses (1693, 1713, and 1826), officials' inventories, and probate data. All creole slaves were identified in all classes of documents with a *van de kaap* toponym. No effort was made to calculate different rates of creolization for the slaves owned by officials, because individual level data after 1732 is too sparse, though much research in their later inventories remains to be done. Because the patriciate purchased many of their slaves directly from the oceanic trade, logically their holdings would not creolize as quickly as would the burghers'.

16. One incident dramatically illustrates the cultural propinquity of the Company's early slaving areas within Madagascar. The Malagasy company interpreter—bought on an earlier voyage—was shocked to see "his aunt" being offered for sale. The company felicitously brought her back to the Cape. Algemene Rijksarchief (AR) Verenigde Oost Indische Companje (VOC) 4034 "Rapport..." (Jan. 1695), n.p.

17. Stephen Gray, personal communication. According to Gray, the manuscript is owned by a person "who does not wish his name revealed for political reasons." A few scholarly doubts have arisen as to its existence. See also Gray (1978), 14-5.

18. According to oral sources. Du Plessis and Lückhoff (1983), 34. Also Shell (1974), 32.

19. For instance, Jan van Laet, a seventeenth century historian, quoted the Political Counselor, Servaicus Carpentier, who claimed when referring to Brazil that:

> The Angolan Negroes were largely employed in agricultural labour but had to be kept at it always with many lashes. The Guinea Negroes are excellent, so that the majority are used for domestic service, for waiting on table, and the like. Those of Cape Verde are the best and most robust of all and they are the ones that cost the most here.

Quoted in Freyre (1971), 303. Cape Verde (sometimes St. Iago in transfers) meant neither the actual cape where Dakar now stands nor the Cape Verde islands [sometimes called the salt islands, cf. Valentijn (1973), 1: 170] but the hinterland of the "Guineau of Cape Verde" stretching roughly from the Cape Verde peninsula to the Sierra Leone river. Slaves from Cape Verde were so expensive at the Cape that only the wealthiest slave trader in the colony, the governor himself, could afford them.

20. Curtin (1969), 155. Also Wood (1975), 152 and notes 64 & 65. Littlefield (1981), 8-32 shows convincingly how stereotypes by origin developed momentum in seventeenth and eighteenth century South Carolina and resulted in different price structures for slaves from different points in Africa.

21. The lodge, with its large numbers of slaves, echoed the pattern of escape in eighteenth century Virginia. Mullin (1972), 34-5.

22. C. 337, *Attestatien*, 20 Feb. 1717, fol. 49-51, Cape Archives Depot (CAD). At the Cape, the equivalent of Mullin's "outlandish" slaves were termed *Nieuwelinge* ("new ones") for at least their first two years at the Cape. Ibid, fol. 50. The slaves referred to in this document must have come from the *Leijdsman* in 1715.

23. Finley (1983), 171.

24. Percival (1969), 288-90.

25. Ross (1983), 20. Slave conspiracies at the Cape were betrayed at the last minute by fellow slaves, usually women.

26. Mentzel spoke with some authority, because he earned money producing embroidery designs for settler wives, who passed them on to their slave seamstresses. Mentzel (1921-24), 2: 127-8.

27. Dominicus (1919), 36-7. Placing women slave workers of such Cape cottage industries in the hall or *voorkamer* was evidently a way of supervising them, as visitors

were obliged to enter the house through the hall. This observation applied only to wealthy households in the western Cape.

28. Morgan (1975), 235; Shell (1992), 1, 15, 24; Borcherds (1861), 204.

29. Sparrman (1977), 2: 152.

30. Shell (1984), 46f.

31. Bird (1823), 73.

32. According to Fritz Heider, the foundation attribution theorist who first defined this arena of human classification, the solipsistic belief in such character traits based on origin was intended to make the world seem a much more predictable and, hence comfortable, place. Heider (1958).

33. Sparman (1977), 1: 102-3.

34. Mentzel (1921-44), 2: 130.

35. Barrington (1794), 34.

36. Bird (1823), 73.

37. In surviving baptismal records, deacons labeled pure creole slaves as *casties* and half creole (i.e., part European) slaves as *heelslag*. Because few burghers baptized their slaves and most half creoles were not sold but remained with the families of deceased estates, only a few cases of the slaves owned by officials suggest this classification.

38. According to court records, including slave witnesses and accused slaves. AR, VOC 4019, "Criminele Rolle, Process Stukken en Justiele Papieren," 1680–1731 (civil cases excluded).

39. "Register van Sententien, 1652–1717," and "Criminele Rechts Rollen, 1717–1741," CJ 278, CAD. In this respect, the Cape differed from early Virginia where, as slaves became more assimilated and more creole slaves were born, their degree of rebelliousness increased. Mullin (1972), 161-3. Mass slave rebellions did occur in the Cape during the 1808 to 1823 period, by which time the creole population exceeded 50 percent. Perhaps only at this time is the south African pattern consistent with Mullin's analysis of the development of creole rebellion.

40. Comparison with Laurence Kotlikoff's work on the nineteenth-century New Orleans slave market shows that Cape slave owners were not unique in paying premiums based on descent. Nineteenth-century American buyers were willing to pay a 10 percent premium for mulatto women, whereas eighteenth-century Cape buyers paid a 15 percent premium for creole women, among whom were the Cape mulattoes. Probably the greater scarcity of women (slave and free) at the Cape inspired the higher premium. Kotlikoff (1975), 9. Kotlikoff could not investigate regional premiums in the nineteenth-century American South, because such distinctions of slave origin had long since disappeared in the slave population. By 1850 the percentage of slaves in the American South who had been born in a foreign country was minimal. Few, if any, distinctions based on region of origin therefore existed.

41. A population pyramid is a demographic diagram that summarizes the age and sex composition of a population.

42. DO, "Transporten," 19 May 1694 (twice), 8 Jun. 1695, 31 May 1697 (twice), 8 Aug. 1709; CJ 3074, CAD; *Obligatien, Transporten van Slaven, ens.*, 1715–19, 11 Oct. 1719, 22 Jul. 1722 (twice).

43. Franken (1926), 35-41, and idem (1930, 18 Jul.), 41, 67.

44. Tas (1969–70), 165, n. 165 [*sic*]. The farm name has survived.

45. AR, VOC 4102, "Criminele Processtukken," "Appendices."

46. Based on a compilation of languages mentioned in all criminal cases, every five

years, in the VOC "Processtukken" (1680–1731). Dutch was normally spoken only by creole slaves.

47. Valentijn (1973), 1: 170-1. Note that Valentijn rank-orders both peoples and languages in a strictly Eurocentric hierarchy. Most significantly, he conflates "nation" and origin.

48. De Kock (1950), 52.

49. Franken (1930, 18 Jul.), 41. As translated in Davids (1989), 74:

This letter comes as a message from Stellenbosch. You sent me. Brother September, I announce that I have been sick for two months and that no human medicine [can cure me]. Brother September, I seek encouragement from you because I know you care about our Buganese people. I request from you brother, if you have compassion, actually for your Buganese race, because I know from the time we spoke with our fellow Buganese people, you said we were suffering and that this concerned you, for we are a broken, suffering people in miserable conditions, thus my request to you, Brother September, if you are compassionate for your suffering Buganese compatriots, will you lead the children who came from the places of Boeloe Boloe and Sanja-c.

50. Kolbe (1968), 1: 363.

51. Kindersley (1777), 66-7.

52. Sparrman (1977), 1: 280 and 40n.

53. Mirza Abu Taleb Khan (1810), 1: 72-3.

54. Sparrman (1977), 1: 58.

55. Mentzel (1921-44), 1: 56.

56. Leipoldt (1976), 17; Shell (1978), 12-16.

57. van Selms (1952), 61-102.

58. For a survey of some recent literature, and a minor example of this never-ending dispute, see Jordaan (1974), 461-95 and *The Cape Argus*, 20 through 26 Dec. 1977. For a fuller discussion of the language problem and the debate over Afrikaans's origins, Valkhoff (1966) and idem (1972).

59. Elphick (1985), 176-7, 179.

60. Requesten en Nominatien, 9 Sep. 1721, C. 228, (also C. 1086, 292), CAD; cf Wednesday, 2 Sep. 1721 in Böeseken et al (1957+), 6: 128-9. Liebbrandt has copied the names incorrectly and translated carelessly. Leibbrandt, *Requesten*, 2: 518 (73 of 1721).

61. Böeseken and Cairns (1989), 74 and n. 35, stating that the delay came about as one of the members of the political council was "absent." Malherbe (1991), 15-6.

62. Wednesday, 9 Sep. 1721 in Böeseken et al (1957+), 6: 129 and n143. Hermanus van Brakel was nominated as heemraad on 14 Dec. 1716 [(no. 156 in Leibbrandt, *Requesten* (1905-1989), 5: 1231] and confirmed on 1 Nov. 1718 (no. 98 in ibid, 1238).

63. Elphick (1985), 182. Venter (1940) makes no mention of this topic.

64. Mentzel (1921-44), 3: 300; cf. ibid, 3: 119.

65. The "apprenticeship" system, so named by Moodie, is not to be confused with the *inboekstelsel* of the VOC period. Moodie admitted that he named the VOC system after the later British system. Moodie (1842), 3: 77, n. 2.

66. For a dicussion of descent system of slavery, Patterson (1982), 135-47.

67. For the Cape, see Theal (1901), 9: 146 (art. 3); Worden (1985), 36, 80; Böeseken (1989), 74-5, 141 n. 37.

68. Beyers (1929), 242-9.

69. Penn (1987), 475-6.

70. Hemmy (1959), 29. Gijsbert Hemmy was the son of Theodor Hemmy, a successful slaving Captain and one of the Cape's wealthiest men.

71. Leibbrandt *Requesten*, 2: 772 (18 Sep. 1771).

72. "Information respecting Cape Good Hope given by Col. Dalyrymple, 1784, 1785," no. 14, A455, CAD.

73. Sparrman (1977), 1: 181.

74. As quoted in Burrows (1988), 43. Article six demanded greater control of "ordinary Hottentot farm retainers brought up by Christians":

> They shall serve their masters up to the age of 25 and not enter another's employ without his consent. No runaway Hottentot shall be allowed sanctary in any *colonie* (kraal) but shall be accosted and warned by the District Officers and despatched directly back to their *Lord and Master*, or else taken in custody by the messenger.

75. "Report from the Select Committee on Aborigines (British Settlements) with the official report and further evidence [minutes of Evidence], Appendix and Index," *Imperial Blue Book*, 1837 nrVII.425, 28.

76. As reproduced in Bird (1823), 247.

77. Philip to LMS directors, Nov. 1826, RCC, XXX: 157-8.

78. Commissioners of Enquiry to Earl Bathurst, 25 Sep. 1823, RCC, XVI: 305.

3

Drosters of the Bokkeveld and the Roggeveld, 1770–1800[1]

Nigel Penn

As the VOC refreshment station at the Cape developed into a colony, it produced a diverse number of fugitives whose greatest desire was to remove themselves from the strictures of its laws. These runaway slaves, deserted sailors, absconding soldiers, "land loopers," vagabonds, escaped murderers, bandits, thieves, and assorted criminals often formed groups, bound together in a particular form of resistance to oppression—flight.[2] By the second half of the eighteenth century, as colonial power advanced further into the Cape interior, the ranks of these fugitives became augmented by new recruits, Khoikhoi and *Bastaard-Hottentot* laborers who, in the eyes of their employers, had broken their contracts and left their place of work. Such groups, increasingly, became known as *drosters*.

A *droster* (from the Dutch, *drossen*, "to run away" or "to desert") was essentially a deserter or escapee from a condition of unfree labor. Though the word had occasionally been applied to runaway slaves, as well as to absconding VOC soldiers and sailors before the 1750s, it acquired a new significance after this date.[3] The changed meaning of the word reflected a growing consciousness among both colonists and their laborers that there was little difference between the condition of being a slave and the condition of being a servant. Perhaps the best way to explore this consciousness and the experience behind it is to examine in detail the *drosters* of the late eighteenth century in the region where they were most active.

The mountains of the Cape interior had always beckoned to fugitives, offering as they did a wild and alluring place of refuge seemingly removed from colonial control. In the heart of these mountains—the Cape Fold Mountain System—lies the range now known as the Cedarberg, the geographical focus of this study. In the eighteenth century the Cedarberg were considered part of the Bokkeveld, a vast and vague area used to describe the mountains that lie east of the Olifants river. It is, in fact, impossible to detach the Cedarberg from the wider environmental context of the Bokkeveld or, for that matter, from the Roggeveld farther east. And these latter two regions formed with the Cedarberg the territory in which *droster* activities were concentrated.

How early the first fugitives arrived in the Bokkeveld mountains is uncertain. Perhaps the runaway slaves recorded as having reached the Charigurikwa Khoikhoi in the 1680s were among the pioneers, for in the seventeenth century the Charigurikwa were sometimes found along the Olifants river.[4] By the eighteenth century it was a common occurrence for both runaway slaves and company deserters to flee beyond the Piketberg. A group of slaves recaptured in 1707 had planned to hide in the *ver berge* ("far mountains") and make their way to the Nama.[5] In 1709 the slave, Simon of Malabar, reported that he along with some other fugitives crossed the Olifants river and entered the territory of the *Cochemans*, who then attacked them and forced them to retreat.[6] Assaulting colonial fugitives was a common response from early eighteenth century Khoikhoi societies, except for the Charigurikwa.[7] In a sense, the Khoikhoi themselves were fugitives from the colony, anxious as they were to avoid the company's reach by retreating farther into the interior. As the colony expanded, the Khoikhoi found it increasingly difficult to isolate themselves from the shock waves emanating from the southwestern Cape, particularly since they were pursued in turn by other colonial escapees. These runaways were often desperate, armed, and ravenous, thus posing a direct threat to the lives and livestock of the indigenous population. The company also encouraged the Khoikhoi, by a mixture of bribery and threats, to capture any fugitives they might find and return them to the colony. Runaways learned, therefore, that it was extremely risky to count on Khoikhoi support.[8]

Gradually the situation changed. Hard on the heels of the fugitive pioneers of the turbulent frontier came the slightly more respectable stock farmers of the colony who, at least in the eyes of the company, had a tenuous legality. But since their activities included the destruction of wild animals through uncontrolled hunting, the seizure of land and water resources, the acquisition of Khoikhoi livestock by fair means or foul, and the seizing of Khoikhoi women and children, their impact on Khoikhoi societies was far more destructive than that of their lawless precursors.[9] Stripped of the means to continue an independent existence and devastated by the 1713 smallpox epidemic, the Khoikhoi were obliged to become the servants of the ever-increasing number of colonists. In 1739 the last overt Khoisan resistance to these processes in the Bokkeveld was crushed. At that point, a common consciousness of oppression between slaves and Khoikhoi laborers came into existence and thereafter gathered momentum.[10]

FIGURE 3.1 The Bokkeveld and Roggeveld, 1770-1800.

Key
Karoo
Mountains
Veld

A crucial stage in this process was associated with the emergence of a new category of colonial subject, the *Bastaard-Hottentot*. Those placed in this category were the children of mixed slave and Khoikhoi parentage. As early as 1721 some freeburghers of the Stellenbosch district had written to the government to ask for permission to bind in service, for a certain number of years, the offspring of slave and Khoikhoi unions.[11] The issue seems to have lain dormant until 1775 when the landdrost and heemraden of Stellenbosch decreed that *Bastaard-Hottentot* children should be bound to serve their masters until the age of twenty-five. The only conditions of service were that such children should be well cared for and that their names, ages, and parents' names should be recorded.[12] Treating *Bastaard-Hottentots* as slaves required but a short step to treating Khoikhoi laborers the same way. A 1781 resolution declared that since runaway slaves were passing themselves off as Khoikhoi, the names of local Khoikhoi should be annually submitted to the authorities by the veldwagtmeesters. After 1787 the earlier suggestion that *Bastaard-Hottentots* be required to carry passes was implemented and extended to apply to the Khoikhoi.[13]

Apart from these onerous laws, the Khoikhoi were a free people in theory. At the level of lived experience, however, there was increasingly little to distinguish their lives from those of other unfree laborers on colonial farms. One of the most important factors in determining their subservient status was the influence on labor relations exerted by the struggle occurring within the frontier zone. The 1739 victory of colonial commandos had resulted in the subjugation of all the Khoisan south of Namaqualand and west of the Roggeveld. Commandos had also enabled frontier farmers to advance beyond the forbidding immensity of the Cape Fold Mountains—for so long inhabited by unconquered Khoisan—and to incorporate into the colony the entire winter rainfall region of the western Cape. Consequently, colonists came into conflict with the Khoisan of the interior escarpment. By 1770 a life-or-death struggle between Khoisan and the frontier farmers was underway, and it intensified as commandos were almost continuously mounted throughout the length and breadth of the frontier zone. Commandos, of course, were used not only to crush enemies without the colony, but also to control laborers within. In 1774 it became virtually compulsory for *Bastaards* and *Bastaard-Hottentots* to serve in commandos, while Khoikhoi, too, were eligible for military service. In response, from 1778 onward, a large number of Khoikhoi and *Bastaard-Hottentots* trekked beyond the boundaries of the colony to the Nama or to the Orange river.[14]

These groups formed the nucleus of societies that became known as *Oorlams*. To some extent the *Oorlams* were larger, more successful versions of *drosters*. They were composed of the same motley collection of colonial fugitives but were distinguished by their having achieved a measure of political independence, economic viability, social cohesion, and military capability that altogether enabled them to secure themselves in a region beyond the reach of colonial commandos. *Oorlams* were not maroon communities, though runaway slaves lived among them, because their many Khoisan and *Bastaard-Hottentot* members gave them a strongly indigenous component.[15]

Drosters remained distinct from *Oorlams*, even though they included many who attempted at least to join those interior communities. Many dangerous days' journey stood between a fugitive and the distant haven of the Orange river. Thus by 1740, runaways were attracted first to the mountainous areas of the Cape interior that lay within, rather than beyond, the colonial frontier (and provided thereby a strong incentive for the determined fugitives who preceded them to flee even farther north). Even *drosters* who had heard of the *Oorlams* of the Orange hesitated running the gauntlet of roving commandos, hostile San, beasts of prey, and the waterless wastes beyond the Bokkeveld. Fugitives continued to make for the mountains, and it is with their struggle that the following discussion is concerned.[16]

The *Drosters*[17]

In early winter 1793, the slave Adam deserted his master, Jochem Scholtz, the younger, of the Roggeveld, and fled to the Ongens (or Ongeluks) river in the Tanqua Karoo.[18] Adam chose his time and place well. Traditionally, the onset of the rainy season occasioned a heightened mobility in the western Cape, as the stock farmers of the Bokkeveld and Roggeveld mountain ranges moved their animals down to their *legplaatsen* on the warmer plains to avoid the freezing rain and snow.[19] For the colonists, living as they did in an area usually too arid to sustain their livestock, the winter rains came at a time of enforced yet welcome sociability when friends and relatives from remote regions were brought together. After the rains, for a brief period, the grazing was good. So too was the hunting, and nineteenth-century descriptions of convivial camp fires and holiday spirits attending transhumance in the Tanqua Karoo may be confidently extrapolated to the eighteenth century.[20] Nor were these seasonal upheavals without benefit for the slaves and servants of the *trekboers*. The long treks with livestock and the mingling and merging of people from different regions in an area where all were comparative strangers provided the shepherds and drovers with circumstances that were particularly conducive to escape. They had legitimate mobility, partial anonymity, and abundant resources of livestock or game close to hand. The landscape, too, seemed to offer a place of refuge. To the west of the Tanqua Karoo rose the brooding massif of the Cedarberg; to the north and south the mountains merged into the vast ridges of the Cape Fold Mountain System. The colonists were in the habit of naming the entire mountain range the Bokkeveld, though, strictly speaking, the district of that name began north of the Cedarberg. Conversely, the southeastern ramparts of the range were known as the Zwaarte Ruggens ("black hills"—a dark name for a grim place). Behind the Zwaarte Ruggens to the west was the Koue Bokkeveld, an area of high mountains and secret valleys. The region was really the southern end of the Cedarberg, and it was sometimes referred to as the Koue Bergen or Koue Veld, though its mountains were also called the Skurweberge. To the Khoikhoi and *Bastaard-Hottentots* who knew the region, the name "Cedarberg" had a mildness that they rejected as incongruous. And, in the mouths of the *drosters* who had lived there, the word underwent a bitter corruption: to Zuurbergen (literally "sour mountains").[21] Regardless of the name, these rugged mountains offered a broken wilderness of weathered sandstone, deep ravines, and thick fragrant fynbos. They were a good place to hide.

Adam, like others before and after him, used the favorable opportunities of time and place to desert. Once the standing water in the Ongeluks river began to dry up, they gravitated toward the western mountains. With him was a Khoikhoi woman, Jannetje, whom he regarded as his wife. She too had worked for Jochem Scholtz. About twelve years before she had given birth to a boy, April, the son of Adam, and therefore a *Bastaard Hottentot*. April had joined his parents in flight, but why had they fled? When Adam was later asked this question, his interrogators must have thought that a man needed a specific, compelling reason to decide, suddenly, to reject enslavement. His answer cannot have satisfied them: He had run away because he had not been given any clothes.[22]

A more plausible incentive, apart from slavery itself, was the milieu from which Adam and his family fled. Jochem Scholtz, his master, had the reputation of being one of the biggest troublemakers in the Roggeveld. He was, as it happened, a "man of immense size, so much so that he could not wear the usual articles of clothing; his daily dress was a night-gown and shirt."[23] The *veldvagtmeester* of the Roggeveld, Gerrit Maritz, described him as a *groot sterk man* ("big strong man") and a *gewelt hebber in moet willige rust verstoorder* ("tyrant and mischievous disturber of the peace"), an opinion based on painful personal experience.[24] By the 1790s Scholtz had registered three farms along the Riet river in the Roggeveld and at least one other in the Skurweberge.[25] His father had farmed in the district since 1756,[26] and his brother, Hermanus, was nearby to lend a hand.[27] Hermanus, in fact, was similar to Jochem in his treatment of laborers. One day in the winter of 1792, he beat the pregnant wife of his Khoikhoi servant, Jan Swart. The woman, Sarmentje, ran away. Jan then ran way because Hermanus was about to bind him for failing to slaughter a sheep quickly enough. The couple hid for a few days not far from the farm before Jan's brother, Claas, joined them. Hermanus had wanted to beat him because he had not brought some oxen to the farm when ordered. Claas's wife, Lena, and their one-year-old child were the next to join the group, while the final adherent was Griet, the sister of Jan and Claas Swart. The fugitives soon moved to the Tanqua Karoo where the Scholtz's had a *legplaats*. Significantly, it was winter. The Swarts did not make their way west but tried to survive where they were. So terrified of discovery was Class that he ordered his wife to bash out their baby's brains on a rock to stop it from crying. Lena did so. Claas then went berserk and beat Lena to death with a *(knob)kierie*; he also inflicted serious wounds on his sister, Griet. The rest of the group, cowed and shocked, were made to promise not to say anything. Such a precaution was necessary, as it was becoming apparent in the veld that there was no food to harvest or livestock to steal. By summer the survivors had returned to Hermanus Scholtz. Hunger and fear had defeated them.[28]

These events suggest that for some Khoikhoi, at least, it was preferable to kill their own child rather than return to service under a harsh master.[29] The Swarts' experiences also point to the difficulties of surviving in the Tanqua Karoo, and it is altogether possible that Adam learned enough from their mistakes to head westward when he made his break.[30]

When Adam and his family took flight in the winter of 1793, other fugitives were already part of the landscape. About a month after escaping, they encountered the runaway slaves, Africa and Cupido, who were in turn accompanied by two Khoikhoi women and their children. The women, Anna and Rosalijn, later testified that they had been forcibly abducted by Africa, the fugitive slave of the influential veldwagtmeester of the Hantam, Petrus Pienaar.[31] Africa had been at large for an unspecified period before he visited one of Pienaar's farms in the Hantam in the summer of 1792–1793 and compelled Anna and her child to join him. At about the same time he also entered a farm belonging to Christoffel Esterhuysen and forced Rosalijn and her child to go with him. Whether the children (girls named Roos and Klijne Flora) were Africa's is unclear, as is his relationship with the women prior to their abduction. At least part of Africa's concern in seizing two women, however, was seemingly to cater for his fellow *droster*, the slave Cupido van Malabar, who had fled from the burgher Frans Joosten. At any rate, when Adam encountered this group, he thought the women were the wives of the men.[32]

Soon they were joined by three Khoikhoi *drosters*: Steenbok, Lammert (or Lambert), and Picqueur. It is not clear why Steenbok and Lammert joined the *complot*, from where they came, or who in fact they were, because their evidence was never recorded.[33] Something *is* known about Picqueur, for he was eventually captured and interrogated. He was about eighteen years old and had been born on the farm of Jan Jacobs in the Bokkeveld. One day, while busy digging white lime for his boss on the farm of Frans Joosten (Cupido's boss) in the Bokkeveld, he was approached by Africa, who urged him to go with him. Picqueur said he was promised food and clothing but in the end claimed to have accompanied Africa out of fear. More than likely Picqueur and Cupido knew one another because both had worked on Frans Joostens's farm.[34] Africa, whose forceful recruiting methods are evidence of his considerable strength of will, emerged as the leader of the group. Gradually Africa's *drosters*, Adam and his family included, made their way to the Winkelhaak kloof in the Koue Bokkeveld.[35]

Considerable difficulties arise in timing the *drosters'* movements, not to mention placing the group's constituent elements when they first met. Certain patterns are clear, however. As the coldest part of the winter receded and the flowerful spring arrived, the colonists left the Karoo and returned to their farms. Soon, the eastern sides of the mountain became even less populated, and the *drosters* felt emboldened to move southward.

They also felt compelled. During the spring of 1793, a great deal of commando activity took place in the mountains above the Olifants river to the west of the *drosters* and in the Bokkeveld to their north. The veldwagtmeesters of these districts imagined that they had uncovered a conspiracy among the Khoikhoi and *orlamse hottentots* of Swellendam, the Hex river, and Namaqualand. The conspiracy was rumored to involve an attack on the Colony by the *"schelm* Donderbos Pokkebos" and 400 of his followers armed with guns. Donderbos was reportedly sighted in the Bidouw (the Pakhuis Pass area) and was believed to be passing through the Bokkeveld in order to reach Namaqualand and raise his army. Further details concerning this fantasy are irrelevant here.[36] What is relevant is the panic it inspired among colonists. Johannes Lubbe, veldwagtmeester of the Olifants river, scoured the mountains of his district with commandos and declared that

> *'t is hoog tyt om onse lant te behouden en swijgen voor de swarte nasie want 't schyn of sy alle op gemaakt is weest gewaapent en gereed* ("it is high time we save our country and (not) to succumb to the black nation, for it seems as if they all have been incited; be armed and ready").[37]

In such circumstances, it made sense for the *drosters* to keep clear of the northern parts of the mountain range.

Africa's group also chose to move to the Winkelhaak kloof in order to place themselves in the proximity of isolated farms. In the western Cape, all *droster* groups were, to some extent, parasites obliged to live off the livestock of the farmers. In the harsh environment of the mountains and the Karoo, natural and seasonal resources such as *veldkos* and game could not always be obtained in sufficient quantities to feed large groups of people. Scarcities were exacerbated by the limited areas in which *drosters* could roam freely in search of supplies. Protecting the secrecy of their where-abouts restricted their movements and made them inefficient hunters and gatherers. In consequence, *drosters* resorted to stealing livestock, though probably only in desperation, because no matter how stealthily executed, stock theft risked drawing attention to themselves and invited discovery.

Africa and Cupido had already managed to obtain some cattle before Adam and his family joined them. With Adam's help a further seven sheep were stolen from Rasmus Esterhuizen and seven from Hermanus Scholtz.[38] The group's resources and numbers were enlarged further when the Meij brothers decided to throw in their lot with the *drosters*.

Rooi and Willem Meij were both about twenty years old and both worked for the burgher, Jan Louw the elder. They were, in the parlance of the day, *Bastaard-Hottentots* who worked on Louw's farm in the Bokkeveld. Louw himself lived at the Tygerberg, near Cape Town, so the management of his farm, Pampoen Kraal, described as *"agter de Scheerfdenberg,"* was in the hands of a *knecht*. In the winter the livestock on this farm, like livestock throughout the Bokkeveld, was driven to the Karoo. This task had likely been entrusted to the Meij brothers, for at some point between the Bokkeveld and the Karoo, Willem Meij fell victim to Africa's persuasive powers. Whether Willem had already decided to desert before meeting up with Africa's *complot* cannot be determined, but he appears to have needed little convincing. In his defence he made no reference to having been forced to desert, testifying instead that he had done so *"om dat ik het daar slegt had en mihn verdiende loon mih onthouden wierd"* ("because I was treated badly and my wages I had earned were held back").[39]

Strictly speaking, as a "Bastaard-Hottentot," Willem was not entitled to a wage, but perhaps that is what rankled him. At least some Khoikhoi on Louw's farm in 1793 were receiving a wage of Rds 12, one *kirsaaije rok* (dress made of coarsely woven fabric), two shirts, and two pairs of trousers for a year's work.[40]

Rooi Meij, his brother, joined the others somewhat later, after having received permission from the *knecht* at Pampoenen Kraal to go to Eylands drift on the Doorn river in the Tanqua Karoo. Quite what business he had to conduct there is not known. Perhaps he had been sent to assist Willem and knew nothing of the *complot*, though his ignorance seems unlikely. For whatever reason, Rooi met Willem and Africa near the Winkelhaak kloof, surely no coincidence, particularly since Adam and Rooi had previously met. One of the Meij brothers had absconded with a musket belonging to Jan Louw, while the other *drosters* already had a gun. At the time Jan Louw was unaware that ten of his cattle had also been "contributed" to the *drosters*. Louw's other cattle were vulnerable, protected only by the risks *drosters* were certain to incur in moving about a larger herd; they committed further robberies when necessary.[41]

The *complot* then numbered fourteen men, women, and children whose common bond was a desire to avoid discovery and capture. Their ambition, it was soon felt, was better served by shifting to the vicinity of Eylands drift, the attraction of which probably lay in the fact that Willem Meij had legitimate business there—a useful alibi.[42] Besides, the robberies in the Winkelhaak area could not go unnoticed forever. In the meantime, months had passed and summer arrived before the *complot* made its way northward.

The group passed between the Skurweberge and the Zwaarte Ruggens, possibly crossed the Katbakkies[43] to the Karoo, and hugged the mountain fringes until they reached Eylands drift under the Zuurbergen.[44] At the drift a Khoikhoi by the name of Isaak, who was there with his family and who worked for Jan Kok, told them that the nearest people in the neighborhood were Oude Rooij and his followers, a group of Khoikhoi who had a kraal, Stille Kraal, further up Eylands kloof. As luck would have it, one of the Oude Rooij's oxen wandered into the *drosters'* vicinity shortly afterwards, and it was promptly butchered and eaten. Only after a good meal did the men begin to wonder whether they had acted wisely. What if Oude Rooij reported the theft? Would it not be safer to silence him?

Oude Rooij's Kraal

Oude Rooij, a Khoikhoi, was known to his mother, Griet, as Jantjie. He was commonly known nevertheless as Oude Rooij, in order to distinguish him from his two sons, Klyn Jantjie Rooi and Rooi Rooi. In 1792 he, along with his mother, sons, his wife Mietje, and his daughter Griet, lived at Klip Fonteyn, the farm of the burgher Arnoldus Vlok in the Zwaarte Ruggens. That year the family was visited by his elder brother, Wittebooij, and his brother's wife, Sara. Too much liquor was consumed and Oude Rooij, while under the influence of alcohol, struck his mother so hard on the head that she nearly died. For good measure he then stabbed her in the leg. Wittebooij, who was also drunk, took exception to this unfilial action and assisted his mother by stabbing Oude Rooij so deeply between the shoulder blades that the knife point protruded from his breast. Far from having a sobering effect, this thrust led Wittebooij to stab his wife, Sara, in the left breast and slash her across the forehead. Although no fatalities resulted, we must conclude that Oude Rooij's 1792 family reunion was not a success.

The very next year, however, undeterred by the unfortunate events which had accompanied his last visit, Wittebooij returned to Oude Rooij's, bringing along Sara and their children, Jan, Trijn, and Leys. The two brothers proceeded to drink brandy, whereupon Wittebooij felt moved to thrash Leys with a bundle of reeds. Oude Rooij attempted to stop him but this made Wittebooij *boos* ("mad"), and a fight ensued. Oude Rooij was flung to the ground and beaten so severely that his son, Rooij Rooij, was forced to intervene. He took his father's musket and shot Wittebooij above the left knee. An hour later his uncle bled to death. His mother, who had also had some brandy, was powerless to influence events; and since Oude Rooij had temporarily lost the use of his arms and legs, the assistance of some neighboring Khoikhoi was required in order to bury the body. Once Oude Rooij had recovered it became obvious to Sara that he planned to kill her and her children in order to prevent them from telling their story. They fled, hiding temporarily in an aardvarks' hole, and made their way to Sara's father, a man called Wissel Bockenveld.[45]

A short time later, Mietje, the wife of Oude Rooij, died. The cause of her death was not recorded, but since Oude Rooij had a reputation for violence, her life alongside him could not have been easy. About the beginning of harvest time (November) in 1793, the surviving members of Oude Rooij's family journeyed to another of Arnoldus Vlok's farms, Eylands Drift, near the confluence of the Doorn and Tratra rivers in the Tanqua Karoo. Unfortunately for the family, Vlok then sold his farm to the burgher Hendrik Smit, who ordered Oude Rooij and his dependents off his property. So they moved, establishing a kraal in one of the kloofs nearby.[46]

Oude Rooij was, however, desirous of female company other than that of his family. With this in mind he visited a kraal, about two days journey away, belonging to a Khoikhoi woman called Anna. He probably knew that Anna's daughter, Flora, was without her husband, Jan Swart Kees, who had been hired for the harvest time by the burgher Jacob Tas of Eselbank in the Cedarberg. Unfortunately, this meant that Jan had to leave behind Anna, Flora, and Flora's young brother, Marthinus, but his absence suited Oude Rooij admirably. When he arrived at the kraal, he told Flora that he was going to take her away and that he would kill her if she resisted. Unprotected, and with Oude Rooij's fearsome reputation to consider, Flora was abducted.[47]

By the time the unwilling woman had been forced to Rooij's kraal (misnomered as Stille Kraal), more visitors had arrived. They were Oude Rooij's daughter, Griet, her husband, Jurie Oortman, and a man called Claas Jaager, also known as Claas Niegerman. Griet and Jurie had a baby girl called Leyn, who was about two years old, so their relationship had presumably been in existence for some time. Jurie worked for Gerrit Cloete, a burgher of the Olifants river area, and he was accompanied by his brother, Kleyne Donderbos.[48] They had arrived at Christmastime.[49] Though it cannot be stated that the family visit was timed to coincide with the holy day, there was to be little to celebrate.

On the third night after Flora's arrival at Stille Kraal, the dogs began to bark. Oude Rooij released them, shouting "*Sa! Sa! Schiet er op!* "in order to scare off any threatening presence. He suspected that *drosters* or predators might be about, and he was right.[50] The dogs eventually stopped barking, and the people returned to their slumbers, but all the while they had been spied on by Lammert. He had been sent forward by Africa, who stayed hidden some distance away with the other men in his band. A decision had been reached earlier in the day to deal with Oude Rooij's kraal. The majority of the male *drosters*—the women were not privy to the discussion—were in favor of murdering the kraal's men. Those taking the hard line were Africa, Cupido, Steenbok, Lammert, and Adam, with the others (the Meij brothers and Picqueur) reluctantly following suit.[51] Toward evening the men had left the women and cautiously approached Oude Rooij's kraal. Around midnight Lammert had crept up to try and gauge the numbers present, but, when the dogs detected him, the *drosters* decided to wait for daylight.

Next morning, before sunrise, Oude Rooij took his bow and his *koker* (quiver) full of arrows to scout and try to find the cause of the previous night's disturbance. The kraal, situated as it was on the bank of the Eylands river, was at that particular time not easily fordable.[52] Oude Rooij crossed the river about a hundred paces from the kraal and began his search. He need not have gone looking for danger. Soon after his departure the *droster* men emerged on the bank opposite the kraal and shouted to Jurie Oortman to show them the way over the river. Altogether they were eight, and since they had muskets, *kieries*, and assagais, they could not be denied. Jurie had an injured foot, so Claas Jager waded over to show them the crossing.

When the *drosters* established that Oude Rooij was missing, Africa sent Donderbos to fetch him. Oude Rooij's heart must have sunk to hear of the unwelcome visitors and, once he returned, his worst fears were confirmed. While Adam and Lammert stood by menacingly with loaded muskets, the other *drosters* bound the hands of Oude Rooij, Jurie Oortman, Donderbos, and Class Jager. The captives were then forced to cross the river and walk away from the kraal up the kloof accompanied by Africa, Adam, Lammert, Willem Meij, Cupido, and Steenbok. Picqueur and Rooi Meij stayed to guard Griet, Flora, and Kleyn Leyn. None knew that Oude Rooij's mother, Griet, had managed to hide herself nearby and was observing the proceedings. About half an hour later the anxious women heard a shot. Young Griet ran toward the river, fearing for her husband, but she was brought back by Picqueur and Rooi Miej. The elder Griet, however, crept through the bushes toward the sound. To her horror she saw her son, Oude Rooij, lying with his head smashed. More shots rang out, as Griet stayed hidden. When it was safe, she fled in the direction of the kraal of a Khoikhoi, Willem Fortuijn, reaching his place by nightfall.[53]

What had happened? Exact details are hard to establish in the case of those men who were eye witnesses or participants in the crime, especially given that those later captured and questioned had to convince the interrogators of their innocence. Pieces of albeit contradictory evidence together seem to suggest that Oude Rooij managed to slip out of his bonds and to make a break for freedom. Adam caught him and bashed his head with a rock, holding him still whilst Lammert shot him. Lammert also shot Class Jager and then, with either Willem Meij or Adam, shot Jurie Oortman and Klyne Donderbos. Africa employed his time by hitting the victims with a *kierie*, while the others stood by. Willem Meij helped himself to the hat of Oude Rooij, who by the standards of his deceased friends was the best dressed. He was the only one in trousers (blue) and a jacket (red). The others wore *karosses*. Claas Jager had a hat, but it was too blood stained to wear.

The murderers then returned to Picqueur, Rooi Meij, and the women, telling them that they had shot the others. Willem Miej gave Picqueur his old hat, and Africa gave Flora and Griet permission to see the bodies. Escorted to the site by Cupido and Rooij Meij, they covered the bodies with branches. Back at Stille Kraal, Africa had discovered two knapsacks full of Oude Rooij's home-brewed honey beer.[54] They consumed it, then loaded the pack oxen of Jurie Oortman and Claas Jager with meat and *karosses*. The *drosters* then moved out, taking Flora and Griet with them and, after a short distance, they were reunited with their own women. After staying a while in the vicinity they once more encountered Isaak, the shepherd, who told them he had heard that a commando was after them. With fearful urgency the group decided to head toward the Bokkeveld.

Dispersal

After two days of scurrying northward, Africa decided that their safety was jeopardized by the presence of Griet and, more specifically, her screaming infant Klein Leyn. He, therefore, drove them away from the group and threatened Flora with death if she ever breathed a word about the murder to the "Christians." On reaching the Bokkeveld mountains, the group split up. Adam, April, Cupido, and Jannetje wanted to go north to Namaqualand. Surviving this route was virtually impossible in the summer because of the lack of water; and Adam, April, and Jannetje eventually withdrew from the plan. The mother and her son then went to the farm of Pieter Langefontein while Adam, having run out of options, returned to the Scholtz's in the Roggeveld. His master, Jochem, was not at home but Jochem's brother, Hermanus, was. One of the Scholtz's Khoikhoi servants, Anthony, had already received word of the evil deeds committed in Eylands kloof, and Adam could not deny that he had been among the *drosters*. He did, however, deny having done anything wrong, which proved insufficient to save him from arrest. He was taken to the Cape for trial. Cupido van Malabar was never captured, and his fate is unknown.[55]

The rest of the group, under Africa's leadership, remained in the Bokkeveld. A craving for certain items of consumption seems to have influenced Africa's next series of commands; he ordered Lammert, Steenbok, and Rooi Meij to steal some spices and tobacco, Picqueur some bread for the children, while Africa, Willem Meij and the women and children went to see what could be found at the farm of Roeloff van der Merwe. The dangerous game of robbing farm houses had begun.

Meanwhile, a commando had indeed been mobilized to track down the *drosters*. As of late December 1793 Gerrit Cloete had been informed of the murder by a Khoikhoi servant of Hendrik Smit. Cloete had been left in charge of the Olifants river district by veldwagtmeester Frans Lubbe, then at the Cape.[56] He therefore commanded Isaac Davel, the baptized Bastaards Carel van Rooijen and David Koopman, and some Khoikhoi servants to accompany him. Griet, Oude Rooij's mother, had managed to tell her story. Since Cloete estimated that the murder had taken place on 28 or 29 December, the news had taken a mere two or three days to travel over the Cedarberg to him. The commando moved more slowly, taking eight days to reach Eylands kloof, searching the mountains as they went but suspecting that the *drosters* had been warned by spies (like Isaak). At the scene of the crime, all they found were two blood-stained, bullet-pierced *karosses*, as well as a blood-stained hat identified as having been Claas Jager's. Signs were present that cattle had been slaughtered and cooked. On the way back a horse and some cattle were found, some of which were dead, and an abandoned musket. Cloete identified it as Jan Louw's—the Meij brothers' boss.[57]

By 20 January 1794 the commando had returned without any *drosters*, but with the news that *die klyne hottentot* Picqueur had been captured. A Khoikhoi servant of the burgher Willem du Toit had caught him. The very next day Africa, Willem Miej, Anna and Flora were discovered and captured by two Khoikhoi servants on the farm of Roeloff van der Merwe. Somehow Africa managed to escape. He was never recaptured.[58]

Rooi Meij and Lammert tried robbing the farm house of the widow of Daniel van der Merwe. Steenbok was not with them as they crept into the garden at night. Realizing that the house was empty, they wasted no time stealing fruit but broke open a window and took what they could find: two rolls of tobacco, a jacket, a pair of trousers, and two women's dresses. Early next morning the widow's son, Erasmus, noticed the broken window and the missing items. He also discovered footprints and quickly summoned two Khoikhoi servants, Coert and Class, to help track down the thieves. That afternoon they came upon the two fugitives in the veld and called on them to stand still. Van der Merwe and his men were armed with muskets but Lammert and Rooi Meij refused to surrender. Instead, they ran. Shots were fired and Lammert fell dead while Rooi Meij was wounded. To van der Merwe's astonishment, Rooi Meij continued running and escaped. The stolen goods were recovered.[59]

Four days later Joseph Joosten, who owned a farm four hours away from the van der Merwe's, was informed by his Khoikhoi servant, Booij, that a suspicious-looking *Bastaard-Hottentot* was among his sheep. Rooi Meij obviously had a craving for tobacco for he was sitting with the shepherd, a slave called Jephta, sharing a pipe. As Joosten rode up on his horse, he recognized Meij as the *opgedroste Bastaard Hottentot* of Jan Louw and called on him to halt. Joosten asked Rooi Meij where he thought he was going and the reply was "to the Bokkeveld," whereupon Joosten accused Rooi of having stolen one of his sheep. This Rooi denied, but Joosten began hitting him with the butt of his musket. As Rooi ran away Joosten fired at him and, seeing the *droster* drop and lie still, dismounted to inspect what he hoped would be a corpse. But as he approached Rooi sprang up, whereupon Joosten hit him on the neck with his musket stock. Joosten then ordered Rooi to lie still and handed his musket to one of his servants for reloading. Before this task could be accomplished, Rooi was on his feet again and running. Joosten followed, using his musket as a club, but Rooi managed to grasp the gun in one hand and stab Joosten with a knife drawn from a knapsack tied to his arm. As the burgher fell back with a wound in his right arm, the battered Rooi Meij made good his escape.[60]

After having been shot and clubbed, the seemingly indestructible Rooi Meij tried to steal a horse to carry his aching body to safety. Close to the widow van der Merwe's farm was a farmer called Rasmus Erasmus,[61] and when one of his horses was found at the van der Merwe's, it behaved as if it had been stolen. Suspicious, Erasmus van der Merwe enlisted Daniel and Louw to help him track Rooi Miej. They caught up with him at the Zoute river. This time he came quietly and was reunited with his brother, then in the custody of veldwagtmeester Pieter Jacobs. Finally, with Adam and Picqueur, Rooi Meij stood trial in Cape Town.[62]

Steenbok was not captured. A later report that he was shot by a shepherd of Frans Jooste has to be weighed against other reports that he remained at large. The authorities could do little more than hope that the slaves Cupido and Africa might have encountered the same fate as Lammert and met their just deserts while engaged in stock theft. Statements were taken from Flora, Griet (Oude Rooij's mother), Anna, Rosalijn, Jannetje, and April, but these women and children were not held responsible for any crime. April and Jannetje were returned to Jochem Scholtz, the latter claiming in 1800 that he had *1 baster genaamd April de welk door den agbaar heer Fischaal mihn als lijf eigenaar is gegeeven* ("one 'Bastaard' named April who was given to me as serf by the honorable Fiscal"). Scholtz also listed a female servant as a Khoikhoi named Jannetje and noted that she was "paired" with one of his slaves.[63] The other women, no doubt, returned to a life of servitude on the farms or to one of insecurity in their kraals in the mountains.

Adam lied desperately at his trial, claiming that he had not been at Oude Rooij's kraal when the murder took place but with the *drosters'* women and children. Nobody supported his story. Willem Meij, who had certainly gone up the kloof with the doomed men, denied having played an active role in their death. He was the only available eye witness to events, but Picqueur claimed that Lammert had told him that Willem had killed Jurie Oortman. Picqueur and Rooi Meij had several witnesses attest that they had stood guard over the women and had, therefore, not played a part in the murder. In Picqueur's favor was his youth and the excuse that Africa had led him astray. Against Rooi Meij was the fact that he had stabbed a burgher, Joseph Joosten (by accident he claimed), an action which could not be condoned. All of the men on trial were of course guilty, at the very least, of stock theft and desertion. Adam and Willem Miej were sentenced to be hanged, and their bodies to be suspended from the gallows until the birds and the air had cleansed their bones of flesh. Rooi Meij was to have a noose put round his neck, his body bound to a pole and then be whipped and branded. After this he would be chained and put to hard labor on the company's works for life. Picqueur's received the same sentence as Rooi Miej's, except that he was given twenty-five years' hard labor and did not have to wear the hangman's noose around his neck.[64]

Conclusions

Droster activity continued after these sentences were carried out, as did the oppressive practices of bondage, as many examples from the Bokkeveld and Roggeveld can attest. One involved two Khoikhoi servants of Willem Sterrenberg Pretorius. After working for nearly ten years, they were prevented by Pretorius from leaving with their wages despite their having received the landdrost's permission. Pretorius flogged them severely and withheld all but a fraction of their earnings.[65] In March 1794 the authorities learned of a young Khoikhoi lad, Jantje, who had been taken from his uncle at least five times, beaten, and chained by Willem Steenkamp of the Roggeveld.[66] That same year Toontje, who worked for Pieter Jooste of the Bokkeveld, wanted to leave and take his wife, Else, with him. Jooste informed him that Else was *ingeboekt*, or "apprenticed" (i.e., a *Bastaard-Hottentot*) and could not leave. Toontje took the matter to the landdrost, who confirmed to Toontje that Else had to stay with Jooste. Toontje, though, was free, so he tried to get a nearby farmer, Wessel Pretorius, to hire him.

When Jooste heard of Toontje's insolent initiative he attempted to tie him up and, after he broke free, shot at him. Fortunately, Pretorius intervened and deflected the gun, but Jooste withheld twenty sheep and a horse that rightfully belonged to Toontje.[67] The list of abuses can be extended, but the examples above are sufficient evidence to explain why Dutch farmers were plagued by the desertion of their laborers.

Correspondingly, during the 1790s, Khoikhoi *drosters* began to link up with the San north of the Roggeveld. In December 1791 veldwagtmeester Maritz reported the desertion of a group of Khoikhoi from the colonists to the San, taking muskets with them.[68] In August 1795 Johannes Karstens reported from the Roggeveld that *Bastaats Hottentotten* were leaving, almost daily, to join the San and that no fewer than eleven had recently absconded with muskets.[69] Three years later Jacob Kriger reported from the same areas that he had sent a commando after a *complot drossende Hottentots* in July, shooting one and capturing a woman and two children. In August he had been obliged to track down *drosters* who were stealing horses and riding away to the Coup. He had also taken the precaution of putting *de bosiman meyt* of Gert Victor in chains to see if this would "tame" her, the reason being that she had been responsible for the death of two Khoikhoi who, on separate occasions, she had persuaded to desert with her and who had then been shot dead.[70]

In the late 1790s the arrival of AmaXhosa groups in the northern frontier zone afforded *drosters* a further option to flight.[71] Not surprisingly Jochem Scholtz was among the first to be affected. In November 1797 he noticed a slave among the followers of the AmaXhosa *inkosi* "Brood," and thinking that one of his slaves who had escaped might be in the group, he approached the group. "Brood" offered Scholtz a welcome by shooting at him with his musket. The gun misfired, giving Scholtz an opportunity to retreat and head for veldwagtmeester Visser's for help.[72] No record indicates that Scholtz recaptured his slave, but the Scholtz-"Brood" incident together with reports of *droster*-San activities illustrate that Khoikhoi and *Bastaard-Hottentots* were establishing a common ground with San and that *drosters* from the Roggeveld were, increasingly, trying their luck to the north instead of the west.

The Cedarberg by no means had lost its attractions. As Johannes Hugo, field-cornet of de Kouwe Velt reported of his district in August 1800, *heet een conterijje is daar veel schelms sig op hout* ("many rogues found themselves in this region").[73] The year before he had reported the desertion of Khoikhoi laborers from several farmers (himself included) with considerable stock theft. According to reliable reports these *drosters* had gone to the Zwaarte Ruggens, which was full of *schelmen* ("rogues"). He had also heard that Khoikhoi from the Roggeveld were congregating in the Zwaarte Ruggens whilst farmers in their winter *legplaatsen* in the Tanqua Karoo had been losing stock to thieves.[74]

The presence of farmers like Jochem Scholtz insured that the mountains would continue to be stocked with *drosters*. Officials on the spot were quite aware of the farmers' oppression of their servants. As the exasperated landdrost at Stellenbosch wrote to Scholtz in January 1799 after having received a complaint from Scholtz's ex-servant:

> Ik kan my niet genoeg[?] deser dat men by u in het veld mit een idee beheeft is als of een Hottentot eens by ejmand in dienst verhuurt is, verplig is geduurende zyn leeftyd te blyven dienen, geluk al weeder een (eaampe) zig voordoet in den Hottentot Cupido Jantje, die hy in den tyd van 13 jaaren gewoond heeft, en (hu) hy heer gaan wil belet jy (hom) did neit alleen maar jy weigert hom zyn vrouw kinderen en vhee af te geeven....("I cannot content myself with the knowledge that there are men in the field with you who have the idea that a Hottentot, once hired by sombody, is compelled to keep serving for a lifetime. The case of the Hottentot Cupido Jantje is another example of this. He has lived with you thirteen years and, now that he wants to leave, not only do you prevent him from doing so, you also refuse to hand over his wife, children, and livestock.")[75]

By the end of the century, the conditions of Khoikhoi *in het veld* were no better than that of a *Bastaard-Hottentot* or a slave. Ross notes that an effect on these groups of an increasingly common condition was greater cooperation.

> [W]ith certain exceptions, the steady reduction of the Khoisan to a position of bondage scarcely distinguishable from that of the slaves led to a slow growth of solidarity encompassing individuals from the two groups and to a slow diminution of estate conflict between them....In the mid-eighteenth century the number of cases...in which slaves and Khoi took opposite sides, as it were, clearly outnumbered those in which they acted together. Fifty years later, the reverse is the case.[76]

What requires further explanation, however, and what the material from the Bokkeveld and Roggeveld helps to answer, is the question of why, though they were becoming more and more like each other and capable of uniting in common associations (i.e., the *drosters*), the oppressed continued to prey on one another.[77]

The events surrounding Africa's *droster* gang and Oude Rooij's kraal illustrate significant developments taking place in the lives of Khoikhoi, *Bastaard-Hottentots*, and slaves in a particular region of the Cape in the late eighteenth century. By virtue of its mountainous remoteness and seasonal marginality, the Bokkeveld and Roggeveld of the western Cape frontier attracted *drosters* as well as Khoikhoi who desired living independently of Dutch farmers. The extent to which the Khoikhoi's ambitions were realized may partially be gauged from the details of the lives of those Khoikhoi connected to the nexus of relationships centered on Oude Rooij's kraal. For instance, in what was a high incidence of seasonal mobility, Khoikhoi servants responded to the rhythms of transhumance and harvest time. Clearly some Khoikhoi did not live on the farms of Dutch burghers year round but spent some time in independent kraals tucked away in kloofs or secluded valleys, staying with friends or family. A farmer might be fairly tolerant of the presence of a Khoikhoi kraal on one of his remote farms, leaving them a large measure of independence and not demanding too much of them. Arnoldus Vlok does not, for instance, seem to have interfered too much in the lives of Oude Rooij and his family. At other times such a presence might be intolerable and Khoikhoi not closely tied into a farmer's labor pool were viewed as vagrants or unwanted consumers of environmental resources. The latter attitude is, perhaps, displayed in the eviction of Oude Rooij's kraal from Eylands Drift by Hendrik Smit when the farm changed hands.[78]

Living on the margins of Dutch farms offered the advantage of greater independence but not necessarily added security. For one thing the land to which Khoikhoi had uncontested access was so marginal that it was hard to survive on year round. One consequence was migrant labor, in which men left their kraals to help with the harvest or to work short contracts. Another was exposure to danger from those other, and more desperate, fugitives from colonial control—the *drosters*. The risks run are evident in the case of migrant laborers, such as Jan Swart Kees, who left his wife and family unprotected, and to Khoikhoi living independently of Dutch farmers, such as Oude Rooij, whose kraal was beset by Africa's *complot*.

In the harsh environment of the Cape mountains, the twin imperatives of fugitives—to avoid discovery and to obtain food—could not both be met at the same time, or at least not for very long.[79] All too frequently *drosters* found it necessary to rob in order to eat, or deemed it necessary to kill in order to remain unreported. Stealing from Dutch farmhouses and herds was riskier, too, than robbing the more vulnerable, outlying Khoikhoi. Some Khoikhoi, such as Isaak at Eylands Drift, were sympathetic to runaways, and others were persuaded to join their ranks. On the whole, however, those Khoikhoi who were resident permanently on colonial farms were far more likely to defend their master's interests (and indirectly their own) by hunting down or shooting at *drosters*.[80] Those in Africa's group who were betrayed, captured, or shot had Khoikhoi to thank for their misfortune. Servants need not be judged harshly; those who were murdered at Oude Rooij's kraal were also part-time servants on Dutch farms.

Violence and brutality were monopolized by neither *drosters* nor colonists. Alongside brutish farmers, such as Jochem Scholtz, may be considered Khoikhoi such as Oude Rooij, Wittebooij, and Claas Swart, who had themselves been brutalized by their harsh life. Oude Rooij, like others who existed in the peripheries of colonial space or endured gross ill-treatment from colonial masters, were subject to fits of uncontrollable rage. His homicidal family rows, punctuated by his violence toward women, though clearly exposing the dangers of Cape brandy, reveal the symptoms of profound social disequilibrium. Though his murder inspires pity and disgust, his death looks much like his life—nasty, brutish, and short. His killers shared his world of pain and fear, and some had had their inhumanity honed by a life of enslavement.[81]

If anything, the position of Khoikhoi women was even less enviable. In Africa's group, as well as Oude Rooij's family, women were little better than chattels, subject to rape, abduction, and assault. Lena, Claas's wife, was forced to murder her own child before suffering the same fate at the hands of Claas. Other women, or at least women in other circumstances, appear to have been valued highly enough to be kept alive, for both *drosters* and Khoikhoi went to considerable trouble to add females to their groups. Women seemingly failed to resist being forced into submission, perhaps because the alternative was to be killed.

Aspirations in the midst of such violence, apart from prolonging escape itself, are difficult to discern, but important clues survive. In the previous events described, commodities and items of consumption of minimal, if any, value for physical survival were acquired often at great risk. Clothes were especially valued by *drosters*. Their nonprovision could cause desertion (Adam's reason), while the prospect of having them could win recruits (Africa's promise to Picqueur). Hats were extremely individualized fashion items that changed heads only in exceptional circumstances (as in the death of a wearer), and male robbers would not hesitate to steal dresses. Tobacco, spices, and bread were items for which fugitives ran considerable risks, while brandy was available side by side with honey beer in Khoikhoi kraals. Muskets, probably the most highly prized of all commodities, bore clear signs of their legitimate owner's identity. Such attempts to shed servile or despised status by accumulating symbols of self-esteem demonstrate why, even in the inhospitable mountains of the Cedarberg, European commodities were in demand. They suggest, too, that the objective of *drosters* and Khoikhoi in the rugged frontier was no different than for the victims of slavery in other societies.

The intent, rather than the means, of *drosters* accounts for the wide alarm they raised. Though these regions seemed empty or sparsely populated they were intersected by a network of human linkages that allowed for the extremely rapid dispersal of news. The whereabouts and deeds of *drosters* travelled especially fast. Once a *droster* group became visible, it was only a matter of time before the noose was tightened. Commandos had a long reach; no landscape, regardless of how bleak or remote, was impervious to colonial power.

Notes

1. This chapter is a slightly revised version of the article by the same title, which appeared in the *South African Historical Journal*, 23 (1991): 15-40.

2. For other studies dealing with fugitive slaves and their relationship with other Cape societies, see Ross (1983) and Worden (1985).

3. The approach of this chapter has been shaped by the belief that language plays an important role in the content of meaning. Understanding the signifier is essential to understanding the signified. For a succinct summary of a vast literature on this subject, see Schöttler (1989). Before the late eighteenth century the words "fugitives" or *het weglopen sijns slaavs, deserteeerden slave,* or *gefugeerde slaaven en andere landlopende vagabonden* were far more common than *droster*. Note also that while slaves and deserters of European origin sometimes joined together in flight before 1720, they rarely did so after.

4. Resolution of 13 Dec. 1696, in Böeseken (1983), 3: 307-8; Ross (1983), 40-1.

5. VC, 5 Nov. 1707, 18, CAD.

6. VC, 25 Jun. 1709, 19, CAD.

7. In January 1712 a recaptured slave died because "The Hottentots beyond the mountain had beaten him most brutally; they had smashed the back of his skull, and with kieries cut his back as if it had been sliced with knives; his lips and eyes were so belaboured that there appeared hardly an hour's life in him." LM, 16 Jan. 1712, 18, CAD.

8. See especially Ross (1983), ch. 4.

9. For an account of slave raiding on the Cape frontier, see ch. 5 of this volume. Also Newton-King (1981a & 1981b), 7, and Penn (1987), 475-6.

10. See Penn (1987).

11. Resolution of 2 Sep. 1721 in Böeseken (1968), 6: 128-9.

12. Regarding the history of these and other indenture arrangements, see Malherbe (1991) and ch. 8 in this volume.

13. For a detailed discussion, Penn (1989). There is some doubt as to whether Khoikhoi had to carry passes. A 20 Nov. 1787 resolution of the Council of Policy said that they ought to. But in January 1797 the landdrost of Stellenbosch informed Floris Visser of the Roggeveld that:

> Ik kan ook niet om heer myn verwondering u.w.te betuigen, waar een zoodaning ordre van daan komt dat een Hottentot een pas hebben moet, did versta ik volstrekt niet, zy zijn vrij, en als jy him tydt hebben uytgedient begeer ik dat zy gaan willen, waar en zig wie zy willen ("I also cannot help expressing my surprise to you about where such an order came from that a Hottentot must have a pass, I do not understand that at all; they are free, and my wish is that, if they have served their time, they should [be allowed to] go wherever they wish.")

v.d. Riet to Visser, 10 Jan. 1799, 1/STB 20/30, CAD.

14. Penn (1989), 13-9; idem (1993).

15. On the origin of *Oorlams*, see du Bruyn (1981) and Legassick (1989). Apart from the maroon community at Cape Hangklip near Cape Town discussed by Ross, no evidence has emerged as yet to suggest that other maroon communities, i.e., formed by runaway slaves, were found in the Cape. Ross (1983), 54-72. Maroons were a common feature in the Atlantic plantation complex and slave plantation areas in Africa. See Curtin (1990), esp. 103-8; Morton (1990), esp. 206-9.

16. Too little space is available here to provide detailed analysis of those instances in which flight took on a form akin to armed rebellion or uprising. Many such instances are known to have occurred in the western Cape during this time, and they illustrate a growing unity among oppressed groups, albeit with a vast preponderance of Khoikhoi involved. See Penn (forthcoming).

17. Of the details that follow, many have been taken from the documents concerning the trial of Willem Meij, Adam, Rooi Meij, and Picqueur. Interpreting events has often required synthesizing scattered and contradictory evidence. As it would be tedious, however, to cite in the notes all the pages that contain the many separate pieces of the puzzle, references have been kept to a minimum. The trial record is found in CJ 454, Crim. Proc. St., 1795: 193-397, CAD.

18. The Tanqua Karoo, situated between the Bokkeveld and the Roggeveld, is known by many names: The Ceres Karoo, the Onder Karoo, and the Bokkeveld Karoo are some of the alternatives.

19. See van der Merwe (1945), 121-46 for a thorough account of this practice.

20. Ibid, 142-3.

21. CJ 454: 345, CAD.

22. For Adam's interrogation, CJ 454: 367-90, CAD.

23. From the recollections of Petrus Borchardus Borcherds, who encountered Scholtz while travelling through the Skurweberge in March 1802. Borcherds (1861), 107.

24. Maritz to landdrost, 16 Feb. 1801, 1/STB, 10/153, CAD. Scholtz had struck Maritz whilst the veldwagtmeester was investigating charges against him.

25. Scholtz's farms were *de Eende kuijl - agter de Roggeveld aan de Riet River* (RLR, 28 Feb. 1786, 34: 154, CAD), *de Elandsberg - agter op de Roggeveld aan de Riet River* (RLR, 6 Jul. 1790, 36: 232, CAD), and *de Baviaans Drift - agter op de Roggeveld aan de Riet River* (RLR, 6 Jul. 1790, 36: 232, CAD). "Elandsberg" and "Eende Kuijl" were taken over by the Olivier family in 1787 and 1788, respectively. See Borcherds (1861), 107, for a description of Scholtz's farm house in the Skurweberge in 1802.

26. Scholtz was known as Jochem (or Joachim) Scholtz the younger because his father, Jan Joachim, was also called Jochem. Jochem senior registered Roggecloof in the Roggeveld on 9 Sep. 1756 (RLR, 14: 180, CAD). Most probably he retired from farming in 1784 when his current farm Drooge Land was taken over by Dan Jacobse (RLR, 31: 86, CAD). The Scholtz family genealogy is in de Villiers and Pama (1981), 2: 856.

27. Hermanus registered *de Matjes Cloof aan de Klipfontein geleegend in Middelste Roggeveld* in 1776 (RLR, 24: 75, CAD). He was eight years older than Jochem.

28. *Relaas van Hottentot Jan Swart, 22 Jun. 1793, Verklarings, Pleidooie en Interrogatorien (Krimineel), 1786–1793, 1/STB, 3/12, CAD*. See also the lament of Pieter Jacobs of the Roggeveld concerning his worthless, wandering, and light-fingered servants. 25

May 1793, 1/STB, 10/162, CAD.

29. Infanticide in slave societies is a formidable and unexplored area of research. An exploration into the psychological devastation that results among survivors, however, may be found in Toni Morrison's novel, *Beloved*.

30. Escape was possible northward but entailed negotiating good terms with the San and crossing the almost waterless expanse of Bushmanland before reaching safety. Some must have tried. In 1791, for example, a group of four slaves were discovered living with a Khoikhoi shepherd over the Renoster river behind the Roggeveld. Maritz to landdrost, 26 Dec. 1791, 1/STB, 10/162, CAD.

31. Anna's statement is found in CJ 454: 287-9, CAD, Rosalijn's in idem, 291-3.

32. CJ 454: 363-90, CAD. Picqueur, at a later stage, said that he had been sent to steal bread for Africa's "children." For his testimony, footnote 34.

33. *Complot*, meaning a plot, was often used as a collective noun for a group of *drosters*.

34. Picqueur's interrogation is in CJ 454: 303-22, CAD.

35. Winkelhaak kloof is close to two other areas of the Koue Bokkeveld that have an interesting history as far as labor relations are concerned. See Penn (1985), which deals with the farm Driefontein, and Ross (1983), 105-16, for the 1825 slave revolt on Houd den beke.

36. Penn (1989), 28-9.

37. Lubbe to anon., 16 Sep. 1793, 1/STB, 10/162, CAD. The Olifants river mountains, forming part of the western Bokkeveld mountains, had long been favorite haunts of *drosters*. In 1802 Willem Burger, field-cornet of the district, was in charge of a commando that tracked down five runaway slaves. Two were shot dead and three captured. One of those shot dead had been at large for thirteen years (to the best of Burger's knowledge), but those who were captured said he had been a *droster* for twenty-five years in the district with a *gekonkkel onder de slave en hottentotte so dat mihn hem nooijt hep kenne kreijge!* Burger to landdrost, 2 Aug. 1802, 1/STB, 10/151, CAD. Another group of four *droster* slaves was caught in the mountains above the Olifants river in February 1776. Two escaped. Schalk Burger to landdrost, 21 Feb. 1776, 1/STB, 3/11, CAD.

38. Presumably Scholtz, a Roggeveld farmer, had his sheep stolen when they were in the Karoo.

39. Willem Meij's interrogation is in CJ 454: 343-62, CAD.

40. *Relaas van Hottentot Piet Claas*, 2 Apr. 1793, 1/STB, 3/12, CAD.

41. Rooi Meij's interrogation, CJ 454: 232-42, CAD.

42. Also possible is that Africa, Petrus Pienaar's ex-slave, knew the area well; fourteen years earlier, in April 1779, EylandsDrift was registered in Pienaar's name. RLR 26: 58, CAD.

43. The present owner of Winkelhaak, Mr. Pohl, assured the author that this route had been a popular one for reaching the Karoo, especially as people with livestock or wagons did not have to go via Karoo Poort.

44. On the Doorn river. Jan Kok farmed at *de Vogelfontein —aan de Osterkant van to Olifants Rivier in t gebergte*. RLR, 20 Dec. 1785, 34: 131, CAD.

45. *Relaas van Hottentottinne Griet*, 14 Mar. 1794, *Crimineele Verklaaringen*, 1/STB, 3/13, CAD; *RelasvanHottentottinne Sara*, 7 Mar. 1794, CJ 454: 271-5, CAD. In 1795 Jasper Cloete reported that Wissel Bokkeveld had come to him to report that all the

other Khoikhoi with him had been murdered by *de vreemde nasie*. Cloete to anon., 28 Jun. 1795, 1/STB, 10/163, CAD.

46. As no Elands river or Elands kloof is marked on the map near Eylands Drift, it is difficult to place the site.

47. *Relaas van Hottentottine Flora*, 14 Feb. 1794, 1/STB, 3/13, CAD; Flora's testimony, CJ, 454: 259-69, CAD.

48. Ibid; also CJ 454: 255-7, 271-5, CAD.

49. CJ 454: 237-8, CAD.

50. Significantly, even Rooi and his followers spoke of *drosters*. *Relaas van Flora*, 14 Feb. 1794, 1/STB, 3/13, CAD; CJ 454: 339, CAD.

51. CJ 454: 303-90, CAD. Naturally, those captured claimed to have had no part in planning the murder.

52. See note 46 above.

53. *Relaas van Griet*, 14 Mar. 1794, 1/STB, 3/13; CJ 454: 271-5, CAD. Regarding Willem Fortuijn, see note 81.

54. Joshua Penny, a deserted sailor who took refuge among the farmers of the Koue Bokkeveld in 1795, describes how honey beer was made: "While among the Hottentots I had learned their method of making a very pleasant beverage resembling metheglin. I was fortunate enough to find an old hollow tree, which I cut off with my knife and seized a green hide on one for a bottom. Into this tub honey and water was put to stand twenty-four hours; then was added some pounded root to make it ferment. This root, in use among the frontier Hottentots, does not resemble any of my acquaintance in America, but makes an excellent drink in this preparation." Penny (1815), 33. Penny's experiences, incidentally, reveal that white deserters did not join *droster* gangs because they were assured of refuge among the frontier farmers, most probably the case from about the 1720s.

55. CJ 454: 202, 363-90, CAD.

56. Frans Lubbe was actually veldwagtmeester of the Biedou area and is not the same Lubbe as Johannes. This area, and the Cedarberg in general, was well known as a reservoir of "*bastaards.*" W.A. Nel of the Hantam was later wrote to Frans Lubbe of *de Bidouw om de bastaards en hottentots die in de Kouwe bergen woont* to call them out on commando. Nel to Lubbe, 23 Jul. 1790, 1/STB, 10/162, CAD. In about 1795 twenty-two men were eligible for commando duty in the Bidouw valley, and sixteen of them were *Bastaards*. Spanneberg to anon., n.d., 1/STB, 10/163, CAD. See also Penn (1989), 29 and footnotes.

57. CJ 454: 237-40, CAD; *Relaas van de gedoopte bastaard hottentotte Carel van Rooijen en David Koopman*, 7 Mar. 1794, 1/STB, 3/13, CAD; *Relaas van Gerrit Cloete*, 5 Mar. 1794, ibid.

58. CJ 454: 229-35, CAD.

59. Ibid: 279-81, 323-42.

60. Ibid: 283-5, 323-42.

61. Was it a coincidence that the widow's son was called Erasmus?

62. CJ 454: 279-81.

63. Scholtz to van der Riet, 4 May 1800, 1/STB, 10/153, CAD. See also CJ 454: 194-227, CAD. At one stage it was suggested that the women serve four months detention in the company slave lodge. CJ 76: 31 Jul. 1794.

64. CJ 454: 194-229; CJ 76: 445-52; CJ 77: 50, CAD.

65. *Relaas van Hottentots Wildschut en Fredrik Platje*, 5 Mar. 1794, 1/STB, 3/13, CAD.

66. *Relaas van Hottentot Jantje*, 24 Mar. 1794, ibid.

67. *Relaas van Hottentot Toontje*, 24 Nov. 1794, ibid.

68. Maritz to landdrost, 26 Dec. 1791, 1/STB, 10/162, CAD.

69. Karstens to landdrost, 15 Aug. 1795, 1/STB, 10/151, CAD.

70. Kriger to landdrost, 18 Aug. 1798, 1/STB, 10/165, CAD.

71. Kallaway (1982), Anderson (1985).

72. Visser to landdrost, 17 Nov. 1797, 1/STB, 10/65, CAD.

73. Hugo to landdrost, 1 Aug. 1800, 1/STB, 10/150, CAD.

74. Hugo to landdrost, 24 Aug. 1799, 1/STB, 10/152, CAD. This picture was confirmed the same month by Jacob Kriger in the Klein Roggeveld: *hier de inloopende Hottentots beginnen balstoorig te worden; en kop te toonen; ook als hun wort neit aanstaal, van hunne Baassen wegloopen.* Kriger to landdrost, 27 Aug. 1799, ibid.

75. Van der Riet to Scholtz, 10 Jan. 1799, 1/STB, 20/30, CAD. The words in parentheses are illegible in the original.

76. Ross (1983), 48-9. Ross hesitates, however, to be definitive:

> That fact [of joint action], though a fact, is fraught with such difficulties of definitional and statistical nature that I would not care to give the precise figure. Nevertheless, such is without doubt the clear impression given by the materials on which the investigation of the lives of the Cape Colony's oppressed can best be based.

77. The composition of Africa's *droster* gang is, in itself, a clear indication that by the 1790s different categories of unfree laborers were being united by a common consciousness of oppression. The group consisted of three slave men, three Khoikhoi men, two *Bastaard-Hottentot* men and one boy, three Khoikhoi women, and two little girls who, if Africa was their father, would have been classified as *Bastaard-Hottentots*.

78. A more radical proposal was that of veldwagtmeester Gerrit Maritz and thirty other colonists of the Roggeveld who had requested in 1787 that no Khoikhoi kraals at all be permitted between the Middle and Klein Roggeveld and that all Khoikhoi should be deprived of their guns. Maritz et al, 3 Mar. 1787, 1/STB, 10/162, CAD.

79. One slave, a certain Reijner, managed to stay free in the mountains for over twenty years. He ran away from his master in Drakenstein in about 1727 and lived in the mountains behind the Berg river until he was recaptured in 1749. 8/9 Jan. 1749, 1/STB, 3/8, CAD.

80. See ch. 4 by John Mason in this volume regarding the incentives offered to slaves in the eastern Cape to prevent, *inter alia*, their flight.

81. A particularly illuminating example of Khoikhoi-on-Khoikhoi violence comes from the Bokkeveld farm of Jan Louw, master of the Meij brothers. At least four Khoikhoi laborers, three Khoikhoi women, and a slave resided on Louw's farm, known as Geduld. One of the Khoikhoi, Klein Booij, had acted as overseer, but once he left Geduld, the slave became *mandoor*. Willem Fortuijn, one of the laborers, accused Piet Claas of sleeping with his wife and of handling oxen badly. The two men fought while harvesting dagga flowers. Claas hit Fortuijn with a *kierie*, but Fortuijn stabbed Claas with the harvesting knife. He was helped up by a certain Willem Stompie and nursed back to health by a slave of the widow Frans Jooste. Perhaps this is the same Willem Fortuijn to whom Griet fled after Oude Rooij's murder. *Relaas van Hottentot Piet Claas*, 2 Apr. 1793, 1/STB, 3/12, CAD.

4

Fortunate Slaves and Artful Masters: Labor Relations in the Rural Cape Colony During the Era of Emancipation, ca. 1825 to 1838[1]

John Edwin Mason

September was a fortunate slave.[2] He was a property owner and a family man, qualities which he shared with a sizable number of other favored slaves, but which set him apart from most slaves in the Cape colony. Like September, many of the fortunate slaves lived on the farms of the rural Cape.[3] They often married and had children, and those with whom this chapter is concerned always owned and disposed of property in much the same way as nonwhite farm servants.[4] Though the slavery reform laws of the 1820s and 1830s—the era of emancipation—offered the slaves some protection in the enjoyment of their property, ultimately slaves possessed this property only because their masters allowed them to do so. The livestock that slave owners permitted slaves to acquire and the garden vegetables that they allowed them to grow and to market were concessions granted in the interest of labor control. Though the possession of property and access to markets allowed fortunate slaves to improve their material well-being in important ways, to be fortunate was not necessarily to be happy, as September's tale will show.

In mid-1835, when a colonial official recorded this story, September was not, strictly speaking, a slave at all. He was an "apprentice." The Abolition Act of 1833 and its supporting legislation had ended slavery, in a narrow legal sense, on 1 December 1834. But the Act had also extended it, in every practical sense, under the guise of "apprenticeship;" meaningful freedom did not come until 1838.[5] Apprenticeship changed September's life very little. He still lived with his wife and seven children, who were apprentices as well, in a straw hut on his master's sheep and cattle farm in the district of Uitenhage. He and his family still worked for their master under compulsion and without the freedom to choose other arrangements. And September still owned the property that he had acquired as a slave. Years earlier his master, Petrus Gerhardus Human, had given him permission to run a small herd of cattle on the farm.

Though several of his animals were valuable dairy cows, September was not content. His master fed and clothed the family poorly, and there was, at the moment, little September could do for them, despite his relative wealth. Sometime in 1834 or 1835, Human had sold five of September's cows without his permission. This was a terrible blow; not only were the cows valuable in themselves, each was "with Calf." Human had promised his apprentice that he would compensate him in cash or in kind, but September said he had "waited patiently" and "received nothing." While the statutes establishing apprenticeship confirmed his right to own and dispose of property, the law could not prevent a determined master or mistress from violating that right.[6] Perhaps because he understood the limitations of the law, September did not seek official help in recovering his property. He lodged a formal complaint against his master only after Human beat him and drove him, his wife, and four of their seven children off the farm.

After the beating, September traveled to Uitenhage and told the special justice, the colonial official whose job it was to oversee apprenticeship in the district, that Human had assaulted him for having been slow to "water the gardens." He insisted that he had done what was required of him, but admitted that he had "fed [his] children first," something his master was not prepared to tolerate. The beating sent September to bed for two days. On the third day, Human forced him out of his hut and back to work. It was then that September decided to complain, provoked as much, it seems, by the injustice of being forced to work while he was still recovering from his wounds as by the accumulated weight of past grievances.

When September returned home from the justice's office, an irate Human ordered him off the farm and told him to take his wife and four of his children with him. He, like so many other slave owners, could not abide a servant who had the audacity to call him before the law to answer for his actions.[7] Human would not, however, allow the three eldest children to leave with their parents. They were girls, working in both the house and the fields, and their labor was too valuable to be lost. A greater misfortune than a whipping or the loss of a few head of cattle now threatened to entangle September and his family. He returned to the special justice, hoping that the law would help him to preserve his family. The justice, uncertain as to whether the statutes governing apprenticeship allowed him to intervene in the matter, drafted a letter to his superiors in Cape Town,

FIGURE 4.1 The Districts of the Cape Colony, ca. 1826.

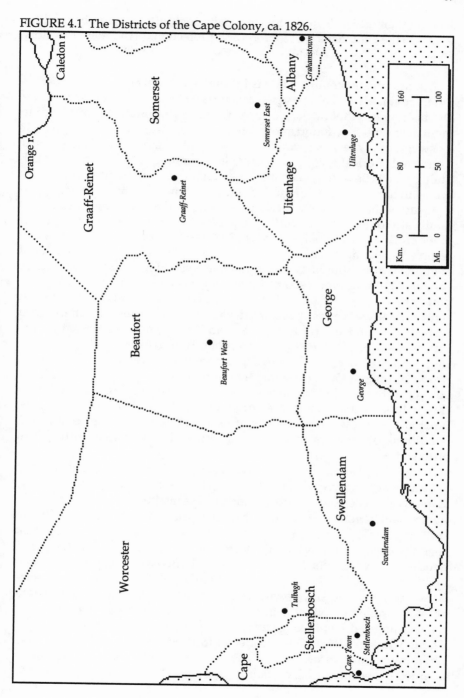

seeking their advice.[8] In the meantime, he committed September and his family to the Uitenhage jail "for food and protection." And there this story ends.

Admittedly, September's tale is in some ways unsatisfactory. Was his family reunited? Did his master ever compensate him for stealing his cattle? Did his property-holdings help to see the family through this crisis, tiding them over until they found another master (there were few other options)? Answers simply cannot be known, for September and his family disappear from the historical record with their incarceration in the Uitenhage jail. Though too little is known about these unhappy events, September's story serves to introduce a different and somewhat more expansive tale.

Many of the elements which shape the narrative of September and his family are common to the stories related about slavery at the Cape of Good Hope and many other parts of the world.[9] To read, for instance, that a slave received a beating can hardly be surprising. Other elements in the plot of September's tale might be more unexpected. Slave families and slave property-holdings, for instance, have rarely been much more than a minor part of the stories that are told about Cape slavery.[10] Yet in the nineteenth century, many slaves, probably most, were indeed members of families that were fragile and easily disrupted. And a large number of slaves, the fortunate slaves of this essay, owned property and disposed of it as though they were free people. The arrangements under which slaves acquired property emerged as a necessary adaptation to the requirements of labor control in the rural Cape and in response to the demands of the slaves themselves.[11] As a result, the conditions under which fortunate slaves labored paralleled the conditions of nonwhite farm servants, that is, the conditions of workers who were in important ways free, rather than enslaved.[12]

To state simply that one person was enslaved by another says remarkably little about the nature of the relationship between the two. Slavery at the Cape, as elsewhere, was an extremely flexible institution. Slaves and slave owners alike were compelled to negotiate the tensions generated by an institution which was, on the one hand, a system of labor exploitation regulated by a judicious blend of terror and indulgence, and on the other, a social structure in which all involved were buffeted about by every human emotion. As Willie Lee Rose so eloquently put it, the interdependence between slaves and slave owners necessarily "invited love-hate relationships, a certain nervous stability, a discernible atmosphere of tension, and a pervading sense of incongruities locked in interminable suspension."[13] Though the legal definitions and ideological underpinnings of slavery were often unyielding, in practice societies recognized that slavery had to be adapted to specific social, economic, and personal circumstances.

Slavery was as much a relationship between individuals as it was a social institution. Slave owners were fully capable of recognizing that while one of the persons that they owned was a "good slave," another was a "bad character."[14] Some slaves, the "good" ones, merited special treatment. Some slaves were never beaten by any of their masters, just as some masters never beat any of their slaves. For their part, slaves knew a "good master" when they saw one, and these masters often got a higher quality of work out of their slaves.[15] Master-slave relationships, however, were not shaped solely by the personalities of the people involved.

Charles van Onselen insists that the social categories into which people place each other also give meaning and substance to their lives. He argues that existing literature on master-servant relations in southern Africa has been insensitive to the nuances of time and place, producing flattened social landscapes and barren analyses. Though he aims his remarks at writings which discuss the period after about 1870, they are relevant to earlier periods as well. "Only urbanized English-speakers," he says perhaps a bit unfairly,

> could gloss over the real distinctions that separate *plaas kaffers* (farm niggers) from *volk* (folk), *mense* (farm people) from *diensbodes* (servants), *basters* (bastards) from *oorlams* (the capable ones), or a *kneg* (serf or bondsman) from a *voorman* (foreman). While most of these words undoubtedly have racial overtones and some are unambiguously racist, others... are more complex and have connotations of social intimacy. It is therefore incumbent on historians to determine more exactly what was the behavior of Afrikaner[s]... when they confronted African wage laborers, labor tenants, or sharecroppers on the land....[16]

While violence, exploitation, and degradation describe certain crucial aspects of slavery and servitude in the eighteenth and nineteenth century Cape colony, the description is only partial, and no part, no matter how vital, can be taken for the whole. Not all subjugated people were slaves, and not all slaves were equally subjugated. If only a slice of life on settler farms is seen, much will be left to explain about subsequent south African history—for instance, the emergence of "Coloured" communities and their vexed, yet familiar and familial relationship with Afrikaners. Taking van Onselen's injunction to heart might mean exploring what it meant to be a fortunate slave.

Like nonwhite servants, favored slaves lived with their spouses and children on their owners' farms and spent extended periods of time out from under their master's or mistress's gaze, leading herds to distant pastures or taking cattle and other commodities to market. The most fortunate of slaves, like some servants and unlike luckless slaves, accumulated property in cattle and other livestock, cultivated fruit and vegetables on plots of land that their masters gave them for the purpose, and bartered, sold, and traded their livestock and produce with their owners and other settlers, with nonwhite servants, and with other slaves. With the profits, they fed and clothed themselves and their families and bought a variety goods their masters did not supply. On occasion, they bought their freedom.

Most fortunate slaves were men. There is no single explanation for the scarcity of fortunate women slaves. There were fewer female slaves than male slaves in the rural Cape, but the discrepancy between the number of slave men and slave women who appear in the historical record as owners of livestock and growers of produce is too great to be accounted for solely in demographic terms. Masters were probably less willing to offer their women slaves livestock, because settler culture understood stock keeping to be a male prerogative. This is perhaps because among the Boer pastoralists, as in most pastoral societies, livestock was the single most important store of wealth. An individual's power and status were thus related to the number of animals that he or she possessed. All women—settler, slave, and servant—had difficulty in gaining access to cattle and other livestock, a fact that both reflected and sustained structures of male supremacy. Perhaps just as important, slave women were a less troublesome species of property than male slaves. Many did indeed stoutly resist their enslavement, but women tended to do so less violently than men, and they ran away less often.[17] Masters did not have to offer women slaves the sort of incentives that they offered male slaves in order to keep them at home and out of trouble.

What was good for the slaves was not necessarily bad for their masters and mistresses. Incentives were important tools of labor control, if only because slaves who had something to lose were less likely to misbehave than those who did not. Forms of labor control that relied more on rewards and incentives than on violence and intimidation were especially important on the farms in the eastern districts of the Cape colony. There unreliable rains and seasonal variations in the quality of pastures forced many masters to entrust their flocks and herds to their slaves and servants, who might live and work without supervision for weeks on end. The possibility of escape was very real. Slave owners had to offer conditions of life and labor that were at the least more attractive than whatever an escaped slave could hope to find elsewhere.

A number of historians, beginning with J. S. Marais, who published his path-breaking history of the "Coloured" people in 1939, have mentioned the slaves' gardens and livestock holdings, but none has made an extended analysis of the subject.[18] For this reason, the experiences of fortunate slaves have stood outside of the central narrative of Cape slavery. This marginalization has made it difficult to see just how important the gardens and livestock holding were—for the slaves who benefited personally and for the future of labor relations in southern Africa. The conditions of labor pioneered by fortunate slaves and the nonwhite servants with whom they worked provided one of the principal models on which labor relations in the interior of southern Africa during and after the Great Trek were patterned. It was a model of subjugation without formal enslavement.

Slavery and Cape Society

Broadly speaking, by the end of the seventeenth century, the Cape economy had assumed a shape that would remain essentially unchanged until the latter part of the nineteenth. Although the colony grew rapidly in size and population, the economy continued to be defined by "two main dichotomies, the first between Cape Town and its agricultural hinterland and, within the latter, between the [wine and wheat farms] of the south-west Cape and the vast [cattle and sheep] ranches of the interior."[19] As Table 4.1 illustrates, legally defined slaves were a much more important part of the labor force in Cape Town and the southwestern Cape than on the stock farms of the northern and eastern Cape. There were fewer slaves in each interior district and, on average, fewer in each slave-owning household.

TABLE 4.1 Average Size of Slaveholding by District, Cape Colony, 1834

	Owners	Slaves	Average Holding
Cape Town	1,218	5,987	4.90
Cape District	603	4,780	7.92
Stellenbosch	1,097	8,595	7.83
Worcester	471	3,270	6.94
Uitenhage	329	1,413	4.29
Graaff-Reinet	540	2,157	3.99
Somerset	429	1,641	3.83

Source: Returns of the Total Number of Slaves in the Various Districts According to the Several Classes and Values, n.d. (1835), SO 20/61, CAD.

In Cape Town, slaves performed almost every kind of labor. They constituted the great majority of the unskilled laborers—longshoremen, porters, and household servants—and a large proportion of the skilled workforce as well—fishermen, cooks, wagon drivers, tailors, seamstresses, smiths, masons, and carpenters. Slaves also predominated on the wine farms and wheat farms of the southwestern Cape. They performed all of the important work on the farms of the southwest, acting as household servants, cooks, field laborers, smiths, carpenters, coopers, and even as distillers, vintners, and overseers.

Slaves were relatively rare in the sparsely populated eastern and north-eastern Cape; they were easily outnumbered by free nonwhite servants, most of whom were Khoisan. In the Graaff-Reinet district, for instance, farmers relied so heavily on free servants that slaves constituted only 12 percent of the local population, while Khoisan and Bantu-speaking Africans made up 40 percent.[20] Slaves lived and worked beside these servants, performing the same tasks—shepherd, cattleherd, field laborer, household servant, and sometimes overseer—and experiencing the same forms of labor control, which was a blend of coercion and incentives.

Several factors determined that there would be fewer slaves on the cattle and sheep farms than in Cape Town and on the wine and wheat farms. Most importantly, stock farmers simply required fewer workers than did wine and wheat farmers. This was just as well; they tended to be less prosperous than farmers in the southwestern Cape and many of the slave owners in Cape Town, and so they could not have afforded to purchase very many slaves even if they had desired them. Ross argues that stock farmers also considered the relative ease with which slaves could escape when they considered whether or not to invest in slave property. "[T]he leakage [of slaves]... away from the farms of the eastern Cape," he writes, "was one of the reasons why there were relatively far fewer slaves on the frontier than in the western parts of the Cape."[21] Ross is probably right, but only because he is referring to a higher incidence of permanent escape. Though scanty, the evidence seems to suggest that slaves ran off just as often in the southwestern Cape as in the east. What southwestern Cape slaves could not do as well was to stay away forever. They were hundreds of miles away from the independent African societies on and beyond the colonial frontier—Griqua, AmaXhosa, BaTswana, and others—that often offered refuge to escaped eastern Cape slaves.

It is difficult to know how many slaves ran away or how often they tried to do so, but the incidence was high enough to worry their masters and mistresses. Only one attempt was made in the nineteenth century to count the number of runaway slaves. In 1835, colonial officials enumerated all of the slaves in the colony as of 1 December 1834 and tallied the runaways separately.[22] The census established that there were 35,745 slaves in the colony, runaways included. Of the total, 427, or 1.2 percent, had run off. The number of escaped slaves, however, varied regionally.[23]

As might have been anticipated, slaves deserted most often in the rural southwestern districts, where the work was heaviest, and in the east, where the probability of permanent escape was the greatest (see Figure 4.1) In a grain-farming subdistrict of the Cape district, 53 or 1.7 percent of the slaves had escaped their masters. In a wine-farming subdistrict of the Stellenbosch district, 57 or 1.3 percent of the slaves had run away. Comparable rates of desertion were found in the sparsely populated stock-farming districts of the eastern and north-central Cape. Fifty-four or 1.7 percent of the slaves had run away from their Worcester district masters. In Graaff-Reinet, the corresponding figure was 35 or 1.6 percent. The highest proportion of deserters in any slave community in the colony was in the far eastern Somerset district, where 54 or 3.2 percent of the slaves had escaped. Slaves ran off the least often in Cape Town, the place of residence for which they commonly expressed a preference.[24] In two representative Cape Town sub-districts, only 9 or 0.6 percent and 4 or 0.3 percent of the slaves were deserters.[25]

Though the number of runaways may not seem particularly high, the absolute numbers are deceptive. A census is a still life. A more accurate picture would show slaves in motion—some in the act of running away, some returning to their masters, either voluntarily or under compulsion, and some eluding capture for days, months, or years on end (particularly in the east). The number of slaves who had, at one time or another, run off would have far exceeded 427; the true figure is no doubt well into the thousands. Many would have been repeat offenders. The number of slave owners who had suffered the sometime loss of their slaves' labor would have been correspondingly large.

The slave owners' fear that their slaves might escape was an especially live issue on the stock farms of the eastern districts. These farms were, of course, relatively close to the sanctuary that independent African communities provided. But for the slave owners, the problem was not simply a matter of proximity. The quality of colonial pastures and the nature of the pastoral economy forced masters to trust their slaves and nonwhite servants to work without supervision for lengthy periods of time. Grazing land in the Cape colony was often poor and much of it was usable only during either the summer or winter months. Farmers adopted a number of strategies to compensate for these environmental constraints. They pastured their animals over wide tracts of land, often splitting the flocks and herds into segments and placing each under the care of one or two slaves or servants, and they moved their animals seasonally as the quality of the pasture shifted. Slaves and servants routinely spent weeks at a time away from the farm. Farmers also sent their livestock to market under the care of slaves and servants and trusted them to return with the proceeds.[26]

Yet, most slaves chose not to run away. For the farmers, escapes were irritants, not crises. The difficulty of surviving as a runaway was surely one of the reasons that slaves stayed home, as was fear of the punishment that would follow an unsuccessful attempt.[27] The chief reason was probably the slaves' calculation that life on the farm was better than life on the run. The livestock that their masters allowed fortunate slaves to accumulate and the garden crops that they allowed them to market would have been crucial factors in this calculation. The rewards and incentives that masters offered the slaves were bribes designed to keep them on the farms, out of Cape Town and the mountains, and away from the sometimes welcoming African societies along the frontier.

Despite the ubiquity of these arrangements, most slave owners seem to have been, in principle, "opposed to the acquisition of property by slaves." According to an assistant protector of slaves in an eastern district—one of the several protectors of slaves who enforced the reform laws of the 1820s and 1830s and interacted frequently with both slaves and slave owners— the farmers feared that property would "render the slave[s] independent." But, he said, slave owners allowed their slaves the privilege of accumulating property because the alternative was to risk losing them altogether.[28] Better an impudent slave than no slave at all. Slaves and slave owners together adapted slavery to the requirements of rural society and the pastoral economy. In doing so, they created a class of fortunate slaves, a process that began to blur the distinction between nonwhite servants and legally defined slaves.

Slaves of Property and Standing

Since at least the 1730s, the slave-owning society at the Cape had recognized that "conscientious masters" allowed their slaves to accumulate property and "to dispose of [their property] as they please[d]." However, the law offered property-owning slaves no protection until the promulgation of the slavery reform laws of the 1820s and 1830s. The reforms made a right of what had been a privilege.[30] By the early decades of the nineteenth century, there were many fortunate slaves in the Cape Colony, and colonial officials, such as the principal protector of slaves, were well aware of their existence.

"The Slaves in the Country," the protector noted in 1833, "have their little gardens out of which they raise much [sic] vegetables... which They sell."[31] "Industrious Slaves," he claimed, earned as much as £5 to £15 a year "by cultivating Potatoes, Pumpkins, Melons, Beans, Peas, Indian corn, etc." and taking them to market in their masters' wagons.[32] He regretted, however, that some of the slaves spent their earnings "Drinking and Gambling."[33] In the "far Districts," he wrote from his office in Cape Town, slaves commonly owned livestock. "Almost all well behaved and Provident Slaves breed goats and Sheep, and...not a few of Them possess Horses and...Cattle to a larger amount which Their Owners allow to run and Graze on their Extensive Cattle Farms."[34] Though the protector did not indicate what proportion of slaves was "well behaved and Provident," the records indicate that it was large.

The mere presence of the sort of arrangement that the protector described was not enough to ensure tranquil labor relations, as the case of a Worcester district farmer will show.[35] About twenty-five apprentices lived on the farm of Isaac van der Merwe, who had granted each of the men a piece of ground on which to raise crops. He also permitted them to use his wagons to take their produce to the village of Worcester for sale. There the apprentices sold or bartered their goods, as free people might have done. One of van der Merwe's apprentices said that his garden earned him Rds 40 (£3) a year, with which he bought his own clothes. Another said that the proceeds from his plot brought him Rds 20 (£1.10) and that he purchased thread and soap for himself, as well as clothing. This arrangement apparently suited van der Merwe well. The incentives kept his apprentices on the farm, and the apprentices largely fed and clothed themselves, saving van der Merwe a considerable expense. But the arrangement did not entirely please his apprentices, and it appalled his sons.

One of the apprentices complained that in over a decade he had received very little clothing from his master—only two pairs of pants, three shirts, and a jacket. His irritation stemmed from his knowledge that van der Merwe had both the customary duty and the legal obligation to supply him with adequate clothing. While some apprentices may have appreciated the opportunity to market produce on their own behalf, this man, at least, resented having to spend some of his earnings on clothes. Van der Merwe's sons, on the other hand, claimed that the relative autonomy that the apprentices enjoyed had made them cheeky. The apprentices, for instance, were often "very insolent," and, when the men returned to the farm in their master's wagons, they sometimes came back drunk.

Slaves did not always look at garden plots as unalloyed blessings, for reasons besides the loss of entitlements such as clothing. Slaves could not always be sure that the energy they expended on a garden would be rewarded. An assistant protector of slaves recorded the grievance of Welkom, a slave of a Graaff-Reinet master, who complained that

> his Master is in the habit of hiring him out with his wife and children, for one month to one person and two months to another, in Consequence of which [when he cultivates] a garden for himself in one place he is obliged to leave it without reaping the fruit of it.[36]

At other times, disputes over the rightful ownership of produce led to trouble between master and slave. In the Stellenbosch district, Isaak, a slave wagon driver, said that his master, Pieter Cillier, beat him "for having put some Chilies upon a wagon proceeding to Cape Town." His master had also accused him of stealing the peppers, though Isaak insisted that he had grown them himself. Cillier told the story differently. He admitted that he had whipped Isaak, but said that his neighbors had told him that his slaves were stealing fruit and vegetables from their gardens and taking them to Cape Town in his wagons for sale. In order to avoid even the suspicion that his wagons were being used to carry stolen goods, Cilliers had ordered his slaves not to place personal property in the wagons. On the day in question, he had dispatched Isaak to Cape Town with a load of wine. He heard the wagon stop just after Isaak drove off and went to investigate. He found Isaak loading a bag of "chilies, onions, and other articles" onto the wagon. Not knowing who owned the chilies and angered that Isaak had disobeyed him, Cilliers punished his slave.[37]

The arrangements involving gardenplots that slaves, apprentices, and their masters and mistresses settled upon need not have caused conflict. Much more is likely to be known about incidents of conflict than about arrangments simply because the information available comes from legal proceedings. Some slaves' "luck," nevertheless, appears to have been quite good. Present, for instance, lived on his master's farm in the Graaff-Reinet district with his wife, who was identifiied as a "Hottentot," and their children. His master provided the family with "all food and other necessaries," as well as "land to cultivate." Present had managed to turn vegetables into animals by bartering the produce of his garden for livestock. In the eight years during which his current master had owned him, he had accumulated two cows, two calves, forty sheep, twenty goats, and a horse.[38] Livestock holdings such as Present's were common. On the stock farms of the eastern Cape, many slaves were fortunate enough to own cattle, sheep, goats, and horses.

No slave's livestock holdings approached the size of white farmers' herds and flocks. In the early nineteenth century, most eastern Cape farmers owned no fewer than 3,000 sheep. Flocks of 4,000 to 6,000 sheep and herds of several hundred cattle were common. The wealthiest stockmen might possess over 10,000 sheep and 1,500 to 2,000 head of cattle.[39] Slaves' flocks and herds were much smaller, similar in size to those of nonwhite servants. Most slaves and servants who possessed livestock ordinarily owned only one or two dozen sheep and goats and less than half as many cattle.[40] Jeptha, a slave on a Graaff-Reinet stock farm, possessed a relatively large number of animals. Over the course of a decade, he acquired fifty-one goats, thirty-one sheep, ten cattle, and four horses.[41] November, a slave belonging to the estate of the late Cobus van Heerden of Graaff-Reinet, owned a good deal more livestock than Jeptha, but his story emphasizes the difficulty with which slaves accumulated property, even though they necessarily did so with their masters' permission.

In 1833, November owned 254 sheep and goats and nine head of cattle.[42] He told an assistant protector of slaves that he had earned, bought, or bred them all. His livestock grazed on his recently deceased master's land and intermingled with the estate's animals. Indeed, all the male servants on the farm, slaves and free nonwhites, owned some stock, and they all apparently ran their animals with those of the estate. To distinguish their livestock from that of the others, both van Heerden and his servants clipped their animals' ears in distinctive patterns. Periodically, all slaves and servants gathered to watch a few of the men count the holdings of each individual. At the time that November spoke the protector, he, another slave, and his master's son had recently counted the servants' livestock, and all concerned had agreed on the number that each man possessed.

For November, the trouble had begun some months before his master's death, when he successfully prosecuted van Heerden for having beaten him "unjustly." The court fined van Heerden, and he seems to have decided to recover his losses by stealing from his slave. In the wake of his conviction, he sold or slaughtered one of November's cows and fifty of his sheep and goats. Van Heerden also gave twelve of November's goats to three non-white servants—"the Hottentots Dragoon and Cout and the Mantatee September"—as wages, without compensating his slave in any way.[43] An additional thirty-five of November's sheep and fifteen of his goats were simply missing. Van Heerden, November said, had gone so far as to alter the marks on some of his animals, making them indistinguishable from his own. After van Heerden's death, his widow had refused to allow November to reclaim his livestock. It took the intervention of the assistant protector of slaves to force van Heerden's estate to make good on November's losses. After lengthy proceedings, van Heerden's widow agreed to return all his cattle to him "together with [another] Cow in lieu of that which was killed and 300 Sheep and goats."

As November's story suggests, slaves and slave owners seem almost to have considered the transfer of livestock to be wages paid for services rendered. Slaves were treated in much the same way as nonwhite servants. However, November's case also demonstrates that the slaves' hold on their property was weak. Although slave owners routinely "paid" their slaves in kind and granted them permission to graze their herds and flocks on the farm, many did so grudgingly. Here, too, the circumstances of free servants were sometimes not very different.

Almost from the beginning of colonial agriculture, payment in kind was a more important part of farm servants' incomes than cash wages. As early as 1695, the conquest of Khoisan lands and the subjugation of Khoisan societies had advanced far enough that many had little choice but to enter the colonial economy as farm laborers. Some were captives; some were not. Many earned a small number of calves or lambs annually, plus tobacco, alcohol, and food. By the early nineteenth century, the practice of paying Khoisan farm workers in kind as an alternative or supplement to cash wages was well established, especially in the northern and eastern districts.[44] A government report written in the 1820s noted that in Uitenhage a servant's annual wages usually consisted "of an ox, or a cow and calf, which are allowed to graze with the cattle of the farmer...." The report added that "in this manner the Hottentots [Khoikhoi] have in some instances been able to accumulate and to preserve the earnings of their labour."[45] The report put the best light on things. In the eighteenth and nineteenth centuries, Khoisan servants often complained bitterly that farmers refused to allow them to take their livestock with them when they left the farms at the expiration of their contracts.

In the 1770s, eastern Cape farmers had also begun to employ AmaXhosa workers and pay them as they had Khoisan servants. The incorporation of AmaXhosa into the settler economy as subordinate laborers accelerated as colonial military forces captured their pastures and agricultural land. In the 1820s and 1830s, other Bantu-speaking Africans—BaTswana and "Mantatees," for instance—joined the ranks of nonwhite servants. They entered the colony as refugees, fleeing warfare and raiding beyond the Orange river. Legislation provided for the employment of these "native foreigners" as contractual workers. The ordinary payment for a year's labor was one cow or its equivalent in smaller stock, the wages of a Khoisan worker.[46]

Slaves and apprentices were well aware of the terms under which their comrades labored. The arrangements that fortunate slaves and their masters agreed upon probably arose in response to the slaves' demand that they be treated in the same way as nonwhite servants. They were, after all, doing the same work. Slaves who understood the workings of the servants' agreements did not hesitate to share that knowledge with their friends. For example, Damon, a slave on a farm in the Somerset district, once earned his master's wrath by telling "a Bechuana [MoTswana] residing on the place that he might if he chose do like other Bechuanas, earn Cattle, Sheep and Goats and select a place for himself to live upon. ...that he might commence Farming for himself...."[47] Though the MoTswana to whom Damon spoke was not a slave, it is likely that slaves and servants on the farms had many similar conversations, ensuring that everyone knew precisely how these arrangements worked.

Slaves seem to have received their livestock in the same way and at the same time as did free workers on their masters' farms. On one farm, the master's sons rounded up the "Young cattle" once a year, and the slaves and Khoisan laborers "claiming the Calves [came] forward and [indicated] which is theirs." The sons then distinguished each man's calves by giving its ears unique marks. In this instance, the calves had come from the farm's herd. On at least one earlier occasion, a slave and a Khoikhoi servant had returned to the farm "from Kaffirland [AmaXhosa territory] with a troop of cattle," some of which were distributed to the slaves and servants.[48] It is not clear whether this episode was a legitimate trading expedition or a cattle raid. Both were common enough on the eastern Cape.[49] There were also exceptional moments at which livestock passed from master to slave. Isaac Pretorious, for example, gave his slave, Jephta, six sheep in compensation for having accidentally broken his jaw.[50]

Once in possession of livestock, the slaves and apprentices bartered, bought, and sold the animals, and lent them out in much the same way as did whites and servants. With the profits they made, they purchased a variety of goods, up to and including their freedom. For example, Adam, an apprentice employed by a Uitenhage farmer, acquired cattle with the produce he grew in his garden and, by means of the cattle, acquired his freedom. Adam's master had given him ground on which he planted both a vegetable garden and a small vineyard. He marketed his crop and over the years purchased several oxen, two of which were trained for the yoke and were quite valuable. Several months before the apprenticeships of the former slaves were due to expire, he sold some of the oxen, earning enough money to purchase his liberty.[51] On other occasions, property-owning slaves paid for the freedom of family members, rather than themselves. Samson, a slave in the Somerset district, once gave Anna Erasmus a cow and twenty-three sheep and goats. In return, Erasmus released Samson's wife, a Khoikhoi woman, from her labor contract.[52]

Sometimes property holdings did no more than give a slave who longed to be free a fighting chance to realize a dream. Cupido was such a slave. He feared the consequences of his mistress's death, telling the assistant protector of slaves in Somerset that her children had never treated him well. He did not want to be inherited by any of them. He wished, instead, to buy his freedom. He owned nineteen cattle and had a claim of Rds 20 (£1.10) against one of his deceased mistress's sons. This, he hoped, would be enough to satisfy his mistress's heirs. When the protector approached family members with Cupido's offer, they agreed to consider the offer.[53]

Slaves and apprentices tried in many ways to build up their property holdings, but the deals that they made did not always work out smoothly. For instance, Isaac, a slave, and Jantje Keyser, a Khoikhoi, argued over the terms of a barter agreement. Isaac took the case to an assistant protector of slaves for adjudication. He claimed that Keyser had undertaken to give him a horse and other livestock in return for two oxen and a cow. Keyser did not dispute the nature of the transaction, but he claimed that he had already delivered the horse. He acknowledged that he still owed Isaac ten sheep and asked for more time to produce them.[54]

Slaves and apprentices also dealt in cash, or tried to. Maria, a slave in the Albany district and one of the rare women slaves who appears in the records as an owner of livestock, went to an assistant protector of slaves in order to recover a debt. Piet Retief—the Voortrekker leader who later came to grief

at the home of the AmaZulu *inkosi enkhulu*, Dingane—owed Maria Rds 249
(£18.13.6) for the 141 sheep and 30 goats he had purchased from her. Maria
told the protector that after eighteen months of "repeated applications for
payment" Retief had yet to respond to her requests for payment. Her
master, Joseph van Dyk, supported her claim. He said that the animals
"were bona fide her property" and produced a receipt that Retief had signed
acknowledging his obligation.[55] It is not clear whether Retief ever made the
debt good.

Like masters and servants, slaves entered into loan-cattle agreements.
These arrangements had long existed in southern Africa. Long before the
arrival of whites, wealthier Khoikhoi had "often lent out their cattle to poor
clients who herded them in return for a percentage of their yield."[56]
Similarly, among Bantu-speaking Africans, "loan beasts would be used by
the borrower until they were reclaimed.... [T]he owner would divide up the
increase, and perhaps the original stock, giving some to the borrower
outright."[57] In both cases, the granting of loan cattle was an exercise in
patronage. Wealthier persons hoped to build a loyal following and, as
Peires says of the AmaXhosa, by controlling cattle, "to control men."[58]
Whites also lent livestock to poorer clients and kin; the borrower gained half
the yearly increase and the lender, perhaps, won an ally.[59]

How and from whom the slaves came to adopt the loan-cattle system is
obscure. Even if the direct influence had come from observing the practices
of their masters, it is possible that their masters had, in turn, learned the
system from the Khoikhoi, as they had so many other aspects of cattle
culture.[60] Whatever the inspiration, slaves did often enter into loan-cattle
agreements. Their aim was, perhaps, to secure a friendship. But more
importantly, they would have wanted to keep their herds and flocks a safe
distance from those of their masters, in an effort to avoid altered marks and
disputes over ownership. To do this, they needed both a cattle herd and a
means of payment. The loan-cattle system provided the answer.

The slaves' loan-cattle agreements duplicated those of other southern
African pastoralists. For instance, sometime during the 1810s or 1820s,
Manas, a Graaff-Reinet slave, gave Roset, a slave woman who belonged to
another master, two cows and two heifers to keep for him in exchange for
half the increase. The arrangement worked well for between ten and sixteen
years (witnesses' accounts vary), but it fell victim to a master's greed.
Manas's cows were prolific, and his herd grew to twenty. However, before
he and Roset thought to divide the herd, Roset's master, Johannes Oberholzer,
took four of Manas's "breed" from her and trained them as draft oxen. Two
of the four died and Oberholzer sold the others, keeping the profits for
himself. Later, he sold a bull and a cow belonging to Manas. When
Oberholzer died, Roset tried to reclaim what remained of Manas's livestock
from the estate but could not. All of Manas's oxen had somehow acquired

Oberholzer's "mark." Neither Manas nor Roset were able to recover their property.[61]

Cases like those of Manas and others seen above emphasize the fragility of the slaves' grip on their livestock. Slave owners continually looked for ways to take away with one hand that which they had given with the other. At times, they simply stole from their slaves. Occasionally, they bothered to contrive an excuse. The slave, James, for instance, charged his master with having commandeered six of his goats. He had given them "to a Mantatee," James said, on the "false pretence of [James] having taken some money from that person."[62]

The slaves' hold on their property was weak because their privileges masked, but did not eliminate, their subordination to their owners. It is true that much of the time well-behaved slaves—those who accepted the terms that their masters offered—lived almost as free servants.[63] But the advantages that fortunate slaves enjoyed never entirely freed them from the realities of slavery. They might be reminded of their status at any moment, as was the slave, Fortuyn. One day on a farm in the Somerset district, two mares, one belonging to Fortuyn, the other to his master, Gerhardus Swart, got into the household garden and began to destroy the crops. After Fortuyn and his master chased the horses out of the garden, Swart caught his horse and began to beat it. He ordered Fortuyn to snare his and bring it to him so that he could punish it as well. Fortuyn refused because, he said, the mare was "heavy in foals and [would] be injured if beaten." When Fortuyn let the horse escape over a fence, Swart beat his slave instead.[64] Violence remained the foundation on which masters built a superstructure of rewards and incentives.[65]

Postscript

Little about the lives and labors of the fortunate slaves of the Cape would have surprised either the slaves or the slave owners in other nineteenth century slave societies. Recent studies of slavery in the United States have tended to show that violence and the threat of violence were the primary means by which American slave owners controlled their slaves. According to Parish, "[a]ll other methods [were] secondary." But Parish insists that secondary methods of control—for instance, incentives such as the garden crops that American slaves tended, the livestock that they raised, and the profits that they made from marketing both—were vital. Within the limits established by a "coercive framework," slaves were "receptive to the idea of making the best of their lot" and accepting some of the rewards that their owners offered. Masters benefited, too. They "avoided, in the daily routine, pushing the logic of slavery to its extremes of inhumanity."[66]

Arrangements of this sort appeared in many other Atlantic slave societies. In the West Indies and Latin America, slaves raised crops and tended livestock, entered the market with what they possessed, and consumed and saved the proceeds. Slaves were so enterprising in producing for the market that some historians have likened them to peasants and have called their market-oriented activities a "peasant breach." This breach was important both because it allowed the slaves to control a major portion of their lives and because it influenced the dreams and aspirations they took with them into freedom.[67] Many former Cape colony slaves also hoped to become independent peasant producers after emancipation, but the limited nature of the slaves' involvement in the market prevented a true peasant breach from developing during the slave era. After emancipation, the freed people found little room to establish themselves as independent producers.[68]

The greater significance of the slaves' property holdings and involvement in the market lies in the demonstration of the adaptability of colonial slave owners and the flexibility of their methods of labor control. The relations between fortunate slaves and their owners, especially in the eastern Cape during the era of emancipation, foreshadowed relations between ex-slave and nonwhite servants and their Voortrekker and settler masters in the Orange Free State and the Transvaal in the nineteenth and early twentieth centuries.[69] A little-known episode involving slave owners in the eastern Cape suggests that having learned to live with anomalous forms of slavery, they thought that they might be able to live without slavery altogether.

In 1826, a group of prominent slave owners in the cattle- and sheep-farming district of Graaff-Reinet put forward a scheme to end slavery in the Cape colony. They proposed that after some unspecified date in the near future "every female child born of a slave woman should be born free."[70] Slavery would thereby be placed on the road to a slow, but inevitable death. Because an act of the British Parliament and colonial legislation had prohibited the importation of slaves after March 1808, the only persons who could be legally added to the Cape's slave population were infants who had been born of slave women. If no more girls and women were added to the slave population, slavery, as the men of Graaff-Reinet foresaw, would expire at the moment that an elderly slave, the last son of the last slave mother, drew his final breath.[71]

While slave owners in the western Cape drafted similar proposals, Watson, who has looked carefully into the matter, believes that only the Graaff-Reinet plan was anything other than a cynical political maneuver. The schemes came on the heels of Ordinance 19 (1826), the first of the slavery reform laws that kept slave owners off-balance and angry during the 1820s and 1830s. The proposals emanating from the western Cape demanded the repeal of Ordinance 19 as the first step towards the emancipation of the slaves. The Graaff-Reinet plan did not. Slave owners there were apparently sincere in their readiness to send slavery down the road to oblivion.[72]

Watson argues that several factors accounted for Graaff-Reinet masters' ability to contemplate the abolition of slavery. Slaves were probably less valuable in the east than in the west, due to the relative ease with which eastern and northcentral Cape slaves could escape. At the same time, Graaff-Reinet seems not to have suffered as severe a labor shortage as most parts of the colony. Farmers there drew on many sources to supply their labor requirements and were, consequently, less dependent on slaves than their counterparts in the western districts. Finally, Watson contends that in Graaff-Reinet the distinction between slaves and legally free, nonwhite servants was "blurred" and that "the concept of *slave* had little meaning."[73] Watson's last point is the most telling.

The slave owners of Graaff-Reinet were less attached to slavery because they had learned that they did not have to own labor in order to exploit it.[74] They, and so many other farmers in the eastern Cape, had adopted a style of labor relations which had indeed blurred the distinction between slavery and other forms of labor subordination. This untidiness was not the result of farmers having transformed free servants into slaves. Rather the farmers had begun the process of turning their slaves into free, though distinctly subordinate, servants.[75] Much of the time, Cape farmers disciplined, indulged, and exploited their fortunate slaves precisely as they did their free, nonwhite servants.

The relationship between masters and their fortunate slaves and their nonwhite servants defined the dominant form of labor relations that the Voortrekkers took to the interior of southern Africa. Beginning in 1836, two years into apprenticeship, groups of Afrikaner farm families collected their possessions, loaded their ox wagons, and left the Cape colony, searching for new land and escaping, as they saw it, the intolerable oppressions of the British. This was the "Great Trek."[76] By 1840, roughly 6,000 settlers had crossed the Orange river, establishing themselves on farms in the highveld and below the Drakensberg in Natal. The Voortrekkers did not travel alone. They took their herds and their flocks, and they took their servants—the people whom Thompson has called "the unregarded members" of the Trek.[77] Many of these servants were apprentices—the former slaves—and most of them seem to have gone willingly. Like their masters, apprentices often traveled with their families and took along their cattle and sheep. In the 1830s and 1840s, masters, ex-apprentices, and other nonwhite servants reestablished in the interior the pattern of labor relations that they had pioneered in the Cape.

Suggestive evidence about the nature of labor relations on the Trek comes from a report written by Gideon Joubert, an astute and resourceful field-cornet from the eastern Cape, who visited several parties of trekkers at the behest of the colonial governor.[78] For a variety of reasons, the trek worried the British. The movement of so many settlers out of the colony and into the interior seemed certain to cause trouble and expense, in part because it was unlikely that the Voortrekkers could avoid antagonizing whatever Africans they encountered. The presence of apprentices among the trekkers also troubled the colonial administration. Officials feared that the farmers had left the colony with their apprentices in order to avoid freeing them on 1 December 1838, the day on which apprenticeship was due to expire.[79] In October 1838, responding to his own suspicions and pressure from the colonial office in London, the governor of the Cape, major general Sir George Napier, ordered Joubert to follow the trekkers into the interior, locate as many apprentices as possible, and see to it that they understood that they were free to leave their masters and return with him to the colony if they so desired.[80] Joubert travelled as far as Port Natal, the future Durban, encountering several parties of Voortrekkers along the way.

Though he spoke to well over 100 apprentices (admittedly a fraction of those who had followed their masters), only 39 elected to return with him to the Cape.[81] Most of the 39 apprentices who reentered the colony with Joubert were "women, children and [the] aged." At least one of the eight men who returned did so reluctantly. This man, Joubert said, had hesitated, "fearing that he would suffer injury by his oxen, goat, Calfs [sic], & lambs." But "his wife begged" him to accept the field-cornet's offer. He agreed and sent his wife, younger children, and possessions (nearly a full wagon-load of pots, pails, beds, and clothes) back to the Cape with Joubert, while he and a son drove the livestock "at leisure."[82] This father, a very fortunate former slave, was one of the few able-bodied men or women apprentices to return to the Cape. Most remained with the Voortrekkers.

Joubert's report suggests that the apprentices did not decline his offer because they feared for their own safety or that of their animals. They seem to have calculated that their prospects in the Cape were simply not good enough to make them want to return. The trekkers also took Joubert's visit in stride; the end of slavery held no terrors for them. They readily agreed to allow Joubert to speak to the apprentices and did not object when he explained to them what the end of apprenticeship would mean. Some apprentices told Joubert that their masters and the magistrates among the trekkers had already declared them free.[83] And, in fact, many of these ex-apprentices had begun to live as free servants.

Some of the ex-apprentices, for instance, had left their masters and hired themselves to new employers, taking their livestock with them to their new homes within the Voortrekker community.[84] Others were comfortable enough with their freedom to hire themselves to new masters after first agreeing to accompany Joubert. Just before Joubert reentered the colony, two women, both of whom had left their masters to return to the Cape, changed their minds and engaged to work for another Voortrekker, much to Joubert's annoyance. (They and their possessions had been difficult to carry across the mountains.) Still other ex-apprentices had no master at all. Though this state of affairs cannot have been common, a few lived, Joubert said, "upon their own." Presumably, they herded cattle and sheep, drawing on their experience as fortunate slaves when buying, selling, and trading their stock.[85] The masters and servants that Joubert encountered seem to have adjusted easily to the end of formal slavery.

This was just as Piet Retief would have had others believe. He was the leader of one of the parties of Voortrekkers and a man who, as is revealed above in his dealings with the slave, Maria, understood the circumstances of fortunate slaves. In 1837, he published a manifesto in which he summarized the reasons behind the settler exodus. He denied that the trekkers had "quit the colony" in order to avoid freeing their slaves. He maintained, in fact, that the Voortrekkers would "uphold the just principles of liberty... [and] take care that no one shall be held in a state of slavery." However, Retief added a significant rider. The trekkers, he said, were determined to "preserve proper relations between master and servant."[86] There is no reason not to take him at his word.

Retief and the other Voortrekkers were indeed ready to let go of formal slavery. What the trekkers objected to was "not so much the freedom of the slaves" as their "being placed on an equal footing" with whites.[87] The Voortrekkers had not repudiated subjugation and exploitation; their record in preserving these aspects of servitude is formidable. Nor had they renounced racism; here, too, their record as historical preservationists is impressive. The trekkers firmly believed that nonwhites were fit only to be servants and that the only good servant was a duly subordinated one. But Retief and the others did jettison formal slavery. They had proven to themselves, while still in the Cape colony and in possession of their fortunate slaves, that the end of slavery did not necessarily mean the end of the proper relationship between master and servant.

Notes

1. My thanks to Jeff Peires, Paul Lovejoy, Rob Shell, and Robert Ross for their many helpful comments on earlier drafts of this essay.

2. The following narrative is drawn from special magistrate, Uitenhage, to secretary to government, 8 Jun. 1835, CO 441, CAD.

3. In Cape Town, the luckiest slaves, most often skilled male artisans, lived and worked almost as though they were free craftsmen, finding their own employment and lodgings, and paying their owners a fixed sum, weekly or monthly, for the privilege. See Bank (1991), 33-60, Mason (1992), 278-92.

4. The term "nonwhite," though personally unpleasant, is preferrred here to "black," which is anachronistic, and to "Khoisan, Bastaard, and Bantu-speaking African," which are clumsy even if inclusive.

5. An Act for the Abolition of Slavery throughout the British Colonies; for promoting the Industry of the manumitted Slaves; and for compensating the Persons hitherto entitled to the Services of such Slaves, 3 & 4 Wm. IV. cap 73; and Cape of Good Hope Ordinance No. 1 of 1835. Parliament believed that for the good of the colonies and of the slaves themselves, the slaves required a period of training in the habits of industry, sobriety, piety, and thrift before they could be freed. Hence, apprenticeship, which came to an end on 1 December 1838.

6. Ordinance No. 1 of 1835, cap. IV, para. 1. Slave property holdings had first been protected by Cape of Good Hope Ordinance No. 19 of 1826, para. 28.

7. This was not a unique response. See, for instance, Mason (1990), 423-45, and Wayne Dooling (1992), 75-94.

8. The Abolition Act protected husbands and wives, and parents and children from separation by sale, but it did not address problems such as September's. (3 & 4 Wm., cap. 73, para. x.)

9. It is true that these events occurred after the formal abolition of slavery and that the 1820s and 1830s had been a time of considerable social and political turmoil, much of it related to the efforts of the British government to "ameliorate" the conditions under which slaves lived and worked. Yet, a decade of reform could not break the habits acquired during 170 years of slavery. The relationship between masters and slaves, and between Petrus Gerhardus Human and his slave, September, were fundamentally unaltered.

10. Slave families at the Cape have recently begun to receive the attention that they deserve. It is now clear that by the turn of the nineteenth century, at the latest, slave families and families composed of slaves and other servants were common features of the colonial landscape. E.g. Mason (1992), 425-526; Shell (1992); van der Spuy (1992), 50-74; and work in progress by Pam Scully.

11. See note 4 above.

12. Throughout this chapter, slaves are distinguished from servants. "Slave" refers only to someone who was defined as a slave or as an ex-slave apprentice under the terms of the Act for the Abolition of Slavery and the Cape of Good Hope Ordinance No. 1 of 1835, and "servant" to nonwhite farm laborers—Khoisan, Bastaard, and Bantu-speaking African—who were legally free, even though some may have been captives or indentured servants working under compulsion. Under the laws of the Cape, slaves were either persons who had been brought to the colony from southeast Asia, the Indian subcontinent, Madagascar, or Mozambique during the era of the slave trade (1652–1808) or descendants of these persons. No indigenous people were ever legally enslaved. For a discussion of legal indentureship, see ch. 8 by Jan Boeyens in this volume.

13. Rose (1982), 29.

14. See Rudolph Cloete's remarks about two of his slaves in Day Book , protector of slaves, Cape Town, SO 5/9, vols. 3, 4, 5, 6, 8, and 9, CAD; report, protector of slaves, Western Division, 26 Jul. 1833, CO 53/56, PRO.

15. Mason (1992), 227-33, and Alexander (1838), 71-2.

16. Onselen (1990), 101-2.

17. Mason (1992), 403-22.

18. Marais (1939), 167, and Worden (1985), 23, 91. Clifton Crais locates property-owning slaves within what he calls the "domestic economy of the unfree," that is, an economy which includes slaves and servants, but his treatments are brief. Crais (1992), 70-3, and (1990), 195-8.

19. Ross (1983), 17.

20. Watson (1990), 63-4.

21. Ross (1983), 84, and 81-9. See also Worden (1985), 125.

22. Circular letter, assistant commissioners of slave compensation to civil commissioners, 28 Nov. 1834, SO 20/4a, CAD.

23. Returns of the Total Number of Slaves in the Various Districts According to the Several Classes and Values, n.d. [1835], SO 20/61, CAD.

24. Mason (1992), 261-3.

25. Figures derived from Returns of the Total Number of Slaves in the Various Districts According to the Several Classes and Values, n.d. [1835], SO 20/61, CAD.

26. Cole (1966), 227-8; Guelke (1989), 84-93; Worden, (1985), 23; and Mason (1992), 54-5, 316-22.

27. The difficulties of marronage on the northern Cape frontier are addressed by Penn in ch. 3 of this volume. Though it was common for masters to assign the job of stock keeper to elderly slaves, the age of slave herders would have been only a minor factor. Because few slaves lived beyond their middle years, most slave stock keepers were young and middle-aged men. Ross (1983), 27-8; Worden, (1985); Mason (1992), 317-23, 437.

28. Report, protector of slaves, Eastern Division, 24 Jun. 1834, CO 53/58, PRO.

29. Statement of the Laws of the Colony of the Cape of Good Hope Regarding Slavery, in Theal (1897-1905), 9: 152-3. See also Mentzel (1921-1944), 3: 129-30.

30. Ordinance No. 19, para. 28.

31. General observations, report of the protector of slaves, Western Division, 28 May 1833, CO 53/55, PRO.

32. These sums are almost certainly optimistic. See below.

33. General observations, report of the protector of slaves, 25 Dec. 1830, CO 53/51, PRO.

34. General observations, report of the protector of slaves, Western Division, 28 May 1833, CO 53/55, PRO.

35. The following narrative is drawn from Criminal Record Book, special magistrate, Worcester, 1835–36, WOC 19/26, CAD, and Register of Slaves, Worcester, SO 6/132, CAD.

36. Report, protector of slaves, Eastern Division, Graaff-Reinet, 14 Aug. 1833, CO 53/56, PRO.

37. Report, protector of slaves, Western Division, Stellenbosch, 25 Jul. 1833, CO 53/55, PRO.

38. Report, protector of slaves, Eastern Division, Graaff-Reinet, 11 Jan. 1833, Ibid.

39. Neumark (1957), 78-9; Burchell (1822-24, 1967), 2: 113; and Thompson, (1827), 1: 55.

40. Giliomee (1989), 431.

41. Report, protector of slaves, Eastern Division, Graaff-Reinet, 28 May 1833, CO 53/55, PRO.

42. The following brief narrative relies on report, protector of slaves, Eastern Division, Graaff-Reinet, 23 Jan. 1834, CO 53/57, PRO.

43. Settlers and officials referred to SeSotho-speaking African refugees, who had fled the troubles to the north and east of the Cape colony and had found work on settler farms, as "Mantatees."

44. Elphick and Malherbe (1989), 17, 30-1, 45; civil commissioner, Swellendam, to secretary to government, 6 Jan. 1830, encl. in governor of the Cape colony to secretary of state, 18 Jul. 1830, GH 26/61, CAD.

45. Report on the Hottentots, Theal (1897-1905), 35: 315.

46. Peires (1981), 104-5, and Newton-King (1980), 193-5.

47. Report, protector of slaves, Eastern Division, Somerset, 28 May 1833, CO 53/55, PRO.

48. Report, protector of slaves, Eastern Division, Graaff-Reinet, 23 Jan. 1834, CO53/57, PRO.

49. Peires (1981), 91-2, 119.

50. Day Book, assistant protector of slaves, Graham's Town, in report, protector of slaves, Eastern Division, 11 Dec. 1832, GR 17/17, CAD.

51. Civil cases, resident magistrate, Uitenhage, 22 Oct. 1838, encl. in governor of the Cape colony to secretary of state, 8 Sep. 1841, GH 28/17, CAD.

52. Report of the protector of slaves, assistant protector, Somerset, 25 Jun. 1831, SO 3/7, CAD.

53. Report, protector of slaves, Eastern Division, Somerset, 14 Aug. 1833, CO 53/56, PRO.

54. Report, protector of slaves, Eastern Division, Graaff-Reinet, 14 Aug. 1833, Ibid.

55. Day book, assistant guardian of slaves, Graham's Town, n.d. [ca. 1827], in GR 17/17, CAD. For identification of this Piet Retief as the Voortrekker leader, see Marais, (1939), 167.

56. Elphick (1975), 62.

57. Beinart (1980), 134.

58. Peires (1981) 32.

59. Neumark (1957), 37.

60. Elphick and Shell (1989), 227-8.

61. Report, protector of slaves, Eastern Division, Graaff-Reinet, 14 Aug. 1833, CO 53/56, PRO.

62. Day book, assistant protector of slaves, Graham's Town, n.d. [ca. 1827], GR 17/17, CAD.

63. Without resistance, of course, masters and mistresses would have had no reason to offer rewards and incentives in the first place. For more on resistance as a way, in Eric Hobsbawm's words, of working the system to one's minimum disadvantage, see Mason (1992), 372-402.

64. Fortuyn resisted. He traveled to the assistant protector of slaves in Somerset and charged his master with having beaten him without cause and with unlawful severity. Swart was convicted and fined on each count. If violent domination was never far below the surface of slavery, neither was resistance to it. Report of the protector of slaves, assistant protector, Somerset, 28 May 1833, CO 53/55, PRO.

65. This turn of phrase from Parish (1989), 35.

66. Ibid, 34.

67. For a convenient introduction to the "peasant breach," see Berlin and Morgan (1991).

68. Mason (1992), 527-90.

69. See, for instance, Beinart and Delius (1986), 23, 36-9.

70. Watson (1990), 60.

71. Ibid, 59-61. Had the Graaff-Reinet plan been adopted and never amended, this event would have occurred in about 1950.

72. Ibid, 59-65.

73. Ibid, 63. Original emphasis.

74. The slavery reform laws of the 1820s and 1830s and the slaves' often clever manipulation of those laws exasperated Cape colony slave owners and lessened their allegiance to slavery as a form of labor exploitation. But they would not have so easily let go of slavery had there not been a readily apparent alternative. See, for instance, Mason (1992), 98-144, and Dooling (1992), 75-94.

75. Although the claim that the line between slavery and other forms of subordinate labor had blurred is hardly original, my emphasis is on the ways that slaves were like servants, not the reverse, which is the usual take. Many other voices have spoken on the matter. For one of the earliest, see Klaas Stuurman, a leader of the Khoikhoi rebellion of 1799-1803, quoted in Barrow (1801), 2: 93-6.

76. There is a vast historiography of the Great Trek. The best treatment in English, and indeed any language, remains Walker (1934).

77. Thompson (1990), 88.

78. My thanks to Dr. Chris Venter of the Department of History at the University of Stellenbosch for bringing this report to my attention.

79. Walker (1934),187. Instructions for the Guidance of Field-Cornet Joubert, on his Mission from the Governor of the Cape of Good Hope, to the Emigrant Colonial Farmers, 16 October 1838, GH 28/13, CAD.

80. Joubert instructions.

81. Report, Joubert to civil commissioner, Colesberg, 19 December 1838, encl. in governor of the Cape colony to secretary of state, 4 Feb. 1839, GH 28/14, CAD.

82. Ibid.

83. Ibid.

84. The search for a new and better master was a phenomenon which ex-apprentices in the Cape colony duplicated after 1 December 1838. Mason (1992), 527-79.

85. Report, Joubert to civil commissioner, Colesberg, 19 December 1838, encl. in governor of the Cape colony to secretary of state, 4 Feb. 1839, GH 28/14, CAD.

86. "Manifesto of the Emigrant Farmers," *GJ*, 2 Feb. 1837.

87. See Walker (1928), 206-7.

5

Slave Raiding Across the Cape Frontier

Elizabeth A. Eldredge

In the nineteenth century the tradition of slave raiding, as practiced by Boers and *trekboers* in the eastern Cape, spread with the advancement of the Dutch frontier. Captive indigenes, the booty of countless commando raids, helped to satisfy the labor demands of these cash-poor pastoral farmers before the abolition of the overseas slave trade and became one of their principal labor sources for decades after. Until the 1820s, their victims were mainly Khoisan men, women, and children, but as these populations dispersed or vanished and *trekboers* and later Voortrekkers moved further into the interior, Bantu-speaking peoples—BaTswana, BaSotho, and Nguni-speakers—served their purposes. The effect on highveld societies was devastating. Such frontier communities as the Bastaards, Griqua, and Kora themselves escaped enslavement by raiding innocent Khoikhoi and BaTswana and exchanging captives in eastern Cape markets for guns and ammunition. The BaTswana of Transorangia had to defend themselves from slave-raids at the same time they were beset with severe ecological crises. In brief, the sustained, high level of violence with which Dutch-speakers expanded their control over land and people beyond the Cape frontier seriously disrupted the demographic and political stability of indigenous societies. In some cases, it destroyed them altogether. The ultimate source of the upheavals of the 1820s and 1830s in the Cape interior predates the arrival of refugees from the east and the formation of the AmaNdebele military state and lays instead in a long-term process of raiding for cattle and slaves that originated on the Cape frontier in the eighteenth century and continued in the nineteenth century as Dutch-speaking pastoralists migrated inland.

Evidence that slave raiding pervaded the frontier is contained in contemporary accounts published by European travelers and missionaries. Their reports indicate that as early as 1797 Cape colonists were already capturing, selling, and buying enslaved indigenous children who origi-nated *beyond* the border and that they were arming frontier renegade groups to conduct raids and provide them with captives. Though few European outsiders toured the Cape's border areas early in the nineteenth century, their testimony exposes these illicit activities in detail and, more signifi-cantly, makes it possible to describe the *process* of enslavement that began in one corner of south Africa and spread to envelop the whole.

Labor Demands and Captive Laborers in the Colony

In districts such as Graaff-Reinet, labor demands on Boer farms were consistently high. Individual Boer families owned up to ten to twelve thousand head of livestock, either sheep or cattle or a combination, and needed many herders. Male slaves and to a greater extent Khoisan boys, referred to by authorities as "apprentices," kept watch over the livestock.[1] Female labor, black and white, also generated its own considerable share of the family income. In addition to providing the goods and services essential to farm members, women produced the farm's only manufactures that earned cash on the market. At the time their work remained largely invisible to male observers; only as a second thought, for instance, does John Barrow reveal their importance:

> The [Boer] women, as invariably happens in societies that are little advanced in civilization, are much greater drudges than the men, yet are far from being [un]industrious; they make soap and candles, the former to send to Cape Town in exchange for tea and sugar, and the latter for home-consumption.[2]

Henry Lichtenstein, who visited the frontier in 1804-06, emphasized the large profits farmers derived from soap produced by their wives and female slaves:

> The children [i.e., "apprentices"] and slaves are sent to collect the young shoots of the Chama bushes. The ashes of these saline plants produce a strong [lye], and of this, mixed with the fat of the sheep, collected during the year, the women make an excellent soap, from the sale of which a considerable profit is derived: large quantities are sent to the Cape town, where it is sold at a high price.[3]

William Burchell, who passed through this area several years later, ob-served that the major earnings from herds of Cape fat-tailed sheep, which did not bear wool, came from selling the soap made from the fat. A Boer family with numerous dependents, including slaves and Khoikhoi appren-tices, thought nothing of slaughtering two sheep a day for their own

FIGURE 5.1 Across the Cape Frontier.

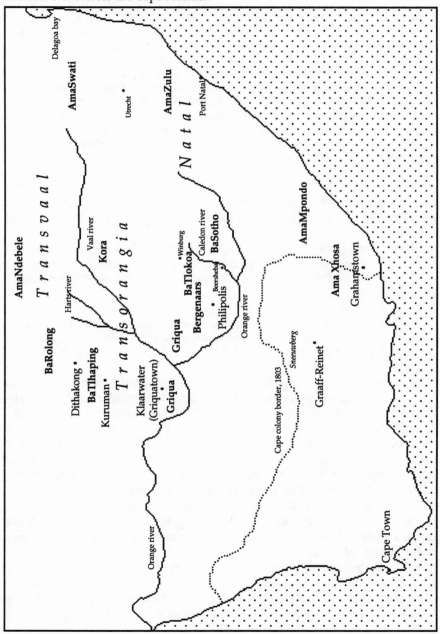

consumption, because the fat was converted into a profitable product. The fat of the sheep

> was considered almost equal in value to the rest of the carcass, by being manufactured into soap. It was, as they informed me, more profitable to kill their sheep, for this purpose, only, than to sell them to the butchers at so low a price as a rix-dollar or less, and even so low as five shillings. Formerly the alkali necessary for this manufacture was obtained here from the *Ganna-* (or *Kanna-*) *bosch*; but that being at length, all consumed through a constant demand for it, another species of *Salsola* growing wild in many parts of the country, was taken as a substitute, and found to be even preferable to the ganna. In the house, I saw a great number of cakes of this soap, piled up to harden, ready for their next annual journey to Cape Town; whither they go, not merely for the purpose of selling it, but of purchasing clothing and other such articles....[4]

Producing articles that earned important levels of cash income explains why women slaves (whether imported or "apprenticed") were in great demand.

Most Boer farmers, and virtually all *trekboers*, lacked sufficient cash income or savings to be able to purchase more than a few if any imported slaves. In the late 1790s Barrow noted that Boer farmers used "Hottentots" as laborers because

> slaves are too expensive. In the whole district of Graaff Reinet there are not more than six or seven hundred blacks [legal slaves], which is about one to each family; and the said district contains about 10,000 Hottentots.[5]

The cost of slaves rose rapidly after the abolition of the overseas trade in 1808. In 1820, eight slaves were sold in the Sneeuwberg area north of Graaff-Reinet for Rds 16,000, the equivalent of £1,600 according to traveler John Campbell. A woman with her nursing child brought Rds 5,000, a female child still nursing Rds 1,300, and a boy, Rds 3,000.[6] During the economic boom of 1806-11, when meat, soap, and agricultural products from the eastern Cape were in great demand, Boer farmers increased their ownership of imported slaves, and on the eve of legal emancipation 20 percent of the colony's legally owned slaves resided in the five eastern districts.[7] In the late eighteenth and early nineteenth century, however, demands for labor in these districts always exceeded Boer farmers' ability to purchase slaves or hire wage laborers.

Meeting the labor shortfall was achieved by tightening controls over the Khoisan in the Cape colony.[8] Their labor was in part mobilized by dispossessing them of their land and stock in the colony, a process that by 1800 was largely complete. It was no secret to the colonists or government at the beginning of the nineteenth century that, contrary to law, indigenous African peoples were also being directly enslaved by white colonists. In fact, Barrow made his trip to the frontier with the intention of witnessing frontiersmen as they enslaved the San on their borders and exposing these abuses in his writing. Other writers tried to discredit Barrow for sympathizing with the victims, but even the defenders of the colonists leave evidence of enslavement and abuse. Enslaving indigenous peoples was accomplished with considerable violence and carried out as official policy, as field commandant G. R. Opperman's instructions to a 1774 commando against the *Bosjesmans Hottentots* bear witness. He instructed the colonists to release the women, permitted them to divide up the males as servants among the farmers, and exhorted them only not to maltreat the captive servants "as has more than once happened with many."[9] In January 1775 a commando killed 503 "Bushmen" (including some injured women and children whose dispatch was justified, chillingly, as having prevented painful death) and returned with 241 prisoners. Some women and children captives "placed" with colonists had their names enumerated and listed in official documents.[10] In 1779 and 1780 commandos were reported to have captured "little ones" (i.e., children), and Dirk Koetse sent with his "Hottentot" replacement a note to his commando leader that "I have desired my Hottentot to catch a little one for me, and I beg that if he gets one, he may be allowed to keep it."[11] Under the first British government (1795–1803), the killing of *Bosjesmans* continued and their permanent state of servitude remained legal. Barrow attributed colonial policy to the propaganda efforts of the colonists.

> In consequence of these representations, [the government] decreed that such of the Bosjesmans as should be taken alive in the expeditions made against them, were to be distributed by lot among the commandant and his party, with whom they were to remain in a state of servitude during their lives.[12]

Colonel Collins, who toured the country in 1809, was told that "the total extinction of the Bosjesmen race is actually stated to have been at one time confidently hoped for," and met men who claimed to have been personally on commandos in which two to three thousand San were killed in a matter of several years.[13] Collins, who claimed that the colonists treated their *Bosjesmens* humanely, acknowledged that "women are sometimes put to death in these expeditions; and it cannot be doubted that the farmers bring away a number of children."[14] William Somerville observed that "the dutch boer...whenever he can murders the parents and enslaves as many of their children as he thinks may prove useful to him."[15] Andrew Smith was told a generation later that " it was very common amongst the farmers to steal Bushmen children, particularly in former days."[16]

Laws prohibiting such raids were promulgated during the first period of British government (1795-1803), but in the outlying areas of the colony they went unenforced. Such was discovered in 1801 by Somerville on a government expedition to the interior. He found deep distrust and hostility between Khoisan on the one hand and the farmers on the other. The "Bosjesmans" hated the Boers, Somerville noted, and for good reason.

> The rigor with which the peasantry treat their Hottentots, the injustice practised by them in defrauding them of their wages, and using them as slaves, did not fail to excite a sincere detestation of these severe masters, who had no way of maintaining authority but by the most wanton and barbarous acts of arbitrary punishment from which they seem not to have been deterred by the laws of the country, probably conceiving themselves beyond the reach of its power from the great distance at which they resided from the cape.[17]

Beyond the Boer frontier Somerville encountered a community of Bastaards who complained of the severe abuses suffered from Boer attacks "[which] forced them to live in this horrible part of the country — The circumstances they related of the oppression and tyranny of the *Wagmeesters* are truly shocking."[18]

Abuses were also widespread within the colony, where thousands of Khoisan laborers were held in bondage. Since 1775 the government had legalized the indenturing of what were termed *inboekelinge* ("apprentices"), the children of Khoikhoi slaves and servants on Boer farms who were bound in the same place until their twenty-fifth year. By 1800 this system was firmly entrenched, and it then enjoyed protection under the first British government, just as it had under the VOC.[19] Khoisan, as well as AmaXhosa and BaTswana, made up its victims.[20] *Inboekstelsel* ("apprenticeship"),as oppressive as slavery from its inception, offered legal protection for farmers who victimized laborers and deprived them of any benefits. Barrow, who toured the colony in 1797–98, was the first publicly to inveigh against conditions of apprenticeship, which he regarded as worse than slavery.

> By a resolution of the old government, as unjust as it was inhuman, a peasant [Boer] was allowed to claim as his property, till the age of five-and-twenty, all the children of the Hottentots in his service to whom he had given in their infancy a morsel of meat. At the expiration of this period the odds are ten to one that the slave is not emancipated....Should he be fortunate enough to escape at the end of the period, the best part of his life has been spent in a profitless servitude, and he is turned adrift in the decline of life (for a Hottentot begins to grow old at thirty) without any earthly thing he can call his own, except the sheep's skin upon his back....Their children are encouraged to run about the house of the peasant, where they receive their morsel of food. This is deemed sufficient to establish their claim to the young Hottentots; and should the parents, at the end of the term for which they engaged, express a

desire to quit the service, the farmer will suffer them to go, perhaps turn them away, and detain their children.[21]

He argued that because apprentices were not transferable property, their lives were valued less than slaves' and they were subjected to less humane treatment.[22] Conditions for Khoisan tied to farms on the eastern Cape frontier were particularly harsh.

> Few of the distant boors [*sic*] have more than one slave, and many none; but the number of Hottentots amounts, on an average in Graaf Reynet, to thirteen to each family. The inhumanity with which they treat this nation I have already had occasion to notice. The boor has few good traits in his character, but this is the worst. Not satisfied with defrauding them of the little earnings of their industry, and inflicting the most cruel and brutal punishments for every trifling fault, they have a constant practice of retaining the wife and children and turning adrift the husband.... [I]t is in vain for the Hottentot to complain. To whom, indeed should he complain?[23]

Regulations under the first British government prohibited farmers from mistreating apprentices and required farmers to compensate all their workers, but enforcement was resisted, particularly on the frontier. According to Barrow, officials who tried to uphold laws protecting Khoikhoi laborers risked their lives.

> The last [landdrost of Graaff-Reinet], who was a very honest man, and anxious to fulfil the duties of his office, was turned out of his district, and afterwards threatened to be put to death by these unprincipled people, because he would not give them his permission to make war upon the Kaffers; and because he heard the complaints of the injured Hottentots. The boor, indeed, is above all law....[24]

By Barrow's time it was already clear that frontier farmers preferred enslaving women and children over men. They were more easily controlled and could be kept indefinitely. Their slavery was more complete than was the case for men, who sometimes retained considerable autonomy herding the animals of their masters.[25] Women were apt to be kept in or near the main house, where they were under constant surveillance and supervision. Slave and Khoisan women had no autonomy, stood ever vulnerable to physical abuse, and remained bound by loyalties to their children, whom they hoped to protect. Sometimes the father of a woman's child was her master.[26] Children were apprenticed to the age of twenty-five, a time itself easily prolonged because of the ambiguity of birth years, and the law insuring their liberation even then was not normally enforced.[27] At best a mother might escape with a child on her back, but normally her only recourse was to flee without her children, and even then her chances of reaching a safe haven beyond the frontier were slim.[28] Conversely, masters had the power to separate permanently a mother from her child. One mother, who refused to abandon her children, was in fact beaten to death, as was recalled years later by her child.

> [A farmer] seized her children, then nearly grown up and strong enough to be made useful on his farm, and drove her away from the place, as she herself appeared too old to render him much service by her labor. He therefore procured Juli [her son, who related this account] and his sister to be registered in the field-cornet's books, as legally bound to serve him for twenty-five years; which was in fact to make them his slaves for that time. The mother clung to her children, wishing to resist this unjust seizure, and desiring to be permitted either to take them away, or to live on the farm with them; but the farmer repeatedly drove her off, and at last, with a resolution to deter her from coming there again, he one evening flogged her so unmercifully that she died the next morning! This, and the harsh treatment which he himself received, were sufficient to drive Juli to despair; and he, in consequence, took the first favorable opportunity of making his escape.[29]

Under the second British government, the apprenticeship system was regulated in more detail but failed to curtail the old abuses. In 1812 legislation limited apprenticeship to ten years, if a farmer had supported the child until the age of eight, or if the child was not in the care of a parent, a predicament not difficult for armed frontiersmen to arrange. New regulations concerning the movement of Khoisan in the colony issued by governor Caledon further strengthened the colonists hold on the Khoikhoi. It became

> legal to compel any Khoisan not in government service to serve the colonists, for without a pass he could not legally be anywhere at all, and it was the colonists who controlled the issue of passes.[30]

That same year on the borders of the colony, William Burchell encountered a party of ten "Bushmen," two men, six women, and two children, all of whom had just left the service of "old Master Jacob," because he had severely beaten one of the women. Their joint act of resistance reveals that these and other "Bushmen," though legally free, were not entitled to leave at will. Another woman "complained that this *baas* had compelled her son to remain in his service against his wish; nor could they by any means obtain leave for him to return with them to their kraal."[31]

Several years later John Campbell visited a frontier farm where "about fifty" Bushmen—men, women, and children—were in the service of Mr. Smit, the owner. At another he found two children, whom, he was told, "a field-cornet higher up the country procured them from their parents to be trained up as servants," alleging, in other words, that they had come voluntarily. Within days the youngsters escaped and "were found half-starved in the wilderness, fast locked in each other's arms."[32]

Slave Raiding Across the Border: Transorangia

Oppression in the Cape colony ultimately promoted slave raiding beyond the colony's borders. Violence was exported in the first instance by persons themselves making their own bid for freedom, as Penn has demonstrated in chapter 2 with regard to the northern Cape in the late nineteenth century. At the same time Khoikhoi, legally free blacks, escaped slaves, and people of mixed descent calling themselves Bastaards migrated across the Orange river and were later joined by renegades and convicted criminals, some of whom were Europeans. They settled in Transorangia, the home of Khoisan and BaTswana of long association. The BaTswana kingdoms constituted amalgamations of small groups of various origin, and they interacted peacefully, also violently, with neighboring Kora, other Khoikhoi groups, and San. Conflict, as well as intermixing and intermarriage, punctuated relations among all these peoples before the advent of the refugees from the Cape.[33] Qualitatively different forms of competition and oppression began to appear in Transorangia, however, when the newcomers, armed and on horseback, began to covet the land and cattle of its inhabitants. Conflict arising in the 1790s following cattle raids against the southern BaTswana became so destructive that widespread death and extreme poverty resulted. The BaTlhaping were particularly hard hit by the raids, which disrupted them politically, weakened for years their ability to resist, and left them exposed as targets for slave raiders in the decades after 1800.

Some of the earliest raids, in the 1790s, were led by European fugitives from justice. Among the most notorious was Jan Bloem, a German who had fled the Cape after murdering his wife. He joined Pieter Pienaar, a renegade field-cornet, and others on attacks against the Khoisan. Captive children were sold to Boer farmers in the Cape.[34] Bloem raided the Kora and compelled San to help in attacks on the BaTswana. In 1801 Molehabangwe, the BaTlhaping's *kgosi* (figuratively "chief") at Dithakong ("Litako") recalled how several years earlier

his people had been attacked by...Jan Blom, and his party, armed with muskets; how their habitations had been burnt and destroyed, and most of their women and children cruelly murdered, some sacrificed in the flames, and the greater part of their cattle captured; and how, though superior in number, they were compelled to succumb, owing to the inferiority of their arms.[35]

Andrew Smith recorded the story of a "very aged Bushman" who took part in the attack:

> Our informant [wrote Smith], with many others of his fellow countrymen, was invited, nay compelled to join in a commando formed by John Bloom about 1794 for the purpose of attacking the Bituanas [BaTswana], and proceeded with it to the Kooroman [Kuruman river] where the Caffres were attacked, many of them shot, and all their cattle, sheep and goats taken, and with which thevictors proceeded toward the colony.... The Corannas [Kora], who formed a very considerable proportion of this plundering band, with the small share of booty which was ceded to them, preferred seeking a new abode to returning to the one they had left, and for that purpose directed their course up the Orange River....[36]

The Kora then set upon nearby BaTlhaping. John Campbell later spoke to two of their victims. One, an "uncle to Mateebe [Mothibi], the King of Lattakoo" related that

> the Corannas made war against the matchappees [BaTlhaping], in which they drove them from Nokanna to Catooss, and afterwards to the source of the Krooman River, capturing almost the whole of their cattle, which were their chief means of support. The loss of these reduced them to the necessity of living upon roots and whatever game they could occasionally kill. During this famine his mother, Picquaney, died....[37]

Another MoTlhaping man stated that the Kora captured all his cattle, leaving him "a poor man, which obliged him for some time to live among the wild Bushmen, in order to obtain subsistence."[38]

Petrus Borcherds, who passed through Transorangia in 1801, heard many reports of similar depredations committed by a party led by the Oorlam, Klaas Afrikaner, whose murders of "Koranahs and Kafirs on or near the banks of the Orange River were numerous and cruel, and their robberies of cattle very extensive." Begged by the BaTswana victims "to obtain them assistance and protection, and to have these banditti punished who kept the country in general terror," several of Borcherd's party joined Adam Kok's Bastaard commando against Afrikaner and recovered stolen cattle.[39] Borcherds considered this a counterattack.

> A Bastard, Hans Luykens, who had served as a guide,....related the most fearful stories of cruelties committed by these banditti upon the namaquas, of whom many had been murdered. Women and children, were tied to trees and, after being ill-treated, killed, and whole communities had been robbed of their cattle; so that these inoffensive tribes, not able to defend themselves with their inferior weapon, the spear, were now wandering about in a state of want and privation, many perishing from hunger.[40]

Raiding became the means for supplying a frontier trade in children. As early as 1797–98, Kora were reported by Barrow:

> not only [to] carry off large herds of cattle [of the BaTlhaping], but...seize and make slaves of their children, some of whom have been brought into the colony, and purchased by the farmers in exchange for cattle.... These people {Kora] make regular attacks, in large parties of four or five hundred.[41]

Such attacks were being encouraged from a distance. Even Lichtenstein, who had attacked Barrow's descriptions of the colonists' brutal treatment of the San, conceded that the Boers were responsible for instigating the emerging frontier slave trade. While in Transorangia in 1804–06 he observed:

> The natives here mentioned do not know anything about the slave trade as they live too far from the coast, but they realised since they met the colonists the advantage of trading their "prisoners of war" for cattle or products from Europe. They offered us even ten year old boys in exchange for one sheep per head. Many a defeated victim has had his life spared by this speculation. The government at the Cape must use all its vigilance, to forestall this dangerous trade and its pernicious repercussions for the coming generation.[42]

Raiding, for cattle and children, moved north as the Dutch frontier expanded. Bastaard and Griqua groups, identified as they were with Dutch colonial culture, also imposed their dominance over their African neighbors by force and enslavement. At the head of one of these groups was Coenraad de Buys, notorious among the European renegades from the Cape then roaming the interior. In 1816 he became the leader of a disaffected Griqua minority at Klaarwater, and "the immediate result of the combination was the plundering of the surrounding Bechuanas."[43]

In response to the raids, by about 1800 the BaTlhaping were strengthening their ties to the stronger Kora and Griqua as a means of protection. Lichtenstein reported that the BaTlhaping were intermarrying with Kora living southeast of Dithakong.[44] Their king, Molehabangwe, married a Kora woman named Leapa, who bore his heir, Mothibi.[45] Regular intercourse between BaTswana chiefdoms and their Griqua neighbors was evident to early travelers. Lichtenstein, for example, was addressed by Adam Kok I in the "Beetjuan" [SeTswana] language, which other Bastaards also spoke fluently. According to Lichtenstein, Kok was said to be "universally known, and, as it appeared, highly beloved" among the BaTswana at the time of Lichtenstein's visit (1804–06).[46] Lichtenstein also discovered that the "Coran" [Kora] language was "understood by many of the Beetjuans, and spoken by them with considerable fluency." At Dithakong he was told by Molehabangwe that he had sent a party to make a treaty alliance with the Kora.[47]

As a result of the incorporation and amalgamation of various people, BaTlhaping society had become stratified, with sharp distinctions between rich and powerful and poor.[48] By 1800, internal servitude was already present. Prior to early nineteenth-century trade contact with Europeans, the system of servitude incorporated captives into the dominant society. A MoTswana tried to sell Lichtenstein two boys, explaining that they had been captured in battle as infants, and he was afraid they would die of hunger as he had nothing to feed them. Though Lichtenstein was unconvinced of the excuse, the offer was made in the wake of prolonged drought and famine, suggesting the MoTswana was speaking truthfully. Lichtenstein described a pattern of servitude which scholars generally refer to as slavery elsewhere in Africa: "All the servants of the rich were in like manner the property of their masters, being prisoners taken in battle, or their descendants."[49] Significantly, Lichtenstein used the term "mutjanka' to refer to a person in hereditary bondage among the BaTlhaping of 1806, and Burchell a few years later spelled the term "muchunka," clearly the term in SeTswana, *motlhanka* (pl. *batlhanka*; the practice: *botlhanka*; SeSotho: *mohlanka, bahlanka, bohlanka*). According to Tlou, who has analyzed the rise of the BaTawana kingdom of Ngamiland and the intensification of their socioeconomic stratification in the nineteenth century, *batlhanka* were dependents, not to be confused with slaves. Most were voluntary clients of wealthy or powerful cattle owners, and a much smaller number, attached to a few BaTawana households, were what he terms "hereditary serfs," who had evolved from the client group. Such persons, though deprived of civil and property rights, were rarely sold internally or for export.[50] Lichtenstein's evidence suggests the practice existed among BaTswana generally and predated the emergence of the BaTawana.

Evidence from the early nineteenth century suggest that Tlou's historical distinction is appropriate, and it indicates that harsher institutionalized forms of *botlhanka* appeared later in the nineteenth century and reflected a process of transformation prompted by new relations of production and exchange related to white frontier expansion from the 1840s. Even before the 1820s, a captive apparently could be sold, but in practice they usually were not and as adults often returned home or were assimilated into the local population. When Burchell noticed a starving child among the BaTlhaping at Dithakong, a man told him

> that it was a *Bushman's child*, and belonged to him; that in an attack on a Bushman kraal, he had seized him, and carried him off as a *prisoner of war*; that he was therefore his by right: and that, if I wished to buy him, I should have him for a sheep![51]

After further inquiries on the subject, Burchell concluded that such captives were not slaves:

> They sometimes also bring away a few *prisoners-of-war*: these are generally retained as servants; and as they in most instances, fare as well as the lower class of Bachapins [BaTlhaping] and, perhaps, as well as they would, had they remained in their own country, they do not, it was said, often take advantage of opportunities for escaping and returning to their own country: nor could I ever, by any outward appearance, distinguish them from the natives. Such captives cannot properly be regarded in any other, than in the light of prisoners-of-war; or if they are to be called slaves (a term which must always sound detestable in the ear of every feeling man), they were not generally considered by their masters as common saleable property; and I have heard of several instances, in which they have been allowed to return home; but whether through the payment of any ransom, or by voluntary manumission, I was unable to learn....Muchunka...confessed that when children fell into their hands, they were carried away, and brought up as servants; and that these were so far rated as their own property, that they were sometimes, though rarely, transferred to another master..., yet they were never, I believe, sold to another tribe or nation. Whenever their parents desired to have their children home again, which often was the case when they were grown up, their masters never refused giving them up for a certain ransom, which amounted usually to the value of an ox and a cow, or a cow and two oxen.[52]

Such practices were qualitatively different than the slavery practiced by Europeans, but they nevertheless made these societies vulnerable to being drawn into a wider network of slave trading linked to European expansion.

Among the BaTswana and San rendered destitute by slave and cattle raiding, some placed themselves under Griqua authority at Griquatown, and others, including entire San groups, were forced to live there. Andrew Bain, who in 1826 hunted in Transorangia, blamed the Griqua for practicing "intolerable slavery" and reported that throughout the Griqua country San and BaTswana were captured and kept under "cruel and degrading conditions."[53] Though oppressive, such conditions did not necessarily constitute slavery. Many Griquatown residents had been driven there by poverty, hoped for some degree of protection and appear to have received it. Those incorporated involuntarily included those being punished for cattle theft. Andrew Smith heard that Andries Waterboer "used to catch such San as stole from his people, and caused them to work in irons about the village; they for a long time have not stolen from him."[54] Few BaTswana and San subjects in Griquatown were sold in the Cape and most were free to resettle elsewhere within several years. Moletsane's BaTaung settled at Griquatown after being attacked by a Griqua and BaTlhaping commando in 1828, and in 1836 left to settle among the BaSotho, first at the Beersheba mission station, then at Mekuatling.[55] Yet, Griquatown was a residence of choice less because of the treatment refugees received at the hands of the Griqua than because of the insecurity prevailing in the surrounding area and the absence of stock, land, and water outside of Griquatown. To those left destitute by raiders, Griquatown represented the least severe of their choices, until African states offering sanctuary on the fringes of the highveld began to emerge in the 1830s.[56]

Destabilization Across the Cape Frontier

The turmoil generated from frontier raids since the 1790s disabled traditional strategies of famine avoidance across the northern border of the Cape Colony, resulting in recurrent famine during a three-decade cycle of drought that began ca. 1800. The influx of migrants from the east in the 1820s came in the depths of this food scarcity, when the local populations were unable to cope politically and economically with the task of absorbing more people. Violent competition for food resources ensued.[57] Legassick has recognized the convergence of white settler interests with those of Griqua and Kora groups, who took advantage of disruptions related to the migrations of the AmaHlubi and AmaNgwana and BaTlokoa in 1822–23. He revealed the presence of slave raiding across the frontier during the 1820s and emphasized its destructive effects.[58] Cobbing tried to show that the *agents provocateurs* in Transorangia were London Missionary Society (LMS) missionaries, but their innocence is easily established. Rather the frontier farmers were responsible, as an abundance of evidence demonstrates.[59] The slave trade arising in the 1820s can be documented, moreover, with the detailed correspondence of John Melvill of the LMS, just as the reports of his fellow missionaries make it possible to describe the pattern of slave trading that continued into the next decade.[60]

Melvill, who first worked among the Griqua as the Cape Colony's government agent, began exposing the slave trade before he joined the mission. In 1824, when the Griqua divided over the decision to cooperate with Cape authorities and respect its laws, including those that restricted Griqua trade with the colonists, Melvill backed the Griqua who accepted the colony's terms and condemned the breakaway group, which became known as the Bergenaars:

> A. Hendrick, his two nephews, Gert. Goeyman and his three brothers, with several others, rebelled against the old chiefs some years before [1821], and having joined a deserter from the colony (one Bergs), they commenced marauding expeditions against the Bechuanna tribes, and were the cause of much disturbance in the country. They were then called Harteneers, from the Hart River, the place where they resided; they are now denominated Bergenaars (or mountaineers), from having taken up their residence among the hills.[61]

The Bergenaars attracted followers because they avoided colonial restrictions on trade and thereby derived huge profits, while those who cooperated with the colonial authorities and their representatives suffered from restricted access to trade. Melvill strongly suspected that the colonists were behind the Bergenaars.

> I have no doubt the landdrosts of the frontier districts have endeavoured to prevent Griquas without passes from entering the colony; still it is a well-known fact that such people have continued their intercourse with the colony, and have trafficked even in guns and ammunition. The Bergenaars have obtained these contraband articles, and they have no other means of obtaining them than from the colony.[62]

"This lawless horde," as Melvill called the Bergenaars, used their guns against neighboring Africans who had none, committing what Melvill referred to as "dreadful depredations....Hundreds of them have been murdered, and thousands reduced to misery and want."

> [T]he King of the Bashootoo tribe, now in Cape Town...relates that his town was unexpectedly attacked by a large party of men on horseback. Being a people they had never seen before, and not knowing the destructive nature of their weapons, the Bashootoos attempted to defend themselves; but seeing great numbers of their people falling down dead, and the enemy, in spite of their utmost efforts, driving away their cattle, they at last gave way, running in all directions, leaving nearly all their cattle in the possession of the plunderers.[63]

The Bergenaars soon returned, and the BaSotho, who decided it was useless to fight, offered no resistance. Many were enslaved. According to the survivors, "four white men collected all the boys [and] carried them off."[64] They also tried to capture some of the women, one of whom failed to escape because she clung to her child. Among the BaSotho, any group that lost its herd in a raid "followed their cattle behind," [i.e., became clients to those who took the cattle and received the cattle back on the loan-cattle system (*mafisa*)]. Inequalities of wealth and the patron-client system were reinforced, but the destitute retained access to their means of survival. The Bergenaars, however, were interested only in the cattle, women, and children as objects for sale.

> Having but a few cattle to subsist on, many of them [BaSotho], rather than starve, resolved to follow the track of their plunderers in hopes of getting something to eat; others said they would not live with those who had reduced them to such misery. When those who followed the plunderers arrived near the residence of the Bergenaars, they were met by some people of the

plundered tribes returning to their country, who said the Bergenaars would kill them if they proceeded. Upon hearing this, many hundreds returned.[65]

As this incident shows, gender and age played a central role in enslavement. Bergenaars were careful to select the more vulnerable children and women for their captives. The latter made easier prey than men in part because they insisted on remaining to protect their children. Raiders desired women and children, because they were easy to control, and killed the men, because they were likely to make rebellious and dangerous captives. For these same reasons, women and children, rather than men, were in demand among farmers.

In 1828 Melvill and fellow missionary, G.A Kolbe, traveled with a view to discovering more about the "Bashutoos," who as a people were still as yet unknown to Europeans.[66] On the trip the missionaries encountered further evidence of Bergenaar depredations. Although BaSotho groups suffered from some cattle raiding at the hands of Nguni-speaking immigrants (the BaSotho termed all of these "Matabele"), they did not fear them. The Bergenaar Griqua posed the more serious threat. At one village Melvill learned:

> it was people under a chief named Chaka [sic], who had deprived these Bafukaings [BaFokeng] of some of their cattle, and that when they fled into these parts to save the remainder, the Bergenaars deprived them of all.[67]

At a BaKoena village Melvill was told that all the cattle of the nearby "Bushmen" had been taken by invaders led by a Bergenaar whom the MoKoena chief named.[68] The pattern was the same: in the wake of the passing through of Nguni-speaking migrants, the Bergenaars moved in as predators.[69] Away from the scene of conflict, Melvill encountered BaSotho refugees living with *some* Griqua in the direction of Griquatown after having been "plundered by the Bergenaars."

> This werf [lit. "kraal"] consists of twelve Griqua, and seventeen Bechuana families. The latter are most of the Bashootoo tribe, which was plundered by the Bergenaars. From the account given by these people, they were driven from their native country by a tribe of Caffers, whom they call matabeele, which is probably the Tambookies[sic]; after this, they were attacked, and entirely impoverished by the Bergenaars, whom they followed into this country. Many hundreds have since found their way into various parts of the colony.[70]

Melvill made his anti-slavery sentiments explicit in a diatribe against the white settlers, in which he exposed their enslaving of Africans:

We hesitate not to say that they [the Boers] are robbers of the oppressed. We are all pleading for the emancipation of slavery, —a christian-like work indeed!—but in Africa christians are daily making slaves. Govt. is continually making regulations agreeable to justice, to punish the Bushmen and other plunderers of Cattle, but we trust the same Govt will prevent the farmers from plundering — we say plundering — the bushmen and Bassutoos.[71]

An 1820s witness to events in the northern Cape frontier, hunter George Thompson, alleged that most Griqua, with the exception of those in allegiance to Melvill and other missionaries at Griquatown, were

> associated into bands of outlaws, who subsist more or less by plundering the helpless natives....They have destroyed or dispersed whole tribes, by robbing them of their cattle and even their children, emulating the ferocity and augmenting the miseries inflicted by the savage Mantatees [sic]. This deplorable state of things now prevails, (or at least prevailed at the time of my visit to Namaqualand) from the sources of the Gariep to its mouth. The Griqua or Bastard population is spread along the banks of that river for an extent of at least seven hundred miles. Their numbers altogether are estimated to amount to nearly five thousand souls, and they have now in their possession, I am convinced, at least seven hundred muskets. Notwithstanding all the proclamations to the contrary, they readily obtain constant supplies of ammunition from the Boers, whom the great profits tempt to carry on this traffic....[72]

In this area, where the BaTlhaping under Mothibi were located, LMS missionary John Moffat also reported that the Griqua and their arms suppliers, rather than any local or other invading group, were the source of conflict.

> Mothibi again asserted, in his usual angry tone, that the heads of the banditti of the country were Griquas, and that they were our friends and servants, who we could command, and with whom we had constant intercourse; moreover, that these Griquas were supplied with guns and ammunition by the colonists, for the purpose of extirpating the Bechuanas![73]

The younger Andries Stockenstrom asserted that Europeans were keeping these captured children in order to "save" them from the ravages of drought, but he accused Adam Kok's Griqua of plundering the San and BaTswana and selling captive children. In their own defense, the Griqua accused white settlers of arming them and sending them to attack "Bushmen" groups.[74]

The Kora were also armed for slave raiding by Dutch farmers of the Cape, as well as by itinerant traders (*smousen*). "For the last eight years," it was reported in 1834 regarding the "Tribes to the Northwards," that:

They have been subjected to the incessant attacks of the infamous Corannas, who have destroyed most of their people, and taken at different times an incredible number of cattle; so that not a single head of cattle is to be found, except at the residence of the chief, Mosheshue, or among some of his people who have ventured from the mountains since the arrival of missionaries among them. For the children another fate is reserved; of late years they have found them to be a lucrative source of traffic among the border farmers who, by their readiness to purchase the children thus violently taken from their country and home, give great encouragement to that practice. Among the Bashutas [BaSotho], cattle have become very scarce, and the commandos do not as usual go out in search of them so much as children, whom they carry off in great numbers, and dispose of them to the farmers who readily give a horse or perhaps an inferior gun for each.[75]

The most notorious Kora leader to emerge at this time was Piet Witvoet, who led raids in the Caledon valley from 1825 until the mid-1830s. Witvoet's people preyed, too, on BaTswana groups moving south from the Transvaal and away from Mzilikazi. In the 1830s Arbousset wrote of the Kora:

They are almost always at war with their neighbours,—not that they delight in war, but they like the pillage by which it is attended. From the time of their emigration to the banks of the Gariep, no tribe in the neighbourhood has enjoyed a moment of repose. Furnished with fire arms, and mounted on good horses, they have pillaged all the tribes around them in succession. With the exception of Hanto,...and perhaps one or two others, their chiefs have filled all their neighbours with terror. They speak of them as *wolves*. We may mention as amongst the most formidable of them, Piet-Witte-Voet, Salres, and Voortoow.[76]

Thomas Arbousset and François Daumas of the Paris Evangelical Missionary Society (PEMS) met a BaKubung chief whose people had been one of Witvoet's victims. The missionaries were told:

These brigands have never ceased to plunder the tribe from the first day that they knew it. They possess no advantage over it, either in numbers or in courage, but that which fire arms gives [sic] over an insignificant assegai [spear], and horses, over a people who go only on foot. More particularly Piet Witvoet has constantly made war against Makuana and his subjects, from whom he hath taken away in succession their herds of oxen, of sheep, and of goats, their millet, their maize, and even their children, to procure in exchange for these little slaves, powder, and brandy from the Cape farmers or from the *smousen* who engage in such traffic. Oh the deadly inequality of arms! Nothing has done so much harm as this to South Africa. A kraal of Lighoyas [BaKubung] is always certain to take to flight before seven or eight Korannas or Griquas on horseback, and who come each armed with his gun. Then all is taken away, and the huts are often burned.[77]

Arbousset and Daumas, clearly disturbed by the raiding and the slave trade in children, confronted their readers with the horrors inflicted by Witvoet, as experienced by the BaKubung of Tikuane river:

> Khomoatsane, the chief of this place related to us how Piet Witvoet had forced him the year before to remove to this place from Makuana's and *to his narration* this man, who was in appearance benign, added, that *'he had not a single child left to him, nor had any of his subjects.'* [emphasis added] We would not at first believe this, but on examination we found that there were none but infants in the village; children from four to twelve years of age there were none, and the poor people assured us that they had been torn from them by the Koranna with an armed force. These poor people were inconsolable. Some of them complained that having recognised their children with the farmers passing through the plain, they went in haste to entreat these whites to restore that which was dearer to them than anything on earth besides, but they hastily replied, 'Get you gone, wicked Caffers; these children are ours; we bought them from the Korannas, and wish only to have to do with them [i.e., the Kora].' Such occurrences are very common among the Lighoyas [BaKubung]. Another call for shame on the inhuman advocates of the most horrible of traffics, carried on as if men were not the property of God alone.[78]

On their travels, Arbousset and Daumas's MoTswana guide made a point, when meeting African groups en route, of distinguishing the missionaries from the raiders. "Do not fear," the guide explained to a chief, "that they want to carry off your children as the Bakotus [Kora] did."[79] A Wesleyan missionary encountered a commando that "professed to be on a hunting expedition." Before the missionary

> left the country, the commando had laid waste to two Bashutas' villages, and taken from thence all the children they could find, after murdering nearly all the women and ten men. Many parts of the country are said to be white with human bones.... Not only Corannas are responsible, but also Bastards, Pienaars, Piet Barend, Piet Davids, and Dergeup, the Corrana Bushmen...also traders, supplying ammunition and contraband goods to Marauders. And lastly, are those farmers who, by their readiness to receive Bechuana children at the hands of the Corannas, furnish an irresistible impetus to the continuance of the inhuman practice of slavery.....[80]

Thus, between 1800 and the 1820s, the nature of slave raiding assumed a regular pattern. Continuity resulted from the simple fact that early raiders had moved further into the interior, embroiling indigenous groups. The Kora and others who were seeking "to avoid being raided or to acquire firearms," joined the breakaway Griqua group, the Bergenaars.[81] The process is exemplified by the notorious Jan Bloem, the white raider who had once been a soldier of the Dutch East India Company, and migrated in the

1780s from the Cape colony to Namaqualand, and then to the Klaarwater area; there he became the leader of the Springbok clan of the Taaibosches, the main body of the Kora. He married an estimated eight to ten Kora wives, by whom he had many children.[82] His son, Jan Bloem, Jr. (1775-1858), who had a Kora mother, succeeded his father in 1799. He was greatly feared; he joined the raids of the Bergenaars for several years, participated in attack on Griquatown in 1824, settled briefly, then resumed raiding.[83] According to Andrew Smith:

> [Jan Bloem, Jr.] has for some years past been an active disturber of the peace of these districts....He has ...almost ever since Mosulacatzi took up his present residence, been a zealous opponent of the Zoolas, and, though in his inroads upon them he has never been particularly successful, but has many times narrowly escaped with his own life, he still perseveres in attacking them, and expresses a determination that he will not desist until he either destroys them or loses his own life in the attempt.[84]

In the years leading up to the Voortrekker movement out of the Cape, *trekboers* and Boers were themselves raiding for slaves in Transorangia. As Arbousset and Daumas reported, their targets were San and BaSotho. The "Bushmen of Ratilabane, and...[San] on this side of the orange River from Philippolis to the malutis," the missionaries wrote, "have all lost a great part of their children...."

> These unhappy beings live in small isolated groups, and rarely do they dwell any where but in bushes and caverns, these being considered the places of greatest safety. But even there the dutch boers discover them, fall upon them, fire on the kraal, kidnap the children, and, when they can, carry off even the adults, and sometimes, with a barbarous refinement on cruelty, tie them, it is said, to the horses' tail. If unhappily the captives make any resistance or attempt to run away they are shot. At all events there remains a sure booty and a more valuable one in the children. *This practice of depredation by the wandering farmers or hunters is so common* [emphasis added] that the cry of alarm and signal for flight amongst the Bushmen is... "Tuntsi, a sea a nge a kunte," "there is the white man; he is coming to take away our children." Tuntsi is employed to designate a white man; it properly signifies a shooter. It is the onomatorpy of the report of a gun, *tuntse*. In ordinary language the whites are called *kho*.[85]

The white farmers also turned their guns against the BaSotho to enslave their children, as Arbousset and Daumas learned from an unnamed BaSotho chief. Referring to this as "bondage," the missionaries reported that:

> They complain that the wandering boers persecute them, seizing almost all their children, dishonouring them if they be girls, and sometimes making

eunuchs of the lads, as if it were not enough to deprive these poor creatures of their liberty, which man values most, and which belong to him and to God.[86]

To some extent the enforcement of anti-slavery laws took effect in the Cape colony in the 1830s, especially after the prescribed period of "apprenticeship" for freed slaves ended in 1838. BaSotho and BaTswana workers from the Cape colony began to reappear at their homes north of the Cape. In 1834 Andrew Smith met BaTswana workers within the colony who wanted to return home, having accumulated some livestock as compensation for their services; he also met people north of the Orange river who had recently returned from the colony with their "small earnings."[87] James Backhouse found in 1839 at Lishuani that "several of the people had been into the Colony to work; they had been careful of their wages, and had procured cattle, and returned with them to their own country."[88] He met BaRolong who had "hired themselves as servants to the Boers, obtaining, a cow for about eight months' labour."[89] Perhaps most poignant was the reunion of Backhouse's guide, a MoSotho named Boesak, with his parents, whom he had not seen since he was kidnapped as a boy.

> In the course of the day, the mother of Boesak arrived, having come on foot about thirty miles, to see her long-lost son, who was strikingly like his mother. She said he was torn from her arms, when a little boy, by the Griqua Bergenaars; and when she turned after them, they told her to run away, but she followed them weeping as long as she could. From that time, she had not heard of him, till the other day, and her heart had mourned over him as dead. Her husband was sickly and could not come to see his son....She also said, that the Bergenaars had took away another son, who, she believed, was among the Boors, and a daughter, of whom she had not heard. Boesak, however, had traced his sister to the neighborhood of Graaff Reinet. This also was joyful tidings to the bereaved mother....[90]

Backhouse encountered living evidence, too, that slavery and enslavement across the frontier was continuing. He discovered Bushmen who had fled to Moshoeshoe to escape forced servitude under the Bastaards, who had "beaten [them] with samboks like beasts"; he also found among the Kora at Bethany the descendants of BaTswana war captives still living with a status akin to that of slaves.[91]

In 1834 the Griqua legislative council at Philippolis publicly condemned the enslavement of San.

> The system of surreptitiously depriving the Bushmen of their children was next discussed and stigmatized as not only highly unjust in itself, but, in the opinion of the council, extremely unpolitic, inasmuch as it seldom failed to

incite the parents to revenge. Instances were adduced of such robberies, *commited not only by Griquas, but colonists* [emphasis added]; and, as it mattered little to the Bushmen to what nation the kidnappers belonged, it was considered extremely necessary to prevent it if possible from being practiced. As a consequence of the system, it was stated that a Griqua subject while travelling with his horse-wagon had been attacked and wounded by a party of Bushmen who, after plundering the waggon, shooting seven of the horses, and disabling the eighth, assigned as a reason for the attack that the Boers, Griquas, and Corannas, through possessing horses, were better enabled to carry off the children of the Bushmen, who were determined not to leave a horse alive.

Andrew Smith, who observed these proceedings, noted the problem of suppressing the slave trade:

> [W]e heard at a village we passed that a number of Bushmen had gone through it on their way to the colony to endeavour to regain some children stolen from them by a party of colonists. They entertained but few hopes of success....[T]he case was also mentioned of the sale of a Caffre lad, who had been bought for a trifling remuneration and carried into the colony. The remarks made during this discussion were in strong reprobation of the practice; yet it was evident that there was no prospect of this [Griqua] government being competent to check it.[92]

According to Smith, colonists living across the border had no intention of returning to the colony because they found land for farms beyond the colony's jurisdiction and therefore paid no taxes to the Cape. He called them "banditti" and identified them as the cause for the "constantly disturbed state of these districts," and even proposed arming Africans so they could defend themselves. [93]

Slavery and the Voortrekkers

After Cape slavery was abolished and thousands of Boers left the jurisdiction of the British by crossing the Cape border, enslavement remained a feature of the moving frontier. Many Voortrekkers who entered Transorangia, Natal, and the Transvaal took part in slave and cattle raids as a way of obtaining stock and labor to develop the land that they had also seized. Boers in Natal in the 1830s readily admitted that battles were waged against the AmaZulu for the explicit purpose of capturing slaves as well as cattle. According to one participant, many Boers thought of the attacks on the AmaZulu "as simply a hunting expedition."

More than one regarded it as the starting-point of his fortunes [in cattle]....and then was it not allowable to bring away three or four young Kafir boys or girls, taken by force from their families, and who by a qualified phrase were called apprentices, in order the better to ward off the idea of slavery? These were destined for household service....[W]hat would my wife say if I did not bring her some? It is so difficult to obtain servants in Natal.[94]

As these words make clear, the system of apprenticeship, which originated in the Cape as a legal form of bondage over indigenous captive laborers, served the same purpose in territories beyond the Cape's jurisdiction. In the interior, children held legally as apprentices were often bound over as "orphans" on the pretext that they had been abandoned by their parents and kin or that they were lone survivors of one disaster or another. Missionaries in contact with the Boers knew better and tried to expose the apprenticeship of orphans. Arbousset and Daumas encountered "a boer, displaying ostentatiously two young matebeles [AmaNdebele] whom he had just captured, and when I reproached him with what he had done, he replied that it was an act of humanity on his part, as the two little slaves were orphans." The missionaries reported, however, that among the AmaNdebele, "there is not, perhaps a single case known of a child being so entirely abandoned as not to have some relative, near or more remote, who would take him under his care."[95]

John Philip of the LMS was among those who accused the Boers of trading in captured children. In September 1841, Philip was told that although commandant-general Andries Pretorius in Natal had proclaimed severe penalties against the sale of children, captives were being sold for Rds 100 to 250 and "the Boers laughed at the proclamation as meant to gull the English and never intended to apply amongst the emigrants [Voortrekkers] themselves." [96] Philip concluded from hearsay evidence and his own observations that:

Not only has an active slave-trade been carried on among the Boers residing at Natal; but it is well known that an active trade in children has been carried on between them and the Boers spread over the Bahurutsi country from the Vaal River to the borders of the colony. Mr. [Rev. Samuel] Rolland at Beersheba, and even in the country of Moshesh, is not able to protect the Bushmen in his neighborhood.... Mr. Rolland is as much feared and respected by the [the Boers] as any missionary in his station can be; and yet they have taken Bushmen children from his kitchen....[97]

The degree to which these farmers attempted to counter charges of slavery contain suggestions that are self-incriminating. A common justification was one of caring for "orphans," without mentioning that often such children lacked parents because the Boers had killed them, as illustrated in

P.J. Zietsman's letter to the editor of the *Zuid Afrikaan* (Pietermaritzburg), in 1841:

> I heard that there is a report in the colony that we are dealing in slaves, to which I must give a most positive denial. Potgieter, when separated from us, I believe, committed such a crime; but since he has been under our rule, no slave-dealing exists at this or the other side of the [Drakensberg]. It once, indeed, happened fraudulently that a trader managed to obtain five Zulus, which he was going to take away with him; but the moment our landdrost got aware of the fact, he sent a patrol off and had the Zulus liberated. Like with the captured negroes at the Cape, so it is at this place with orphan Zulus, who, if unable to earn a livelihood, are indentured to certain persons, under a strict penalty against any bad treatment.[98]

Weeks later, Natal commandant H.S. Lombaard assured *Zuid Afrikaan* readers that apprenticeship laws were being enforced and slave trading strictly prohibited.

> The Zulu children who after the war fell into our hands as orphans, or who were brought to us by their parents, who had been robbed of all their cattle by dingaan, lest they should perish by starvation, are indentured here by the Landdrost—the boys until they shall attain the age of twenty-five, and the girls that of twenty-one years. And the landdrosts have been directed to watch with a vigilant eye that no fraud be practised in this respect. It is also strongly forbidden that any dealing in these apprentices shall take place, or that they be removed beyond our limits, under a penalty of Rds. 500.[99]

Such denials of slave dealing were taken at face value by some observers. LMS missionary J. Archbell believed that war orphans were legitimately apprenticed and then to "respectable men." Archbell was convinced that the Voortrekkers were opposed to slavery.[100]

Other observers make it clear, however, that "apprentices" were normally acquired by forceful capture and were liable to be sold. Rather than wages, they received mere upkeep in a system that rendered individual masters free to treat their "apprentices" at will and maintain them in a state of slavery. J.J. Freeman, sent by the LMS in 1848 to visit their south African mission stations, reported that knowledge of Boer slaving activities was widespread. At Kuruman, where he visited the Moffats, Freeman met a man who had walked ca. 200 miles from the east to tell Moffat about

> the difficult circumstances in which the people his district were being placed. He related, that some time since, a party of armed Boers came and demanded of the chief the *orphans* who might be there. The people affirmed that they had none who were friendless and destitute, since all orphans were taken care of by some of the friends and relatives of the deceased parents. After much

altercation, and the steady refusal of the chief to give up the orphans, *the Boers demanded the children of the people*. The mothers ran to hide their children; the Boers began to seize them and put them in their wagons; the men interfered; the Boers fired, and in the result most of the men were killed defending their families, and the wagons were loaded with the children and driven off as booty! Against such outrages there seems no relief. The natives cannot withstand the power and fire-arms of the Boers; and the latter are too far away, too numerous, and too scattered, to respect the remonstrances of the British Government, even supposing the latter in earnest in checking such unjust and cruel proceedings. But by such proceedings, many of the aboriginal tribes of South Africa, in all these extensive regions which have been taken forcible possession of by the Boers, are diminishing, being in the first instance reduced to slavery, and must ultimately perish, unless timely aid be afforded.[101]

Among those who was particularly interested in slave raiding, and attempted to use his offices to restrict it, was Joseph Orpen, landdrost of Winburg. Orpen believed that raiding for the purpose of capturing children was occurring in all areas into which Boers were expanding, and he tried to expose it. He reported the raid against Dingane, launched by Mpande with 400 Boers, which netted 400 children, and a raid in southern Natal in 1840, which "was got up with the intention and for the sole purpose of carrying off children." He had heard as well of a commando under Potgieter that plundered "a peaceful tribe" of their cattle and children.[102] Orpen regarded Boer slave raiding as the cause of violence across the entire frontier, because "it is the sight of children, and even grown men and women, carried off into slavery that rankles in the breast of the native."[103]

In his reminiscences, Orpen portrays at length the slave raiding activities of Boers who took children from Natal. While surveying farms in the Upper Valsch River ward in 1855, Orpen encountered two young children who had been reported as runaway servants by a Mrs. Odendaal. Orpen was known at the time for his opposition to slavery, so it is understandable that his driver reported to Orpen the following account, as told to him by the two children:

> he [Orpen's driver] said they had just been telling him that they had been taken by force from their parents and that their brother had been murdered and that the elder one, a little girl, apparently ten years old, said that they had run away from the master who had captured them, because her little brother, apparently about five years old, had been beaten.[104]

From field-cornet Englebrecht, Orpen learned that the children were probably Mrs. Odendaal's "two little servants." Orpen asked him "whether he knew how they had been obtained or where they came from and whether they were apprentices or not. He said he thought not and that probably they were some of a lot of children brought by the Odendaals and others from Zululand where they had been on a hunting expedition." He then questioned the children.

> They spoke Zulu and said they were Bushman folk, though they were darker than most Bushmen, and that they had gone at nightfall from their parents' hut to fetch water at a spring near it, when several Boers rushed at them from behind some bushes where they had been concealed, caught them and then ran to the hut, caught their sister there and took an elder brother prisoner and put a rope round his neck. They demanded of him to know where more Bushman children were to be had, and took him away and as they heard from the servants, he had led them in the night close to the kraal of 'ringheads' (Zulus or Amaswazi) upon which they [the Boers] had killed him for alleged treachery. A number of other children had been captured by the party and divided among them, and how because her little brother was beaten, they were going 'home.' That meant going several hundred miles through country, much of it, infested by lions.[105]

These children were then kidnapped again by the Odendaals and rescued by Orpen, who held an inquiry into the "hunting expedition," leading to the freeing of other children. After further investigation, Orpen found that "several persons, mentioned by name and resident under the jurisdiction of the three countries in question [OFS, Natal, and Utrecht] had been implicated more or less in the system of kidnapping and traffic in native children...."[106]

Orpen further widened the investigation. He enlisted the aid of his brother, Arthur Orpen, and the Natal secretary for native affairs, Theophilus Shepstone, and gained support from J.N. Boshoff, newly elected OFS president. Boshoff informed Orpen that such instances were anything but new:

> [H]e had had experiences of just such difficulties in the old times in Natal, where he had been landdrost and secretary to the Volksraad. He said that when [Andries] Pretorius had started on that expedition which captured a number of children from Ncapayi near the Umsimbuvu, it had been given out that they were going to deal with some Bushmen thieves, but that he heard they were really going to capture children and he had written to warn Pretorius that the result would be that the British Government would take their independence from them, which, in fact happened. But he said his letter was ineffectual, and they did capture children. I said 'Yes,' and that the wife of my native constable was one of them [captured children].[107]

Orpen was also accompanied on his formal investigation by Jantje Potgieter, his "Zulu constable...who had himself been captured as a child in Zululand and 'indentured'."[108] Along with other, Boer, commission members they were joined by "two of Shepstone's best indunas, men of importance, whom he had employed in embassies to Panda [Mpande], the great chief of the Zulus."

The source of trouble appeared to be Utrecht. [109] In this tiny republic in northern Natal, as elsewhere, the taking of children was portrayed as rescuing orphans. Utrecht residents overlooked that even receiving children from middlemen fueled the system.

> Cornelius van Rooyen [Utrecht field-cornet] then told us that the Amaswazi in their constant 'eating up' of tribes and individuals, captured native 'orphans,' to obtain whom by barter, he considered a Christian and charitable act, also that some friends of his name Meyer, had just arrived at his farm from Swaziland with seven children and some strange tribe. These he had bought from the chief Umswazi for an ox. He invited us to come and see them. A man named Rensburg told us he also had two which had bartered from Umswazi and that we should probably meet on our journey two kaffirs, whom he had sent to the same quarter to barter for another. It turned out, too, that Commandant Klopper himself, had three such children, obtained in the same way.[110]

Through the AmaZulu indunas, Orpen elicited statements from the AmaSwati subject chief, Nyama-inja (Nyamantja); he said that "Zulus" took children in wars and alleged that whites did, too.

> He said he had heard that white people had carried off the children violently, threatening to shoot the parents if they tried to prevent them. In answer to some further questions and some cross questions (in more senses than one) from other members [of the commission], it was elicited that the so-called Bushmen were to some extent Zulu half breeds, that they cultivate a little and were timid, particularly afraid of white men and ran away and hid their children if they saw these approaching, that white men afterwards came and just took the children by force and made them barter them under compulsion. They had done this so often that there were hardly any children left. He said that some of his own people also captured Bushmen children and bartered them to the whites and concealed the fact of their having done so from him.[111]

At this point the Boer commission members (who themselves owned captured children) refused to continue the investigation with the Orpen brothers, arguing that "Nyama-Inja, though he was the chief to whom the children belonged, did not seem to interest himself in the matter" and that "they saw no possibility of discovering the parents of the children since they were a wandering people."[112] The Orpens persisted alone and convinced Nyamantja to continue helping them although the chief was "in great dread" of field-cornet van Rooyen. With his aid, Orpen met the "Bushmen" whose children had been stolen and recorded their stories. After returning to the OFS, Orpen learned that Nyamantja suffered reprisals from the Boers and fled into Lesotho.

In the Orange Free State itself, according Orpen, slave raiding was carried on until the Boshoff's administration (1855–60) with the knowledge and approval of the republican government. Some Volksraad members themselves purchased slaves. A man on the OFS anti-slavery commission purchased two slaves and took them home, and one Volksraad member "received a present of a few of these little 'trophies' [captured children] from Mr. M.W. Pretorius, now President of the TransVaal Republic."[113] In Orpen's words, "the rise, progress, and establishment of slavery as a domestic institution in South Africa will still be regarded as a myth by some. It is nevertheless true....The Free State Government is too weak to suppress it, though it makes a show of doing so, and, therefore, connives at it."[114]

The British presence in the Orange Free State, Orpen's notwithstanding, also contributed to slave raiding, because the Boers commonly refused to participate in British-led commandos without children as booty.[115] In 1851 a commando led by Major Henry Warden, the Cape government's representative in Bloemfontein, attacked the AmaThembu and returned with sixty children. They were retained by the Boers on the grounds that they had no parents, in spite of the fact that some of the children's parents followed the commando and tried to claim back their children. The children were then sold.

> The mother [of two captured AmaThembu children] afterwards came to Voussie, and begged for the children, and was refused them. She then begged to be allowed to serve along with them, and was permitted to do so. She soon afterwards ran away with them. After a time, Mr. Voussie met one of them in the possession of a Boer in the Albert district, and asked where he got it [her]. He said he had bought it [her] from Baillie. Voussie produced his title-deed [to the child], and recovered possession, and upon asking the child "Sara," how she came there, she stated that she had been recaptured, and that her sister had been sold to a Boer in Aliwal.[116]

Upon investigation Orpen learned that all sixty children were still in slavery, having been sold to various farmers in the OFS and the Cape for prices ranging from a horse to several cows; one magistrate stated that it was legitimate to acquire these children by giving "food money" if they had no father. The opportunities for unfettered enslavement created by such rulings on apprenticeship "regulations" are obvious. Five years after Warden's commando captured and sold these children, the governor at Cape Town, Sir George Grey, was still trying to determine what became of each of them. He learned, too, that Warden had ordered a detachment of the Cape Corps to capture 107 "Bushmen," who were then distributed to farmers.[117] The slave trade, which emanated from the Cape, was beyond the British government's will to stamp out in the interior.

Notes

I would like to thank Leonard Thompson and Fred Morton for their comments and suggestions.

1. Campbell (1822), 2: 330-1; Burchell (1822), 2: 81. Burchell visited the farm of the "greatest sheep-grazier in the colony" and was told he had 30,000 sheep, as well as cattle. Ibid, 123.

2. Barrow (1801), 2: 402. The economic significance of female labor in the nineteenth century and, for that matter even since, has gone unrecognized by South African scholars.

3. Lichtenstein (1928), 1: 154.

4. Burchell (1822), 2: 81.

5. Barrow (1801), 1: 163.

6. Campbell (1822), 2: 325.

7. Newton-King (1980), 178-9.

8. In spite of their common origins, Khoikhoi and San are recognized in this chapter as distinct historically on a social and economic basis. References to Khoikhoi and San as distinct categories of people were commonly made by Europeans in the setting of the early nineteenth century, although it is clear that Cape policy at the time was predicated on often mistaken assumptions of identifiable distinctions between the two. Regarding evidence of common origins of Khoikhoi and San, see Elphick (1985), xxi-xxii, 3-42 and Elphick and Malherbe (1989). Differences among various Khoikhoi, San, and groups of mixed descent are nevertheless highly ambiguous, because on one hand observers used inconsistent or vague references and, on the other, individuals referred to often straddled what observers perceived as distinctions. For instance, intermixing and intermarriage of Khoikhoi and San with IsiXhosa, SeTswana, and SeSotho-speaking persons was common. Europeans commonly referred to San as *Bosjesmans* or "Bushmen" hunter-gatherers and to Khoikhoi as cattle keeping "Hottentots." Yet Khoikhoi, BaTswana, and BaSotho who lost their cattle resorted to hunting and gathering, and San were known to acquire livestock. Europeans tried, too, to distinguish "Bushmen" as much shorter than "Hottentots," but exceptions were noted among the former who kept cattle, indicating that diet rather than genetics underlay any distinction based on such a crude measure as physical appearance. Linguistic analysis demonstrates both common origins and differentiation, and linguistic differences were described by early travelers who attempted often unsuccessfully to distinguish between Khoikhoi and San. Yet, Khoisan people did belong to groups that identified themselves politically, socially, and/or linguistically, difficult as it may now be to identify them using the surviving record. The Kora (na) may be distinguished from other Khoikhoi groups, because they spoke a distinct Khoikhoi dialect and regularly intermarried with their BaTswana neighbors. Some Bastaards retained their designation as a way of distinguishing themselves from the Griqua, even though both groups in language and culture resembled the frontier Boers. Though such derisory

terms of identity as "Bastard" originated among outsiders, they became common usage among literate south Africans and are retained in quotations of original sources. The reader should understand that such terms are not accepted here at face value and should be free to judge the intentions and assumptions contained in the primary sources.

9. Opperman, 19 Apr. 1774 , in Moodie (1842), 3: 28-9.

10. Ibid, 3: 40-50.

11. Ibid, 3: 84-5, 10-4-5.

12. Barrow (1801), 1: 235-6, 241. Enslavement of San must have been occurring long before Barrow toured in 1797–98, because he was told that some Sneeuwbergers were fluent in the "Bosjesman" language (as distinct from Khoikhoi) as a result of being raised by Bosjesman nurses. Ibid, 1: 290.

13. "Journal of a Tour to the North-Eastern Boundary, the Orange River, and the Storm Mountains...in 1809," ibid, 5: 7-8.

14 . "...Report on the Bosjesmen [omitted in the Parl. Papers]," ibid, 5: 35. Collins recommended that colonists be permitted to pursue and kill "Bushmen robbers" as far as the colony's border (37).

15. Bradlow and Bradlow (1979), 60.

16. Lye (1975), 284.

17. Bradlow and Bradlow (1979), 25.

18. Ibid, 183. The Bastaards had suffered from such attacks since the 1770s. Legassick (1989), 374. Wagmeesters, later titled field-cornets, were frontier officials responsible for law enforcement in frontier areas.

19. Giliomee (1981), 85. See also du Toit and Giliomee (1983), 37. Boers had sought legal sanction for legally binding Khoisan apprentices as early as 1721, but a forced labor system was only informally countenanced until the 1775 regulation.

20. Especially children. In 1803, as part of the peace agreement following the third Frontier War, the AmaXhosa signatories agreed with the British government to return slaves who had escaped from the colony as soon as "all Caffre children which have fallen into the hands of the colonists shall be given up." Lichtenstein (1928), 1: 385. AmaXhosa residing within the colony were threatened with the loss of liberty if they did not enter the service of farmers. Ibid, 1: 272, 464; 2: 220. For BaTswana children held as apprentices in the Cape, Campbell (1815), 165, 209.

21. Barrow (1801), 1: 146-7.

22. Ibid, 1: 145, 291.

23. Ibid, 1: 404-7.

24. Ibid.

25. See ch. 4.

26. Barrow (1801), 1: 148, in an oblique manner, revealed the particular vulnerability of Khoikhoi women to rape: "The Hottentot girls in the service of the colonists are in situations too dependent to dare to reject the proffered embraces of the young peasantry [Boers]."

27. For a fuller discussion of Khoisan in the colony, see Elphick and Malherbe (1989). The myth of apprenticeship was earlier discussed by Macmillan (1927), 166-8.

28. Khoikhoi fathers, apparently, were the more likely to abandon their children in bondage. Barrow encountered, for example, several Khoikhoi men who "had preserved a sort of independence, and supported themselves, partly by the chace

[hunting], and partly from the labors of their children who were in servitude." Barrow (1801), 1; 149.

29. Burchell (1822), 2; 114. The fate of the sister was not recorded. Juli, a "Hottentot of mixed race," accompanied Burchell into the interior. Rather than leave behind his wife and newborn child at Graaff-Reinet, he took them along until they could be left in safety with the Griqua of Klaarwater (129).

30. Newton-King (1980), 177.

31. Burchell (1822), 2; 68-9. The woman who had been beaten was "a young girl of harmless engaging appearance as all girls of her nation [she was] of very small and delicate frame. "The diminutive stature of many of the enslaved increased their vulnerability. Barrow found that the Sneeuwberg commandant brought home a "Bosjesman" man with two wives and a child. "The man was only four feet five inches high, and his wives were still of a shorter stature, one being four feet two, the other four feet three inches." Barrow (1801), 1; 241.

32. Campbell (1822), 1: 21 & 28.

33. Legassick (1969), 68, 252.

34. Ibid, 132-48; See also Lye (1975), 148. Bradlow and Bradlow (1979), 71. Pienaar was later killed by a son of the well-known Khoikhoi raider, Klaas Afrikaner. Afrikaner's sons also worked for Pienaar, and one killed Pienaar and his brother for seducing their wives while they were away, after which the entire Afrikaner family fled north. Two white brothers, Jacob and Carel Kruger, escaped from prison on Robben island and made their living as raiders across the frontier in the early years of the nineteenth century. Some of the most predatory leaders were white renegades who, like the Krugers, moved into the interior and built their own followings with the promise of booty from raids.

35. Borcherds (1861), 82.

36. Lye (1975), 178.

37. Campbell (1822), 2: 172.

38. Ibid, 2: 186.

39. Borcherds (1861), 93.

40. Ibid, 95.

41. Barrow (1801), 2: 403.

42. Spohr (1973), 75.

43. Lye (1975), 286. For de Buys, Wagner (1974).

44. Spohr (1973), 79.

45. Bradlow and Bradlow (1979), 121.

46. Lichtenstein (1928), 2: 335-6, 364.

47. Ibid, 371, 384. In 1815 John Campbell met a Griqua captain whose cattle and sheep were tended by "faithful herdsmen," Bushmen, who received for their labor the use of the milk. In the town of Klaarwater [Griquatown], Campbell heard five languages spoken: Dutch, Kora, SeTswana, "Hottentot," and "Bushman." Campbell (1822), 162, 243. Campbell's is a good example of travelers who distinguished related Kora, Khoikhoi, and San languages. According to Breutz (1987), 149, BaTlhaping-Griqua [Khoikhoi?] relations date to the first half of the eighteenth century. Molehabangwe's mother, and great wife of Mashwe, was of Khoikhoi/Griqua origin. Two to three generations of such close contact appear to account for the multilingualism observed in 1806.

48. Eldredge (1993), 18-24, 28-34.

49. Lichtenstein (1928), 2: 397.

50. Tlou (1977).

51. Burchell (1822), 2: 334.

52. Ibid, 2: 377-8.

53. Lister (1949), 136.

54. Kirby (1939-40), 1: 388. Many San settled voluntarily around Griquatown and became Griqua themselves. Waterboer was himself of San descent.

55. Macgregor (1905), 66, and D.F. Ellenberger (1912), 214.

56. Lye (1975), 39. Most early missionaries failed to discern the severity of choice afflicting those seeking security and turned a blind eye to the mistreatment they suffered at the hands of the Griqua. John Moffat of LMS station at Kuruman approved of the Griqua forcing San to move to Griquatown, because he saw it is an improvement over the previous Griqua policy of extermination. Legassick (1969), 224.

57. Eldredge (1992).

58. Legassick (1969), 327, 342, , 353-4.

59. Cobbing (1988). For a lengthy refutation of Cobbing's accusations against Melvill and the missionaries, see Eldredge (1992).

60. By far the most thorough of Melvill's descriptions of slave raiding is found in his lengthy report to the colonial secretary. See Melvill to Plasket, 17 Dec. 1824, parts of which were published in Philip (1828), 79-84. A nearly verbatim version appears as "Extract from a Report by Mr. Melville[sic]...," Great Britain, Parliamentary Papers (1835), 212-19. [see full citation in bibliography]

61. Ibid, 213.

62. Ibid, 216.

63. Ibid, 217. The account was given by an unidentified, lesser BaSotho chief, not Moshoeshoe. Other sources suggest he was Ketlani.

64. Ibid.

65. Ibid.

66. Prior to the arrival of French missionaries in Lesotho in 1833, Melvill's accounts provide the earliest written references to the BaSotho, who were among those people identified vaguely in the Colony as "Mantatees." The original account of Melvill and Kolbe's journey is found in "Extracts of the Journal of Mssrs. Melvill and Kolbe, addressed to the Rev. Richard Miles..," 25 Nov. 1828, CWMA. An edited version, dated 18 Nov. 1828, appears in Melvill (1829).

67. Melvill (1829), 126.

68. Ibid, 125.

69. Melvill provides no evidence that Nguni-speaking immigrants were responsible for widespread human suffering among the BaSotho groups or for the loss of all their cattle. His general references to the Nguni-speakers are dispassionate, apparently reflecting the equanimity with which his BaSotho informants described the "Matabealees." Melvill did not implicate Mzilikazi's AmaNdebele in any way with the ongoing disruptions in the area. He was very casual when he mentioned their recent departure, and made no reference whatsoever to any troubles caused by them, outside of the earlier remark that they had once raided a portion of cattle from a BaFokeng group. Significantly, the BaSotho with whom Melvill talked in 1828 feared the Bergenaar Griqua, not the "Matabele":

On the opposite side of the river, we saw a deserted Matabalee village, and exceedingly high mountains to the eastward. The Matabalees are a people exactly (as we were informed) resembling in their dress and language, the Caffres who reside on the eastern borders of the colony. They are a different tribe from the Bashutoos, who are the Bechauana nation. The country through which we were now riding, had been lately left by the Matabalees, who had sought pasturage for their cattle along the banks of the Caledon.
Ibid, 93.

70. Ibid. The derogatory designation "Caffres," while ambiguous, was used in this period to indicate isiXhosa-speaking people east of the Colony.

71. "Extracts of the Journal of Mssrs. Melvill and Kolbe, addressed to the Rev. Richard Miles..," 25 Nov. 1828, CWMA.

72. Thompson (1827), 2: 68-9.

73. Moffat (1842), 431. Melvill and Moffat 's credibility has been questioned by scholars both accepting and rejecting the evidence about slave raiding across the northeastern frontier. Cobbing has accused them of planning and executing slave raids for their own profit, and of covering up an illicit slave trade in which they played key roles. Melvill and Moffat's evidence notwithstanding, the accounts of persons other than these missionaries attest to frontier slave raiding during the 1820s and 1830s.

74. Hutton (1887), 1: 214, 229, 376.

75. "Investigatus," *GJ*, 30 Jan., 6 Feb. 1834.

76. Arbousset and Daumas (1852), 26. For Witvoet, see also Legassick (1969), 357.

77. Arbousset and Daumas (1852), 26, 210-1. See also Kirby (1939-40), 1: 357.

78. Arbousset and Daumas (1852), 228.

79. Ibid, 194.

80. As reported by "Investigatus," *GJ*, 6 Feb. 1834.

81. Quotation from Legassick (1969), 356. Legassick notes that those Kora communities who failed to join forces with the raiders were themselves raided and had to seek alliances with the BaTlhaping and others for protection. Ibid, 358-9.

82. Kirby (1939), 1: 149.

83. Ibid, 404. See also Bradlow and Bradlow (1979), 110 and editor's note. Jan Bloem, Jr. was said to have 20,000 people living under him on the Vaal river in about 1825. "Frederick Opperman: Cape Slave," *Christian Express*, Jul/Aug. 1891, reprinted in Wilson and Perrot (1973).

84. Lye (1975), 148.

85. Arbousset and Daumas (1852), 228. Andrew Smith heard when attending the Griqua legislative council in 1834 at Philippolis that "colonists," in addition to Griqua groups, were conducting slave raids against the San. Lye (1975), 140. See also Kirby (1939-40), 1: 179, 182, 195.

86. Arbousset and Daumas (1852), 252.

87. Lye (1975), 20, 30.

88. Backhouse (1844), 389.

89. Ibid, 414.

90. Ibid, 376-7.

91. Ibid, 424.

92. Lye (1975), 140. See also Kirby (1939), 1: 179, 182, 195

93. Lye (1979), 47.

94. Adolphe D'Elegorgue, quoted in Wilson and Thompson (1969), 367 n. 4.

95. Arbousset and Daumas (1852), 138.

96. Macmillan (1923), 222.

97. Quoted in ibid.

98. 5 Jan. 1841, reprinted in Bird (1888), 623-4.

99. 10 Feb. 1841, reprinted in ibid, 632. Lombaard admitted that some slave trading may have occurred "on our northern boundaries," but argued that in light of "the extent of these countries, the habitations, and the distance of the magistracies," along with other difficulties, that "offences of this sort might have taken place, with which we were unacquainted, and which we could not prevent."

100. Archbell to editor, *GJ*, Sep. 1841, reprinted in ibid., 655.

101. Freeman (1851), 260-1.

102. Orpen (1979), 30-1. For slave raiding in the Transvaal, see chs. 6, 7, & 8 in this volume.

103. Ibid, 148.

104. Orpen (1964), 303.

105. Ibid, 303-4.

106. Ibid, 311.

107. Ibid, 313.

108. Ibid, 314.

109. Ibid.

A republic [which] was formed of farmers from the other republics and the northern part of Natal, who had obtained a land concession from Panda in consideration of their aid in subjecting a branch of the Swazi tribe under...chiefs who were living on and northward of the sources of the Pongola and Umkonto Rivers. The Bushmen were said to be living among the people of those chiefs.

110. Ibid, 316.

111. Ibid, 319.

112. Ibid, 320.

113. Orpen (1979), 151.

114. Ibid, 15.

115. Ibid, 138.

116. Ibid, 88.

117. Theal (1964), 2: 187-9. Warden did resist pressure from the farmers to separate children from the parents on the pretense of their being "orphans."

6

Delagoa Bay and the Hinterland in the Early Nineteenth Century: Politics, Trade, Slaves, and Slave Raiding

Elizabeth A. Eldredge

During the eighteenth and early nineteenth centuries commercial activities at Delagoa bay (Maputo bay) stimulated the economy of the region and prompted economic and political competition at the bay and in its hinterland. Control over trade and trade routes to the interior allowed for ambitious leaders to begin to consolidate wealth and power, and strong chiefdoms began to subdue weaker competitors in a process of political consolidation that was evident by the late eighteenth century. Competition among chiefdoms gave way to overt conflicts during periods of scarcity when production and trade were disrupted. Droughts and disruptions in the trade with Europeans during the Napoleonic wars catalyzed ongoing processes of struggle and consolidation among African societies just as these were confronted with renewed European imperial expansionism in the early decades of the nineteenth century.

The purpose of this chapter is to trace the rise of slave raiding in Delagoa bay and its hinterland, and to analyze the links between African politics, Delagoa bay commerce, especially the export slave trade, and the rise of slave raiding after the mid-1820s. In the late eighteenth and early nineteenth centuries the balance of power shifted frequently, both among Delagoa bay chiefdoms and between the Africans and the Portuguese, according to the economic circumstances and military alliances that prevailed at any given time. Tracing this political history, this chapter demonstrates that shifting political and economic factors in Africa and Europe caused the expansion of the slave trade at the bay in the mid-1820s and the subsequent rise of slave raiding, first in the immediate vicinity and later in the north and west. The slave trade was not new at Delagoa bay, but the export of relatively small numbers of human captives had remained secondary in importance to ivory exports throughout the eighteenth century. This earlier trade in slaves caused occasional losses from bay chiefdoms, but it was never so extensive as to undermine the viability of communities and chiefdoms in the region. Conflicts remained small and localized, and they generated only sporadic and limited supplies of slaves for export. The limited availability of slaves in turn suggests the absence of systematic slave raiding in the hinterland in this period.

Research conducted by various scholars on trade in the Delagoa bay region has remained largely unpublished, which has hindered the analysis of political change and the rise of the slave trade at the bay.[1] Julian Cobbing's hypothesis that the volume of slave exports from Delagoa bay expanded dramatically between 1800 and 1815, prompting the defensive emergence of the AmaZulu state, is shown to be false by the evidence collected here and in earlier unpublished studies, which demonstrates that the slave trade did not expand until after 1823.[2] The appearance of Cobbing's article, which rested on the mistaken assumption that relevant research had yet to be undertaken, emphasizes the need to fill some of the void in the historiography of Delagoa Bay. In subsequent work Cobbing argued further that the AmaZulu under Shaka were actively involved in slaving activities linked to Delagoa bay, but his case again rested on an inadequate consideration of the evidence, which is presented here.[3]

In 1823, at the same time that the rising demand for slaves from southeastern Africa for the Brazilian and American markets stimulated an interest in exploiting all potential supplies, economic and political circumstances in the region of Delagoa bay changed, bringing new supplies of human captives onto the market. Thus, changes in both demand and supply caused a dramatic increase in the volume of slaves exported out of Delagoa bay after 1823. Within two or three years, slave exports jumped from what was estimated to be an average of a dozen slaves per year, to between one and four thousand per annum.

In the 1820s slave raiding was confined to the vicinity of Delagoa bay. Entire communities were destroyed, falling victim to both famine and enslavement. In the 1830s, however, slave raiding reached further into the Delagoa bay hinterland, primarily affecting African societies north of the bay. To the south, the AmaZulu state under Shaka pursued and maintained legitimate trade with European traders operating out of Delagoa bay and Port Natal. Shaka's power was based on his personal control over wealth in cattle, which were valued within his own society, and in ivory, which was of primary value for export. Shaka's interest lay in consolidating his control over people through a patronage system, which involved the careful allocation of cattle won as booty in battles, and through a tributary system in which, among other things, all ivory belonged to the king. Shaka's primary goal of accumulating a large population under his control was antithetical to enslavement and slave trading, which were never in evidence in the AmaZulu state during his reign.

The expanding white frontier altered trade links between Delagoa bay and the highveld. Tenuous trade contacts which extended as far as the Kalahari desert had existed before the nineteenth century. In the 1820s, highveld peoples who greatly feared the European, Griqua, and Kora renegade slave raiders in the area displayed no similar fear of slave raiding from the east, and they retained their tenuous trade links with Delagoa bay traders. In the 1830s, however, slave raiders supplying the Delagoa bay slave trade began to operate in the northern and eastern Transvaal at the same time that the expanding Boer frontier brought raids and turmoil to the region. For the next few decades, Africans across a wide area, from Natal to the Transvaal, were subject to enslavement and sale both at Delagoa bay and in the newly established Boer societies of the Orange Free State and Transvaal, as the slaving frontiers in Natal and the Transvaal converged.

Chiefdoms and Politics at Delagoa Bay, ca. 1550–1824

Throughout the eighteenth century peoples around Delagoa bay were organized in a number of chiefdoms, from the Mpfumo, Magaia, Mambe, and Matake and Madolo (Matoll) on the northern side of the bay to the Tembe, and eventually, Mabudu (Maputo) on the southern side.[4] The peoples of these chiefdoms have been referred to variously as Ronga, Thonga, and Tsonga, designating peoples in the "east," but these labels remain ambiguous because no historical origins, boundaries, or linguistic or cultural attributes clearly define the peoples around Delagoa bay.[5] More appropriate designations refer to chiefdoms, some of which are associated with specific origins or cultural attributes in oral traditions.

The Tembe dominated the area south of the bay during the late eighteenth and early nineteenth centuries. They are reputed in the traditions to be linked to a "Makalanga chief" (i.e., of western Shona origin), who had long before migrated into the area.[6] Although the tracing of historical and cultural origins is inconclusive, a chiefdom referred to by the Portuguese as Tembe was present at Delagoa bay by the 1550s.[7] The Tembe rose to prominence with the demise of an earlier power, the Nyaka, sometime in the mid-seventeenth century, and traded ivory with Europeans in the 1720s.[8] By mid-century the domains of the Tembe had become so extensive that the chief divided them among his three sons, giving the area southeast of the Maputo river to his son Mabudu (Maputo). Following the death of the Tembe chief in the late 1750s or early 1760s, Mabudu broke with his elder brother, who kept the portion of Tembe next to the Bay. In the meantime, Mabudu subdued the local people, including groups of Khumale, Gumede, and Ngubane; some of these left the area and others recognized Mabudu's authority. By the 1790s the Tembe and Madolo were competing for trade with whalers at the bay. The Tembe had regained power relative to the Mabudu chiefdom, which after Mabudu's death in the 1790s had fallen to his grandson Makhasane. Nevertheless Makhasane turned the chiefdom's reputation for military strength to his advantage. *Amabutho* (military regiments) were in use by the time Makhasane came to power, and Dingiswayo of the AmaMthethwa sought out an alliance with him.[9]

FIGURE 6.1 Delagoa Bay and the Mozambique Channel.

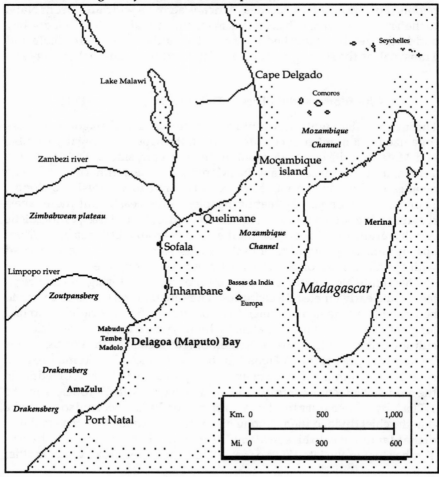

Political consolidation around Delagoa bay can be explained in terms of the environmentally strategic locations of chiefdoms, and the productive strategies of people in the area. Hedges concludes that "the Tsonga were not such passive victims of the environment, but controlled it systematically."[10] However, some environmental constraints could not be overcome, such as periodic droughts which upset the demographic balance. Similarly, African traders could not control variations in European trade patterns and levels of demand and supply. Hedges links periods of centralization with periods of stress and argues that "if, however, the upsetting and reestablishing of the equilibrium [between human needs and resources] was periodic, as the ecological evidence suggests, rather than once-for-all in 1805, a more continuous and less revolutionary accretion of chiefs' powers must be supposed."[11] The consolidation of both Tembe and Mabudu power indeed occurred during the stressful decade of the 1790s. The Delagoa bay ivory trade had begun to decline by 1789, as the British East India Company honored the Portuguese monopoly. French corsairs began raiding the coast for booty in the 1793, raising the risks for traders, and the French expelled the Portuguese in 1796. The ivory trade never recovered even after the Portuguese returned in 1799, because Indian merchants found readier and closer supplies on the Swahili coast further north and did not revive the Delagoa bay link. In the meantime, the turmoil in the Indian ocean caused by the Napoleonic wars deterred whalers from coming to the bay.[12] There were also several years of drought in the 1790s, which disrupted food production just as trade-dependent chiefdoms had become more reliant on selling cattle and other foodstuffs.[13]

Hedges, therefore, associates political centralization in the 1790s with intensified competition resulting from declining trade in ivory, as "a scarcity of valued imported goods would appear to be a more pressing motive for conflict than a superfluity."[14] He attributes the emergence of the Mabudu to "changes in productive forces in the final decade of the eighteenth century resulting from the sharp decline in the ivory trade and its replacement by trade in cattle [to foreign whalers at the bay]."[15] The internal political economy of chiefdoms was tied to regional production and trade:

> While preceding [political] changes had been associated with the disposal mainly of a commodity of low local value [ivory], accompanied by small numbers of cattle, such [political] centralisation had now to be maintained (reproduced) by the export mainly of a commodity with a very high local value, the basis of internal exchange and social investment; cattle stocks were also the most durable form of food storage available. The result of the demise of the ivory trade was a strong incentive to dispose of a further part of the cattle surplus and to organise its replacement from outside the chiefdom by use of the *amabutho....*[16]

According to Hedges, competition for cattle to meet demands for consumption and trade was intensified by the drought of 1801–1802, which spurred the further organization of societies around *amabutho*. Regiments were organized for raiding in order to ensure a steady influx of wealth, through the accumulation and exchange of booty acquired from plunder.[17]

The chiefdoms of the Delagoa bay area, notably the Tembe and Mabudu, thus emerged before the AmaMthethwa chiefdom under Dingiswayo began expanding in the territory south of the bay. The AmaMthethwa and Mabudu forged a mutually beneficial alliance, as the AmaMthethwa supplied the Mabudu with ivory and cattle and the Mabudu controlled access to the bay for trade from the south. The Mabudu went as far as to support the AmaMthethwa with musket-bearing soldiers in a battle against the AmaQwabe, and as a result Dingiswayo continued to send all of the ivory hunted by the AmaMthethwa, which he monopolized as king, to the Mabudu.[18] After Dingiswayo's death the Mabudu chief, Makhasane, opened commercial relations with Zwide, *inkosi* of the AmaNdwandwe, but eventually (about 1821) the forces of either Zwangendaba or Zwide defeated the Mabudu and imposed AmaNdwandwe dominance. Subsequently, these AmaNdwandwe were pushed out by Portuguese and AmaZulu pressure, and by mid-1824 the Mabudu had fallen under the sway of the AmaZulu state. Their virtual submission to the AmaZulu appears to explain why the Mabudu were spared the AmaZulu depredations against other people of the bay, including the neighboring Tembe, in the early 1820s.[19]

Three migrant groups led by AmaMthethwa and AmaNdwandwe chiefs visited Delagoa bay between 1821 and 1824. The activities of these groups are not always distinguishable because they were referred to indiscriminately as "vatuas" or "vatwahs" by the Portuguese, but not all of their activities were disruptive. One of the most disruptive invasions of the bay came in June and July 1821, involving a reported 5,000 troops.[20] The Tembe responded to the invasion by abandoning their lands temporarily to the invaders, and then regrouping and returning. They initially won their counterattack but eventually suffered defeat, lost many people, and saw their crops and cattle raided. Tembe resistance may have provoked the invaders, who attacked only those people who defended their property.[21] Nevertheless, no captives for sale as slaves were reported to have been taken, and these raiders were clearly seeking cattle and food. The raids coincided with a period of severe drought and food scarcity in the region that had already intensified the struggle for food. The ensuing battles further disrupted food production, exacerbated food shortages, and ultimately brought famine.

Muhadane, the Tembe chief, opened negotiations with the Portuguese in order to forestall the continued threat posed by the invaders. The Portuguese agreed to pay a ransom to the so-called "Vatwahs," who moved north and invaded the Madolo of Machechane and the Moamba of Collele. These groups retreated to safety and, driven by dire circumstances, allied with the Portuguese. The invaders threatened the fort twice but refrained from attacking after they were convinced through negotiations that the Portuguese could not pay the cattle, beads, and copper which they were demanding. In the meantime the Portuguese governor, Caetano Matoso, quickly came to terms with the Madolo and Moamba, offering protection in return for one tusk from every elephant killed in their lands. The Portuguese somehow convinced the invaders to withdraw; later the British claimed that it was by agreeing to buy captive slaves from the "Vatwahs." This seems an unlikely demand for the invaders to make of willing Portuguese buyers from whom other concessions might have been extracted, and the claim was never substantiated.[22]

A period of relative calm followed until the Tembe chief, Muhadane, died in 1822 and a succession dispute followed. His designated heir, Mayethe, was challenged by a cousin, eventually resulting in the breaking away of a small chiefdom, Panyelly, in 1823. The Panyelly chiefdom was located on the banks of the Tembe river, where Soshangane's AmaNdwandwe had established themselves the previous year, suggesting that an alliance between Panyelly and Soshangane had enabled the former to secede from the Tembe.[23] This year was also marked by a severe drought and the arrival of famine in the Delagoa bay area.[24] Even the Portuguese ran short of food and supplies. In the wake of invasion, rebellion, drought, and hunger the Tembe sought to negotiate with the Portuguese, but they were forcibly rebuffed by the new governor, Miguel Lupe de Cardinas.[25] The Tembe were thus driven to deal with the British. Unwilling to tolerate a British presence, the Portuguese renewed their efforts to exert their dominance, introducing conflict and strife, which ultimately opened up the floodgates of the export slave trade.

The Export Slave Trade at Delagoa Bay

Traders hailing from various European nations sporadically operated at Delagoa bay during the eighteenth century, and their exports included relatively small numbers of slaves. The east coast trade was directed towards India and the Indian ocean islands, including Madagascar, Mauritius, and the Mascarenes, and was tied primarily to the trade winds which blew only as far south as the northern coast of modern Mozambique, in the vicinity of Moçambique island. The Dutch operated a trade factory at the bay between 1721 and 1730, but high mortality from disease rendered it unsuccessful; over the course of a decade Dutch traders exported a total of 288 slaves, who comprised only a small portion of the value of their exports. Slaves thus were included in the sporadic export trade from Delagoa bay in the eighteenth century, but their numbers remained low, largely because slaves were only occasionally available following local conflicts. Early reports indicate that the peoples living around the bay did not like to enslave their neighbors; when they did raid for slaves, they elected to victimize the Tshopi further north. By 1729 they had already become reluctant to attack the Tshopi, who had become better at defending themselves.[26]

British, French, and Portuguese traders vied for control over Delagoa bay during the second half of the eighteenth century. British traders were drawn to the bay in the 1750s and 1760s to obtain ivory for trade to India, and an Englishman serving under the Austrian flag controlled the bay trade from 1777 to 1781. In the 1780s the French and Portuguese fought for control of the growing ivory trade from the bay. The Portuguese won tenuous control and imposed a monopoly on trade from the bay. They were expelled by the French in 1796, but returned in 1799. During the early years of the Napoleonic wars the British ended all French shipping around the coasts of southern Africa and in the Indian ocean, and the trade in slaves to the French islands declined temporarily at the turn of the nineteenth century.[27]

The Portuguese were less successful at trade than had been their English and Austrian predecessors at the bay. They brought inferior goods, refused to pay the prices demanded by their African trading partners, and relied on middlemen because they did not use boats to go up rivers and deal directly with producers.[28] Unlike their predecessors, the Portuguese were unwilling to stay during the best trading months, May to October, because the monsoons began blowing south in October, preventing departure for the north for another season.[29] The Portuguese also did not attempt to reach inland markets, whereas the Austrian company had intercepted ivory bound for Inhambane or Sofala and exported it via Delagoa bay.[30]

The Portuguese were too weak to establish a successful slave trade at Delagoa bay in the 1790s and early 1800s. Even when they interfered in local politics they could not establish their dominance and often found themselves at the mercy of local chiefs.[31] They could not generate a regular supply of slaves. The small number of slaves that came into their possession, like other exports, were only transported on the Portuguese ships, which were sent annually from the seat of government at Moçambique island to Delagoa bay with provisions for the Portuguese officials and which returned from Delagao bay with whatever slaves and ivory had been procured since the previous year. Slaves at Delagoa bay (and Inhambane) therefore had to be held until they were picked up by the annual ships, and it was generally not easy or profitable to keep slaves at the fort for long periods.[32] For the most part, the Portuguese also kept foreign slavers out of the bay. A British trader evaded the Portuguese monopoly in 1801 and took on a cargo which included slaves, but because of the interruption of trade from the Napoleonic wars the next English ship from the East India Company did not arrive until 1815.[33] The French apparently had the strength to bypass the Portuguese, but they took most of their slaves from the northern Mozambique coast because of the proximity of these ports to their Indian Ocean possessions and because of the patterns of the trade winds which did not extend further south.[34] Barrow reported a trade in slaves from the northern ports of Moçambique island and Sofala, he but indicated that the Portuguese were not, as of 1803, enslaving Africans for export at Delagoa bay:

> To the southward of the Portugueze [sic] settlement of Rio de la Goa, the natives are Kaffers; but from the description given of them they appear to be a degenerated race. They are however *free* [his italics]; nor has Portugueze avarice yet dared to attempt to make them slaves. This is not the case to the northward. At Mozambique and Soffala the black people are all negroes, not however at the present day, natives of the sea-coast, but such as are brought down from the interior as articles of trade. From Mozambique they have now, as appears from the information of a Portugueze slave merchant, a direct communication across the continent with their settlements of Congo, Loango, and Benguela, on the west coast, between which negro merchants are established in different parts of the country.[35]

The Portuguese refurbished their fort in 1815 and managed to keep out the first English trading ship that had tried to land since 1801. By that time, because the demand for and supply of ivory had decreased, profits at the bay lay in whaling and in supplying whalers with locally produced food-stuffs, including cattle. The Portuguese therefore worked to establish a whaling operation in 1818 and to monopolize local commerce at the port.[36]

After the British slave trade was abolished in 1807 and Anglo-Portuguese treaties limited the slave trade to the southern portion of the African continent in 1815 and 1817, slave prices in the New World rose, making it profitable for slave traders from the Americas to obtain slaves from the more distant markets of southeastern Africa. Accordingly, the northern coastal slave markets at Moçambique island, Sofala, and Quelimane expanded rapidly. Traders favored these ports over those further south because mechanisms for procuring and marketing large numbers of slaves were already in place, and because they were connected to established shipping routes from the Atlantic that passed east and north of Madagascar and avoided the unpredictable, often treacherous Mozambique channel.[37] The proximity of the bay to Brazil remained irrelevant to the slave trade until 1824, because exports from Delagoa bay were still being taken to Moçambique island on Portuguese ships sent annually to collect all trade goods for re-export further north.[38] Nourse indicated that in late 1822 the

Portuguese were still trying to maintain "the exclusive right of traffic with the natives" at the bay, and that "all the ivory etc. which they procure is sent to Mozambique by a vessel which comes for that purpose at stated periods."[39] Nourse observed that non-Portuguese ships traded only under Portuguese supervision.[40] According to Owen, who toured the east African coast between 1822 and 1824, until the 1817 negotiations between Great Britain and Portugal, the slave trade at Delagoa bay "had never before existed beyond the purchase of a dozen a year, but where by this permission means *will be found* to keep the whole country in a state of disorder and warfare, for the purpose of having slaves in greater numbers."[41] In other words, Owen was predicting in 1823 that the slave trade would expand, even though the location of the port had not yet caused an expansion. Indeed, Portuguese slave exports must have been nil in the years 1821 to 1823. As of 1823 the 'annual' ship from Moçambique to the southern ports had not sailed for three years, forcing Portuguese officials to transport personnel and documents on British ships.[42] The Portuguese were also not yet powerful enough to engage in slave raiding. When Owen arrived in September 1822, the Portuguese requested (but did not receive) British assistance in defending the factory and repelling invaders from the nearby Mpfumo chiefdom.[43]

Owen's reports make it clear that there was not yet a lucrative slave trade at the bay. The only way the Portuguese could make a profit at the fort, he noted, was by maintaining a monopoly over the trade in food supplies, "which they bought from the natives for a mere trifle, and sold to us at a gain of about six hundred per cent."[44] Some slaves were included in the Portuguese trade, however. Commodore Nourse of the HMS Andromache learned from captain Owen

> that the Portuguese upon the appearance of the [British] surveying vessels, sent 180 natives (slaves) from their fort, in order that they should not by seen by the english men of war, probably fearing they might be seized. I mention this circumstance to shew there is a traffic in slaves from Delagoa Bay. I believe them to be carried to Mozambique [island], and from thence exported to the Brazils, and that numbers are sent from Mozambique to Madagascar and that some are conveyed to the Seychelles and to Bourbon.[45]

Captain Owen, describing "The Bay of Delagoa," emphasized the diversity of trade goods sold by Africans in the region, and noted that the Portuguese hold in the area was weak, but at the same time indicated the presence of a limited slave trade in May 1823:

> The Portuguese shew not the shadow of pretension to interference with any of these people, and indeed have great dread of them. The commerce of all these people is similar; that is beads, brass and cottons [from European

traders] for Elephants' Teeth [ivory], ambergris, Rhinoceros Horn, and Hippopotamus Teeth, they also barter their Cattle, Poultry, Pigs, boats, and Grain, as also the skins of wild animals....Like all other African Nations all the countries around the Bay make Slaves of their enemies, but of the enemies only. The proximity of this point and the Bazaruto Isles to the Cape and to the French Islands offered to the Cupidity of some Europeans too strong a temptation to resist. English, French, and Dutch vessels have been known to visit these places to entice the people on board and then steal many of them, so that even now the Inhabitants have no confidence in Europeans, but watch the slightest symptoms of movement to make their escape, until they have acquired some knowledge of the parties. The Portuguese merely buy such as are caught from the Vatwahs of the interior, or some of the native women to make a market of their prostitution, thus feeding the worst passions of our nature. War among the surrounding tribes furnishes them Slaves and famine [furnishes them] Women at a low price to let out to such Ships as may visit the Bay. There are however very few slaves exported from this place, and the natives have a decided aversion to the trade.[46]

The Portuguese were not able to expand the slave trade prior to 1824. They could not control events, much less organize slave raiding to provide for an export slave trade, during the turbulent period of migrations, conquests, and political intrigues that consumed the Delagoa bay region from 1821–1823. Conflicts between Africans sometimes generated captives who were available for sale, but the Portuguese were in no position to take advantage of this circumstance. Owen's evidence, partially quoted by Cobbing, says that "The devastation of the Vatwahs, and consequent famine, brought slaves to the fort for almost nothing..."; however, Cobbing neglects to cite the remainder of the same sentence: "...but fortunately, the fort itself was in want, and could not sell food for slaves."[47] According to Owen, then, in early 1823 the Portuguese were too poor themselves to buy any slaves, and were awaiting relief supplies because no ships whatsoever had arrived at Delagoa bay. In this case, there cannot have been a slave-trading-profit motive operating to induce slave raiding at that time.

The upturn in the slave trade came in 1823–1824 in the wake of political turmoil, drought, and food scarcity. The oppressive activities of the Portuguese, including their slaving, impelled the Tembe king to ask Captain Owen to "accept the cession of the Kingdom of Temby to His Majesty," and a document formalizing this cession was signed on 19 March 1823. The British captain was desperate for African seamen to replace crew members who had fallen sick or died, and the king had agreed to let twelve of his men embark on the ship only on condition that he cede the territory, "taking this act for the security of their persons and to assure their return."[48] Among the Tembe concerns noted in the document was a complaint against the Portuguese that they "were not only at peace with our invaders [the

'Olontontes' or 'Vatwahs']; but, on such amicable terms as to buy their plunder of slaves and cattle, and to carry on other peaceable traffic with them; whilst my people were reduced to a famine by the effects of the said war."[49] Thus, the young Tembe king, Mayethe, who had succeeded his grandfather (Makhasane) just before the arrival of the British, turned to the British for protection, but the British provided no actual protection as their ships continued on their voyage up the coast.

Apparently Tembe vulnerability forced Mayethe to continue dealing with the Portuguese as a means of self-defense. In mid–1823, Henry Fynn reported that in the Delagoa bay area only the Tembe sold slaves. According to Fynn, Mayethe's subordinate chief Mohambie was

> the only Chief at Delagoa who takes prisoners, which are conveyed across English River to the Portuguese to whom they are sold as Slaves for trinkets and cloth which he shares with his King. These Slaves are kept in the Fort till the annual vessel comes to carry them off.[50]

Once the British had departed in December 1823, Mayethe was confronted with renewed Portuguese aggression as the Portuguese sent soldiers to raise their own flag in Tembe. Instead of resisting, Mayethe's people fought for the Portuguese against the king of Madolo, only to turn against them once more when the Portuguese withheld their promised payment in cattle.[51]

The upsurge in Delagoa bay slave exports after 1823 was the result of conflicts caused by brutal Portuguese actions designed to establish their dominance and prevent further British interference.[52] Nineteenth century Portuguese historians dated the expansion of the slave trade to the disruptions associated with migrations from south of the bay in 1823, but they failed to report the central aggressive role played by the Portuguese. According to Manso:

> As the *vatuas* from the Natal coast had invaded in 1823 the interior districts of Laurenco Marques, then began in the colony the traffic, in which the Portuguese bought slaves from the *vatuas* and sold them to the French who frequented the port.[53]

Significantly, although his interpretation is unreliable, Manso refutes an 1824 report that the trade in slaves at Delagoa bay had stopped. His evidence indicates the changing content of trade in 1824–1825. A royal decree of November 1824 created a commercial company with exclusive control over all trade in the bay; notably, the agreement specified the exclusive right to the ivory trade.[54] The company began operations in January 1825 but was not particularly successful because by then profits lay in exporting slaves, a trade which the governors allowed foreigners to conduct upon the payment of bribes.

The available evidence suggests that slaving activities expanded at Delagoa bay in 1824 or soon after. Both a drought in 1823 and political and military conflicts provoked by the Portuguese generated supplies of slaves. Drought conditions and consequent raiding disrupted food production and induced famine, although there is no evidence from this period that crops were deliberately destroyed by Africans trying to weaken and enslave others for sale to the Portuguese. By October 1823 the Portuguese at Delagoa bay were generating more captives through their involvement in local conflicts, which Owen reported:

> From Inhambane however, the trade in slaves is very limited compared with that of Mozambique and Quillimane, the neighbouring tribes being very averse to it; nevertheless wars are excited solely to make slaves to pay for merchandize. The same also occurs at English river to a still smaller extent, yet sufficiently so to keep the neighbouring tribes in a ferment and continual state of warfare.[55]

In 1824 Delagoa bay became a focal point of Portuguese political intervention. The Portuguese responded to Owen's interference and signing of treaties with Delagoa bay chiefdoms by attempting to assert their own dominance in the area much more aggressively.[56] Aware that the ivory sold by the Mabudu originated south of them, Cardinas sent a mission to ask Shaka's permission to open a trading station south of the Mabudu, but Shaka refused.[57] Undaunted, Cardinas marched into Tembe and Mabudu and forced them to renounce their treaties with the British. Cardinas then enlisted the Mpfumo in a successful effort to subdue the Madolo chiefdom and one of its tributaries to the north of the bay. Emboldened, Cardinas went personally to take formal possession of Madolo. In retaliation for their mistreatment, the Madolo ambushed and killed Cardinas and his companions on their return to the fort.[58] The Madolo also attacked the Mpfumo allies of the Portuguese and burned their villages. The most senior surviving official, lieutenant Teixera, became the new governor, and with Machechane's Madolo troops menacing the fort he pursued a policy of appeasement. He simultaneously negotiated for protection from the Tembe king, Mayethe. The resulting alliance led Machechane to attack the Tembe just as some Nguni-speaking traders were arriving with cattle for sale at the fort, and the Tembe-Nguni forces defeated the Madolo. The Portuguese reneged on their agreement to pay the Tembe, however, and Mayethe had Teixera killed. The defeated Madolo left the vicinity just as the last Nguni-speaking invaders passed through, bringing an end to the local fighting in about mid-1824.[59]

With a second governor killed in one year, the Portuguese at Moçambique were forced to react. A relief force traveling overland from Inhambane had to turn back, but new troops arrived with a new governor, Xavier Schmidt von Belliken, in late 1824. Von Belliken was just as determined as his predecessors to enforce Portuguese control, block foreign traders, and defy the British. Owen's ship had returned from its journey to the Swahili coast, and he replanted the British flag in Tembe. Provoked, the governor captured a private British trading ship, which Owen rescued by turning his guns towards the fort. Owen's ship departed thereafter, however, leaving the port to the Portuguese.[60] The Portuguese continued to promote conflicts between themselves and various chiefdoms at the bay that generated captives and also awakened outsiders to growing slaving prospects there.

A succession of Portuguese governors then pursued their personal interests by accepting bribes from foreign slavers in exchange for permission to trade.[61] The Portuguese government was disturbed more, however, by the loss of tax revenues than by the fact that the trade was contraband, and returned Caetano Matoso to the governor's post. He and his immediate successor, Jose Antonio Teixera, proved no better. In 1829, Dionisio Antonio Ribeiro became the governor of Delagoa bay, and under his command slave raiding to supply the slave trade became common in the Delagoa bay hinterland.[62]

Slave Raiding in the Delagoa Bay Region After 1823

A precipitous rise in slave exports from Delagoa bay was evident in the presence of French slavers reported by Owen in late 1823 and 1824, and in the numbers of French and Brazilian slave ships which visited the port in 1826 and after.[63] As slave trading picked up in 1824, people in the immediate vicinity of Delagoa bay were at increased risk from slave raiders. In his diary, written years later, Fynn pointed out that conflicts among groups living in the vicinity of Delagoa bay "were beneficial to the Portuguese, for they purchased the prisoners captured by the rival parties and made slaves of them."[64] He points out that "those who were made prisoners were sold whilst those who escaped were caught in the woods in a famished state, owing to their corn having been destroyed." Although he gives no dates for these events, he links them explicitly to the Tembe king, Mayethe, who acceded to the kingship in 1823; hence, Fynn is clearly referring to 1823 or after.[65] In addition; he refers only to people in the immediate vicinity of the bay, and there is no evidence that these activities reached further afield at that time.

An 1828 inquiry into the slave trade to Mauritius provides more evidence that the destructive slaving of the Portuguese commenced after 1823. It states:

> The settlement made by Captain Owen in Delagoa Bay in 1823, having been subsequently [in 1824] destroyed, a connection is stated to have been formed between the Portuguese and the French slave traders, and a marauding system commenced, the object of which was the capture of the peaceable tribes inhabiting the interior of that part of Africa, to which cause has been attributed the appearance since 1823, of great numbers of starving people upon the frontier of the Cape colony. The slave traders at Delagoa Bay, are said to have gone out in armed parties to drive off their cattle, and destroy their grain, in the expectation that a large proportion of these wretched people would repair to the coast, in quest of subsistence, where they might be seized and embarked in the slaving vessels.[66]

This evidence shows that slave raiders began to induce famine deliberately, but it also states explicitly that slave raiding activities began only after the British settlement (established in 1823) was destroyed in 1824.

By 1829 European traders were directly involved in slave raiding. This year marks the arrival of the governor Ribeiro, who engaged in slave raiding as well as slave trading. Soldiers employed by Ribeiro complained that he sent them on slave hunting expeditions and mistreated them if they returned with too few slaves.[67] Ribeiro must also have received captives who were taken in local conflicts in the late 1820s, some of which he deliberately instigated. By 1828 the strength of the Madolo was such that they seized control of the Mpfumo, who received no aid from their former Portuguese allies. Eventually, the Portuguese did send guns to rally several chiefdoms, including the Mpfumo, against the Madolo. The Madolo were forced to submit and began paying the Portuguese tribute in 1831. Apparently, the Portuguese from Delagoa bay established good relations with the powerful AmaNdwandwe chief, Soshangane, who aided them in establishing control over the chiefdoms in the north. The Portuguese from Inhambane were not as wise: in October 1834 they instead sent almost 300 soldiers (including Portuguese) to attack Soshangane and lost the entire force. Portuguese officials contrived both to establish control and to profit from slaving, but beyond the immediate vicinity of their forts they were continually reminded of their military weakness relative to the more powerful chiefdoms and kingdoms of the region.

Only by playing off one chief against another were they able to generate slaves for export, the supply of which increased dramatically after 1824 as a result of their machinations. Over time Portuguese slave raiding to the north became more systematic. Smith presents a series of Portuguese documents from 1830 which demonstrate that:

Expeditions in search of captives were sent to the mouth of the Limpopo River, where both the Portuguese and French acquired Tshopi slaves. Although they were sometimes obtained by purchase, the Portuguese also engaged in capturing them. Portuguese traders and soldiers from Inhambane also visited this area to purchase or to hunt their victims.[68]

The Portuguese do not appear to have engaged much in slaving south of the bay, but the peoples on the southern part of the bay clearly suffered to some extent. Andrew Smith, making notes in part from what he learned from Fynn on his 1832 trip, wrote without further explanation:

> Found a nation of women between the Maputa and the Portuguese. First the Portuguese had made slaves of the men and the women had had all their arms carried off by a tribe from the interior. In a starving state, eating the bark off the trees.[69]

The Portuguese themselves were not in a powerful enough position to raid for slaves south of the bay, or to sponsor and protect others who might do so for them. Throughout the period in which the slave trade expanded, the Portuguese pursued policies of appeasement with the Mabudu and AmaZulu to the south, and they were unable to establish their dominance. In 1828 the Portuguese had to send presents to both Soshangane and the AmaZulu after a battle between the two chiefdoms closed trade routes which they wanted reopened. Similarly, after Makhasane closed off trade routes in 1829, Ribeiro sent an embassy to negotiate.[70] Frustrated, Ribeiro tried to establish cordial relations with Dingane after he succeeded Shaka in 1828, but the plan backfired when Dingane was insulted by a gift of what he considered inferior goods. Ribeiro placated Dingane, who proceeded to send the Portuguese some cattle as a sign of good faith. Thereafter, AmaZulu trade continued to be funneled north in spite of increasing competition for this trade from British traders operating out of Port Natal.[71]

Governor Ribeiro's relations with Dingane remained friendly for several years, and then deteriorated dramatically. In December 1830 Ribeiro sent tribute to Dingane in the hands of musket-bearing African soldiers, and in 1831 Dingane responded to Ribeiro's request for AmaZulu soldiers to help defeat the Madolo. Ribeiro then sent ten musket-bearing soldiers to help Dingane defeat one of his own neighbors.[72] Ribeiro was aided by the AmaZulu in his expeditions against chiefdoms north of the bay as he extended Portuguese authority in that direction in 1831 and 1832. Soon thereafter, however, Ribeiro decided that Dingane was too demanding, and in 1832 he refused to send some goods requested by Dingane. Dingane stopped all trade with the Portuguese by gaining the compliance of all the chiefdoms around the bay. In July 1833 Dingane's soldiers menaced the Portuguese fort until they were placated with goods, while Machechane's

Madolo raided nearby. When Dingane learned that his troops had let off the governor so easily he sent them back, ordering all the nearby chiefdoms to mobilize for war. In the end it is not clear whether it was Madolo or AmaZulu soldiers who captured and killed Ribeiro, but at the formal execution they expressed dissatisfaction because governor Ribeiro had taken Madolo lands, made war in the area, raised the Portuguese flag, and— most importantly— enslaved people and sent them to Moçambique island. The grievance expressed explicitly against the export slave trade appears to exonerate the Madolo and AmaZulu from charges of being slavers themselves. Meanwhile, the Portuguese traders from the nongovernment company trading in ivory had managed to distance themselves from the Portuguese government, and they were spared because they did not trade in slaves, indicating that the grievances harbored by the AmaZulu were directed against Ribeiro's slaving and not all Portuguese traders.[73]

Dingane and the head of the Portuguese trading company established a good working relationship until the company also found that it could not supply Dingane with the goods he demanded. The Portuguese at the trading factory had been under threat from the Madolo, and, when they requested Dingane's help, a force of AmaZulu, Tembe, Mabudu, and Magaia marched against the Madolo in June 1834. The AmaZulu were motivated not by a desire to obtain and trade slaves but to restore profitable, legitimate trade with the bay. Far from being victims of slave raiders operating out of Delagoa bay, the AmaZulu remained dominant in the region to the south. Their interest lay in subduing and absorbing their neighbors in order to increase their military might; there is no evidence that at any time the AmaZulu themselves engaged in enslaving other peoples for sale to Europeans.

The AmaZulu State and the Slave Trade

European trade at Delagoa bay fueled regional trade networks, as ivory was traded to the port in relays, and beads in particular found their way far into the interior. This trade fostered socioeconomic stratification and political consolidation in the hinterland, but slave exports from the bay were too sporadic and the numbers too low to account for the turbulence and political change which ensued in the late eighteenth and early nineteenth centuries. The slave trade did not expand until after the emergence of regional kingdoms beginning in the late eighteenth century, and therefore cannot account for the rise of the AmaMthethwa of Dingiswayo and its successor state, the AmaZulu kingdom of Shaka. Contrary to Cobbing's assumption of early regional slave raiding, there is no indication in the primary sources referring to the Delagoa bay hinterland in the 1810s and 1820s that slave raiders were operating beyond the immediate vicinity of the bay prior to 1823. In addition, no evidence has yet surfaced of slave raiding in the interior, from the east, through the remainder of the 1820s. Yet, had there been active slave raiding to supply the Delagoa bay trade, captives destined for the bay would have required armed transport over long distances. Captive male warriors would have been especially dangerous and difficult to transport unnoticed. The absence of navigable rivers feeding Delagoa bay from the west or from AmaZulu territory necessitates overland transport, and caravans of captives could not have passed through the area unnoticed. The evidence from Africans and Europeans recounts battles, migrations, hunger, and the consolidation of chiefdoms through voluntary and involuntary subordination. There is no evidence from either side, however, of slave raiders or captives being transported out of the area and sold. A conspiracy of silence on the part of the AmaZulu and their enemies, as well as the rival European powers, is not likely.

Shaka earned notoriety not for capturing people for sale as slaves to Delagoa bay, but for killing people in battle or incorporating them into his kingdom as subordinates. He centralized authority and privileged a core group of followers by the imposition of authoritarian rule, sometimes involving the arbitrary use of terror to enforce compliance. Hence, the general status of most people incorporated under AmaZulu state authority was one of relative powerlessness; slavery as a separate institution did not emerge. The strength of the state rested on the accumulation of people for the sake of political and economic dominance and military security; therefore the sale of captives was not in the interests of the AmaZulu state.

The large-scale slaughter of people in battle was also contrary to AmaZulu state interests. Unpredictable acts of terror gave Shaka a reputation for widespread destruction and induced fear and compliance, but stories suggestive of the wholesale slaughter of men, women, and children may be misleading. In at least one instance his stated intentions of exterminating an entire chiefdom were not carried out, and the people were allowed to live after they surrendered their animals and accepted his authority. In this case Shaka used threats to coerce the British trader, Isaacs, and his party into subduing a branch of the AmaKhumalo who were resisting his domination in their mountain stronghold. Isaacs claims he ordered them "not to leave alive even a child, but exterminate the whole tribe." Shaka explained to Isaacs that the women and children had to be killed because "they can propagate and bring children, who may become my enemies."[74]   No slaughter resulted, however, and none of these resisters were captured or sold as slaves. The day after the attack they surrendered; and according to standard practice, they were accepted as Shaka's subjects:

The [AmaZulu] chiefs did not wait to hear their propositions, as they have only one term [for accepting surrender], namely, to give up their cattle, and become tributary to the conqueror. They did not hesitate to comply with this, but promptly brought forward their half-starved cattle and goats.[75]

According to Isaacs, Shaka's regiments were motivated by "booty in cattle, the main object for which the Zoolas go to war," and as such were "not fighting any particular tribe, but maintaining a kind of predatory warfare."[76] It is particularly unlikely that women were killed indiscriminately, as women were valuable because of their productive and reproductive functions. One European observer noted that there was no limit for men "in the number of concubines they may choose to take," and these concubines must have come from the ranks of captive women, given the social protection afforded unmarried women by their male kin.[77] Isaacs noted the presence of concubines and indicated that "there is a great excess of females over males," strengthening the probability that captive women were subject to concubinage, itself a form of enslavement grounded in violence.[78]

Shaka certainly maintained trade contacts with Africans living in the vicinity of Delagoa bay and trading with the Portuguese, but no evidence indicates that he or his people sold any captives as slaves. In his diary, Fynn included a lengthy description of the "natives of Delagoa and the surrounding country," and over several pages addressed their lives and activities.[79] He began the section on trade by noting that "the situation of the [Delagoa bay] tribes [i.e. chiefdoms] for trade purposes is very advantageous, for they have the Zulus on one side and the Portuguese, and formerly the Ndwandwes to the north." He continued:

During the chieftainship of Jobe, father of Dingiswayo [chief of the Mthethwa tribe], the natives of Delagoa traficked very little with them [*the AmaMthethwa*], but Dingiswayo monopolised the whole market until he was killed by Zwide [chief of the AmaNdwandwe], which induced the Delagonians to open up a trade with the latter [*the AmaNdwandwe*]. They [*the natives of Delagoa*] continued [after Dingiswayo's death] to trade with Shaka, by whom they were looked upon as being the only people who possessed beads and brass [copper]. The former article gave rise to many conjectures. Some supposed them to be found on the sea coast of Delagoa at low water; others, that they grew in bunches on trees, which ideas still exist here and there among the Zulus. As these people [*the natives of Delagoa*] were looked on as being the sole merchants, they were left unmolested by both the powerful chiefs referred to [*Zwide and Shaka*], to both of whose markets they carried monkey and genet skins procured by hunting and catching them in traps. For the beads, brass and blue cloth (dungaree) that were brought they [*the Delagonians*] received in return elephant and sea-cow ivory, iron and tobacco. Trade with the Portuguese factory, on the east side of the English River, was equally beneficial [*for the Delagonians*]. The ivory [*the Delagonians*] procured from the Zulus and

Ndwandwes together with the prisoners taken in their [*the Delagonians'*] wars
(which they sold as slaves), they [*the Delagonians*] bartered with the Portuguese for beads and brass.[80]

In this passage Fynn continued to write about the activities of the "natives
of Delagoa," and it is these "Delagonians," not AmaZulu or AmaNdwandwe,
who Fynn says took prisoners in their local wars, some of whom they sold
as slaves to the Portuguese.

There is also no suggestion in the evidence that the European traders who
visited Shaka, whether British from Port Natal or Portuguese from Delagoa
bay, were slavers. Had either the British or the Portuguese been collecting
slaves in the region under Shaka's control, they would have had to do so
either with his consent and complicity or without his knowledge. African
oral traditions, which portray treachery and severe repression on the part
of Shaka, could not have neglected to reveal any slaving activities in which
Shaka might have been involved.[81]

Commercial relations between the AmaZulu and European traders
instead involved legitimate trade goods. Isaacs, surprised to encounter a
Portuguese trader at Shaka's, learned "though [he was] perhaps employed
by his government in some military office, that he had arrived there for the
purpose of purchasing cattle."[82] Shaka himself was occupied with ensuring monopoly control over ivory, as Isaacs discovered when he was unable
to purchase ivory because "messengers from the Zoola king" were active in
keeping track of how much had been collected.[83] The importance of ivory
is evident in that Shaka, and later Dingane, sometimes mobilized their
regiments for the purpose of hunting elephants.[84]

Isaacs' credibility may be questionable, but it is hard to imagine how he
himself could have been secretly engaged in slaving at that point without
having such activities exposed by Africans and by Europeans with anti-
slavery sentiments. Moreover, his companion Charles Rawden Maclean,
known as "John Ross," was more familiar with the area between the
AmaZulu state capital and Delagoa bay than were the other Port Natal
traders by virtue of a journey he had made in the company of AmaZulu
guides. His writings show that he was ardently opposed to slavery and the
slave trade, and he openly described and condemned the export of slaves
from Delagoa bay. Nevertheless, in his later exposé of events during his life
among the AmaZulu and among the Port Natal traders, Ross mentions no
capture, enslavement, or transport of conquered peoples from the south for
sale to the slave market at Delagoa bay. Rather, he noted that the fate of
those conquered by the AmaZulu was either death or incorporation as an
impoverished remnant group lacking wealth in cattle. Among these groups
he noted in particular "a class of natives called Maphisi who make it their

special business to hunt these animals [hippopotami], as well as the elephant, for the means of subsistence."[85]

AmaZulu society was characterized by extreme disparities in wealth and power, but there is no evidence of slave trading. D'Elegorgue, who exposed "apprenticeship" among the Voortrekkers as slavery, believed that "the slave-dealers have never found their way to these people, probably because the Zulus had a reputation of unusual ferocity, and also because of their ideas regarding war. They think it absurd that a conqueror should spare the life of his adversary, and they kill any they meet in fight."[86]

A more likely explanation for the absence of slave raiding and slavery within the AmaZulu kingdom lies in the interests which motivated the AmaZulu. They stood to gain more from subordinating their weaker neighbors and trading with the Mabudu who had access to European traders at Delagoa bay. The Mabudu were a tributary of the AmaZulu state from 1823; AmaZulu officers resided at the Mabudu capital, and the AmaZulu refrained from attacking them when they made forays against the AmaMthethwa and AmaNdwandwe who had migrated towards the bay.[87] According to Hedges:

> Notified of the royal demand after the harvest by Tshaka's messenger, Makhasane collected at his court the required quantity of local animal products of Mabudu hunters—the skins and furs of animals such as buck and monkeys; and articles such as calabashes, beer baskets and other goods made of materials common in the north-east lowlands. Mabudu carriers then transported the goods to Zululand along with the beads, brass wire and cloth acquired from European ships and the Portuguese factory. On arrival at the Zulu court, the carriers were given cattle and shields for the Mabudu *ihosi* [chief], and ivory and horn when the Zulu king required goods from the Europeans.[88]

Shaka and Dingane had much to gain by perpetuating legitimate trade relations with the Mabudu and European traders. A trade in human captives was inimical to those interests, and did not play a role in AmaZulu commercial relations with traders operating out of Delagoa bay or Port Natal.

The Highveld and Delagoa Bay

Eighteenth-century Portuguese sources confirm that goods such as ivory, gold, and copper reached Delagoa bay from the highveld, apparently brought from long distances.[89] According to oral sources and traveler reports, from at least the early-nineteenth-century trade was maintained between Delagoa bay and the VhaVenda, the copper miners of Musina, and BaTswana kingdoms as far away as the Kalahari desert.[90] Early European travelers to the highveld, from the edge of the Kalahari to the Drakensberg in the east and the Limpopo river in the north, noted indications of contacts with Delagoa bay. Written European and oral African sources make clear the presence of long-distance trade in ivory, precious metals, cloth, and beads, but make no mention of slave raiding or enslavement by agents operating out of Delagoa bay.

Traders from somewhere along the Mozambique coast brought goods to some BaTswana chiefdoms. In 1801 Somerville was told that the BaTlhaping were visited by traders from the north, who were flat-nosed and resembled his cook, a Mozambique slave.[91] These people were said to live with white people near the water, from whom they received their cloth; a MoTlhaping man had a piece of Indian calico acquired in this way.[92] Similarly, the BaHurutshe had regular trade contacts to the northeast. Campbell found that they had acquired beads by selling ivory to traders to the east. They had heard of the "Mahalaseela" people living near the ocean, from whom beads and inoculation against smallpox originated.[93] By the early nineteenth century VaTsonga traders had come as far inland as BaHurutshe territory, penetrating from the coast both via the lowveld Limpopo valley in the northeast and across the plateau directly to the east.[94] Nevertheless, Campbell was told by the BaHurutshe that "they knew of no nation who sold men," which indicated that slave raiders from the east or northeast had not penetrated that far inland as late as 1820.[95] By the 1820s the BaNgwato also had trade links to the east coast, and received beads and cloth for their ivory. According to a MoNgwato who had been to Delagoa bay, east coast traders in boats traveled as far as northeastern Transvaal on the Limpopo river; he also stated that there was no slave raiding or trading outside of the immediate bay area.[96]

Peoples living as far west as the Kalahari may well have maintained trade contacts extending as far as the Zambezi river and beyond to the east coast via the Zimbabwe plateau. Andrew Smith was told in 1834–1835 that the BaNgwato traded with the BaKalanga and the MaShona to the northeast, which might indicate links to the Zimbabwe plateau and northern Mozambican ports.[97] In 1834 Smith observed, in his report to the Cape government on the "Northern Frontier," that the BaKwena chiefdom of the BaTswana was connected to the trade network to the coast:

> The Baquaina, in the days of their prosperity, were visited by native traders from the neighbourhood of Delagoa Bay, who, in return for their ivory and cattle, supplied them with European articles, such as they desired. The Bakalaka also, who, judging from report, had a more direct and regular communication with the coast, were also in the habit of visiting the Baquaina with foreign commodities and with metallic ornaments manufactured by

themselves.   Large and coarse beads of Portuguese origin are often seen adorning the necks of the natives towards the Tropic....[98]

David Hume, a trader resident at Kuruman, visited the "Bakaas" south of the BaNgwato (at modern Shoshong) in 1833 and found that:

> During one month the Portuguese traders had been twice to deal with them. The Bay was eight days journey from them. The Portuguese conveyed their goods on pack-oxen and never approached the kraal but remained in the fields and sent to the people to come. Probably adopted to prevent its being known to Masalacatzie that traders had been to barter with them. They preferred teeth between 40 and sixty pounds; those would not take cow teeth so that the teeth most commonly presented to other traders are those of females and very large male teeth. The Portuguese will not take teeth with broken points.[99]

Ivory reaching Delagoa bay was reported to have been transported by wagon from the Kalahari region, by boat from Kosse, and in caravans of porters going to Kosse or all the way to the bay.[100] Hume noted that the Portuguese were trying to escape the notice of Mzilikazi, who might have interfered with their trade; certainly large-scale transporting of goods could not have gone unnoticed and unreported by Africans in the region. The absence of a record of slave raiding and slave trading in African oral traditions from the region strongly suggests that no captives were being transported or used as carriers to the coast. Instead, reports were made of legitimate VaTsonga traders who had begun to travel further afield and had become known by a variety of names; they were identifiable by their dress, scarring on the face, and language.[101] VaTsonga traders reached the western Transvaal in the mid-1830s using pack oxen for transportation, but they were known for their strength because they carried the ivory themselves.[102] Mzilikazi's AmaNdebele, when located in the Transvaal, were in the mid-1830s primarily fearful of the Kora and Griqua threat from their southwest, and of the white settlers who had been taking the lands of the AmaXhosa.[103] At that time they evinced no fear of traders from Delagoa bay, who were apparently not yet taking slaves from the interior; Mzilikazi was in possession of Portuguese beads from the bay.[104]

Miscellaneous reports of people vaguely described as long-haired, or light in complexion, have fueled speculation that Portuguese slave raiders had penetrated the interior in the 1820s.[105] The evidence cannot easily be explained as referring to Europeans or even Afro-Portuguese, however, since both Europeans and Africans made doubtful observations of this nature. Somerville noted in 1801 that among the BaTlhaping were people of various descriptions: "some are of a swarthy hue and others are certainly as fair as a native of Portugal."[106] Intermixing and intermarriage were common between the BaTlhaping and their Kora and Bastard neighbors;

reports of light-skinned raiders might therefore be traced to any of these groups.[107] Somerville mentioned that the BaTlhaping were more surprised by the length and texture of Europeans' hair than by the color of their skin. Liechtenstein's Cape slave, who may have been of Malay origin, was considered "white" by the BaTlhaping in the interior.[108] In 1815 Campbell was told that the "Bushmen" could distinguish the Boers from their other enemies (i.e., Griqua and Kora on horseback bearing guns) only because they wore hats.[109] Backhouse noted that the AmaXhosa and AmaTembu referred to Khoikhoi as white people.[110] Bain, traveling through the area in 1829, observed that the AmaMpondo had countenances like "lascars," lighter than the AmaXhosa, and believed that it was because various Europeans had intermarried with them, including the white mother of a chief.[111] Smith noted that the AmaMpondo "wear their hair smeared with red and hanging down the back in long tassels."[112] The AmaHlubi, who crossed the Drakensberg from the east in 1821 or 1822, were noted for wearing their hair in long tails. By the early 1820s, Kora and Griqua who rode horses and dressed as Europeans, as well as renegade Europeans such as Coenraad de Buys, were raiding BaSotho to the east and BaTswana chiefdoms far to the north.[113] The AmaNdebele mistook the first Voortrekkers for Griqua, and mistakenly attacked them in retaliation for an earlier Griqua raid. On the other hand, when they visited Motlomo on the Sand river in 1836, Arbousset and Daumas were told that the inhabitants "had never before seen white men," although they had been raided by the Kora.[114] Clearly, Africans could not readily identify Europeans according to any single criterion, and the confusion of color and culture renders their identifications unreliable. Reports of long-haired or "white" raiders may be accounted for in many ways, and are certainly not evidence that Portuguese traders were raiding far into the interior from their base at Delagoa bay in the 1820s.

French missionary Thomas Arbousset's accounts of his travels northeast of Lesotho in 1836 and 1840 contain no references to Portuguese agents raiding on the highveld. Among the first Europeans with a knowledge of the local languages to travel through the area, Arbousset talked to groups who had recently been dislocated. Arbousset reported neither stories of massive death and destruction from wars and battles nor other evidence of the so-called *"mfecane"* to which other Europeans attributed the deserted villages full of skeletons that they encountered in the region.[115] The accounts given to Arbousset by Africans throughout the area dwelt on the struggle for cattle, crops, and stored grain; African informants attributed deaths on a large scale not to battles but to starvation. Even more significant is the absence of any evidence that Europeans or slave raiders of any origin had ever penetrated into this part of the interior of southern Africa from the east, or from Delagoa bay. It is highly unlikely that Arbousset would have ignored such evidence from any of his many African informants or omitted it from his account. Arbousset held strong anti-slavery views; moreover he was aware of the slave trade off the Mozambique coast and had denounced it. Arbousset related a story told to him "by the natives" that a group of people identifying themselves as BaFokeng followers of Sebetoane had wandered all the way to the Indian ocean where some were tricked into boarding a slave ship; others refused and returned to tell the tale, leading Arbousset to conclude that "that diabolical trade has spread even to the foot of the Maluti mountains." He was then referring, not to slave raiding in the interior, but to the capturing of people at the coast. Arbousset concluded that "I do not suppose that it [the slave trade from Delagoa bay] has reached further on the southern side of this continent."[116]

Arbousset's conclusions seem convincing considering that his informants included people who had emigrated away from the Natal area under AmaZulu domination. Among the new subjects of Moshoeshoe were IsiZulu-speaking immigrants who had fled from Dingane. They had adopted SeSotho clothes and customs, and were already speaking SeSotho among themselves; one told Arbousset's guide: "Dingane, I served him for a while; I have also served his father....But both of them have been the death of me. Believe me, friend, Dingane is nothing to me any more, nor to my family. We are Basotho."[117] Such migrants, who had moved west from the southern hinterland of Delagoa bay and spoke with disfavor about both Dingane and Senzangakona, were the most likely sources for reported abuses taking place in the area of AmaZulu state control, but they did not mention slave raiders or a slave trade.

Clearly in the 1820s Portuguese slave traders or their agents were not raiding for slaves far into the interior. They could not have been doing so without Africans living in the region reporting these activities. The only evidence in the early decades of the nineteenth century regarding slave raiding in these areas pertains to Griqua, Kora, Bergenaar, or white outlaws from the Cape colony, all of whom frequented the area and were indistinguishable to Africans living there. There is no indication that Portuguese agents raided on the highveld to supply the Delagoa bay export market until after the arrival of the Voortrekkers in the 1840s.

Delagoa Bay and the Northern Transvaal

By 1840, the Transvaal had become the center of violence associated with hunters and raiders connected both with the Delagoa bay trade and with the expanding Boer frontier of settlement.[118] Since the 1820s, the sons of the renegade Coenraad de Buys, themselves of mixed descent, had settled in the eastern Transvaal and pursued their father's pattern of destructive raiding.[119] VaTsonga traders had settled among the VhaVenda and BaPedi before the Voortrekkers arrived in the Transvaal.[120] Not surprisingly, the Voortrekkers sought links with Delagoa bay to escape their dependence on British lines of trade and communication. Moreover, they were encouraged to do so by an Amsterdam trader who sailed into the bay in the *Brazilia*, in June 1843, and waited for their arrival. After a disappointing wait into 1844, the Dutch trader was ready to leave the bay when twenty-four Voortrekkers under Potgieter "adequately armed and well mounted, rode into Delagoa Bay, followed by three hundred slaves."[121]

The Portuguese did not welcome the Voortrekkers at first, however, and discouraged links with them, because they feared both British and Boer expansionism in the region. Potgieter's people settled the new village of Andries Ohrigstad and in 1848 resettled at Schoemansdal in the Zoutpansberg. They maintained slave dealings with Portuguese not connected with the government through the agency of João Albasini. Of vague Portuguese origins, Albasini left Delagoa bay to settle among Soshangane's people, supposedly as a trader, and became known as the white chief of the "Shangaans."[122] A somewhat mysterious figure who appears to have fabricated his ancestry, Albasini joined the sons of Coenraad de Buys in plundering the frontier for captives. He became the focal point of the violent hunting frontier which brought back human captives as well as elephant tusks.[123] According to Wagner, the documents which name a Boer from Ohrigstad as an agent for a business house in "macazula" belonging to João Albasini and Carlos João Trigardt establish that there was indeed "a business association between Albasini and Carel Trichardt, son of the trekker Louis Trichardt, for the development of trade from Lourenço Marques with the new Boer colony of Ohrigstad."[124] Albasini kept his stores of goods at his place in Makaxule, which was halfway between Lourenço Marques in Delagoa bay and Ohrigstad and ideally placed for such an enterprise.

The role of Albasini in despatching African raiders to hunt ivory and capture children in the northern Transvaal was exposed in early official inquiries into slavery in the Transvaal.[125] Less is known about his links between interior slave raiding and Delagoa bay, but miscellaneous evidence about Albasini suggests his use of *opgaaf*, or involuntary, tributary labor. For example, Martins notes that only human transport was possible between Lourenço Marques and Makaxule because of tse tse flies, although between Makaxule and Ohrigstad it was possible to use ox-wagons. According to Martins, "whenever Albasini wanted to send ivory to Lourenço Marques or bring back provisions he never lacked for porters which the obliging chiefs gladly furnished him."[126] Albasini left Makaxule and moved into the interior of the Transvaal in 1851, and by 1853 he was settled on his fortified farm, Goedewensch, in the Zoutpansberg. Goedewensch became the new center for trade in legal and illicit goods transported by his VaTsonga "MaGwamba" or "Shangaan" followers. His activities in the 1850s and 1860s, described by Jan Boeyens in chapter 8 of this volume, were also noted by Martins: "In the intermittent wars that continued after 1865 between the Boers and the VhaVenda, while he lived in the mountains of Zoutpansberg, Albasini and his people always fought on the side of the whites."[127] As Boeyens shows, these "wars" generated the captives who filled the ranks of "orphans" then apprenticed to Boers as *de facto* slave laborers.[128] The ongoing link between illicit activities in the interior and at Delagoa bay persisted through the efforts of Albasini, who served simultaneously as an official "Superintendent for Natives" for the ZAR from 1859–1868 and from 1859 as the vice-consul representing the Portuguese government in Mozambique to the Transvaal government.[129]

The Delagoa Bay Slave Trade and Historians

This study of politics, slavery, and slave-raiding is part of a larger concern to reinterpret the early nineteenth century and discredit the old paradigm, which portrays the developments of this period as deriving solely from AmaZulu agency. Delagoa bay has lately assumed special importance because Cobbing has attempted to undermine the paradigm of a so-called *"mfecane"* by adopting a false chronology of events in order to attribute the rise of the AmaZulu state to slave raiding from Delagoa bay. The ensuing debate over the origins of conflict and demographic dislocation in the 1820s and 1830s has naturally focused on the issue of when Europeans and their agents became involved in raiding for slaves in the hinterland of Delagoa bay.[130] This chapter establishes a chronological basis for correlating the Delagoa bay slave trade with events in the interior. It contradicts Cobbing's assertion that the rise of the AmaZulu state and the aggression of the AmaZulu and their neighbors are to be attributed to slave raiding activities that fed an extensive Delagoa bay slave market before 1823. The evidence clearly demonstrates that the volume of the slave trade did not expand until after 1823, by which time the AmaZulu state was well established under Shaka. Cobbing's assertions with regard to slave dealing by traders at Port Natal, also, have been discredited by Hamilton.[131]

In portraying the rise of Shaka's AmaZulu state from 1817 as a defensive reaction to a slave trade out of Delagoa bay, Cobbing has argued that the Delagoa bay slave trade must have been extensive prior to 1817 and that there must have been concurrent destructive slave raiding in the interior, feeding the external trade.[132] Evidence from the hinterland of Delagoa bay in the 1820s undermines Cobbing's theory that agents connected to the Portuguese at Delagoa bay or to the British traders based at Port Natal were operating as slave raiders in the interior regions (from the highveld in the west to the coastal areas of Zululand and Natal) in the 1810s and 1820s. Given the congruence of evidence from many groups who had conflicting and often hostile interests, it is not credible that slave raiding and a slave trade on the scale proposed by Cobbing could have gone unrecorded and unreported in European and African sources alike. Contrary to what Cobbing has argued, the region which came under AmaZulu state domination in the 1810s and 1820s was not a vortex of slaving, and Shaka and the AmaZulu were not engaged in slave raiding.

Cobbing's postulation of an enormous scale of slave exports is based on only a hypothetical model which assumes that because the slave trade was extensive in the late 1820s, a period for which there is evidence, it must have increased at a steady pace over the previous two decades. Cobbing assumes, in other words, that an export curve is fixed and immutable, ignoring that trade in a given item can jump dramatically at any time depending on supply or demand factors. Cobbing hypothesizes that *if* 5,000 slaves were leaving Delagoa bay per year "for the latter half of the 1820s,"

> working backwards, this would produce about half that volume (c.2,500 per annum) for 1821-25, half that again for 1816-20, and so on, a procedure which produces total slave exports from Delagoa Bay between 1805 and 1830 of approximately 45,000-50,000, with perhaps nearly half those being exported in the middle and later 1820s. With inland losses this could mean that as many as 80,000 people disappeared or perished as a result of the European slaving system in that quarter of a century, to which would have to be added losses from the migrations that are known to have occurred. Although the number of slaves lost increased in the mid-1820s, a critical threshold would have been reached before then, when the actions of slave raiders reached perhaps an extractive capacity of 1,000 slaves or so per annum, and with an upward trajectory, a moment which is likely to have been reached at some stage of the 1810s.[133]

Subsequently, Cobbing conceded that "the evidence for slaving at the Bay between 1800 and 1821 has so far not surfaced."[134] At that point Cobbing still mistakenly believed that no one had searched the Portuguese archives in Lisbon and in Maputo. In fact, a number of prominent scholars have done just that, and there is abundant countervailing evidence indicating that Cobbing's hypothesis about the chronology of slave trade expansion is wrong.[135]

Political amalgamation involved conflict and conquest, and oral history records various battles which marked this process. It is a mistake to assume, however, as does Cobbing, that every battle and military engagement in the first three decades of the nineteenth century was really a conflict between slave raiders and their victims. In seeking to discredit the Zulucentric paradigm, Cobbing has sought an alternative explanation for the violence of the early nineteenth century in which, ironically, the AmaZulu appear once again as the aggressive victimizers of their weaker neighbors. In his search for slave raiders perpetrating violence, Cobbing has revived the notion of a predatory state distinctive from the *"mfecane"* version only in that it was driven by the prospect of profits from the slave trade.

There is no evidence to support Cobbing's assertion that the AmaZulu or neighboring chiefdoms were engaged in slave raiding for the purposes of selling slaves for profit at Delagoa bay before 1823.[136] It is possible to begin to piece together the sites and timing of local conflicts and battles and to identify the participants, but it is not possible to conclude from the evidence now available either that the fights were initiated by slave raiders or that captives were taken to Delagoa bay and sold. As Hamilton demonstrates, Cobbing's arguments remain hypothetical; they rest on evidence which he admits "has not yet come to my hand."[137] It is beyond credibility that, as he argues, 80,000 captives disappeared or perished in the hinterland of Delagoa bay between 1800 and 1825 as a result of European slaving and that all traces of the violence were covered up or lost. Tragedies of this nature become part and parcel of the historical memories of the peoples affected, and there is no reason why Africans would have remained silent about slave raiding. Furthermore, his mistaken assumption that thousands of slaves were exported from Delagoa bay from 1800, rather than from 1824, forms the basis from which he argues that slave raiding in the hinterland must have been extensive, and must account for the conflicts which arose in this period. Similarly, he mistakenly assumes that when the trade did expand in 1824, it was supplied primarily with slaves captured from the west and south. Cobbing's assumption that slave raiding was widespread prior to the disruptions which began in 1817 rests on a circular argument based on conjecture.

The Delagoa bay trade was clearly important in the accumulation of wealth and the allocation of political power regionally in the eighteenth as well as nineteenth centuries. The content of the trade fluctuated along with the participants, and the impact of the trade on the hinterland varied accordingly. The Europeans involved in trade and politics did not hold the balance of power in the eighteenth and early nineteenth centuries, and Portuguese control remained tenuous even after the deliberate and sustained application of force, leading to the expansion of the slave trade, from 1825. The roots of centralization lay in African trade initiatives and political contests dating back to the eighteenth century, and the African initiative was never lost in the emerging contests with Europeans. The Portuguese intent to extend their domination was evident from the time they contested the British presence in 1823 and in the slave raiding expeditions sponsored by governors from 1825. The murder of Portuguese governors (by Africans in 1824 and 1833, and AmaZulu efforts to end the slave trade and restore the trade in legitimate goods in 1833 and 1834, illustrate ongoing African resistance to slaving and Portuguese domination in the Delagoa bay hinterland.

Notes

I would like to express my thanks to John Wright and Carolyn Hamilton for their comments and suggestions. I am also grateful to the late Alan K. Smith for his earlier advice about my research on Delagoa Bay.

1. Of particular value are the unpublished doctoral dissertations of Smith (1970) and Hedges (1979).
2. Cobbing (1988); see Eldredge (1992).
3. Cobbing (1990).
4. The following is taken from the reconstruction of the early history of chiefdoms at the bay in Hedges (1979), *passim*.
5. Hedges notes that "the inhabitants of Lourenco Marques district called themselves Ronga, a term which permutes to Thonga when spoken by people of modern Zululand." Hedges (1979), 253. Smith uses the term Ronga to refer to those VaTsonga who lived around Delagoa bay, acknowledging that these are linguistic classifications not made by the peoples themselves; he traces the historical emergence of various identities over several centuries. Smith, (1970a), 8-27. Neither of these historians attempts to use the terms with any precision because of the presence of multiple cultural influences in the area. Harries has traced the process by which missionaries constructed ethnicities and languages in southeastern Africa. Harries (1988 & 1991).
6. Smith (1970a), 28; Hedges (1979), 115.
7. Hedges (1979), 115.
8. Ibid, 116-21.
9. The preceding historical survey is based on Ibid, 134-54.
10. Ibid, 9.
11. Ibid, 8.
12. Ibid, 145-7.
13. Ibid, 151.
14. Ibid, 12.
15. Ibid, 198.
16. Ibid.
17. Ibid, 199.
18. Smith (1970a), 247.
19. Ibid, 248-50; Hedges (1979), 228.
20. Smith has argued that the so-called "Vatwahs" of this incident were Zwangendaba's AmaNdwandwe, but Hedges suggests they may have been the AmaMthethwa of Nyambose. Smith (1970a), 250; Hedges (1979), 228.
21. Smith (1970a), 251-2.
22. Ibid, 253-6.

23. Ibid, 256-9.

24. Newitt, (1988), 14-35. See also the discussion in Eldredge (1992), 12-3.

25. Smith (1970a), 261.

26. Ibid, 345-6.

27. Klein (1978), 77-8. Barrow, important in exposing the enslavement of Africans on the frontiers of the Cape colony, wrote that "In the late war our cruizers from the Cape kept the Southern Ocean completely clear of the enemy's [French] ships, and allowed the Indian squadron to make such choice of their cruizing ground, that between the two, not a French frigate escaped, nor scarcely a single privateer remained on the Mauritius station for some time before the close of the war." Barrow (1804), 183 and 238-9. On Barrow's activities in the Cape colony see ch. 5 by Eldredge in this volume.

28. Smith (1970a), 237-8.

29. Ibid, 238.

30. Ibid, 321. The Austrian company sent Indian employees upriver on the Nkomati and Maputo rivers in shallow draft longboats, which could carry several tons of freight. Boats going up the Nkomati river reached the territory of the Kosse where ivory porters from the interior took their goods. Hedges (1979), 127, 131.

31. In April 1790, when soldiers in the Portuguese garrison (presumably most were African) led a mutiny against the governor, the local Madolo (Mattoll) chief and his army freed the governor from the fort. In 1793, a new governor helped a claimant to the Tembe chieftaincy come to power, for which the Portuguese received a piece of land. In 1795 the chief of Madolo sought aid from the Portuguese. Soon after the Madolo came to the aid of the Portuguese against the Tembe. When the Portuguese were forced out of the port by the French attack in 1796, Madolo lost power to the Moamba. Upon their return, the Portuguese ingratiated themselves with the Moamba and in 1813 sent soldiers to help them crush a revolt. Captives from these conflicts must have fed the slave trade on a sporadic basis, but it is clear that the initiative in these events remained with the Africans and that the Portuguese were not able to dominate the region. Smith (1970a), 212-2. This dissertation, based on a comprehensive use of oral and archival sources, provides a detailed reconstruction of this entire period.

32. Ibid, 348.

33. Ibid, 224, 236.

34. The French slave trade at Moçambique island peaked between 1785 and 1794. Zimmerman (1967), 19, 21. Trade by foreign ships was legally prohibited off the coast except for the years 1789 to 1800 out of the port of Moçambique, and illicit trade cannot be traced. However, an incident in 1785 indicates that slaves were not available at Delagoa bay when a French ship stopped there. Lobato (1949), 1: 127. The Portuguese had begun to regulate the foreign traffic in slaves, mostly French, by the mid-1780s, but official prohibition on foreign trade at Moçambique island remained in effect until 1853. Although the monopoly in trade held by Moçambique island was broken and other ports were given the right to trade, until 1814 all ships still had to stop and pay import and export taxes at Moçambique, which explains why Quelimane did not emerge as the preeminent slave port until after this time. Zimmerman (1967), 17; Capela and Madeiros (1987), 32-3. It is misleading to designate this as completely "free trade" as does Klein (1978), 77-8.

35. Barrow (1804), 2: 118. Note that Barrow then goes on to make physiological

distinctions between "Kaffers" and "Negroes."

36. de Castilho (1881), 11-2.

37. Both navigational and economic reasons explain why the level and type of trade activity that was going on further north developed later at Delagoa bay. Delagoa bay was the Mozambican port closest to Brazil but in fact proximity was not the main consideration. Ships coming around the tip of Africa were reliant on winds which took them far to the east, and they returned to the east coast by going to the east and north of Madagascar. The first coastal port for the ships was in the north rather than the south, and regulations required that they go to Moçambique island. The trip to Delagoa bay was thus longer than the trip to the north. If a ship could fill its hold with slaves in the north, there was no obvious reason to proceed south. In addition to the extra distance, crews landing at Delagoa bay suffered high morbidity and mortality from disease.

French traders, who dominated the Mozambican slave trade, gained the east African coast from the north side of Madagascar. Their ships did not frequent the Mozambique channel at least in part because French mariners were afraid of its unpredictable weather. The passage was well known to the Portuguese but appeared too dangerous to the French because of the currents and the winds. Sailors were afraid of the Banc de l'Etoile on the southern tip of Madagascar, and of the isles of Europe and les Bassas da India in the channel, and some actually believed that the Isle Juan de Nova was a floating island. French ships thus stayed north and east of Madagascar, and only occasionally sailed as far south as Moçambique island, which was itself just below the furthest point south at which the trade winds could be caught. British ships also took the wide route to the east of Madagascar and did not pass close to Delagoa bay.

The trip to Delagoa bay thus represented exceptionally high costs for a trader. Only steep competition and increased prices at the northern ports, or large supplies and reduced prices at Delagoa bay, would have made the costs of obtaining slaves at Delagoa bay competitive with those to the north and have induced ship captains to go there in spite of the perceived risks. Following the 1820 abolition of the slave trade from Merina-dominated Madagascar, however, French slavers became reliant on Mozambican slave outlets, and increasingly came to Delagoa bay beginning in the early 1820s. Filliot (1974), 107-8; Cooley (1833), 316.

38. Cobbing questioned the delayed expansion of the volume of the slave trade at Delagoa bay because of its location relative to the market for slaves in Brazil. This led Cobbing to quote part of a statement by the British sea captain Owen that "the port is more convenient than any other for direct communication with Brazil," and draw a mistaken conclusion that as the slave trade expanded out of the Mozambican coast "Lourenço Marques received an additional priority because of its excellent harbourage, [and] the 'freshness' of its slaving hinterland." Cobbing (1990), 5.

39. Nourse to Croker, 5 Jan. 1823, in Theal (1903), 9: 20.

40. Smith (1970a), 269.

41. Owen to Croker, 11 Oct. 1823 in Theal (1903), 9:37-9. Also quoted in Eldredge (1992), 11.

42. Hedges (1979), 230-1.

43. Smith (1970a), 262. The Portuguese and British did not cooperate with each other. While the British ships under Owen were in the area, the Portuguese governor Cardinas seized two private English ships and planned to confiscate both ships and

cargo to send to Moçambique island; Owen returned in March 1823 and recovered the vessels only with threats. Ibid, 264-5.

44. Owen comments that "this traffic being their only resource, they take great care to prevent any direct trade between the whalers and natives." This latter passage also suggests that whalers and other traders were still being successfully prevented from trading independently at the bay. Owen (1833), 1: 73, 79, 118. Owen clearly found the company of the Portuguese *degredados* at the fort distasteful, noting that the adjutant had reportedly murdered his father or brother and that the lieutenant had murdered a priest.

45. Nourse to Croker, Sep. 26, 1823, in Theal (1903), 9: 32. The slave trade from the bay was technically in accordance with the Anglo-Portuguese agreements, but the British were nevertheless eager to maintain surveillance over the trade in order to deter its expansion. The British therefore had reason to report the size of the slave trade, lending credibility to British reports.

46. Owen, "The Bay of Delagoa," 1 May 1823, in ibid, 2: 478. An excerpt from this description appears under the label "Extracts from a letter from Captain Owen to the Reverend Dr. Philip," in ibid, 9: 23-4.

47. Cobbing (1991b), 9; also quoted in Eldredge (1992), 12. Cobbing cites the very evidence which refutes his position but, by selectively quoting only part of the evidence, argues the reverse of what the evidence shows. Owen to de Botelho, May 1825, in Theal (1903), 9: 57.

48. Owen to Croker, 7 Apr. 1823, in ibid, 9: 22-3.

49. Cession of the Kingdom of Temby, signed by Kapell, Stengelly, Capenfinick, Shamaguava, encl. in Nourse to Croker, 8 May 1823, in ibid, 9: 25-6. Writing much later about his experiences at Delagoa bay from about June to December 1823, Fynn recorded in his diary that "Mayetha, chief of the Tembe country at the time of my visit, had recently been defeated and many of his subjects sold into slavery. It was, therefore, natural that Mayetha, from seeing the terror of the Portuguese in the presence of a British man-of-war, should rejoice at the opportunity of ceding his country to the British Crown, in prospect of protection for himself and the remnants of his tribe." Stuart (1969), 43.

50. Fynn, "Delagoa Bay," in Theal (1903), 9: 487.

51. Whitworth to Nourse, 29 Apr. 1824, in ibid, 9: 47-8.

52. Portuguese determination and brutality were in frequent evidence, e.g., "The king [of Matoll] then sent a messenger to the governor, suing for peace, and proposing terms, but the governor cut off his ears, nose, and lips, and returned him [the mutilated messenger] to the king with a message that he would destroy them." Whitworth to Nourse, 29 Apr. 1824, in ibid, 9: 47; Whitworth indicated he was writing on behalf of Reverend Threlfall.

53. Manso (1870), 11. Translation mine.

54. The company was given further privileges by a proclamation of 27 October 1825. The agreement permitted the company to establish a factory in Lourenço Marques and another in Inhambane within the year, and to send a ship to both places at least once a year; in return the company was granted the exclusive right to trade ivory for twenty-four years. Had there already been a thriving export trade in slaves prior to 1824, it is highly unlikely that either a commercial company or the Portuguese government would have been preoccupied with monopolizing the ivory trade. Ibid, 11-3.

55. Owen [from Moçambique island] to Croker, 9 Oct. 1823, in Theal (1903), 9: 33. However, in 1824 French slave traders still had to rely on ruses to lure unwitting Africans on board, indicating a dearth of captives already available for enslavement. Eldredge (1992), 11.

56. In addition to the cession treaty signed with the Tembe, Owen signed a co-operative treaty with the Mabudu under Makhasane. Smith (1970a), 267-8.

57. Ibid, 269.

58. Ibid, 272.

59. Ibid, 273-5.

60. Ibid, 275-6.

61. According to the Anglo-Portuguese treaties of 1815 and 1817, slaves leaving Portuguese territories were only permitted to be exported to other Portuguese territories; the trade going to Brazil met this condition, but that in the hands of the French did not.

62. The slaving abuses of these governors were reported by the nonofficial Portuguese traders of the *Companhia do Comercio de Lourenco Marques e Inhambane* who were angry because they had been granted a trade monopoly for the bay in 1824 and were being deprived of profits by the illicit traders. Smith (1970a), 278-83.

63. Ibid, 352; Harries (1981).

64. Stuart (1969), 47.

65. Ibid, 46-7. His description of "destruction" does not necessarily imply anything other than theft of standing crops by hungry people, and there is no indication these Africans had deliberately induced starvation as a strategy of enslavement.

66. *British Parliamentary Papers 292 (1829): Report of the Commissioners of Inquiry upon the Slave Trade at Mauritius, 12 March 1828* , Slave Trade series 76 (Shannon, 1969): 38, cited in Cobbing (1991b). The reference (in the same passage) to immigrants arriving on the frontier of the Cape colony since 1823 fails to demonstrate that the Portuguese were engaged in slave raiding prior to 1823. The appearance of the starving people at the Cape frontier was reported to have been "since 1823," and there is no reason to suppose that it would take years to cover the same ground that could be covered in a matter of months, following either a coastal or an interior route. European travelers passing through the area in the first three decades of the nineteenth century covered comparable distances in trips that lasted for months rather than years. Even if the evidence given to this 1828 inquiry is reliable, it fails to close the chronological gap between the disturbances which began between 1816 and 1818 and the slave trade at Delagoa Bay which expanded after 1823. The reported arrival of refugees on the borders of the Cape Colony after 1823 cannot demonstrate either the existence of a massive slave trade out of Delagoa Bay prior to 1823 or related slave raiding in the Delagoa bay hinterland prior to 1823, as argued by Cobbing.

67. Smith (1970a), 283.

68. Ibid, 351.

69. Kirby (1955), 76-7.

70. Smith (1970a), 287-8.

71. Ibid, 290-2.

72. Ibid, 294-5; Hedges (1979), 243-4. The British traders from Port Natal were also involved in this expedition.

73. Smith (1970a), 297-301.

74. Isaacs (1836), 1: 160. However, Isaacs may have fabricated this conversation since he was intent upon depicting Shaka as a tyrant, as he wrote explicitly in a letter to Fynn. Hedges (1979), 2, citing Isaacs to Fynn, 10 Dec. 1832.

75. Isaacs (1836), 1:166. This is one incident argued by Cobbing to have been a slave raid by the Natal traders, which he assumes was later disguised by the author and participant, Isaacs. I do not find it credible that accounts such as that by Isaacs were written at such a deep conspiratorial level, when incriminating incidents could just as easily have been omitted from the narrative. Hamilton questions Cobbing, noting that he points only to the evidence that one of Isaacs' companions suggested that "they should give ten young maidens by way of cementing their friendship by nuptial ties," but there is no further evidence that this ever happened. Hamilton (1992), 43, n31.

76. Contrary to common perceptions that Shaka retained all of the booty, Isaacs reported that after giving lieutenant King seventy-eight cattle for his help, Shaka "distributed the remainder of the captured herd among his people." Isaacs (1836), 1: 180.

77. Gardiner (1836), 93. Hence, when women were taken captive in conflicts, their fates were presumably determined by whether their male kin had survived. Gardiner notes here that the prohibition against marriage was not designed to limit the sexual activity of men, but merely to prevent them from developing social attachments that would distract them: "I have heard [the prevention of marriage] gravely asserted as one of the wisest enactments for rendering a soldiery efficient, by keeping them thus aloof from family attachments, and unshakled by domestic attractions."

78. Isaacs (1836), 2: 254.

79. Fynn learned about these commercial relationships during his six-month stay at Delagoa bay in 1823. A close reading of the passage indicates that the pronouns "they" and "these people" refer to the "Delagonians," rather than the AmaZulu, which has been a source of confusion in the interpretation of this passage. Viewing these passages in full reveals the continuity of Fynn's references to the "natives of Delagoa," presumably the Tembe and Mabudu on the southern side of the bay, who evidently remain the active subject throughout the text. The misreading and misinterpretation of this passage has been used to argue that the AmaZulu and AmaNdwandwe captured and sold slaves.

80. Stuart (1969), 47-8. Underlined names in brackets are mine; passages in brackets which are not underlined are additions found in this edition of the diary. Fynn retained grammatical correctness in ensuring that the subject of each statement throughout this entire passage was the Delagonians. The "Zulus and Ndwandwes" appear only as the objects of a preposition in this passage and never as the subject.

81. Oral traditions must be used carefully, but informants interested in discrediting Shaka are unlikely to have covered up any slave raiding and slave trading in which Shaka was involved. Informants such as those recorded in the James Stuart Archive reported atrocities committed by Shaka but mentioned no enslavement or transport of captives into the hands of Europeans during his reign. Their silence on the issue of slavery constitutes a strong contraindication for Cobbing's thesis that the AmaZulu under Shaka were involved in slave raiding and slave trading. See the James Stuart Archive of Recorded Oral Evidence, vols. 1-4.

82. Isaacs (1836), 1: 58. At one point Isaacs discovered that Portuguese traders seeking ivory had preceded him at one location but, like himself, had been unsuccessful in obtaining it. Ibid, 205. Fynn reported that at the time he left Natal in July 1831, "a company of Portuguese soldiers from Delagoa Bay" arrived. Kirby (1955), 72. This passage is taken from notes copied from Fynn's original diary by Smith in 1834 before the original was buried with Fynn's brother.

83. Isaacs (1836), 1: 149.

84. Ibid, 2: 236.

85. Maclean (1992), 99.

86. D'Elegorgue [Delegorgue] (1847), reprinted in Bird (1888), 473-4.

87. Hedges (1979), 229.

88. Ibid, 230.

89. Smith (1970a), 322. Smith notes that some traders were said to have spent six or seven months traveling.

90. Ibid, 324-5, 335-6. Parsons notes that trade goods from both coasts had reached the Tsodilo hills in the Kalahari by the eighth century, presumably by a relay trade. He concludes that through the mid-eighteenth century trade in the interior remained in the hands of "Kgatla-Pedi" and "Palaborwa-Pedi." Parsons (forthcoming).

91. Bradlow and Bradlow (1979), 141.

92. Ibid.

93. Campbell (1822), 1: 242, 256. Parsons discusses evidence about VaTsonga traders in the interior, noting the various names by which they were known, including Malukwe, Malokwana, and Makwapa or MaGwamba. He repeats the assumption of other scholars that the term Mahalaseela derives from "*ma-hale-tsela*" ("people from down the road"). A more likely origin would come from the word for cloth, *lesela*, rendering *ma-ha-lesela* as "people from the place of cloth." See Parsons (forthcoming).

94. Parsons (forthcoming).

95. Campbell (1822), 2: 242.

96. Parsons (forthcoming), citing information from missionary Robert Moffat.

97. Kirby (1939), 2: 222. This 1834 reference may be one of the earliest European references to MaShona, the IsiNdebele term for Rozwi and later used for the people otherwise known as BaKalanga, MaKaranga, etc. This source predates the arrival of the AmaNdebele in southern Zimbabwe, indicating either a prior knowledge of these people on the part of the AmaNdebele, or the adoption by the AmaNdebele of a name already in use by other groups in the region.

98. Lye (1975), 297.

99. Kirby (1939), 2: 42-3.

100. Smith (1970a), 325-6.

101. Ibid, 327-8. Specialist traders had emerged by the nineteenth century, and they relocated themselves to the Transvaal as middlemen in the ivory trade. Ibid, 343.

102. Parsons (forthcoming).

103. Lye (1975), 236, 238-9.

104. Kirby (1939), 1: 266. Not long afterward, however, the combination of threats from AmaZulu and AmaSwati enemies to the east and Griqua and Boer enemies to the southwest drove the AmaNdebele north of the Limpopo river.

105. Cobbing (1990), 10.

106. Bradlow and Bradlow (1979), 118.

107. See ch .5 by Eldredge in this volume.

108. Lichtenstein, (1928), 2: 405.

109. Bradlow and Bradlow (1979), 135; Campbell (1815), 299.

110. Backhouse (1844), 203.

111. Lister (1949), 103.

112. Kirby (1955), 34.

113. Ch. 5 by Eldredge in this volume.

114. Arbousset and Daumas (1846), 110.

115. Arbousset (1991).

116. Those who were enslaved were duped into boarding the ship voluntarily; they were not captured by armed slave raiders operating on land near the coast, much less further inland. Arbousset and Daumas (1852), 161-5. The same incident is discussed by Parsons (forthcoming). He speculates that Arbousset was told this story in encoded form to see if he knew what they knew about the slave trade and assumes the BaFokeng never went east before their migration west. The detail included in the story of the ship off the coast suggests, however, that it originated from eyewitnesses; a group of people might easily have covered that amount of territory in a short time. If only a small portion of people identifying themselves as BaFokeng took this journey, their story would still have had time to have entered into the lore of the entire group by the time Arbousset visited them a dozen or so years later. Two further conclusions can be drawn from this passage, however. First, if further rumors or reports of slave raiders penetrated the highveld and reached Europeans opposed to the slave trade, such as Arbousset, they would have reported them. Second, if the first decision of migrants was to go east, and the second alternative chosen subsequently was to go west, it suggests the serious disruptive pressures were coming from the southwest, i.e., the vicinity of the Kora and Griqua who *were* raiding for human captives to sell into the Cape Colony as slaves. See ch. 5 by Eldredge in this volume.

117. Arbousset (1992), 107.

118. Wagner (1980), 313-49.

119. For more on Coenraad de Buys see ch. 5 in this volume. For the de Buys sons see Wagner (1980), 318, 321, and *passim*; ch. 8 by Boeyens in this volume; Agar-Hamilton (1928), 66-9 and *passim*.

120. Smith (1970a), 343-4.

121. Jackson Haight (1967), 287.

122. Albasini claimed that his father was an Italian naval captain and that he himself was born in Portugal in Oporto, but no evidence has surfaced to support these claims. All biographical information about Albasini has been collected from himself or his descendants without independent confirmation of any kind, and investigative efforts to uncover information about his purported father revealed that neither the Italian navy nor Portuguese records contained any information about him. Only at the insistence of an old friend, who said that he knew for certain "by other means" did Ferreira Martins include this biographical sketch, which he himself doubted. Martins (1957), 103-4 n.2. His untraceable past, his physical appearance, and the fact that he was the only person to escape being killed by rebel Africans when the Portuguese fort at Delagoa bay was attacked in 1836 all point to

the strong possibility of mixed European and African ancestry. For the photo see Martins, frontispiece; he also reports that Albasini was the only survivor at the for(p.19). See also ch. 8 by Boeyens in this volume.

123. Albasini claimed to have arrived at Lourenço Marques in 1831. Sometime in the early 1840s he moved to the interior of the Portuguese territory of Mozambique. From there, in 1846, he went to live among the Dutch; by his own account he married Maria Magdalena Van Rensburg from Ohrigstad in 1847. Albasini died in 1888. Martins (1957), 13-29. Boeyens provides additional information on Albasini in ch. 8 in this volume.

124. Wagner (1980), 343, n49.

125. Agar-Hamilton (1928), *passim*; ch. 8 in this volume.

126. Martins (1957), 21.

127. Ibid, 27.

128. That he retained the means to mobilize involuntary labor is evident in the fact that "he was able to furnish blacks to work in the first gold mine in Eersteling south of Pietersburg when, in 1873, it was impossible to find them (blacks), from any other source." Ibid, 28. The provision of laborers as *opgaaf*, a form of tribute or "taxes" collected by the military forces of Buys and Albasini, who were employed as officials in the ZAR government, indicates that the enslavement of Africans continued with government sanction long after slavery and slave trading within the Transvaal had been outlawed. See Agar-Hamilton (1928), *passim*, and ch. 5 by Morton and ch. 8 by Boeyens in this volume.

129. Agar-Hamilton (1928), 69, 192, 215; Wagner (1980), 321, 325; Martins (1957), 29.

130. Cobbing (1988); Eldredge (1992).

131. Hamilton (1992). Hamilton has worked with John Wright, a specialist in AmaZulu history and in the recorded oral traditions of the AmaZulu, to produce the most recent, authoritative summary of the period. Wright and Hamilton (1989), 49-82.

132. Much of his work remains unpublished, but its presentation at a major conference in 1991 led to the wide dissemination of arguments which rest on conjecture and hypothesis. Cobbing (1990, 1991a, & 1991b). In a cover note to the last paper, Cobbing indicated that it was a "first draft" and requested that anyone wishing to quote it should first contact him. As I subsequently presented him with countervailing evidence, including that which appears here, and as none of these three papers or portions thereof have appeared in published form, I have refrained from holding him responsible for errors which appeared in them. I am obliged, however, to refer to some of the evidence he raised in order to reexamine it more carefully.

133. Cobbing (1990), 7.

134. Cobbing (1991a), 14.

135. Capela and Madeiros have devoted extensive energy searching the Maputo archives for nineteenth century slave trade data; Cobbing was apparently not aware of their work, perhaps because it is published in Portuguese. Capela and Medeiros (1987) and personal communications, July 1992. Alan K. Smith used the Lisbon archives for this period and was aware that certain stratagems were necessary to try to ensure nothing was withheld by the archivist; a new search could confirm this. The Lisbon archives have been copied and provided to the Maputo archives,

however, so this has already been part of Capela and Madeiros' research, as well as that of David Hedges and Gerhard Liesegang. Hedges and Liesegang support the interpretation of Portuguese sources and conclusions about the chronology of the Delagoa bay trade presented in Eldredge (1992). Personal com-munications, July 1992. It is hard to believe that there was a conspiracy of silence by the nationals of four countries (i.e. the British, French, Portuguese, and Dutch) regarding Delagoa bay but not the rest of Mozambique for the first two decades of the nineteenth century; it is also hard to believe, if evidence of an extensive pre-1823 Delagoa bay slave trade exists, that these highly respected researchers looking for the evidence have not found it.

136. This is Cobbing's primary contention in (1990).

137. Ibid, quoted in Hamilton (1992), 44.

7

Captive Labor in the Western Transvaal After the Sand River Convention[1]

Fred Morton

Following the 1852 Sand River Convention, at which Boer leaders agreed to prohibit slavery and slave trading north of the Vaal river, slave raiding on the peoples of the Transvaal border continued as did the institution of slavery (in the form of "registered labor") at least up to 1870. Initiative in raiding was taken by the western Transvaal Boers, who operated independently of the AmaSwati-Boer slave trade in the eastern Transvaal of the 1860s documented by Bonner and Delius.[2] Western Transvaal Boers procured women and children as slaves and used them as domestic servants and plantation workers. Slave raids took place with regularity, and those captured probably totalled in the thousands. Determining actual volume is difficult, however, because information was suppressed by the Zuid-Afrikaansche Republiek (ZAR). Although ZAR laws prohibited slave raiding and slavery, ZAR officials, including president Marthinus W. Pretorius and commandant-general Paul Kruger, led raids and owned slaves. Boer raids against the many African communities along the ZAR borders were part of an official policy that was conducted, inter alia, for the purpose of procuring slaves. African subjects of the ZAR were required to assist in these raids and were encouraged to raid on their own for the same purpose. In the post-Convention period, slaves were captured, traded, and used in all parts of the Republic. And, for generations, slave descendants remained in this region.

Existing studies of the Transvaal have dismissed the notion that slave raiding and slavery were part of Boer state policy. Beginning with Agar-Hamilton's *Native Policy of the Voortrekkers* (1928), the literature has certainly conceded that such practices existed in the ZAR but concluded that they were localized, isolated, and erratic.[3] In Walker's words, the "trekkers as a body were certainly neither slavers nor slave-owners."[4]

Agar-Hamilton argues that slave trading and slave holding were confined almost entirely to the eastern Transvaal, and briefly at that, a conclusion that has been supported by more recent work.[5] Even while noting that ZAR officials, including president Pretorius, had "apprentices" or "orphans" in their domestic service, the suggestion that the state condoned, if not promoted, slavery has not been entertained. Instead, ZAR officialdom has been given the benefit of the doubt. Agar-Hamilton argues that the Volksraad lacked the power to prevent the odd individual (especially Bastaards and Portuguese) from enslaving Africans, but its constitution and laws prohibiting slavery and slave trading show that Boer leaders regarded these acts as crimes. Moreover, since Agar-Hamilton, South African English historians in particular have regarded the Boers as too quarrelsome and weak to establish a real government and therefore too powerless to run a slavery system.[6] Afrikaner historians, suspicious of the anti-slavery campaign that reached its climax prior to Britain's annexation of the Transvaal in 1877, portray the clamor over slavery in the ZAR as a red herring for British imperialism.[7]

Registered or bonded labor (*inboekstelsel*), which was widely practiced by Transvaal Boers as it was by whites in the Orange Free State, Natal, and the Cape Colony, has been described as a form of labor service rather than slavery. Agar-Hamilton argues that the Boers adapted the "precedent" of "apprenticeship" (as the system was named in the British Cape) to conditions in the Transvaal, where, he asserts, children were frequently abandoned or sold by their parents. Rules governed the raising of orphans registered as apprentices, "turning them to good account," and releasing them at maturity.[8] A recent assessment argues that "apprenticeship" may not properly be termed slavery on the grounds that Britain prevented the establishment of a formal system of slavery, complete with open trading and a slave code. Instead of being used and traded as chattel, *inboekelinge* were incorporated into settler society as a "dependent servile class." The position of each *inboekeling* depended on demands of the Boer settler and on the ability of the *inboekeling* to resist them. Rather than slaves, they were "unfree servants of white households."[9]

Evidence is now available to challenge these views and to provide a sketch of the western Transvaal slave system. Scattered references found mainly in travellers' accounts published in books and in contemporary newspapers in the Cape, Natal, and Transvaal suggest that slavery was more important than previously thought. Research into newspaper sources, heretofore untapped, has been conducted by Barry Morton and Dan Galbraith.[10] My own historical research on the BaKgatla baga Kgafela and other highveld BaTswana groups, and my study of the missionary correspondence in the Dutch Reformed Church archives has turned up ex-slaves among the BaKgatla in Rustenburg district and produced leads for sleuthing in the region.[11] A fuller description of western Transvaal slavery than the outline that follows will await research in the Transvaal archives in Pretoria, the Hermannsburger Missionary Society archives in Potsdam, and systematic field work among the mainly SeTswana-speaking peoples of the Transvaal. Slave studies based on additional sources may have to mark time, too, until fuller descriptions of the western Transvaal itself become available. So far, a lesson learned from studying slavery in this region is that scholars (this writer included) remain profoundly ignorant of the subjects of Boer rule in the nineteenth century.

Slave Raiding After the Sand River Convention (1852)

At Sand River, Great Britain and the Transvaal Boers under Andries Pretorius readily agreed to prohibit slavery north of the Vaal because both parties knew the prohibition would be a dead letter.[12] Britain was withdrawing its official presence from the interior, and as compensation the Convention signatories were pretending that the Queen's moral influence would remain. Convention euphemisms abound. Britain's "guarantee" of the Transvaal Boers' "right to manage their own affairs," for example, meant that Britain was powerless to abrogate it. The agreement to outlaw slavery carried the same empty force. By signing the Convention, however, Britain was by no means abandoning its interests in the interior or leaving to chance its relations with the Transvaal Boers. Both contracting parties at Sand River considered themselves partners in the ultimate white conquest of south Africa. As one signatory wrote, the

> gradual increase of the white race must eventually though slowly ensure the disappearance of the Black. Providence vindicates this its unalterable law by rendering all the philanthropic efforts that have been made to avert such a destiny subservient to its fulfillment.[13]

The goal of a white south Africa was served by those Convention provisions that Britain did have the power to enforce. Britain obligated itself to disclaim alliances with any of the "colored nations," to prohibit arms sales to Africans, and to provide the Boers with continued access to guns and powder in the Cape colony and Natal.[14]

Officials enforcing anti-slavery regulations in Britain's south African colonies also understood that Boers in the interior practiced slavery. Avoiding laws governing slavery ranked high among the Voortrekkers' motives, and instances of Boer slave raiding and slave trading were reported in most of the years between the trek and the Convention of 1852. As of 1842, John Philip of the London Missionary Society reported that:

> Not only has an active slave-trade been carried on among the Boers residing at Natal; but it is well known that an active trade in children has been carried on between them and the Boers spread over the Bahurutsi country from the Vaal River to the borders of the Colony.[15]

Other references to slaving on the highveld, some involving officials of the Orange River Sovereignty annexed by Britain in 1848, lend support to Philip's broad assertion.[16] British expansionists confined their concern regarding slavery to the Cape because they were seeking Boers in the interior who would accept British authority and pay the taxes to maintain it. The slavery issue would have undermined these efforts. Britain found few supporters, anyway, and soon withdrew its presence. It did so, however, with declarations of friendship toward the Boers and with offers of support in the form of open trade for the development of their states.

In the months following the Convention, Boer raids on African communities increased dramatically. The largest commando of the year, under ZAR Marico district commandant P.E. Scholtz, launched an attack in August against Mosielele's Mmanaana BaKgatla and Sechele's BaKwena. Scholtz's commando killed between sixty and 100 BaKwena, captured 3,000 cattle, and seized as many as 600 women and children, including Sechele's own son.[17] According to Paul Mebalwe, Livingstone's fellow missionary among the BaKwena, captured children were put in sacks up to their necks and hung over the side of the Boers' horses.[18] "Many mothers," wrote Livingstone several months later, "have lost all their children, and many mothers have not yet escaped from the Boers."[19] In September, ZAR commandant-general Hendrik Potgieter led a commando into the eastern Transvaal against Sekwati's BaPedi, who were robbed of 5,000 cattle, 6,000 small stock, and an undetermined number of children.[20] In December Montshiwa's BaRolong, on the western border of the Transvaal, were attacked; they retreated north to gain refuge with Gaseitsiwe's BaNgwaketse.[21] And in early 1853, a large commando raided Mapela's BaLanga and Mughombane's BaKekana in the northern Transvaal, following which the "children of the tribe...were *ingeboekt*, that is to say portioned out among Boer families."[22] Word of frequent Boer raids, all associated with the enslavement of women and children as "apprentices," reached Natal months later.[23] Appeals to British officials at the Cape gained no response. Sechele himself journeyed to Cape Town via Bloemfontein and Port Elizabeth in hopes of sailing to England, but he ran out of money.[24] Cape officials chose neither to relay his grievances to London nor lodge complaints with the Transvaal government; instead, they carried out Britain's obligations under the Convention that weakened African defenses against Boer commandos. The Cape prohibited merchants fro selling

FIGURE 7.1 The Western Transvaal, 1852–1870.

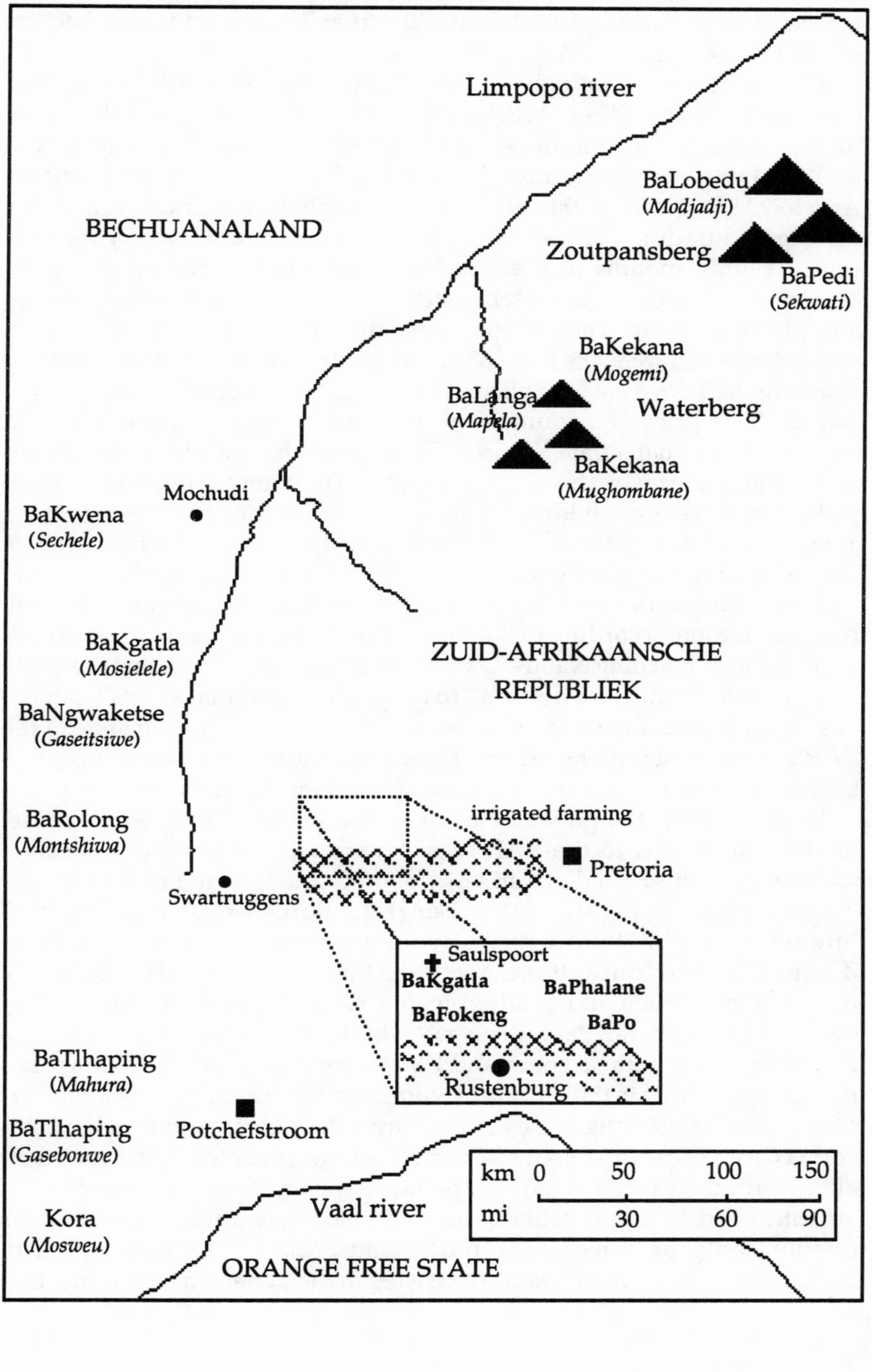

arms or ammunition to Africans, and police arrested Transvaal African laborers leaving the Cape for home with either. Gunpowder soon became scarce in areas outside ZAR control.[25]

The ZAR, too, complied with the Convention by legislating against slavery and slave trading. Articles 10 and 224 of the ZAR constitution duly incorporated the slave-trade/abolition provisions of the Convention, and in 1857 Pretorius proclaimed that ZAR officials publicize and enforce Article 224.[26] None of this was taken seriously in the Transvaal, where raiding and trading seemed the natural response to anti-slavery declarations. Within months of Pretorius's proclamation, commandos set out against Mapela's BaLanga, Gasebonwe's BaTlhaping, Mahura's BaTlhaping, and Mosweu's Kora. The raids produced thousands of cattle and hundreds of children.[27] In 1859, the *Natal Mercury* published the account of a recent visitor to the Transvaal who alleged there were many buyers and sellers of slaves. "The price of a young Kafir is from £5 to £20; they are inbooked [*inboekt*] at the magistrate's office...."[28] Most of the trade was fed by Boer raids, particularly in the northern and northeastern Transvaal, which yielded hundreds of children. The raid on Modjadji's BaLobedu in 1861 alone netted 400 captives.[29] But by 1859 a small-scale Boer-AmaSwati slave trade was underway, lasting until the mid-1860s and involving Boers who exchanged cattle, horses, and dogs for children captured by the AmaSwati. Annual volume, according to Bonner, approximated several hundred children. Reports reaching Natal and the Cape at the time alleged that the Boers and the AmaSwati were doing a "roaring trade" and that slaves from the Transvaal were being were traded as well in Delagoa bay.[30] In spite of the ZAR's legal prohibitions, ZAR officials monitored the Boer-AmaSwati traffic, and children were in some cases passed on to president Pretorius. [31]

In 1866, when the governor of the Cape colony, Philip Wodehouse, finally complained to the ZAR regarding reports of slavery and slave-raiding, Pretorius issued a fresh series of proclamations and notices forbidding slave trading, registering (*inboeking*) of children, or transferring indentured children.[32] Within months, slave raiding resumed with attacks on the Zoutpansberg and on the BaKekana under the regent Mogemi ("Machem"), from whom women and children were seized. These raids were led by commandant-general Paul Kruger.[33] In 1868 Kruger returned to the Zoutspansberg with a commando 900-strong and attacked Mapela's BaLanga, resulting in the capture of women and children.[34] In the same year Montshiwa's BaRolong were attacked by a Boer commando under field-cornet Cronje. The inhabitants of two villages were captured and carted off along with their cattle.[35] At this point, however, British interest in such atrocities had become keener than in the past, given that since 1867 the interior had proven resources in diamonds. Slavery became topical in Parliament, whose members were assisted in their concern with a substantial 1869 command paper, entitled *Correspondence Relating to the Alleged Kidnapping and Enslaving of Young Africans by the People of the Trans-Vaal Republic*.[36] Uys has noted that Britain's interest in slavery in the Transvaal disguised its imperial ambitions and those of the settlers in Natal and the Cape, but his suggestion that allegations in the command paper were trumped up for this purpose ignores many instances of slave raiding and trading that had been reported steadily since the Sand River Convention.[37]

Slavery in the ZAR

Children and women captured during commando raids or purchased from African suppliers such as the AmaSwati were supposed to be registered by the ZAR as *inboekelinge* (registerees) and to remain in service until adulthood. Estimates of the number duly registered, together with those transferred extralegally to new owners, range from several hundred to 3,000 per annum.[38] In 1866, Gideon Steyn of Potchefstroom estimated the total population of *inboekelinge* in the ZAR to be "at least 4,000."[39] Using Steyn's figure with somewhat later estimates of Transvaal's white population suggest that *inboekelinge* constituted at least 10 percent of the Boer community.[40] Few descriptions of *inboekstelsel* have been uncovered pertaining to the western and central Transvaal, where most Boer farmers in the ZAR lived. According to Delius and Trapido's description of "apprenticeship" as it functioned in the eastern Transvaal, Boer owners kept *inboekelinge* on their farms, where they were taught skills, used as herders, and put to work in the fields. Many learned methods of stone cutting and building, brickmaking, roof thatching, wagon repair, hunting, gun maintenance, cookery, veterinary and folk medicine, and ploughing. Children grew to maturity speaking Dutch, and *inboekelinge* raised in wealthier homes were often literate and familiar with the Dutch Bible and catechism.[41]

Though legally entitled to good treatment and ultimately their freedom, *inboekelinge* were abused and seldom manumitted. As early as 1844, the Adjunct Raad at Potchefstroom included in its thirty-three articles governing the Transvaal a law governing "masters and servants." The Raad recognized the master's "right to maintain discipline properly among his servants. But there shall be no ill-treatment; if that does take place, the servant ill-treated shall be taken away and the master shall be punished...."[42] In 1859, the ZAR Volksraad introduced a similar code regulating the treatment of "colored servants" and instructed field-cornets to enforce it. Servants were to be "well treated," ill-treatment was punishable by fine, and selling of servants was prohibited.[43] Yet the evidence indicates that ZAR officials ignored the code, just as they had violated legal prohibitions against slave raiding and slave trading, and recognized the absolute authority of an individual Boer owner over the *inboekeling* as property. Among reports of mistreatment of *inboekelinge* in the Transvaal, only one example exists of an owner who was divested of his servants, that following evidence of extreme abuse. The divestment case involved a British resident of Rustenburg, named Fitzgerald, who had tortured two of his eight-year-old female *inboekelinge* by inserting a hot poker in their vaginas. Their bodies were covered with burns and bruises. He was arrested and sentenced to a year's hard labor, but the sentence was remitted, and he was ordered to pay a small fine.[44] Other press reports appeared regarding unpunished and unfined acts of torture, beating, or killing of *inboekelinge,* though one man was fined for killing a "kaffir" trying to "entice away his servants."[45] In practice the *inboekstelsel* was a permanent condition enforced by the Boer community. As one observer stated in 1859:

> I never saw a full grown Kafir sold, and they are reputed free; but in case of endeavoring to escape are caught and punished.... They will tell you that they are...apprenticed till the period of manhood, when they are freed. Don't believe it. Unless they make a run for it...they are slaves for life.[46]

Upon reaching adulthood, *inboekelinge* were known to marry, raise families, and even to begin farming on their own. But they settled close to their former owners and remained ever liable for service, as did their children. On Schaapkraal, a farm in the Rustenburg district where twenty such families lived, as late as 1888 the children were often sent to work for their former "baasen."[47]

Slaves were procured through raids and purchase in the 1850s and early 1860s when irrigated, cash-crop agriculture was being developed in the central and western Transvaal. On a line between Swartruggens and Pretoria, and primarily in the hills around Rustenburg, Boer farms produced sugar cane, coffee, maize, wheat, as well as tobacco, cotton, oranges, and other kinds of fruit.[48] Most of these crops were being raised as early as the 1851–52 growing season.[49] Cash crops, together with cattle, wool, and the usual products of the hunt and interior trade—ivory, ostrich feathers, and karosses—were exported to the Orange Free State, to Natal, and, via Potchefstroom, to the Cape.[50] Profitable markets for products other than game trophies and cattle failed to materialize in the years before Kimberley, however, and periodic droughts also prevented the plantation districts from succeeding.[51]

Though no direct evidence is available to prove it, the chances are that slave raiding increased because cash cropping was being attempted. In Rustenburg, for example, large groups of women were seen in the early 1860s weeding the fields of the commandant-general.[52] There is no question that the demands for labor in western and central Transvaal districts such as Rustenburg were substantively different than in areas of the eastern Transvaal, where hunting and herding dominated the local economy.[53] It remains necessary nonetheless to explain how these farms were brought into production; the evidence so far is unavailable. Approximately 70,000 African (mainly BaTswana) subjects of Boer rule lived in the cash-crop districts, but it is doubtful that the Boer community had sufficient power to coerce them into providing all its labor requirements. BaTswana leaders resisted having their subjects meet Boer labor demands that interfered with their own seasonal farming and herding requirements.[54] These leaders, or *dikgosi*, accepted the authority of ZAR field-cornets and other officials and provided some labor as tribute, but they retained their cattle, hunted and traded ivory and other game trophies, raised crops (including cash crops), and acquired substantial wealth. Boer officials protected the position of *dikgosi*, whose privileges and material standard of living exceeded most Boers, because they and their people assisted the Boers in obtaining ivory and in raiding other Africans for slaves.

African Auxiliaries in the Rustenburg District

The Boers of the Rustenburg district participated in nearly all of the recorded commando raids that resulted in young captives, and they were customarily assisted by armed regiments provided by BaTswana *dikgosi*. Featuring prominently in this respect were Kgamanyane's BaKgatla, Mogale's BaPo, Mokgatle's BaFokeng, and Ramokoka's BaPhalane. These groups were allied with the early Voortrekkers of Hendrik Potgieter in repulsing attacks from Mzilikazi's AmaNdebele and in Potgieter's initial raids on Mankopane's BaLanga and Sekwati's BaPedi in the northern and eastern Transvaal.[55] Ivory trading also factored into the Boer-BaTswana formula. Potgieter settled next to Mokgatle and not far from Pilane (Kgamanyane's father and predecessor), both of whom were already in contact with ivory traders beyond the Limpopo.[56] After Potgieter removed to the northern Transvaal, Rustenburg's leadership was assumed by the young field-cornet Paul Kruger, who in 1852 became Rustenburg district commandant. Rustenburg was by then a slave trading center with its own resident dealer.[57] Between 1852 and 1868, Kruger took part in all the commando raids against Africans in the northern Transvaal and was accompanied by African auxiliaries from the Rustenburg district in all cases.[58]

African auxiliaries owned guns and used them to subordinate weaker groups under the authority of their *dikgosi*, and to hunt for game trophies, principally ivory. Kruger also prohibited Boer farmers in the district from coercing their nonmilitary labor. As a consequence, these men and their followers acquired wealth in cattle, plantations, tools, buildings, and dependents. In 1862, the combined population under Kgamanyane and Mogale alone was estimated at 11,000.[59] Between 1852 and 1862, the town of Mokgatle's BaFokeng more than doubled in size, from 300 to more than 600 houses.[60]

Proper ways or streets ran through the village, about 30 feet broad.... Each place consisted of a circular wall, about 4 1/2 feet high, plastered much more evenly than any ordinary Dutch house I met with in the country.... The thatching was done with a fine grass, laid with great compactness and regularity, and secured on ribs of white rattan, this whole having a better appearance than any thatching I have seen in this country.... Many of the doorways were supplied with good plank doors on hinges, secured by lock, padlock, or bolt, which latter they buy in town, but the door was made by themselves from planks sawn in the bush, and I counted nine pit and cross-cut saws at the Chief's Kraal.... The floors were carefully cemented.... Some of the superior houses had an inner circle wall, for a bedroom, with a small doorway, also polished to imitate a door frame, and a few had cupboards built up, in which they put their various little traps, and took great pride showing their mode of fastening them. One large house belonging to one of the principal wives of the Chief, had a number of compartments beautifully moulded and polished, with great taste, and furnished among other utensils with Basins, Cups, and Saucers, Pots and Pans, and even Foot pans, bought at Rustenburg, there was also a Box of Tools in one corner of the house, which were turned to good account, for they sat us down upon chairs made after European models, though somewhat roughly, and Tables the same.

We found our way to the house and courtyard of the old Chief.... He had an intelligent countenance, was dressed in European clothes, and was engaged in making a gun-stock, which was admirably carved, and fitted to the barrel as well {as it could be done]. He was using several carpenters' tools in its manufactures. [Mokgatle] has twenty-six wives and seventy sons.... Moshesh [Moshoeshoe] had sent him six of his daughters for wives the month before, being desirous to have an alliance with him...against the Boers. [Mokgatle] is however, ever, himself on the best terms with the Boers and all around him, partly in consequence of the wise and just policy of Paul Kruger, the Commandant, who has prevented, by his influence, any injustice being done to the tribe by any in the district, and the old Chief bears a good character with all.... [Mokgatle] has been in the present spot twenty-six years....

We then proceed to inspect his wagons, of which he had several, and what is more, Wagon-houses to protect them from the weather; there was also a splendid Stone Cattle Kraal, in extent about an acre and a half, which, like the piggeries, were kept in excellent order; there was pottery of all sizes and shapes...which were used for storing mealies. In one yard there were vices, Grindstones, Ploughs, Candle Moulds, and many other Instruments of Manufacture, besides tools, and there must have been a considerable sum laid out in this way.[61]

The central town of Kgamanyane's BaKgatla was surrounded by ten to twelve smaller settlements. In addition to wagon houses, horses, cattle, and guns, Kgamanyane maintained forty-eight separate households, one for each of his wives.[62] Part of the wealth accumulated by BaTswana *dikgosi* and their subjects was derived from independent ventures. Kgamanyane traded in ivory north of the Limpopo, and some of Mokgatle's men worked in the Cape colony, where they purchased guns and manufactured goods.[63]

Wealth and power belonged to *dikgosi* who served the Boers. In their successive reigns, Kgamanyane and his father, Pilane (d.1850), attached seven previously independent African groups to their authority, some forcibly.[64] Among these were Bohosi's BaBididi, who were placed at the disposal of local Boer farmers. Bohosi was killed, and his son Mochela Mfatlha (called "Zwaartbooi" by the Boers) lived on the farm of Theunis Snijman. Zwaartbooi, who accompanied the Boers when they visited Mzilikazi in 1857, was governed by Kgamanyane and later by Mokgatle.[65] Kgamanyane's regiments also delivered captured children to the Boers, as the Kgatla themselves remember in one of their *maboko* (praise songs) to Kgamanyane:

Rona kafantle retshaba Kgalemi,	We who are outside flee from the Rebuker,
retshabile Kgalemi wagaPilane;	we've fled from the Rebuker, Pilane's son;
ogapa dikgomo, ogapa legatho, ogapa leditantane, Tumisi,	he seizes cattle, he seizes people, too, the Famed One also seizes infants still at the breast;
ogapa lebanyana babaanyang banyana obagapa asabarue, obanaya banna babahubidu.	but the infants he seizes he does not keep, he gives them to the white [literally "red"] men.[53]

BaTswana allies were also expected to retrieve runaway slaves. In 1848, David Livingstone's party encountered four BaLanga children at the farm of Johannes Pretorius near Rustenburg and tried to induce them to escape. "They said they had often run away," wrote Livingstone, "but Mokhatla [Mokgatle] caught them and returned them to their owners."[67] Mokgatle, who reigned from 1837 to 1889, was later remembered by the BaFokeng as a *kgosi* who "did what the Boers wanted...."[68]

The BaTswana-Boer partnership increased the power and wealth of leaders in both camps. Commandant-general Kruger owned thirteen farms in Rustenburg district, on two of which Kgamanyane and most of his BaKgatla lived.[69] Kruger had his own skilled African work force, including sawyers, tanners, masons, thatchers, ploughmen, wagon drivers, and elephant hunters, not to mention women agriculturalists who worked his fields. As head of ZAR commandos and their African auxiliaries, Kruger also controlled the supply of *inboekeling* labor to the Boer community.[70] After the mid-1860s, however, the close relationship between Kruger and his African auxiliaries deteriorated for reasons that are not yet clear, though parallel events are suggestive. As weak markets for cash-crops undermined their plantations, large landowners such as Kruger pressed their auxiliaries to pay them in cash and livestock for rights to land and, through the Volksraad, introduced taxes that Kruger and his relatives, as the local officials, collected. Not long after diamonds were discovered at Kimberley, Kruger began forcing Africans in his district to build dams and irrigation works. Attempts were made, too, to disarm them. In 1870 Kgamanyane's resistance to these measures resulted in his flogging by Kruger before the *dikgosi* of the district, soon after which Kgamanyane and most of his followers emigrated to Bechuanaland.[71] During these few years, at least four other African groups fled Rustenburg district.[72] As Africans were pushed out, land values rose, properties were subdivided for sale, and large farmowners became involved in land speculation.[73]

Apparently, in the late 1840s and early 1850s, slaves were captured on raids for the development of plantations from which little capital was ever realized. By the early 1860s, labor was plentiful in the Rustenburg district, but unemployable. When diamonds spurred the revival of irrigated farming, Kruger and others turned to their African clients to deliver the necessary labor and to join in fresh commandos that produced slaves. But raiding without censure became impossible by 1868, by which time diamonds had been discovered and Britain had taken up once again the issue of slavery in the ZAR. In that year Kruger, with regiments from Kgamanyane, Mokgatle, Mogale, and Ramokoka, raided the VhaVenda in the northern Transvaal and returned with young captives, but the ZAR Volksraad ordered Kruger to return them.[74]

The Consequences of Slavery

Most slaves, when adults, were incorporated into African societies in the Transvaal, especially after the mid-1860s. Though wrested away from their parent societies as children, older slaves had little difficulty intermingling with Africans in the neighborhood of their Boer owners. Their artisanship, as well as knowledge of the Boers and the Dutch language, were in demand in Transvaal African communities. Some ex-slaves tended to retain the stamp of Boer culture and live clustered in towns or on farms as *Oorlams* ("civilized", i.e., Dutch-speaking people), known to the Boers as *Oorlam Kaffers*.[75] For the most part, however, *inboekelinge* were readily absorbed into African societies and sometimes entered royal families. *Kgosi* Mokgatle formally married the female servant of one of his Boer neighbors and repeated the nuptials once contact with her family had been established.[76] Full appreciation of ex-*inboekelinge* in Transvaal African societies awaits the collection of family histories and close examination of governmental and missionary records, but the information available from Dutch Reformed Church (DRC) correspondence and other sources regarding the BaKgatla of Saulspoort and Bechuanaland suggests that ex-slaves played a central role in the transformation of African societies during the mineral revolution.

When missionary Henry Gonin arrived in Rustenburg in 1862 for the purpose of establishing a DRC station in the area, he encountered ex-slaves in Rustenburg town and on the surrounding farms. At Welgeval, where Gonin opened his first station, his first enquirers were Dutch-speaking Africans who had grown up on Boer farms and homes. Among them were "Januari," who worked for Gonin as a servant and interpreter and was eventually christened "Petrus," and Vieland, christened "Stephanus" by Gonin. When a boy, January was among the women and children stolen by a large Boer commando during their raid on the BaKwena capital of Dithubaruba, near Molepolole, in 1852. Vieland, too, was captured when young.[77] Gonin also baptized two brothers, Petrus and Abraham Phiri, who as boys had been taken from the Pilansberg, north of Rustenburg, and sent [or perhaps traded?] to the Cape, where they worked as domestic servants until their majority. Gonin was also befriended by a man named David, who taught Gonin how to speak SeTswana and served as his interpreter. David spoke and read SeSotho and SeTswana and understood IsiXhosa, Dutch, "and a little English." He had been converted by the Wesleyans in Grahamstown in the eastern Cape.[78]

Gonin's mission at Welgeval also attracted ex-*inboekelinge* living nearby. Welgeval was situated amidst the farms of Paul Kruger's son-in-law, Sarel Eloff, within riding distance of Saulspoort, one of Kruger's farms. Nearly all the *inboekelinge* who sought out Gonin in the 1860s were residents on the farms of these two landowners. They came to Gonin already able to read, and their skills enabled Gonin to build his mission station.[79] They were also the subjects of *dikgosi* and their headmen, whom the Boers termed *kapteins* ("captains," "chiefs"). Several settlements were located near Gonin's farm of Welgeval and were known by the name of their *kapteins*—Sentswe, Moseleketse, and Tshomankane. The largest settlement in the district was Kgamanyane's, located at the northeastern fringe of the Pilansberg, on Kruger's farm, Saulspoort. By law, only four *inboekelinge* could be kept on a single farm and then for only a bonded period.[80] There was no restriction, however, on the number of ex-*inboekelinge* who collected on a farm and no limit on the number of African settlers providing labor in return for the use of the land. Such tenants were not protected from the farmer by ZAR officials, and Gonin cites examples of attempts by farmers to coerce them, but in the 1860s Boers provided inducements for ex-*inboekelinge* and African settlers to remain on the farm and keep them from running away.[81] Ex-*inboekelinge* gravitated to Saulspoort and other settlements, where they were employed as interpreters, artisans, and given farmland for themselves and their families.[82]

Kgamanyane's flight to Bechuanaland in 1870 transformed the history of the BaKgatla and created new opportunities for ex-slaves to join Kgamanyane's community. Kgamanyane and his son, Linchwe, who soon succeeded to the throne, established a new capital at Mochudi beyond Boer control and began the process of transferring his BaKgatla followers in Saulspoort to their new home. Saulspoort remained a Christian center with an ex-slave core. Ex-*inboekelinge* joined the congregation and served as teachers, catechists, and servants to missionaries. Linchwe (1875-1920) brought over from Saulspoort to Bechuanaland a number of Christianized ex-*inboekelinge* to work as teachers and interpreters in Mochudi and other BaKgatla villages. The BaKgatla village of Sikwane, located on the Madikwe (Marico) river, was headed by a priest named Leoke Mariri, of *inboekeling* origin, and was for years the largest Christian community among the BaKgatla.[83] Thomas Phiri, son of one of Gonin's early ex-*inboekeling* converts, headed the congregation at nearby Mathubudukwane.[84] Leading members of the BaKgatla royal family married women from this Christian group and adopted important features of its social outlook. Linchwe needed the Saulspoorters to educate talented members of the royal family, establish English-medium schools, and in other ways assist the BaKgatla in interpreting events and holding their own in a volatile region. Friendly contacts maintained by African DRC ministers proved especially valuable. Mariri's friend, David Matsawi, was an LMS priest in the Cape colony north of Kimberley in the early 1880s, when English land-grabbing became endemic. Matsawi, whose two daughters married Linchwe's closest brothers, Ramono and Segale, helped prepare the BaKgatla in the 1890s to deal with the threat posed by imperialists operating in the Cape colony against the BaTswana kingdoms of Bechuanaland.[85] Matsawi and other ex-*inboekelinge* also enabled Linchwe to gain control of the DRC establishment inside the BaKgatla kingdom.

Future studies of slavery in the Transvaal might therefore pay close attention to the formation of mission communities and developments within African societies during and after the period of slavery. Uncovering kinship and other connections between ex-*inboekelinge* and free African communities will be difficult because of the stigma attached to persons of slave origin. Informants with *inboekeling* origins are likely to conceal the fact.[86] Patient genealogical research nevertheless may reveal how individual ex-*inboekelinge* were spliced to royal and commoner lineages, just as a survey of ward and surname identities can suggest how clusters of ex-

inboekelinge were absorbed into entire societies. Focused studies are still possible, it would seem. Whole villages bearing the earmarks of ex-*inboekeling* origin, such as Sikwane and Mathubudukwane, await field research.

Unexplored, too, is the question as to when, if ever, slavery was effectively abolished in the Transvaal. Uys alleges that, during Britain's temporary annexure of the Transvaal (1877–81), Transvaal administrator Theophilus Shepstone "perpetuated the apprenticeship system by assigning large numbers of women and children to Transvaal farms."[87] Widespread ownership of slaves was alleged at the time.[88] Slavery continued after the restoration of the ZAR, according to one observer, at least until the South African war (1899–1902).[89] For certain, as late as 1895 Transvaal Boers were buying female slaves at Nkomati for £40.[90] And during the South African war, as Nasson notes, the *agterryers* (African auxiliaries) riding with Boer commandos contained a significant *inboekelinge* element.[91] In other words, slavery, and its by-products, persisted in some form during the mineral revolution, the establishment of a migrant labor system, and the spread of British rule in southern Africa.

Notes

1. This is a revised version of "Slave-raiding and Slavery in the Western Transvaal after the Sand River Convention (1852)," *African Economic History* (1992), 20: 99-118.

2. Bonner (1983), 81-4, 90-3; Delius (1984), 35-6, 136-47.

3. Agar-Hamilton (1928), 169-95, esp. 193.

4. Walker (1957), 281.

5. Agar-Hamilton (1928), 169-195; Bonner (1983), 81-4, 90-3; Delius (1984), 35-6, 136-7.

6. Agar-Hamilton (1928) 93. De Kiewiet (1929) attributes slavery (or rather the "abuses from which the apprenticeship system suffered") to a weak government unable to curb the excesses of a minority of the white population, mostly in the Zoutpansberg: 105-7, 242-56. In other accounts, ZAR ineptitude during this period is stressed usually without mention of slavery. Cf. Thompson (1969), 424-46; Davenport (1981), 106-7, 120-26; Omer-Cooper (1988), 95-7; Thompson (1990), 96-107. Macmillan (1963) portrays ZAR rule as outright conquest resulting in deprivation of African civil and land rights, but he makes no references to slavery, esp. 358-61. Two recent surveys assert that ZAR officials sanctioned slavery and benefited personally, but they provide few details and cite no primary sources. Cf. Parsons (1982), 120-21 and Saunders (1988), 144-9.

7. Uys (1933); Kistner (1952).

8. Agar-Hamilton (1928),169-82.

9. Delius and Trapido (1983); See also Trapido (1976).

10. Graduate students in History at Indiana University. Morton, who has contributed ch. 9 to this volume, is conducting his own research on nineteenth

century Ngamiland in northwestern Botswana, Galbraith on nineteenth-century western Transvaal African communities.

11. Morton (1988), Morton (1985).

12. Part of the Convention reads: "It is agreed that no slavery is, or shall be, permitted or practised in the country to the north of the Vaal River by the emigrant farmers." Eybers (1969), 358.

13. William S. Hogge quotation in Galbraith (1978), 257-8.

14. For the text of the Convention, Eybers (1969), 357-9.

15. Macmillan (1963), 222.

16. See ch. 5 by Elizabeth Eldredge in this volume.

17. Ramsay (1991), 1: 102-3. Kgari was later returned to Sechele by M. W. Pretorius. Ibid, 108; for the attack on Mosielele at Mabotsa, see report of R. Edwards, ca. 1853, in Schapera (1974), 140-1. Also Wallis (1945), 1, 154; Schapera (1960), 84-91.

18. Jousse (1853), 17. Scholtz's commando may have attacked the BaKwena in part because they regarded Sechele's territory as a refuge for their runaway slaves. According to Mebalwe, Sechele told the Boers before the battle that he would give them any Bushmen that had fled to his territory, but he would not hand over Mosielele and his followers, who had fled to Sechele's after being attacked by the Boers at Mabotsa. Ibid, 16. I am grateful to Barry Morton for this reference.

19. Livingstone to Mary Livingstone, 14 Jan. 1853, in Schapera (1959), 2: 200.

20. Delius (1984), 38.

21. Sillery (1952), 173.

22. Kruger (1969), 47. See also ibid, 42-3.

23. *NM*, 9 Jun. 1853; see also ; *GJ*, 30 Dec. 1854; *NM*, 31 Jan. 1855.

24. *NM*, 28 Apr. 1853; Schapera (1974), 144-51; Sillery (1952), 19. Sechele's case did reach the Secretary of State for the Colonies in a memorial presented by the London and Wesleyan missionary societies, the Aborigines Protection Society, and the British and Foreign Anti-Slavery Society. Ramsay (1991), 1: 110-2.

25. Theal (1969), 1: 435; *NM*, 9 Jun. 1853, 20 Dec. 1854; Schapera (1974), 89n.

26. C. 4141: 6; Eybers (1969), 364, also 414-5 for Pretorius's detailed instructions to field-cornets regarding the treatment of "coloured servants"; Walker (1957), 28 & n. See also Kistner (1952), 237-8.

27. Theal (1969), 1: 434; *NM*, 3 Jun. 1858; *GJ*, 7 Dec. 1858 and 26 Mar. 1859; Collins (1965), 155-6; Shillington (1985), 19-20. See also Wallis (1953), 140, re in LeHurutshe a Dutch-speaking boy known as January (by context probably MoTlhaping), who "had been caught young by the Boers."

28. "The Transvaal Country," by "a Recent Traveller (an intelligent young Englishman)," *NM*, 13 Mar. 1859. These figures agree with Struben (1920), 86-7, and Holden (1855), 388. See also *NM*, 9 Jun. 1853, 11 Apr. 1855, & 4 Aug. 1868.

29. Das Neves (1879), 191-2. See also statement of J.H. Roselt, editor of *TA*, in C. 4141: 45.

30. Report of E.T. Rathbone, *NM*, 26 May 1859; Bonner (1983), 81-3; 91-2. For reports of very active trading, reprint of the Cape journal, *Wekker*, in *NM*, 12 Sep. 1861, reprint of *Cape Mail* story in *NM*, 18 Jul. 1862, and *NM*, 6 Dec. 1864. Trading "black ivory" from the Zoutpansberg into Delagoa Bay was also reported in the mid-1860s. *NM*, 24 Feb. 1866, quoting report from the *Republican*(Pretoria). See also ch. 8 by Boeyens in this volume.

31. Delius (1984), 98, 139. See also Burke (1969), 114.

32. For Wodehouse's letter, Aborigines' Protection Society (1881), 2-3; for Pretorius's proclamations, Cory (1940), 179; reprint from the Pretoria *Republican* in *NM*, 24 Feb. 1866.

33. Kruger (1969) 98-101; *NM*, 13 Oct. & 24 Nov. 1868; *TA*, 2 Mar. 1868; Theal (1969), 1: 484f; Delius (1984), 104; Struben (1920), 90. For Kruger's attack on Mogemi, see also Jackson (1982), 22-3, which omits mention of children captives.

34. Annexures H, I, & J in C.4141: 72-4; M. Lynch to editor,*TA*, 4 Aug. 1868; *TA*, 5 Feb. 1868; *NM*, 19 May & 1 Jun. 1868; Theal (1969), 1: 487.

35. Montshiwa to editor, *NM*, 4 Nov. 1868. Montshiwa referred to the people of one of these villages as "Balala," indicating that they were probably *batlhanka* or servile BaKgalagadi or BaSarwa under the BaRolong. See ch. 9 in this volume; for Cronje's attacks, see also ibid, 4, 17, & 19 Nov. 1868, 25 Feb. 1869; TA, 3 Nov. 1868; Matthews (1945), 19.

36. C. 4141.

37. Uys (1933), 74-6.

38. Harries, (1981), 326. The lower estimate, based only on the Boer-AmaSwati trade, is from Bonner (1983), 92, and Delius (1984), 138. The larger figure, which assumes all forms of procurement, is from letter extract 27 Apr. 1868, C. 4141: 42.

39. Steyn to Wodehouse, 12 Mar. 1866, C. 4141: 4.

40. The figure of 40,000 Transvaal whites is taken from *a late 1870s estimate* in Silver (1877), 6, 44; For similar figures, War Office (1881), 63, 69; Aylward (1881), 16; Uys (1933), 319.

41. Delius and Trapido (1983), 53-81.

42. Eybers (1969), 356.

43 . See articles 37-46 & 54 in Instructions to the Field-Cornets, 17 Sep. 1858, in Eybers (1969), 413-5.

44. *NM*, 14 Mar. 1867, 6 Oct. & 14 Nov. 1868; *TA*, 21 Feb., 14 Mar., & 16 May 1867.

45. *NM*, 24 Mar. 1868; For unpunished crimes, see *NM*, 6 Oct. 1868, 31 May and 31 Dec. 1870; *TA*, 4 Dec. 1866, 10 Jun. 1868.

46. "The Transvaal Country, By a Recent Traveller [an intelligent young Englishman]," *NM*, 13 Mar. 1859; see also Holden (1855), 388-9.

47. Gonin to DRC, 27 Apr. 1888, 438-9, 15/7/2(C), DRCA. Translation of all DRC correspondence from the Dutch by Mr. Wom van den Akker, Gaborone. See also Delius (1984), 145.

48. *NM*, 30 Dec. 1852, 21 Jul. 1859, 11 Dec. 1866, & 30 Apr. 1867; *TA*, 29 May, 12 Jun., 17 Jul., 25 Sep.1866; Child (1973), 39; War Office (1881), 52-4. Farms in the Marico area north of Zeerust also raised coffee, sugar cane, and cotton. *TA*, 31 Jan. 1867.

49. Sanderson (1860), 246-7.

50. *NM*, 11 Dec. 1866; *TA*, 29 May & 26 Jun. 1866; Sanderson (1860), 243, 246-7.

51. *NM*, 11 Dec. 1869, 9 & 30 Apr. 1867. The 1865–66 drought killed an estimated 10,000 sheep in the Swartruggens area alone. Ibid, 25 Jan. 1966; See also *TA*, 12 Jun. 1866.

52. *GJ*, 11 Oct. 1862, reprint of a *Zuid Afrikaan* article, "The Natives in the Transvaal."

53. Delius and Trapido (1983), 62-4, often citing Wagner (1980).

54. The population figure is based on War Office (1881), 69, using estimates for Heidelberg, Pretoria, Rustenburg, Potchefstroom, and Marico districts [See Silver

(1877), 6]. For resistance to labor demands, principally through emigration, Agar-Hamilton (1928), 51-2; Breutz (1953), 91, 183 and Breutz (1987), 413-4.

55. Breutz (1953), 18, 341, 413; Schapera (1959), 2: 57-8.

56. *GJ*, 8 Aug. 1844; D'Elegorgue (1847), 2: 340, 410-5, 434. Pilane was also among those prosperous *dikgosi* who supplied ivory, along with grain and skins, to Mzilikazi before his migration north from the western Transvaal. Two men who travelled through Mzilikazi's territory in 1832 and 1833 noted that "Pilni[Pilane] has under him several villages of quite considerable size." Lemue (1834), 271. Thanks to Barry Morton for this reference and a translation thereof.

57. Holden (1855), 388.

58. BaTswana regiments also accompanied Kruger's commando against Moshoeshoe's BaSotho in 1858 and 1865. Schapera (1965), 63n, 66-7, 68n, 69-70; Schapera (1942), 10; Breutz (1953), 275; *TA*, 5 Feb. 1868.

59. *NM*, 7 Jan. 1862. Transvaal BaTswana lived in large settlements before, but seldom during, Boer rule. See Mason (1968), 167-80.

60. Sanderson (1860), 248.

61. From an anonymous traveler's account published in the *NM*, 11 Dec. 1866; see also Child (1973), 40.

62. Gonin to DRC, 13 May 1862 & 15 Apr. 1866, 15/7/2(E) and 13 Jun. 1862, 9 Aug. 1862, & 22 Sep. 1870, 15/7/2(A), DRCA. For a list of Kgamanyane's wives, Breutz (1953), 341; for his descendants, I. Schapera, "Kgamanyane—Agnatic Male Descendants," Schapera papers, PP 1/3/8, BNA. In the Transvaal, apparently only Sekhukhune of the BaPedi had more wives than Kgamanyane.

63. *GJ*, 21 Sep. and 19 Oct. 1850. Purchasing guns was possible only prior to the Sand River Convention.

64. Breutz (1987), 474; Schapera (1965), 64n, 68n; Schapera (1952), 113.

65. Breutz (1953), 473-4; *Notule van die Volksraad van die Suid-Afrikaanse Republiek*, 2 (1851-3): 371; Kruger (1925), 97, 162

66. Schapera (1965), 66, 68.

67. Mokgatle denied the charges. Mar. 1848, Schapera (1959), 1: 236.

68. Bruetz (1953), 65. See also Bozzoli (1991), 40

69. Kgamanyane's capital was located on Kruger's farm, Saulspoort 269, and a satellite village on Middelkuil 564. For a list of Kruger's farms, Trapido (1980), 366n26.

70. *GJ*, 11 Oct. 1862, reprint of a *Zuid Afrikaan* article, "The Natives of the Transvaal."

71. Based on correspondence of the DRC missionary, Henry Gonin, at Saulspoort, Kgamanyane's capital. See especially Gonin to DRC, 11 Oct. 1864, 5 Dec. 1866, 12 Jan. 1869, 6 Mar. 1869, & 22 Sep. 1870, 15/7/2(A), DRCA; Schapera (1942), 10-1; Trapido (1980), 350-68.

72. Mabe's BaTlhako, Senthsu's BaRokologadi, and two others (one under "Bothman" [Letsebe?]. Breutz (1953), 288, 291; Breutz (1987), 420; Gonin to Nov. 1865, 15/7/2(E) and 1 Jul. 1866 & 2 Dec. 1867, 15/7/2(A), DRCA.

73. Trapido (1980), 350-68; Gonin to DRC, 6 Mar. 1869, 3 & 27 Apr. and 4 Jun. 1888, 27 Nov. 1891, Dec. 1894, 1 Mar. & 7 Sep. 1895, 15/7/2(A)-(D), DRCA; Theal (1919), 1: 500. Throughout this period, persistent fears of African revolt also encouraged limiting the size of, and breaking up, African settlements.

74. *NM*, 13 Oct. 1868; *TA*, 2 Mar. 1869; Kruger (1969), 101-2. Delius (1984), 146-

7, identifies these raids as spurring a Volksraad clampdown in response to outside pressures. Kruger's forces fought in the northern Transvaal when raids on the VhaVenda were being mounted from many quarters. See ch. 8 by Boeyens in this volume.

75. Delius and Trapido (1983), esp. 75-81.

76. Mokgatle (1971), 37-51. The woman, the author's grandmother, had been stolen in a Boer raid on Mapela's BaLanga in approximately 1849.

77. Gonin to DRC, Jan. 1865, 12 Jun. 1867, and note to his of 23 Sep. 1867, DRCA. Vieland had been taken by the Boers during Potgieter's attack on Mzilikazi's capital of Mosega in 1838, became the possession of Jacobus Venter, acting president of the Orange Free State, and after Venter's death was handed on to Paul Kruger.

78. Gonin to DRC, 13 May 1862 and 19 Jun. 1863, DRCA.

79. Gonin to DRC, 19 Jun. 1863, n.d., 15 Jul. 1864, 18 Oct. 1864, 22 Feb. 1866.

80. Gonin to DRC, 11 Oct. 1864.

81. Ibid; 1 Jul. 1866; 2 Dec. 1867.

82. They likely came from the groups earlier captured by the BaKgatla and placed in the service of the Boers. See footnote 64; also Morton (1988).

83. Mariri's report, n.d.[1894], 15/4/3/1, DRCA.

84. Phiri to Reyneke, 30 Dec. 1923, 15/4/3/18, DRCA.

85. Morton (1988), 12-7.

86. Ibid, 2-3 regarding Professor E.S. Moloto and Francis Phiri.

87. Uys (1933), 76.

88. Aylward (1881), 150-1. See also Peterson (1973), 203; Aborigines' Protection Society (1881), 8.

89. Wilson (1901), 198-200.

90. Harries (1981), 322.

91. Nasson (1983), 145-55. Nasson's assertion that *agterryers* represented "a numerically small element in the republican camp" (147) has been disputed by Pretorius, who estimates that *agterryers* constituted as much as 20 to 25 percent of burgher forces. Pretorius (1988), 380-401, esp. 395-6. I am grateful to Jan Boeyens for these two references and for translations of portions of the latter. See also Delius and Trapido (1983), 78.

8

"Black Ivory":
The Indenture System and Slavery
in Zoutpansberg, 1848–1869[1]

Jan C.A. Boeyens

In Zoutpansberg, the northernmost district of the Transvaal, or *Zuid-Afrikaansche Republiek* (ZAR), the indenture system often graded into a form of slavery, in particular with regard to the manner in which young children classed as *inboekelinge* (so-called "apprentices") were obtained, traded, and controlled. Some children were gifts from Africans, but most were captives, such as *buit* ("booty") distributed by Boers among themselves after commando raids on African communities or claimed as "war bounty" from their African auxiliaries in military campaigns. Demand for children and young women was fed partly by local domestic needs, but the hundreds of *inboekelinge* whom the Zoutpansbergers obtained annually far exceeded their internal labor requirements. Until 1855 captives were produced by wars waged to open up certain areas of the far north for white settlement; thereafter the clashes resulted mainly from African resistance to attempts by the Boers to enforce their newly acquired authority by demanding labor and *opgaaf* (tribute). Zoutpansberg was, after all, an "open frontier" where the authority of the whites was continually challenged, resulting in regular clashes and wars with local African communities. Rather than building towns, farms, and herds, the few burghers of the district invested their capital in hunting game and increased it by exporting trophies; children were taken as spoils of war because they, too, had export market value. The Zoutpansberg, which on the coast was known as a major source of "white ivory" and other game products, was reputed in the Dutch interior for its capacity to supply "black ivory." From there children were transported by wagon to other parts of the ZAR and the Orange Free State and sold to local burghers. Apprenticeship laws of the Boer republics prohibited the exchange, sale, or purchase of *inboekelinge*, but until 1870 landdrosts, field-cornets, commandants-general, and presidents alike connived in the traffic, as discussed in chapter 7. Some contemporary observers viewed the legal apprentice system, which permitted whites to indenture African children up to a certain age as laborers, as a disguised form of slavery.[2]

Legal Indentureship in the Transvaal

The indenture system that was sanctioned in the Transvaal until the late nineteenth century originated in the Cape colony. In chapter 1 of this volume, Shell notes that during the Dutch occupation of the Cape, a de facto arrangement existed as early as 1721 by which the children of male slaves and Khoi women could be indentured to the age of twenty-five years. Because such children could not become legal slaves, indentureship recompensed slave owners for the maintenance of children for whom they were not legally responsible. Eventually, indentureship formally included all Khoisan children.[3] Legal indenture was institutionalized and regularized after the second British occupation of the Cape in 1806.[4] After the emancipation of slaves in the Cape colony in December 1834, the indenture system was used to bridge the transition from slavery to freedom and prevent a labor shortage. New laws provided for the indenturing of freed slaves to their previous owners for four years and stipulated that slave children under six years at the time of emancipation or children born to freed slaves during the transition period could be indentured until their twenty-first year if no other means of support was available to them. In December 1838, after criticism mounted against these laws and resultant malpractices, the indenture system in the Cape Colony was abolished.[5]

The Voortrekkers took their knowledge and experience of Cape labor laws into the interior. Cases of indenturing were recorded in the Transvaal at least as early as 1848.[6] The legal indenture system in the Transvaal dates from May 1851 with the Apprentice Act.[7] Under that legislation, Transvaal burghers could, at place of the landdrost or a field-cornet of a district, indenture "any child, orphan or orphans [who] were given as gifts or obtained in other legal or voluntary manner" from Africans. The "apprentices" were thereafter compelled to remain in the service of these burghers until at most, twenty-five years of age, after which they were regarded as exempted from "all compulsory labor obligations."[8] The burghers were required in turn to treat indentured laborers well and accept responsibility for their upbringing. Persons who illegally obtained and/or ill-treated apprentices were liable for punishment.

Apprenticeship represented a complete break with traditional African provisions for orphans. In precolonial African societies, children who had been orphaned or had lost one of their parents were sheltered by kinship ties

FIGURE 8.1 Zoutpansberg, 1848–1869.

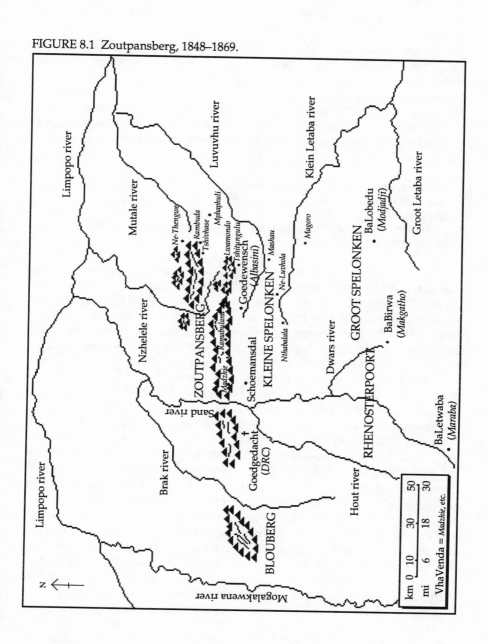

as well as a set of guardianship rules.[9] Though promulgated ostensibly to provide for the care of African orphans, the Apprentice Act facilitated the procurement of labor, which was its underlying purpose. In the Transvaal, the Voortrekkers frequently experienced labor shortages, and their attempts to force African groups to supply labor to the burghers often met with resistance.[10] The slave owners' tradition played its part, as did the mentality of many white Transvaal settlers, who looked down on certain forms of manual labor associated with Africans.[11] The economics of labor use, however, which as yet remains undetermined for Zoutpansberg, was probably more important.[12] Clearly, large-scale dependence on African labor was prevalent in Zoutpansberg, as one long-term settler observed:

> The most remarkable thing to me was that I never saw the farmers working; when it was time to sow, the *meiden* (African women) were called to pick up the ground and plant the maize, and when it was time to reap they were again called upon to harvest the crop. I never once, during that time, saw a plough in the ground.[13]

Under the indenture system, many such laborers were obtained through capture or trade. The Apprentice Act is unclear about what constituted "illegal" procurement of indentured laborers. It required that apprenticed children be defined legally as orphans or as having been relinquished voluntarily by their parents, guardians, or custodians. According to instructions received by Lydenburg military officers in November 1851, for example, only children who were found "helpless" at least half a day after a military clash could be taken and indentured.[14] Yet it was common practice in this and other military campaigns for children of opposing Africans to become legal apprentices of commando members or other burghers, who claimed that the children had been orphaned as a result of combat. Also, under its provisions for the "transfer of apprentices," the Apprentice Act made it possible for children to be legally traded, though not across ZAR borders. Indentured laborers could be "transferred" from one Transvaal burgher to another, and heirs of a deceased person who had indentured laborers in service could transfer them to someone else. Transfer was legal as well for persons who through poverty "or any other cause" were forced to "dispose of" their indentured laborers, on condition that the laborers concerned be re-registered by a landdrost or field-cornet and that the "owner" could claim a maximum of Rds 30. Admissibility of transferring indentured persons according to such vague definitions made it difficult to convict anyone of unlawful trade in African children.[15]

Legal indentureship was also used by Transvaal leaders as proof that the ZAR upheld Article 4 of the January 1852 Sand River Convention, which forbade slavery.[16] Similar effect was intended in 1866, when fines for contravening "the law prohibiting slave trading" (*de wet tot wering van slavenhandel*) were drastically increased and a term of imprisonment could be imposed if the culprits neglected to pay the fines. Officials could also be fined if they failed to insure that the provisions of the law were upheld.[17] The Voortrekkers and their successors opposed legal slavery, not so much from moral repugnance as from the practical consideration that to do otherwise might induce outsiders to interfere with their newly acquired independence. On the eastern frontier, from where the Voortrekker majority came, farmers had minimal exposure to the early nineteenth-century philanthropical world view; Old Testament beliefs exercised far more influence on their attitudes regarding enslavement and the relationship between master and servant.[18] Their leaders condemned slavery on legal rather than religious or ideological grounds, which explains in part why the private actions of some Transvaal burghers, including government officials, were at variance with official state policy in this regard.

In the historical literature, most references to the ZAR indenture system emphasize its legal aspects and confront the "guilt question," namely the accusation that it was a disguised form of slavery. Few have analyzed the historical processes and underlying forces that influenced the system. In chs. 4 and 7, respectively, Mason and Morton have drawn attention to Agar-Hamilton as the first to note that the indenture system led to practices bordering on slavery, particularly in the northern and eastern areas, although slavery as such was legally forbidden by the ZAR. Even president M.W. Pretorius, who took a strong public stand against slavery, participated occasionally in the illegal trade in African children.[19] A more apologetic treatment of accusations leveled at the Boers characterizes the discussions of Venter (1934), Pieterse (1936), Greyling (1944), Kistner (1945 and 1952), and Moolman (1975). They stress the legal steps taken by the central ZAR government to combat the slave trade and to control labor practices, while acknowledging that irregularities sometimes occurred. They provide evidence that some charges against the Boers with regard to slavery were false, that their accusers did not understand the complex contact and labor situation in the Transvaal, that their charges were colored by an ideological and philanthropical viewpoint, and that these charges were seized upon and misused by protagonists of the British imperialist cause in their efforts to undermine the independence of the ZAR. Though truth is contained in these arguments, these historians were frequently overenthusiastic in their efforts to justify the Boers and to show that the indenture system was instituted primarily on the humanitarian grounds of providing for the care and upbringing of "destitute" African children. Some of this work, such as Kistner's, is nuanced but fundamentally apologetic. The approach is summarized most saliently by Moolman:

There is no proof that Bantu children were carried off by the Boers after punitive expeditions primarily in order to obtain labor. The indenture system merely insured that private individuals who acted out of charity in such instances received a measure of compensation for their trouble. On the other hand, the children concerned learned a trade and were assured of a secure living.[20]

Only the "revisionist" historians, who have studied the development and functioning of social classes in South Africa, have begun to provide a social and economic context within which to understand the indenture system in nineteenth-century Transvaal and the historical processes which influenced it. Their work draws attention to the origin, status, and role of indentured laborers in the new social order arising from the northward Boer migration. In an exploratory essay, Trapido stresses the importance of indentured laborers in the Boer economy, in which he regards them as nothing more than slaves, thereby typifying the Boer economic system as a "slave mode of production."[21] Trapido subsequently abandoned describing indentured servants as slaves but retained with Delius the view that the indenture system alleviated the serious labor shortage among the Voortrekkers who settled first at Ohrigstad and later at Lydenburg. They also argue that after 1860 the Zoutpansberg Boers played a dominant role in the "apprentice" trade into the central and western Transvaal. Colloquially, these children were referred to as "black ivory," a euphemism drawing its analogy from the other main Zoutpansberg export item, the white ivory obtained from elephant hunting.[22] The Boers obtained some of these indentured laborers through exchanges with Africans. Bonner's study of the AmaSwati, the main suppliers of African children to the eastern Transvaal Boers, shows that these soon-to-become indentured laborers were carried off mostly during raids on communities outside the borders of the AmaSwati kingdom. Before 1860 the AmaSwati handed over some children to the Boers to conclude or confirm a political alliance with them against other African groups. In the 1860s, as Boer military and political power weakened, the goods exchanged for the children attained greater significance in these transactions.[23]

A problem persisting in the discussions of labor practices in the Boer republics concerns the appropriate terminology in describing the nineteenth-century system of unfree labor and child bondage. Lovejoy, for example, asserts that British diplomatic pressure compelled the Boers to disguise by means of euphemisms their practice of a "modified form of slavery."[24] The fact that legislators and burghers in the ZAR used "apprentices" almost without exception to refer to indentured children should be attributed, however, to their familiarity with the English terminology used during the operation of the indenture system in the Cape Colony.[25] The term "apprentice" itself creates confusion, because the generally accepted meaning of this term misrepresents the position of the indentured laborers in the ZAR. Probably for this reason several English-speaking historians avoid "apprentice" and use "inboekseling" with reference to unfree laborers.[26] Yet, at least insofar as the Zoutpansberg record is concerned, "inboekseling" does not occur in Dutch or Afrikaans, and is most likely a corruption of "inboekeling." The term "inboekseling" may erroneously have been derived from the term "inboeksel," which was used by Transvaal Boers with reference to the written proof obtained when an African child was indentured.[27]

Rather than pursue an inclusive term for all forms of unfree labor present in the ZAR, a more useful lead to follow is provided by Malherbe, who regards apprenticeship, indenture, and slavery in South Africa as distinct but often overlapping labor forms.[28] The Zoutpansberg case below illustrates that although the Transvaal Boers commonly used the term "apprentice" to refer to their unfree laborers, the legal provisions of the Apprentice Act of 1851 were typical of an indenture system, which in practice often graded into a form of slavery, in particular with regard to the manner in which so-called "apprentices," predominantly young children, were obtained and bound to their white masters.

Zoutpansberg

The period 1848 to 1869 covers the first, fully-fledged white settlement phase in Zoutpansberg, located on the northern frontier of the Transvaal. Permanent settlement dates from the arrival from Ohrigstad of Voortrekker leader Andries Hendrik Potgieter and his followers, who founded the town of Schoemansdal at the southern foot of the Zoutpansberg mountain range. Schoemansdal was occupied less than twenty years. On 15 July 1867 it was evacuated following a protracted conflict with the VhaVenda. (For an 1865 sketch of Schoemansdal, see Plate 3.) For two years the ZAR government tried to subdue the VhaVenda by diplomatic and military means but abandoned their attempts at the end of 1869. Thereafter the ZAR governed the northern part of the Zoutpansberg district in name only; the few impoverished whites who continued to live in the vicinity of the abandoned Schoemansdal posed no threat to the VhaVenda, who remained de facto independent.[29] After 1869, with the burgher exodus from Zoutpansberg and the collapse of white authority in the district, the indenture system there virtually ceased.[30]

Reconstructing the indenture system in Zoutpansberg is impaired by the paucity of documentary evidence. Almost the only landdrost records to survive are correspondence with officials of the central government. An indentured laborer register, similar to that in the archives of the Lydenburg landdrost, has yet to be found.[31] Most relevant records were apparently lost during the evacuation of Schoemansdal.[32] And, according to an 1864 commission of inquiry, which made an inventory of the landdrost's office, the district's record keeping was chaotic and incomplete.[33] The literacy level among white settlers was generally low, and even some officials had difficulty compiling reports.[34] Moreover, as could be expected, few irregularities regarding the indenture system were ever documented, because of the penalties attached to them. The Berlin missionaries, who while residing in the eastern Transvaal recorded valuable information on indentured laborers, entered Zoutpansberg only after effective white settlement.[35] Dutch Reformed Church (DRC) missionary Alexander MacKidd settled among the Buys family in the western part of the district in 1863 but died within two years. Stefanus Hofmeyr, his successor, evacuated the DRC Goedgedacht station in mid-1865 because of the Boer-VhaVenda conflict.[36] Scarce documentation for Zoutpansberg reflects its frontier nature: local administrative arrangements, distant from central government control, were seldom documented properly; the area was infrequently traversed by observant or educated visitors; and most whites who settled there were too caught up in a struggle for survival to concern themselves with recording their thoughts or activities.

Zoutpansberg was a typical "open" frontier, to use Giliomee's definition, in that it was a "disputed area" in which "two or more ethnic communities co-exist with conflicting claims to the land," and where "no authority is recognised as legitimate or is able to exercise undisputed control over the area." In such zones, competing communities rely on "coercive power, i.e. the ability to realise aims forcibly in the face of opposition from others."[37] Although the Boers with their guns held a military advantage over the African communities of the north and tried to maintain it by banning the sale of fire-arms to Africans, white supremacy in Zoutpansberg was never unquestionable or absolute.[38] In fact, Zoutpansbergers were frequently forced to assemble in laagers for their own protection, especially during the hunting season from mid-June to mid-October, when many men were away in quest of ivory.[39] During the 1848–69 period, only a small portion of the Zoutpansberg was occupied by whites, who had no settlements north of the Zoutpansberg range, or to the east in the malaria-infested lowveld. According to the hunter-trader Alexander Struben, his hut, erected in 1864 about 64 km. (40 mi.) east of Schoemansdal, was the farthest outpost of white occupation.[40] One visitor reported that in 1855–56 Zoutpansberg district's white population numbered approximately 1,800 and comprised about 260 families.[41] Schoemansdal had a small population; in 1861 only about seventy houses stood in the town, and the latest archaeological findings suggest that the town contained probably no more than 100 families.[42] In the 1860s Schoemansdal's population and that of the district declined dramatically due to the slump in the ivory trade and increased conflict with African communities.[43] The political authority of such a small group of whites was therefore never accepted unconditionally by an African population numbering many thousands.[44]

Relations between the Zoutpansbergers and neighboring African communities gradually assumed a pattern that shaped the indenture system. The Zoutpansbergers divided African communities into two categories, namely Africans "doing service" (*dienstdoende kaffers*) and Africans "rendering tribute" (*opgaaf kaffers*). *Dienstdoende* Africans were those living in the immediate vicinity of whites and therefore subject to greater control. *Dienstdoende* chiefs had to provide laborers to the whites and were exempted from paying *opgaaf*. In exchange for their labor some of the smaller groups were permitted to remain in their original dwelling places, even those allocated as part of white farms.[45] In contrast *opgaaf* chiefs lived on the fringes of white influence and retained a larger measure of independence.[46] *Opgaaf* was in essence a form of tribute collected directly from chiefs by Zoutpansberg government officials on behalf of the district or ZAR; it was made up of cattle, sheep, goats, grain, hoes, ivory, copper ingots, or leopard skins.[47] Tribute, an established practice among African communities, accorded recognition to the military and political authority of a specific group or leader in an area.[48] It would appear, however, from the limited documentary evidence available, that the majority of African children indentured to the Boers, particularly after 1860, were abducted during military clashes with African groups who were expected to pay *opgaaf*.

Boer interest in developing their laboring class from captive children, who could be easily controlled and trained to specific tasks, may have been partly influenced by their failure to obtain suitable labor from *dienstdoende* chiefs. The labor corps from the latter, though supplied generally on demand, was ill-prepared for many of the tasks required. Also it was difficult to bind or coerce *dienstdoende* laborers, as they were apt if unsatisfied to leave their "employers" at any time and return to their homes nearby. Cases occurred in which field-cornets attempted to confine such laborers by redistributing them to burghers in other parts of the ward, but burghers who had developed stable labor relations with Africans in their service resisted.[49]

Unlike the eastern Transvaal, the Zoutpansberg had no dominant African group with whom whites could ally for mutual benefit. No specific African group, like the AmaSwati, acted as the main supplier of children to the Boers. The VhaVenda, northern BaSotho, and northern AmaNdebele of the region were divided into many chiefdoms, none of which commanded a power base approaching that of the AmaSwati or were in a position to undertake raids and military expeditions for the purpose of abducting children. Zoutpansberg whites therefore played a more direct role in the procurement of indentured children than did their compatriots in the eastern Transvaal. Before 1855, whites waged war to open up the Zoutpansberg territory for settlement. They also attached to themselves VaTsonga refugees from Mozambique, using them as laborers and soldiers against Africans of the Zoutpansberg. The VaTsonga influx, particularly into the Spelonken ward, gained momentum after the Portuguese, João Albasini, established himself among the Boers in Zoutpansberg in 1853 (see Eldredge's chapter 6).[50] The concentration of VaTsonga strained relations with the VhaVenda, old inhabitants of the Zoutpansberg, and led to further clashes between on the one hand the Boers and VaTsonga and on the other the Zoutpansberg indigenes, from whom the Boers took African children as booty. After 1860, Boers and their African auxiliaries conducted raids against scattered chiefdoms for the purpose of subjugating them and capturing children. These instances of child kidnapping and slave trading by Boers in Zoutpansberg are documented *largely* by their own inadvertent accounts, which strengthen, incidentally, the case for the reliability of other reports of slave raiding derived from "outsider" sources.[51]

Involved in many of these raids were the official collectors of *opgaaf* in the Zoutpansberg, Michael Buys and João Albasini. Michael, son of Coenraad de Buys, was appointed in 1855, Albasini in 1859.[52] Both were placed in charge of *opgaaf*, because they had the military power needed to collect it. About 300 people attended the first service held by Alexander MacKidd among the Buyses in 1863, and an estimated 15,000 to 20,000 Africans recognized Michael Buys's "chieftainship," or rather were placed under his jurisdiction.[53] Albasini built his power base by offering shelter on his farm, "Goedewensch," especially to VaTsonga groups fleeing Mozambique from Soshangane, the VaNgoni leader. "Juwawa," as they dubbed Albasini, was considered to be the "white chief" of the "Knob-noses," or the MaGwamba. In 1864 he was reported to be able to summon an estimated 4,000 VaTsonga supporters by merely beating a drum.[54] Albasini and Buys employed a large number of African marksmen in the hunting-field and on raids for children. Albasini's hunters had about one hundred elephant guns, while Buys and his "shots" hunted, according to the Hunting Act of 1858, "for the benefit of the [ZAR] Government."[55] These forces, together with local commandos and volunteer units sent by the ZAR government, provided the means to establish Zoutpansberg's indenture system.

Procuring "Black Ivory"

Years before the semblance of an official collection system began to operate, some of the early Boer settlers in Zoutpansberg were raiding

Africans for stock and children. In August 1850, scarcely two years after the founding of the Zoutpansberg settlement, the traveler, Thomas Baines, was informed that a few months before a Zoutpansberg commando led by commandant-general Andries Hendrik Potgieter had attacked some local African villages. Potgieter's commando killed many of the occupants and captured ca. 1,500 cattle, ca. 1–2,000 sheep, and a substantial number of children. According to Andries Jacobus, a "coloured person" who had accompanied his employer, the trader F. Pistorius, to the Zoutpansberg, the captured African children totaled about 200, including fifteen for Potgieter and at least ten for a certain Duvenage, although Pistorius considered these figures to be inflated.[56]

Early in 1855, approximately three months after defeating Mughombane I's BaKekana in the siege of Makapansgat in revenge for the murder of a number of Boers at Moorddrift on the Mogalakwena river, a Zoutpansberg commando moved against another northern AmaNdebele chiefdom, the BaLetwaba of Maraba, regarded as Mughombane's ally. Two thousand BaLetwaba were reportedly killed and 400 children abducted.[57] The following year, two more raids were launched. Zoutpansberg commandant J.H. Jacobs led a patrol against Rasikhuthuma, son of the VhaVenda chief, Ramabulana, after João Albasini had accused Rasikhuthuma of stock theft. In the attack on Tshitungulu, Rasikhuthuma's stronghold in the Spelonken ward, 25 of his subjects were shot and 76 cattle, 108 sheep and goats, as well as 13 young Africans, were taken as plunder and divided among patrol members.[58] In November Jacobs reported that field-cornet L.M. Bronkhorst had raided "Rambu[b/l]aan," presumably Ramabulana. Eleven Africans were killed, and five children were divided among members of the commando.[59]

These early raids assumed no uniform pattern, as distinctions between *dienstdoende* and *opgaaf* Africans had yet to settle into practice, insofar as indenturing children was concerned. The economic benefits to be gained by refraining from taking violent action against and abducting the children of *dienstdoende* groups, who were beginning to provide labor, were yet to be realized. That child-kidnapping raids against such groups made no sense was, however, apparent to local burghers by 1860. In November of that year, Spelonken ward field-cornet Jan du Plessis led a commando against Mashau, a *dienstdoende* VhaVenda chief, because reportedly he was disobedient. After the raid, white farmers complained to Pretoria that commando members had divested Mashau's people of their cattle, sheep, goats, hoes, grain, and women and children, as spoils of war.[60] From this point, raids were confined almost entirely to Africans from whom the Boers claimed *opgaaf*, which as tribute became increasingly equated with indentured children.

In January 1861 landdrost N.J. Grobler reported that Michael Buys had under his instructions led a patrol against chief "Makakabula." Ten of his subjects were killed and fourteen children carried off. When Makakabula sued for peace, Grobler considered returning the children in exchange for ten elephant tusks to cover the costs incurred in the campaign, but he then sought approval from Pretoria.[61] In May or June 1861 the Zoutpansbergers sent a commando against Modjadji, chieftainness of the BaLobedu and her VaTsonga vassal, Xiluvana, because they refused to pay *opgaaf*. According to D.F. das Neves, a hunter-trader then in Schoemansdal, the commando plundered a large number of cattle, sheep, and goats and abducted 400 children.[62] In October 1863 Albasini, by then superintendent of African chiefdoms, despatched a VaTsonga force under Munene against the VhaVenda chief, Rambuda, because he refused to pay *opgaaf* and had closed the hunting trail through his territory. Munene's force failed to defeat Rambuda but killed seventy-seven and abducted a number of women and children.[63] By the mid-1860s, according to his own claim, Munene had been sent by Albasini on frequent raids against Africans refusing to pay *opgaaf*. He also abducted children and put them aside for Albasini: five after the Rambuda campaign, two after a skirmish with Ne-Thengwe, a VhaVenda chief, and five and ten, respectively, after attacks on "Sanieka" and "Lesieka."[64] Perhaps as a consequence of such raids, chiefs at this time wanting to remain on good terms with Albasini, such as the VaTsonga's Sikwalakwala, began to include children as part of their *opgaaf* payments.[65]

Of increasing significance in these raids was the involvement of Africans armed with guns. Elephant hunting and the ivory trade were the most important economic activities of Zoutpansbergers, who depended increasingly on African marksmen as elephant herds retreated north into the tsetse belt, where draught and riding animals could not carry white hunters, or east into the malaria belt, where whites had trouble surviving. Few Zoutpansbergers abided by the law prohibiting African marksmen from hunting without white supervision. Thus many African hunters were equipped with guns by Albasini and others. Marksmen were as aware of the white demand for indentured laborers as for elephant tusks, and they used their guns while on expeditions to raid settlements for "black ivory." *Dienstdoende* chiefs provided whites with marksmen, who in turn provided whites with captured children. This is apparent in a statement made by M.W. Pretorius in his address to a Volksraad commission in 1865. Pretorius became convinced, he said,

> by two young African children (*Kaffer-kinderen*) from the kraal of Katlachter, who were driven by hunger to his laager, that the African hunters (*jagt Kaffers*) had the habit of capturing children from other Africans (*Kaffers*) and declaring these to be orphans.[66]

"Katlachter" was the Boer name for Madzhie, a VhaVenda chief whose capital was situated in the mountains above Schoemansdal. He was a *dienstdoende* chief who supplied labor to the white community, including a considerable number of African marksmen.[67]

By 1865, the Zoutpansberg whites had become dependent on such men to do their fighting. After the 1864 death of the VhaVenda chief, Ramabulana, white involvement in the succession dispute between his sons, Makhado and Davhana, caused conflict that spread to other parts of the Zoutpansberg. In August 1865 the VhaVenda leader Magoro, who occupied a stronghold south of the Klein Letaba river, was besieged and then attacked by a force of approximately sixty whites supported by 1,000 armed VaTsonga. The Boers claimed that Magoro had colluded with Makhado, by then hostile to the Boers, and refused as well to pay *opgaaf*. The Boers and VaTsonga prevailed, killing Magoro and ca. 300 of his subjects. Adult males, not in demand, faced a gruesome death, as Alexander Struben's eye-witness account makes clear:

At the foot of the hill I witnessed a fearful scene. They had brought down a lot of prisoners and then ensued a work of butchery which was fearful to behold—with a refinement of cruelty one was thrust forward and ordered to run and a short start was given to him. He was a well made athletic man but exhausted by thirst and hunger—and without a word he sprang forward and bounded swiftly down the glade. For about thirty yards he ran without interruption and then with a fierce yell and whoop about a dozen warriors clutched their assegais and tore away in pursuit. They draw nearer and nearer – in another moment they will be upon him—one has already raised his arm to strike, but with a fearful effort he rouses all his failing energies and with a look of terror springs forward and regains the start he has lost but it is the last effort of exhausted nature; slower and slower he runs now and his body is swaying to and fro and his limbs trembling beneath him. God help him for it is his last moment upon earth. A huge savage clad in a long hunting shirt of tiger skins bounds forward with a fearful yell of triumph and with his long keen assegai stabs him in the back. He sinks to the earth clutching the tufts of grass wildly with his hands and biting the ground in agony. Warrior after warrior approaches and uttering his war whoop plunges his assegai into his yet breathing body or whirling his tomahawk above his head brings it down upon the warm yielding flesh. One then clutches the leg of the dying Maccatee and with wild yells and bounds, their feathers tossing fiercely in the wind, they drag the moaning body over the rough ground, and then casting it loose they spring away to repeat the performance upon another—and lying there bleeding, torn and mutilated the soul of the Maccatee warrior passes to its last account. [For Struben's sketch of the battle scene, see Plate 2.]

The captured VhaVenda women and children were more highly prized; women captives were given to the VaTsonga combatants, and each white commando member took two children to be indentured to him. Their lot was no less tragic, as Struben recalls:

> [I]t was a sad, sad heart-rending sight to see children, some of whom were yet hanging at their mothers' breasts, torn shrieking away, the parents yielding them in tearful silent agony.... One woman as she was being led away fell down upon her knees to her owner and prayed him to get back her child—"it is so small," she said, "see it can scarcely stand, it suckles yet — it is no good to anyone but me — get me back my child," and she knelt wringing her hands and the tears streaming down her face. The warrior to whom she belonged pushed her up and led her out of the camp and so finished that morning's work.[68]

The raid, though successful, failed to reverse declining Boer control of the Zoutpansberg, occurring as it did less than two years before the evacuation of Schoemansdal. The raid also drew unflattering attention to the Zoutpansbergers. British circles held up this action as an example of Transvaal slavery, and the ZAR summoned the leaders of the commando— assistant commandant-general F.H. Geyser, commandant S.M. Venter, and superintendent Albasini—to appear before the supreme court on charges of "illegal actions and child-stealing."[69]

Thereafter the ZAR increasingly assumed direct authority over the Zoutpansberg and took command of military actions against Africans who did not recognize it. ZAR officials, in turn, became involved in procuring children as spoils of war. After the evacuation of Schoemansdal in July 1867, Pretoria sent Stephanus Schoeman with a volunteer corps to subjugate the VhaVenda and their allies. In October Schoeman's forces attacked Mashau, a VhaVenda chief, taking a few women and five children after the battle. They then fought with one of Modjadji's headmen and took a number of women and seventy-four children as their booty. Later, children above three years when captured were assigned provisionally to Schoeman's volunteers and a few local whites. Fifty-five children were distributed accordingly. Children under three were returned to their mothers, while captured women were allotted to VaTsonga who took part in the campaign. In December 1867 Schoeman's volunteers attacked Makgatho's BaBirwa in the Groot Spelonken. They captured a number of women and children, who were transported to Albasini's farm. Shortly after, in late January 1868 Michael Buys led a patrol against Serakalala, a northern BaSotho headman under Madzhie. A few women and children were brought back.[70]

When the campaign to subdue the VhaVenda failed, the ZAR called on the aid of Africans outside the Zoutpansberg, such as Mzila's VaNgoni of Mozambique and the AmaSwati. In October 1869 an AmaSwati army launched a campaign against the VhaVenda. A month later they left the

Zoutpansberg with 4,000 cattle, 200 guns, and 400 women and children.[71] Before reaching Swaziland, however, the AmaSwati and their booty apparently were set upon by Africans in the lowveld and virtually eliminated.[72]

Thus ended the taking of women and children as war spoils in the Zoutpansberg. The women were normally given to the African allies of the Boers who supported them in their military expeditions. In this regard Albasini's VaTsonga force played an important role: they were considered *gouvernementsvolk* ("government's people"), and as such were frequently sent under their own commanders against African groups resisting white authority.[73] Few if any Zoutpansberg commandos or patrols comprised whites only, and in the ensuing skirmishes African auxiliaries usually bore the brunt of the fighting.[74] After large-scale conflict between the Zoutpansbergers and the VhaVenda erupted in the 1860s, the Schoemansdal military council specifically decided that African women captured during military expeditions and who were too old to be indentured to burghers were to be given to Albasini's VaTsonga as a way of encouraging them to continue to participate in these expeditions.[75] They were also recompensed for their military services by land which formerly belonged to the VhaVenda. For instance, after a successful campaign against the VhaVenda chief, Ne-Luvhola, in July 1865, his former abode was allocated to the VaTsonga headman, Njakanjaka.[76]

Although some orphans resulted from war, the indenturing of children arose for other than humanitarian reasons. Rarely was the term *weeskinderen* ("orphans") used in military reports. Boers preferred *kleingoed* ("little ones") or, as the Zoutpansberg commandant on occasion used without pretense, *buit* ("booty").[77] And they were accepted as such by high-ranking ZAR officials. Stephanus Schoeman, then acting state president, and his secretary, H.C. Stiemens, visited Zoutpansberg in January 1862. There Michael Buys presented Stiemens with a boy of ten years, named Silovela. Stiemens demurred until Buys claimed to have forty such children whom he could not feed. Albasini also presented to Stiemens a young child with a card around his neck, reading "Present for the gentleman Stiemens." Stiemens accepted the child, wrapped a handkerchief around his waist and that of Buys's "gift," and, as Stiemens later wrote, took them with him in the back of the wagon as a "surprise" for his wife.[78] African leaders in the Zoutpansberg understood, too, that ranking ZAR officials accepted children as "gifts." In 1868 or 1869, when Schoeman in his capacity as "diplomatic agent" was still attempting to subdue the VhaVenda, one VhaVenda chief, Lwamondo, presented Schoeman with twenty cattle and two African children. What prompted this gesture is not recorded but was probably inspired by Lwamondo's desire for support in his struggle against Tshivhase, another VhaVenda chief. Lwamondo had twice approached Schoeman, first in his capacity as commander of the volunteer corps and later as "diplomatic agent" among the Zoutpansberg Africans, for military assistance against Tshivhase.[79]

Determining the exact number of children indentured in the Zoutpansberg is impossible, but according to information received in 1866 by the two Berlin Society missionaries, H. Grützner and A. Merensky, the annual total amounted to about 1,000.[80]

Exporting "Black Ivory"

As a consequence of military clashes with local African communities, the small white population of Zoutpansberg acquired as booty more African children than they could absorb, and they were consequently distributed to other areas of the country. By 1855 the Zoutpansberg burghers were known as important suppliers of African children within the Transvaal and beyond as far away as Cape Town.[81] The Cape newspaper, *De Zuid-Afrikaan*, reported that:

> [in] Zoutpansberg, where the farmers have the most hostile contact with the indigenes, and where the greatest number of captives is assured, there is a regular export of these to other parts of the Republic, and sometimes to within the boundaries of the Orange Free State.

According to this report, "apprentices" were sold at £10 to £15 each.[82] Children were also exchanged for cattle and other goods.[83] Indentured laborers from the Transvaal were taken across the Vaal river, contrary to the Apprentice Act of 1851, as was apparent from commandant-general Stephanus Schoeman's proclamation before the local residents in Zoutpansberg on 5 October 1855 to the effect that the export of "apprentices" was punishable.[84]

Open trading of African children was common practice in Zoutpansberg and was known to highly placed government officials. Whites who illegally obtained these children faced few difficulties in obtaining the necessary *inboeksel* so as to indenture them. The law was vague regarding transfers of indentured laborers and was interpreted by government officials who themselves sometimes condoned or even participated in the trade. In 1856, Orange Free State president, J.N. Boshof, admitted before the Volksraad in Bloemfontein that local burghers purchased children from their Transvaal neighbors. The Volksraad responded by legislating the indenture system so as to prevent slavery but left a loophole for transgressors by providing for the indenturing of children outside Free State boundaries.[85] Transvaal president M.W. Pretorius's proclamations of September 1857 and March 1858, "against the transport of black children (*naturellen-kinderen*)" across the Vaal, show that the practice continued.[86]

Pretorius's proclamations were issued most likely because he and other officials feared the impact of slaving reports on public opinion outside the ZAR, rather than opposed slavery itself. Only months before, he had informed Schoeman of accusations being leveled against the Zoutpansbergers by a certain Tobias Mostert, who had painted Schoeman in "hellish colors." Mostert claimed he had bought two children from a man named Landsberg, with the knowledge of the local authorities, and intended to take them to the Cape as proof of slave trading in Zoutpansberg. (Landsberg was presumably the Schoemansdal shopkeeper, August Landsberg, who later sat on the Zoutpansberg heemraad.[87]) Pretorius was afraid that Mostert's story would get out.

[I]f we want to maintain our freedom we must oppose the *careless* traders in African children (*kleine kaffers*) and keep this practice as far as possible within our own borders, but people such as Landsberg who have done nothing for our freedom undermine it by participating in the trade for their own benefit. [emphasis added] [88]

Agar-Hamilton long ago noted that Pretorius himself participated in the traffic. In 1864 he arranged for purchases of six children in Schoemansdal through Piet Vercueil, brother of landdrost Jan Vercueil.[89] Commandant-general Schoeman, of course, was involved in the trade, as other ZAR officials were aware. Pretorius's nephew and Pretoria district field-cornet, "Swart Martiens" (also with the initials M.W.) Pretorius, was one of Schoeman's loyal supporters when he became the ZAR's acting state president. Swart Martiens looked to Schoeman, in turn, for occasional favors.

Dear friend, do not forget to consider my need for laborers when you arrive in Zoutpansberg, and if you could obtain a young girl for my wife I would be very grateful, but you must not pay more than six or seven pounds, because they are nothing more than a handful of flies.[90]

One of the clearest indictments against the Zoutpansbergers' trade was published by Rev. Charles Murray, DRC mission inspector, who with missionary Henry Gonin visited Stefanus Hofmeyr at Goedgedacht in mid-1865. On their return while passing through Makapanspoort, near Piet Potgietersrust, they encountered Gert Duvenage, who was on his way to sell children to burghers in other parts of the Transvaal. Gert was without doubt part of the well-known Duvenage family who had entered Zoutpansberg in 1848 with A. H. Potgieter and settled in Schoemansdal and the Rhenosterpoort ward.[91]

Gert Duven(h)age, son of T, previously of Hope Town...had a strange cargo that he was going to trade. In the back of the wagon I saw about eight small African children packed tightly together, in the same manner that I, as a child, was wont to observe in drawings of slave ships. To my question as to where he came from, where he was going and what he had on the wagon, he replied that he had come "from the back," that he was going "ahead" and had "wood and such goods" on the wagon. "And," I asked, "whose children are sitting in the back?" "Mine" was the answer. It appeared that he had traded them "at the back" for two head of cattle each, and that they would be traded "ahead" for six head of cattle each. In the meantime they were being badly treated, one can even say abused. At night in the bitter winter cold they lay on the bare ground in the open sky, some even with their bodies naked. The youngest child was, I would say, not more than four years old, and many times it was heart-rending to hear them cry during the night because of the cold. When the man spoke to me about his journey, I became extremely angry and told him that his trading practice was one of the reasons why the Lord held back his blessing on the land; it was enough to bring a curse on the Republic. His reply was that I should not see this as slave trade. "It is sanctioned by an *inboeksel* [a certificate of indenture], Sir." Of the *inboeksel* I saw nothing, because whoever wanted them could have one for six head of cattle.[92]

At the time, hunter-trader Alexander Struben, brother of the Transvaal trader and later Volksraad member, Harry Struben, entered Zoutpansberg in order to hunt elephant. Instead he became involved in the war between the Zoutpansbergers and the VhaVenda and joined the laager on Albasini's farm, Goedewensch, from which commandos were launched against the VhaVenda. From the laager, Alexander wrote to his brother Harry that two traders, Calverley and Haversman, had visited the laager and respectively obtained £200 and £150 worth of ivory, cattle, cash, and "niggers" for trade goods.[93]

Apparently in 1865 the export of African children underwent a brief resurgence due to disruptions in elephant hunting and ivory trading. In 1864 the Zoutpansbergers had a row with the VaNgoni leader, Mzila, over the repatriation of the fugitive headman, Munene, and as a result, Mzila closed the Mozambique hunting fields to white hunters and their African marksmen. At the time, whites were also involving themselves in the succession struggle for a *dienstdoende* chieftainship following Ramabulana's death by siding with Davhana against Makhado, the eventual victor. Makhado retaliated by withholding labor from the Boers and instructing his marksmen to retain the guns of their white employers until the pro-Davhana Zoutpansbergers, who included Albasini, recognized his claim. Ivory trading, already in decline due to the injudicious, large-scale killing of elephants in the region, thus came to a standstill.[94] Conversely, the trade value of African children taken as booty during these conflicts, including the campaign against Magoro, rose at this time, as did demand for labor in the southerly areas of the Transvaal.[95]

Increased publicity over instances of selling, however, began to embroil the ZAR in controversy and led in 1866 to stricter laws to curtail slave trading. In early December 1865 word spread that a Carl Schmidt of Makapanspoort and "Frederik" Haenert of Zoutpansberg had brought wagon-loads of African children which they had obtained in Zoutpansberg and were planning to sell them to the Boers of Makwassie in the western Transvaal. According to reports, Schmidt had nineteen children and Haenert, seventeen. While passing through the Waterberg, Haenert encountered a local resident, P. J. van Staden, and told him that he had only sixteen children as one had died of the cold on the way. He left another with van Staden because the child had sustained burns.[96] The British governor at the Cape, P.E. Wodehouse, after receiving a report from Gideon Steyn of Potchefstroom about the dealings of Haenert and Schmidt, protested to ZAR president Pretorius.[97] The Transvaal government speedily arrested Schmidt and Haenert, but Schmidt was fined only Rds 100. Considering the fine too lenient, the ZAR reopened the case, but administrative bungling and neglect on the part of the state attorney resulted in Schmidt's acquittal in May 1866. Haenert appears to have been spared further legal proceedings.[98]

Apologists have sought to minimize the role played in the trade by prominent Boers. Schmidt and Haenert, for example, have been portrayed as inconsequential white residents operating clandestinely, but both were well-known residents of the Transvaal.[99] Claims that the "Portuguese" section of the Zoutpansberg population was particularly guilty in this respect have also been misleading.[100] Certainly Portuguese-speaking settlers were present in Zoutpansberg, and Albasini played an especially prominent part in the procurement of and trade in "black ivory." Nevertheless, it is also true that most Portuguese-speakers, some of Goan-Portuguese descent, were incorporated into the Boer community through marriage.[101]

Indentureship in Zoutpansberg

Little information on African children of Zoutpansberg after their indenture to whites is available in the sources. According to Morrison Barlow of the British administration of the Transvaal (1877–81), indentured children were, on the whole, treated reasonably well despite the constraints of the system. When asked in 1881 if he was aware of cases of slavery among the Boers, Barlow replied:

> I have come across that peculiar class of servant who receive no pay of any kind or description; they get their food given them and their clothes.

> When I have asked them where they came from, they say they have been with their master ever since they were quite small. I have said to them, "Where are your father and mother?" "I do not know; I have never seen them." "Where do you come from?" "I do not know." I have seen scores and scores of cases like that, but at the same time the Boers treat that class of servants remarkably well. I mean to say, that they always mix on an equality; they are treated well; they get their clothes and food and everything else, in fact, they are far too valuable a class for the Boers to ill-treat.[102]

However, as incidents involving Schmidt, Haenert, and Duvenage clearly reveal, ill-treatment and abuse occurred, even though these children held value for their owners as either trade items or potential laborers or servants. *Inboekelinge* belonged to a servile class and remained subject to the will and whims of their masters.

Whether ill-treated or not, children indentured by the Boers underwent an acculturation process that tended to separate them from their cultures of origin, and particularly so for Zoutpansberg children indentured to burghers in other Transvaal districts. A few children were able to return home, such as "Kaatje" and "Dammio," two girls who made it back from Pretoria, but such cases must have been rare.[103] Children above three were for the most part easily controlled, cared for, and trainable in those skills important to the white household and hunting industry.[104] When Rev. Piet Huet of the DRC arrived in Schoemansdal in 1858, he was struck by the large number of African children or so-called *inboekelinge* in the streets, most of whom were carrying around small white children they had to look after.[105] Many indentured laborers upon maturity became marksmen, who supervised other African workers and hunters.[106] And because the indenture system was administered indifferently, adult indentured laborers were not necessarily released at the age of twenty-five or otherwise as determined by law.[107]

The longer detached from their origins, the more indentured servants tended to develop a bond with their masters. Marriages between indentured laborers also strengthened their master's hold, impeded escape, and facilitated the acculturation process. Spouses from different ethnic groups were especially inclined to become estranged from their origins and receptive to Boer culture. The "apprentice" Manungu, Albasini's chief elephant hunter and "head chief" of his VaTsonga following, remained with Albasini until the latter's death in 1888.[108] Manungu was either of VaTsonga or AmaZulu origin and married Lya, who was captured by the AmaSwati during a raid on the BaPai, an eastern BaSotho group, and had been traded by them with the Boers for "cloth and beads."[109] Manungu's service to the Zoutpansbergers was fundamental in their attempts to dominate the region. He was a mediator in their negotiations with Mzila, the VaNgoni leader, and on several occasions commanded African auxiliary troops in the conflicts between the Boers and the VhaVenda.[110]

As Delius and Trapido have noted with regard to the Lydenburg area, indentured laborers, no matter how devoted to their masters, underwent simultaneously the processes of incorporation into and exclusion from white society, the latter process often initiated by indentured laborers themselves.[111] They were involved in all activities in the Boer household but were excluded from certain rights and privileges in Boer society on account of race. In a sense they formed a marginal group between the white community and "traditional" African societies. From available evidence, a large percentage of the so-called "oorlams Kaffers," frequently referred to in nineteenth-century literature on the Transvaal, were or had been indentured laborers. "Oorlams" Africans largely became westernized and often spoke only Dutch/Afrikaans. From their ranks came a large number of the first African urban dwellers in Boer towns. In Zoutpansberg, references occur to "oorlams" who cared for the farms of their employers while the latter were congregated in laagers during times of conflict with the VhaVenda.[112] "Oorlams" also were among the first Africans to convert to Christianity in the Zoutpansberg and to become actively involved with the DRC mission.[113] Thus because of the Boers' indenture system, dependent as it was on children seized as booty, a new social stratum or grouping in the Transvaal African population emerged, and Zoutpansberg, as export center of "black ivory," played a crucial role in this transformation process.[114]

Notes

1. This chapter is a revised, English version of "'Zwart Ivoor': Inboekelinge in Zoutpansberg, 1848-1869," which appeared in the *South African Historical Journal,* 24 (1991), 31-66. All quotations from the original Dutch or Afrikaans sources have been rendered into English.

2. Chesson (1869); Huet (1869); Nixon (1885), 62-77; anon. ["One who knows more than the Boers care about"], 20 May 1881, in *TA,* 21 May 1881. See also ch. 7 in this volume.

3. Venter (1934), 23; Giliomee (1981), 85. See also chs. 2 and 4 in this volume.

4. Giliomee (1989), 452; Malherbe (1991), 16.

5. Liebenberg (1959), 37-47, 50-8, 62-4.

6. Minutes of the Volksraad, Ohrigstad, 7 Oct. 1848, SAR Tvl, no. 1: 86.

7. The complete act was published in ibid, no. 2: 29-32: Resolution of the Volksraad, Lydenburg, 9 May 1851, and Jeppe and Kotzé (1887), 8-11. Quotations in this chapter are derived from the latter source.

8. In Lydenburg gender distinctions were sometimes made, by which boys were indentured to the age of twenty-five, girls to twenty-one. See "Register van Naturelledienskontrakte," 65, in LL (landdrost Lydenburg), vol. 172: 40, TAD. I

have not found, however, any legislation or any reference to legislation containing such a provision.

9. Van Warmelo and Phophi (1949), 941-5; De Beer (1986), 339-41.

10. Delius and Trapido (1983), 62-3; Viljoen to Schoeman, 6 May 1861, SS 37, R 4384/61, TAD; van Heerden to Geyser, 15 Oct. 1864, SS 60, R 905/64, TAD; Preller report on Kaffercommissie, 28 Jun. 1872, SS 152, Supl 104/72, TAD.

11. Trapido (1976), 25.

12. The economics of labor use remains as an open field of investigation as pursued tentatively by Fred Morton in ch. 7 of this volume.

13. Recollections of N.T. Oelofse, n.d., A 1721, 61, TAD. Oelofse entered this district in 1860.

14. Instructions in connection with the planned campaign against Sekwati and Mabhogo, art. 9, Lydenburg, Nov. 1851, SAR Tvl, no. 2: 255-6.

15. An 1866 Volksraad resolution making the government "co-guardian" (*toeziende voogd*) of all African orphans narrowed the loophole regarding transfer. Heirs of persons with apprentices in their service or under their care at the time of death could still obtain control over them, but in all other cases the power to appoint a "guardian" for African orphans rested with the government. Volksraad minutes, 16 Mar. 1866, art. 423 & 427, SAR Tvl, no. 5: 117.

16. Art. 4 of Sand River convention, 16 Jan. 1852, SAR Tvl, no. 2: 289. See also Eybers (1969), 358 and ch. 7 in this volume.

17. Government Notice, Pretoria, 23 Jul. 1866, SAR Tvl. no. 5: 426-7.

18. In connection with Old Testament influence on their beliefs, Moolman (1975), 25-8.

19. Agar-Hamilton (1928), 169-95, 218-9.

20. Moolman (1975), 96. In a similar vein, Venter in a recent article regarding indentured slaves accompanying the Voortrekkers suggests that "the positive statements of the majority of the indentured slaves [about the treatment they received] are to the credit of the Voortrekker community and the Voortrekker leaders, and are indicative of sound labor relations." Venter (1991), 29. For another view of master-servant relations in the Voortrekker community, see Mason's concluding remarks in ch. 4 of this volume.

21. Trapido (1976).

22. Delius and Trapido (1983). In connection with the term "black ivory," see Grützner to ZAR state president, 10 Feb. 1875, SS 184, R 436/75, TAD; W 182 (H.C. Stiemens collection), 51, TAD; Struben (1920), 87.

23. Bonner (1983), 80-4, 90-2.

24. Lovejoy (1983), 222, 234.

25. With regard to the use of the term "apprentice" in the Cape colony, see Liebenberg (1959), ch. 3. The Voortrekkers' preference for this term is evident from documents on the indenture system included in the series, SAR Tvl, nos. 1-8.

26. Delius and Trapido (1983), 53; Trapido (1976), 25; Delius (1984), 35-7; and Wagner (1980), 332.

27. Haenert to Pretorius, 8 Dec. 1868, SS 104, R 1424/68, TAD.

28. Malherbe (1991), 5-6.

29. Boeyens (1990), 110; Tempelhoff (1988), 269-70.

30. Slave trading in Zoutpansberg may have continued. According to Morrison Barlow, special commissioner for Waterberg and Zoutpansberg during the British

administration of the Transvaal, the VhaVenda chief Mphaphuli offered him first two and later three children in exchange for a Martini Henry gun. Mphaphuli apparently took the children from the VaTsonga chief, Xikundu, whom he had beheaded. Barlow also reported that "certain white Traders, I regret to say, Englishmen, are carrying on a regular slave trade with some of the Chiefs in the Zoutpansberg Mountains; they come from 'Bamangwato' in 'Sichele's' country, bring with them guns, powder and lead, which they exchange for young Kaffirs obtained from the Chiefs 'Pafuri [Mphaphuli], 'Magato [Makhado]' and 'Servass' [Tshivhase]: they put them in Australian 2-wheel carts drawn by oxen and then convey them by the back and northernmost side of the 'Zoutpansberg' across the 'Limpopo River' into Sechele's country where they are readily disposed of." Dahl to government secretary, 30 May 1877, SS 238, R 2171/77, and Barlow to Osborne, 2 Oct. 1877, SS 249, R 3704/77, TAD. Slave trading between the northern Transvaal and the BaKwena and BaNgwato in the Kalahari region at this late date, however, seems unlikely. See ch. 9 in this volume, as well as Theophilus Shepstone's note of 15 Feb. 1879 in SS 327, R 376/79, TAD, that Barlow apparently wrongly assumed that "Bamangwato means any place in Sicheli's country." For additional reference to Mphaphuli, Barlow and Dahl report, 28 May 1881, C. 3219: 62-3.

31. Gaps in the Zoutpansberg record were noted long ago by Agar-Hamilton (1928), xv. Cf. the Lydenburg sources, Delius and Trapido (1983), 67-8.

32. Boeyens (1990), 67.

33. Survey of the Office of the Landdrost of Schoemansdal, 10-12 Aug. 1864, SS 58, R 569/64, TAD.

34. Witness the difficulty with which burghers signed petitions, e.g. Vorster and 66 others to Pres. and Uitv. Raad, 3 May 1858, SS 20, R 2050/58 and Herbst and 5 others to Pres. and Uitv. Raad, 9 Apr. 1863, SS 48, R 294/63, TAD. A. P. Duvenage, an official who found it difficult to compile a written report and who referred to himself as "such an ignorant man," held at one stage three posts—field-cornet, superintendent of African chiefdoms, and justice of the peace. Cf. Duvenage to Uitv. Raad and Pres., 22 Jan. 1866, SS 74, R 64/66, TAD.

35. Delius and Trapido (1983), esp. 65, 70-1, make much use of missionary A. Nachtigal's diary.

36. Maree (1962), 36, 49-60; Boeyens (1990), 33-4.

37. Giliomee (1989), 426-7.

38. The ban proved unsuccessful. Pace Jeppe and Kotzé (1887), 110-1: *Wet met betrekking tot den handel met de aan deze republiek ondergeschikte kafferstammen*, approved 22 Sep. 1858. See Buys statement, 3 Jun. 1858, SS 20, R 2103/58, and Albasini to Uitv. Raad, 14 Oct. 1864, SS 60, R 902/64, TAD.

39. Pretorius et al. to Pres. and Uitv. Raad, 3 May 1858, SS 23, Supl. 3/58, TAD; recollections of J.H. Coetzer, A 1594, 2, TAD; and Churchill letter, 13 Sep. 1856, A 17, TAD.

40. Struben account, n.d., A 595 (Le Roux Smith—Le Roux collection), 31, 35, TAD. See also Churchill letter, 13 Sep. 1856, A 17, TAD.

41. Pater Joaquim de Santa Rita Montanha account, 1 Oct. 1856, A 81, 93, TAD.

42. Boeyens (1987), 182-6; Das Neves (1879), 140; Miller and Tempelhoff (1990), 36.

43. ZA, 28 Jan. & 12 May 1864.

44. Du Plessis and Duvenage report, 2 Aug. 1864, SS 57, R 521/64, and van Nispen

to State Pres., Marawasland, 19 Nov. 1867, SS 92, R 1164/67, TAD; Potgieter (1958), 23.

45. Van Rensburg to Pres. and Uitv. Raad, 10 Apr. 1863, SS 48, R 300/63, TAD; Duvenage "Voorstel van wetten voor de kaffers stammen," 1865, SS 73, Supl. 63/65, TAD; Albasini to Vercueil, 6 Apr. 1866, SS 76, R 393/66, TAD; Struben account, n.d., A 595, 31, TAD; *ZA*, 12 Nov. 1855.

46. A geographical analysis of Albasini's list (26 Dec. 1867, SS 72, R 1964/67, TAD) shows that the residential areas of *opgaaf* communities were sometimes situated far from the center of white settlement.

47. Report of meeting chaired by Schoeman, 27 Feb. 1855, SS 7, R 774/55; du Plessis and Duvenage report, 2 Aug. 1864, SS 57, R 521/64; "Monene" interview, 11 Apr. 1864, SS 55, R 210/64, TAD.

48. Delius (1984), 52; Bonner (1983), 33, 88-9.

49. Du Plessis and Duvenage to Pres. and Uitv. Raad, 1 Aug. 1864, SS 57, R 513/64, Duvenage to Uitv. Raad, Mar. 1866, SS 76, R 370/66, and Moulder et al. petition, Mar. 1866, SS 76, R 371/66, TAD.

50. De Vaal (1953), 20, 66; Junod (1905), 232, 235; Albasini to Schoeman, 2 Apr. 1862, A 248, vol. 1: 153-4, TAD.

51. It has always been a strong argument in the apologist literature that the accusations of slavery against the Boers were based on the reports of outsiders (travelers or missionaries) who were often unsympathetic to the Boer cause.

52. Gabriël Buys, Michael's brother, was originally assigned this task but died the same year, whereupon Michael assumed his position. Report of meeting chaired by Schoeman, 27 Feb. 1855, SS 7, R 774/55, and Geyser, Jacobs, and le Grange report, 31 Mar. 1863, SS 52, Supl 28/63, TAD. Albasini was instructed to collect *opgaaf* from Africans to the east, northeast, and southeast of Schoemansdal. Upon Albasini's appointment as superintendent of African chiefdoms for the same area on 9 Apr. 1863, his main task remained the collection of *opgaaf*. Albasini to Schoeman, 23 Jan. 1862, SS 41, R 61/62; Albasini to Grobler, 1 Feb. 1861, SS 37, R 4234/61; van Rensburg to Albasini, 3 Apr. 1863, SS 8743, no. 19; and Albasini to Uitv. Raad, 5 Aug. 1864, SS 58, R 551/64, TAD. When two additional superintendents were appointed a few years later, initial confusion over their jurisdiction was clarified by the central government, which indicated that *dienstdoende* Africans in their various wards had been placed under the control of field-cornets, whereas *opgaaf* Africans were under superintendents. Van Nispen to Duvenage, 29 Jan. 1868, SS 96, no. 205/68, TAD.

53. Maree (1962), 49; MacKidd to Murray, 27 Feb. 1865, Soutpansberg collection, DRCA.

54. *ZA*, 28 Jan. 1864; de Vaal (1953), 5, 20; Anon (1972), 29-32; also n. 49 above. For further details on João Albasini and his slave-raiding activities, see ch. 6 by Eldredge in this volume.

55. *Wet tot betere regeling der jagt....* Jeppe & Kotzé (1887), 107 (art. 7).

56. Kennedy (1964), 113-4, 123, 130-1, 307. I am grateful to Daniel Galbraith for this reference.

57. *ZA*, 12 Nov. 1855, report on "De Transvaal."

58. Jacobs report, 29 Feb. 1856, SS 11, R 995/56, TAD.

59. Bronkhorst remarked that many of the stronghold's inhabitants apparently had left before the attack "as very few women and children were seen and found."

Jacobs report, 15 Nov. 1856, SS 11, R 1242/56, TAD.

60. Weeber complaint, 1 Feb. 1860, SS 37, R 4237/61; Grobler to Schoeman, 10 Dec. 1860, SS 35, R 4179/60; and Grobler trial, 6 Apr. 1863, SS 47, R 281/63, TAD.

61. Grobler to Schoeman, 24 Jan. 1861, SS 37, R 4224/61, TAD. As yet no reply to Grobler's request for instructions in this regard has been found in the Transvaal archives.

62. Das Neves (1879), 191-2; Albasini to Schoeman, 11 May 1861, SS 39, R 4903/61, TAD.

63. Albasini to Uitv. Raad, 13 Nov. 1863, SS 51, R 865/63, TAD.

64. "Monene" interview, 11 Apr. 1864, SS 55, R 210/64, TAD.

65. Ibid. Sikwalakwala's domain was situated north of the Limpopo in present-day Mozambique. He apparently paid tribute to both the Boers and the Gaza kingdom founded by Soshangane's VaNgoni. Cf. Das Neves (1879), 122-5.

66. Volksraad minutes, 6 Mar. 1866, art. 268, SAR Tvl, no. 5: 104.

67. Du Plessis and Duvenage report, 2 Aug. 1864, SS 57, R 521/64, and Duvenage report, 25 Apr. 1865, SS 66, R 495/65, TAD.

68. Struben account, A 595, 41, TAD. According to Struben, he declined to take his share of this "booty," as well as the four head of cattle he could have claimed instead.

69. The case lapsed after the court ruled that the men, whose alleged acts having taken place under conditions of war, had to be tried only by a military court. Boeyens (1990), 36-9.

70. Schoeman to State Pres. and Uitv. Raad, 12 Feb. 1868, SS 96, R 206/68; Schoeman to Pretorius, 2 & 13 Dec. 1867, SS 93, R 1226/67; Albasini report on the BaLobedu campaign, 13 Nov. 1867, and Albasini to Henderson, 6 Dec. 1867, and Skinner's list of individuals to whom children were allocated, 4 Jan. 1869, SS 114, R 1209/69; Schoeman to State Pres. and Uitv. Raad, 15 Feb. 1868, SS 96, R 179/68; and Maré to State Secretary, 26 Mar. 1875, SS 186, R 748/75; Buys report, 1 Feb. 1868, SS 96, R 205/68, TAD. See also "Ooggetuigen" letter, Feb. 1868, in *TA*, 18 Mar. 1868.

71. Albasini to Kruger, 13 Nov. 1869, SS 123, R 680/70, TAD.

72. Bonner (1983), 115.

73. Albasini to Uitv. Raad, 28 Sep. 1863, SS 50, R 735/63, Albasini to Uitv. Raad, 13 Nov. 1863, SS 51, R 865/63, and Albasini to Venter, 5 May 1865, SS 67, R 540/65, TAD.

74. Boeyens (1990), 35, 38, 41-2.

75. Military council session, Schoemansdal, 14 Jul. 1865, A 26 (F.V. Engelenburg collection), TAD. In his seminal essay on the Zoutpansberg, Wagner (1980), 333, argues that female captives referred to as *meiden* were young girls indentured exclusively to Transvaal Boers, but the correct translation of this Dutch term is "women," and adequate evidence shows that as a rule they were handed over to the Boers' African auxiliaries.

76. Albasini to Schnell, 16 Sep. 1872, SS 149, R 1461/72, TAD.

77. Jacobs report, 29 Feb. 1856, SS 11, R 995/56, TAD.

78. W 182 (H.C. Stiemens collection), 50, TAD.

79. Schoeman to State Pres. and Uitv. Raad, 12 Feb. 1868, SS 96, R 206/68, TAD; Schoeman journal, cv. 1 & 8 Oct. 1868, SS 118, Supl 1/69, TAD; and Uitv. Raad, 26 Oct. 1869, art. 21, URB, vol. 3, TAD.

80. Grützner to SAR State Pres., 10 Feb. 1875, SS 184, R 436/75, TAD. See also

Delius and Trapido (1983), 67-8.

81. Delius and Trapido (1983), 68, err in suggesting that only in the 1860s did Zoutpansberg play a dominant role in the trade in African children, before which time captive children "were principally disposed of locally."

82. Report on "De Trans-Vaal," *ZA*, 12 Nov. 1855. These price estimates tally with those in Struben (1920), 87. In 1881, A.K. Murray noted that during his residence in the Transvaal over a seventeen-year period, "I have witnessed the sale of boys and girls—at Zoutpansberg for £10 each, but this is in confidence." [Murray still had family in the Transvaal]. Murray to British and Foreign Anti-Slavery Society, 20 Jun. 1881, S. 22, G13, Transvaal Aborigines Protection Society Papers, Anti-Slavery Papers, RH. I am grateful to Barry Morton for this reference.

83. Prinsloo statement, 5 Dec. 1865, SS 72, R 1291/65 and van den Berg statement, 26 Jun. 1868, SS 102, R 998/68, TAD. See also Murray letter, *De Volksvriend*, 19 Aug. 1865.

84. Schoeman proclamation, 5 Oct. 1855, SS 8, R 915/55, TAD.

85. Van Aswegen (1971), 251-3.

86. Jeppe and Kotzé (1887), 32-3, 72-3.

87. Schoeman to Pretorius, 24 Nov. 1858, SS 322, R 2452/58, TAD; Grobler (1919), 221.

88. Pretorius to Schoeman, 12 Jan. 1857, SS 14, R 1277/57 and du Toit to Pretorius, 26 Oct. 1856, SS 12, R 1227/56, TAD.

89. Agar-Hamilton (1928), 218. Piet Vercueil was a well-known Zoutpansberger who lived in the vicinity of the VhaVenda of Mashau on his farm "Beaufort" in the Kleine Spelonken, part of the Spelonken ward. Schoeman to State Pres. and Uitv. Raad, 12 Feb. 1868, SS 96, R 296/68, and J.F. Goodwin diary, vol. 1: 138, M 1637, TAD.

90. Pretorius to Schoeman, 6 Jan. 1862, SS 41, R 8/62, TAD. Swart Martiens was one of a small group of burghers who died in 1864 fighting in Schoeman's "people's army" against Paul Kruger's "state army." Ferreira (1978), 308; Liebenberg (1977), 12, 107-8. This letter arrived prior to Schoeman and Stiemens's departure for Schoemansdal, where Stiemens received "gifts" of children from Buys and Albasini. See above.

91. Grobler (1919), 218-9.

92. Murray to "de heeren Lubbe, Biedouw, enz.," *De Volksvriend*, 19 Aug. 1865. For Henry Gonin's recollection of the case, Gonin to Pres. 15 Feb. 1875, SS 185, R 458/75, TAD.

93. Struben (1968), 146.

94. Boeyens (1990), 12; *ZA*, "Beschryving der Transvaalsche Republiek," 28 Jan., and Zoutpansberg report, 12 May 1864.

95. Delius and Trapido (1983), 68-73.

96. Pretorius to van der Linden, 5 Dec. 1865, SS 72, R 1297/65, van Staden, de Clerck, and Prinsloo statements, 5 Dec. 1865, SS 72, R 1291/65, and Uitv. Raad minutes, 5 Dec. 1865, SS 72, R 1289/65, TAD. P.J. van Staden of Waterberg is not to be confused with Petrus Johannes van Staden, the Rustenburg landdrost who was instructed by the ZAR to investigate the case.

97. Steyn to Wodehouse, 4 Dec. 1865, and Wodehouse to Pretorius, 8 Jan. 1866, c. 4141: 1-2, 7 (the original of the latter is in SAR Tvl, no. 5, 450); see also Kistner (1952), 240-2.

98. Pretorius to van der Linden, 18 Dec. 1865, SS 72, R 1333/65, and Munnich to

Pres. and Uitv. Raad, 10 Feb. 1866, SS 75, R 172/66, TAD; Kistner (1952), 241; Pieterse (1936), 53.

99. Agar-Hamilton and Kistner assume Haenert operated his trade out of a cave near Schoemansdal, because his residence is listed in the documents as in "den Spielonk." This merely indicates, however, that he lived in the Spelonken ward in Zoutpansberg. Though sometimes referred to as "Frederik," Haenert's real first name was Ferdinand. He was the successful owner of the farm, Driefontein, also known as "The Last Hope." The town Haenertsburg was later named after him. Like Carl Schmidt, Haenert was of German extraction, a fact that was stressed by Kistner to lessen the censure on the Transvaal Boers. Agar-Hamilton (1928), 212; Kistner (1952), 241, 154-5. For more information on Haenert and confusion over his Christian names, see Changuion (1987), 16-7. Changuion's claim that Haenert's farm was probably situated between Mara and Vivo is incorrect. See van Nispen to Pretorius, 17 Jan. 1867, SS 84, R 63/67 and Spelonken census list, 3 Mar. 1873, SS 165, R 2160/73, TAD; de Vaal (1953), 137.

100. De Vaal (1953), 127; Hofmeyr (1890), 27; Lys to Burgers, 12 Feb. 1875, SS 200, R 3034/75, TAD.

101. Wagner (1980), 345, n. 65.

102. Barlow report, 28 May 1881, C. 3219: 62.

103. Most probably the girls had been taken as booty during the volunteer corps campaign against Mashau's VhaVenda in 1867 and allotted to the corps' physician, B.G.A.D. Arnoldi. In July 1870 Arnoldi complained that one of Mashau's people had taken the two girls from him and that Mashau had failed to compensate Arnoldi after promising him four heifers. "Orphans" list, 4 Jan. 1869, SS 114, R 1209/69, and Haagen to Albasini, 17 Jul. 1870, SS 125, R 993/70, TAD.

104. "De Trans-Vaal," *ZA*, 12 Nov. 1855.

105. Huet (1869), 19-20, 32-3. At night the *inboekelinge* had to sleep either in the open or in the outer kitchen on their master's erven (premises).

106. In the 1858 draft of the Hunting Act, "kaffer apprenticen" were among the four categories of Africans who could be despatched without white supervision on game hunts (*Wet tot het beter regelen der jagt...*). EVR, vol. 199: 114. Cf. Wagner (1980), 332; Trapido (1976), 25.

107. Steyn to Wodehouse, 4 Dec. 1865, SAR Tvl, no. 5: 450-1; Delius and Trapido (1983), 73.

108. De Vaal (1953), 7, 143-4.

109. Ibid, 7-8. According to De Vaal, Manungu was of AmaZulu origin, but other sources suggest he was of VaTsonga extraction. Cf. Motenda (1940), 69, and Junod (1905), 232.

110. Wagner (1980), 332-3; De Vaal (1953), 7; Struben account, A 595, 38 and Albasini to Uitv. Raad, 14 Oct. 1864, SS 60, R 901/64, TAD. Another indentured servant who acted as go-between in negotiations between the Boers and local African leaders was Anthon, the "apprentice" of landdrost Jan Vercueil. See meeting attended by Vercueil and Albasini, 19 Aug. 1864, SS 58, R 594/64, TAD.

111. Delius and Trapido (1983), 70-5.

112. In an 1865 attack launched by Ne-Luvhola and Nthabalala's VhaVenda on Jacobus Botha's farm, Vleyfontein, in the Spelonken, two "oorlams" were killed. Du Plessis to Maré, 20 & 23 Jul. 1865, A 26 (Engelenburg collection), 27, 31, TAD.

113. Maree (1962), 93. To what extent any of these former *inboekelinge* or "Oorlams"

were assimilated into the mainstream African population, as certainly occurred, requires further investigation. See Delius and Trapido (1983), 75-81, and ch. 7 by Fred Morton in this volume. A noteable case is that of Mughombane II, the heir apparent to the northern AmaNdebele chiefdom of BaKekana. He was captured by the Boers after the siege of Makapansgat in 1854 in which Mughombane I was defeated. Mughombane II was then "apprenticed" to a white farmer in the De Wildt area near Pretoria, where he was employed as a cattle herder and acquired the Dutch/Afrikaans name of Klaas. In the late 1860s, he was brought back by his compatriots to the northern Transvaal to be prepared for the assumption of his chiefly duties. De Beer (1986), 37-9.

114. In pre-ZAR days Africans of the area had abducted women and children, as happened following internecine conflicts, although Boer demand for indentured laborers greatly increased the value of African children for exchange purposes. Van Rensburg, 23 Aug. 1864, SS 56, R 287/64, TAD. War captives had as a rule been incorporated into the dominant group, sometimes over several generations, and a "slavery-to-kinship continuum" existed in the Zoutpansberg, as it did in other African societies. See Miers and Kopytoff (1977), esp. 7, 16, 19-20, 22-4, 77; Harries (1981); Cooper (1979), 103-6; Delius (1984), 50; Bonner (1983), 80; Motenda (1940), 54.

PLATE 1. On commando (1833). Sketch by Charles Davidson Bell. *Source:* Bell, Charles Davidson. ART 179/3. © The Brenthurst Library, Johannesburg.

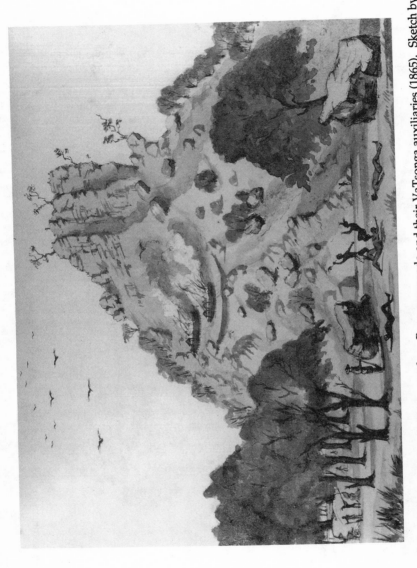

PLATE 2. Attack on the VhaVenda of Magoro by a Boer commando and their VaTsonga auxiliaries (1865). Sketch by Alexander Struben. *Source:* Mrs. R. Krause.

PLATE 3. Schoemansdal (1865). Sketch by Alexander Struben. *Source:* Transvaal Archives Depot, Pretoria.

PLATE 4. Slave riding (1869). The Ngamiland slave expedition of Jan Viljoen, Lucas Marthinus Swartz, and Hendrik Van Zyl. Water color by Thomas Baines. *Source:* Wallis (1946), frontispiece.

9

Servitude, Slave Trading, and Slavery in the Kalahari

Barry Morton

Though indigenous systems of African servitude have received steadily increasing attention for the past quarter century, the issue has yet to be raised insofar as the region south of the Zambezi is concerned.[1] This gap is most apparent when perusing the standard compendia on African slavery, in which the multitude of southern African societies are represented in sum by only two case.[2] Of these, Isaacman describes how slavery was imported by the Portuguese into the lower Zambezi valley and then was adapted by indigenes, and Tlou argues that the indigenous form of servitude practiced by the BaTawana in northwest Botswana was a form of "clientship."[3] Judging, therefore, from published research on southern African history, a field itself enjoying sustained growth the past fifteen years, Africans south of the Zambezi escaped the scourge of indigenous slavery, just as they avoided becoming ensnared in the export trade in human beings.[4]

Further research in Ngamiland, the area studied by Tlou, and a survey of sources relevant to the Kalahari region of present day Botswana indicate that slavery was indeed practiced by the BaTawana as of the late nineteenth century and that forms of servitude, referred to locally as *botlhanka* or *bolata* (pers. sing. *motlhanka*, *lelata*; pl. *batlhanka*, *malata*), were present in the Kalahari at least a century earlier.[5] Prior to the so-called "mfecane" period, the BaTswana of the Kalahari subjugated the Khoisan-speaking BaSarwa (SeTswana for "bushmen," also the derisory "Masarwa") and BaKgalagadi and used them as cattle herders, hunters, agricultural laborers, and domestic servants. After being themselves dislodged in the 1820s by Sebitwane's BaKololo (BaFokeng) and the 1830s by Mzilikazi's AmaNdebele, the BaTswana moved further into the Kalahari and virtually enslaved the BaSarwa and BaKgalagadi living there and controlled them with startling brutality. For the remainder of the nineteenth century, these subjugated

216

FIGURE 9.1 Botswana and Southern Africa.

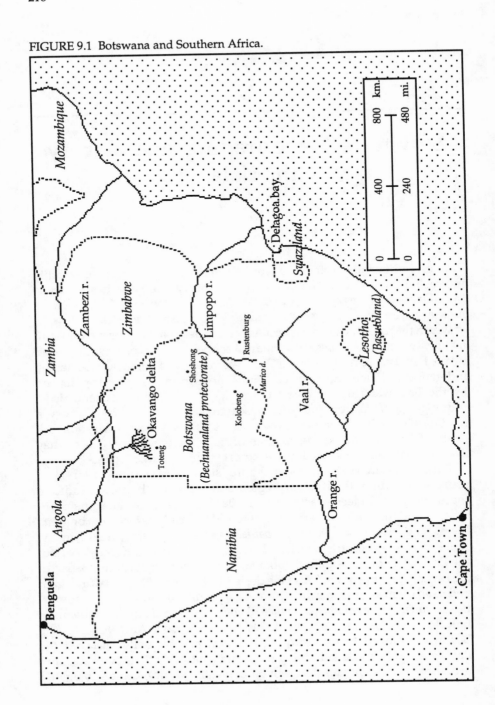

peoples enabled the BaTswana elite, and the heirs to whom they were passed on, to increase their political and economic control over wide expanses of territory. They herded their master's cattle, magnified their rangelands, created leisure time for them to engage in public affairs, and hunted, dressed, and transported ivory and skins to the capital from which the BaTswana elite traded these articles for guns, horses, and other goods arriving from the Cape and Namibia. As early as the 1850s their children were sold by some BaTswana rulers to Boer traders from the western Transvaal. Although their importance as a source of trade revenues declined with the close of the hunting frontier in the late nineteenth century, their value to the maintenance of large cattle herds, on which the dispensation of political and economic favors within BaTswana society was based, continued into the twentieth century.

Botlhanka/Bolata "Studies"

Isaac Schapera, to this day the most eminent scholar of the BaTswana, is the first to have portrayed *botlhanka/bolata* as a form of servitude. In his standard works on the BaTswana, Schapera terms *malata* "serfs," though noting that in precolonial times persons known as *batlhanka* "were treated almost like slaves." *Malata* performed domestic service, hunted, herded, and otherwise labored for the BaTswana elites. They lacked property rights, legal protection, were liable to lose their children, could be transferred among BaTswana masters, and were inherited. In modern times their condition improved, though *malata* remain a stigmatized group often without protected legal rights.[6] Schapera asserts that such persons were not chattel, citing David Livingstone: "Never in any case, within the memory of man, has a Bechuana chief sold any of his people, or a Bechuana man his child."[7] Yet, Livingstone's own correspondence reveals, and Schapera has acknowledged in his later work, that *batlhanka* children were "occasionally" sold to Boer traders, and that Khama III upon his succession as *kgosi* (senior royal, king, pl. *dikgosi*) of the BaNgwato in 1875 took the step of prohibiting the sale of BaSarwa children and the "transfer of serfs from one man to another."[8]

Recent scholars adhere nevertheless to Schapera's standard interpretation of *botlhanka/bolata*. According to Wilson, "BaTswana chiefs and certain leading families had Sarwa families attached to them...but Sarwa could not be bought or sold."[9] In the early 1960s Silberbauer and Kuper at a village in Ghanzi district interviewed BaSarwa who said they had been "owned" by the BaKgalagadi for generations, but Silberbauer and Kuper characterized their status as "serfs," because these "Bushmen...are free to marry, raise families and enjoy their traditional social life to a degree which forbids the description of their condition as 'slavery.'"[10]   Other ethnographers and anthropologists have remained aloof from the *bolata/botlhanka* question, all the more surprising given the voluminous "Bushmen" literature.[11] Historians, beginning with Tlou, have instead addressed it. Tlou's study, often cited, elaborates in detail Schapera's concept of serfdom and provides an historical outline of the institution. According to Tlou, *botlhanka* began in the post-*mfecane* period, when the BaTswana were rebuilding their societies, and was relatively unimportant to the new BaTswana economies, which he claims "did not require intensive labor....[T]he number of serfs was small in relation to the total population...."[12] *Batlhanka* may not be considered as slaves on the added grounds that "a virtual absence of buying and selling" of *batlhanka* took place. Moreover they were treated fairly because "the King could intervene on behalf of the batlhanka [and thus] mitigate abuse."[13] Tlou and others writing since have argued that serfdom became established through an evolutionary process whereby BaTswana first employed BaSarwa and BaKgalagadi as hunters during the ivory trade era, and, as the game on which they depended for meat disappeared or migrated, these heretofore independent hunter-gatherers gradually became dependent on BaTswana cattle owners.[14]

Two studies by University of Botswana undergraduates provide a more critical view of the *botlhanka* system but refrain from challenging Tlou's interpretation. Gadibolae, who did field research among the BaSarwa of Nata, maintains that *botlhanka* was a colonially inspired institution, beginning only in 1890. It was "a form of involuntary servitude in which persons were obliged to perform duties for others under conditions of social inferiority and restriction." Still, he asserts, *batlhanka* could never be bought or sold.[15] Mautle took the first step in asserting that BaTswana owned *batlhanka* as "slaves," with reference to the BaKgalagadi conquered and exploited by the BaKwena after 1840.[16] His study of *botlhanka* emphasizes the dehumanization central to the institution. The BaKwena economically exploited their BaKgalagadi *batlhanka* for labor and tribute, used female *malata* for sexual gratification, routinely abused *batlhanka* physically, and in general treated them as sub-humans. His research interviews, attached to his original thesis, record *malata* descendants bristling with anger when recounting how their families had been treated in the past.[17] His description of BaKwena *botlhanka* as slavery is dissipated, however, by ignoring the *batlhanka* literature, as well as that on African slavery, and focusing attention instead on theoretical distinctions between slavery and an "asian mode of production." Other undergraduate researchers have also conducted interviews relating to this topic.[18]

Delay in coming to terms with the *bolata/botlhanka* issue stems in part from the persistence of what may be called "kgotla research." Among SeSotho- and SeTswana-speaking people, the *kgotla* has served as the focal point for political and judicial activities, but until recently participation was limited to adult men with full legal rights. All women and *malata/batlhanka* were excluded, and in practice so were the poorer men, who could not afford the time to attend. A common characteristic in historical studies of the BaTswana is the reliance on the opinions of those who dominate the *kgotla* (i.e., the ranking male BaTswana, and historically the large cattle owners). With regard to the historical literature on *bolata/botlhanka*, an important source has been the *kgotla* testimony of the BaNgwato regent, Tshekedi Khama, before an LMS inquiry in 1935.[19] Apart from the pioneer studies of Schapera, Silberbauer and Kuper's interviews at Kuli, and the recent work of several Botswana university students, research has not been based on interviews or other evidence derived from the *batlhanka* and *malata*, from their descendants, or from observers who stood outside the system. Ironically, the very traditions collected by the above mentioned constitute a rich repository of evidence for viewing *botlhanka* as slavery, at least from the mid-to-late nineteenth century. The Botswana National archives, which holds an extensive collection of colonial district reports and correspondence dating from the 1890s, is an excellent resource on this topic.[20] Also incompletely tapped have been the journals, correspondence, and recollections of the many nineteenth century European missionaries, traders, and hunters who passed through areas where *bolata/botlhanka* was practiced. Much of their writing has been published. Taken together, the existing interviews, archival records, and nineteenth century literature provide a detailed perspective on *bolata/botlhanka* that stands apart from the testimony of leading BaTswana. With these sources, *bolata/botlhanka* may be viewed as a system of extorting labor and goods from conquered BaSarwa and BaKgalagadi peoples, who were subordinated over time through the use of physical force and psychological dehumanization and rendered liable to exchange in both internal and external markets.

The Origin of Bolata/Botlhanka

Before the 1820s BaTswana societies forcibly subjugated many of the peoples in the regions of the Kalahari sandveld they colonized.[21] Those conquered were used to hunt and provide tribute or herd cattle. Presumably women were used as domestic servants, as suggested in a nineteenth century usage of *lelata* then understood by southern BaTswana to mean "female domestic servant" or "female slave."[22] No other information regarding female *malata*, however, has as yet come to notice. Prior to the

1840s the BaTswana apparently subjugated peoples of various origin, but difficulties arise in pinpointing exactly what form this subjugation took. No detailed eyewitness accounts of the Kalahari in the pre-1842 period are available, and oral traditions do not provide specific information about the nature of servitude. Because BaTswana societies were devastated during the 1820s and 1830s, eyewitness testimony about later periods may not be used to reconstruct the pre-1820 period.

The sources available demonstrate nevertheless some form of subjugation took place as early as ca. 1600 AD in the Kalahari, when groups now known as "BaKgalagadi" forcibly conquered some of the region's indigenous BaSarwa inhabitants.

> The Kgalagadi Chief ordered that the Bushwomen and the small Bushman children should be rounded up and brought home. Beginning here, in the time of Chief Seloilwe I, the MaKalagadi began to own the Bushmen....They were owned because of the defeat inflicted upon them...[23]

Balala, as these subjugated BaSarwa were classified by the BaKgalagadi, were also passed down through inheritance. [24]

In the seventeenth century SeTswana-speaking BaKwena began to dominate the southern Kalahari, the territory earlier controlled by BaKgalagadi. The four major BaTswana polities of a later era—BaKwena, BaNgwaketse, BaNgwato, BaTawana—were offshoots of this BaKwena group. By all accounts the original BaKwena defeated the BaKgalagadi of southern Botswana and subjugated those who did not flee to other regions. The nature of this subjugation is difficult to establish precisely, but paying tribute in the form of hunting trophies was involved. As appears to have been the case, BaKgalagadi were "owned" in groups by the BaKwena *dikgosi* and their relatives. As two BaKgalagadi elders said with reference to the BagaMeetlo, *Kgosi ya bo e le Teteng, Monye wa bo too Segootshane, kgosi ya ga Ngwaketse* ("Their chief was Teteng, their owner [master] was Segotshane, chief of the Ngwaketse").[25] The notion of group service as an inherited, rather than voluntary, part of BaTswana-BaKgalagadi relationships is clear in this tradition collected from three BaKgalagadi:

> When we were born our fathers were owned by the BaTswana...Our fathers did not tell us anything about how it came about that the BaNgwaketse came to own them.... We just found ourselves being owned. They own us because we are the children of their servants, as they owned our fathers. [26]

A MoKgalagadi headman of Lehututu in the Kwena district recalled that the BaKwena conquered his forefathers when governed by Mokgwatleng II (Moriti) five reigns prior to the 1943 interview.

Morhityi e see i-ye e da kga nno too go baKwena ba he biza baSaga. Ha be rhe baSaga go rhua bathanka ("Moriti was already here when the BaKwena started to call us BaSaga. When they say BaSaga they mean servants.") [27]

Botlhanka, a term apparently derived from the SeTswana root, *go tlhanka* denoting subordination, is in most common use in Botswana among central and northern SeTswana-speakers. The corollary term, *bolata*, meaning "to follow" or "to go to," is more common in southern Botswana.[28] Confusion over the meaning of these terms sometimes arises in that *botlhanka* is often applied with regard to various commoners and even royals in BaTswana and BaSotho societies to indicate a client who borrows cattle from a patron, or to commoners who are appointed as regional officials by the chief. In the nineteenth century, however, the only available definitions of the SeTswana term *botlhanka* restrict the meaning to "servitude, a state of servitude" or "slavery" and *batlhanka*, to "servants," "inherited servants," or "slaves."[29] A further complicating factor arises when comparing various BaTswana polities, each of whom subjugated neighboring populations at different times and developed accordingly their own vocabularies of rule. Inquiries into the topic are beset also by the general thinness of the sources. For many periods, understanding *bolata/botlhanka* is dependent on the imprecise impressions of itinerant travelers and missionaries or on the apologetics of the BaTswana masters.

When various other BaTswana groups came into existence as they separated from the BaKwena beginning in the mid-eighteenth century, they conquered or drove out people from the areas newly occupied.[30] After breaking away from the BaKwena in ca. 1740 the BaNgwaketse moved west, where they defeated BaKgalagadi. Captives were distributed among various wards, although the royal lineage of the defeated group was allowed to remain free and form a ward of its own.[31] In 1834, the BaNgwaketse under Sebego I moved further west to avoid AmaNdebele rule and beset the BaKgalagadi of the Matsheng area. Those refusing to submit were dealt with in the following manner:

After having confiscated their goats, [Sebego I] had men, women, and children put into their huts, which he then burned down.[32]

When the BaNgwato split from the BaKwena in 1770, they conquered BaKgalagadi in the eastern Kalahari. Apparently they also conquered some local BaSarwa, because in the early nineteenth century the BaNgwato fought a small neighboring BaTswana group, the BaKhurutshe, after the latter refused to give their BaSarwa to the BaNgwato as "tribute."[33] BaNgwato traditions date what Schapera calls the "enslavement" of BaSarwa and many BaKgalagadi to the reign of Kgari I, ca. 1817–28, though there is reason to believe the process of conquest began earlier.[34] According to Simon Ratshosa, a MoNgwato royal:

> The Masarwa before this time were living a nomadic life, wandering all over the vast Kalahari without permanent master or habitation. They were collected from their various places and with tribal cattle were distributed amongst the headmen.... [35]

Ratshosa claimed that BaSarwa became the herders of the BaNgwato headmen, who were permitted to pass them on to their children as long as the family remained loyal to the BaNgwato *kgosi*. The BaNgwato also transferred BaSarwa among themselves. As stated by another member of the royal family in 1934, "long ago when we were at Shoshong...[t]here was a certain amount of exchanging Masarwa for goods...."[36] The BaTawana, who split from the BaNgwato ca. 1795, and who are discussed at some length below, took BaKgalagadi with them to Ngamiland and subjugated the BaYei, another group they found there.[37] By the time BaTswana began to trade systematically with the Cape in the 1840s, most of the BaSarwa and BaKgalagadi of the Kalahari region lived under their authority. In general, they belonged only to BaTswana royals and other wealthy BaTswana cattle owners, who passed on to their descendants these servants and their children.

Joseph Miller has suggested that BaTswana, at least those located in the northwestern Kalahari, may have been involved in producing slaves for the Benguela market between ca. 1795 and 1825.[38] Little evidence from the Kalahari itself is available to confirm this thesis. HaMbukushu living in the modern day Caprivi sold slaves north, but there is nothing to suggest that others to the south were involved.[39] In this respect, an Angolan who worked as a slave trader in Benguela in the early nineteenth century noted that the Portuguese were uninterested in purchasing BaSarwa, whom they considered too "dwarfish."[40] One oral source collected a decade ago on the fringe of the Okavango delta alleges that when the BaTawana subjugated the BaYei ca. 1800, the latter were living in "anarchy" and that *botlhanka* was created to stop BaYei selling themselves into slavery and mistreating their own servants.[41] Though the BaTawana were themselves in a position to sell BaYei to the HaMbukushu, with whom they traded in other respects, it is doubtful they did so, because no evidence shows that the OviMbundu slavers ever journeyed to the southern reaches of the Okavango.[42]

Ivory, Botlhanka, and the Slave Trade

Following the upheavals associated with Griqua, BaFokeng, and AmaNdebele movements on the highveld and sandveld between 1820 and

FIGURE 9.2 The Kalahari Sandveld.

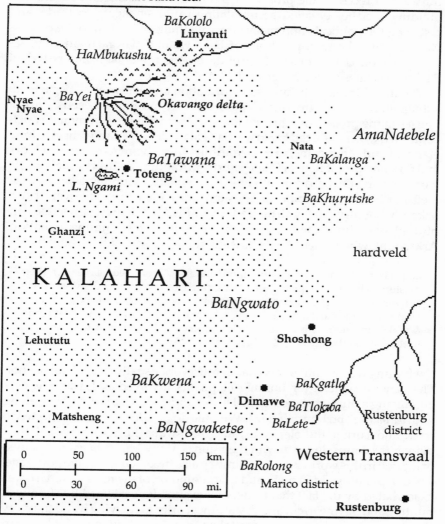

1840, BaTswana groups declined or divided as a result of raiding, or were destroyed or absorbed by their attackers. BaTswana groups who survived intact sustained large losses of cattle. In the 1840s, when the last of these threats had receded, the process of BaTswana reconstruction began. Rebuilding societies entailed accumulating cattle, engaging in trade, and restoring the political supremacy of royal families. Central to the process was *botlhanka*; large populations of BaSarwa and BaKgalagadi were severely exploited as a consequence of the emergence of large and powerful BaTswana states on the fringe of the Kalahari sandveld.

The initial impetus behind state formation and BaSarwa/BaKgalagadi subjugation was the growing Cape market for hunting proceeds. Royal houses in the process of rejuvenation, together with the commoner wards connected to them, forced BaSarwa, BaKgalagadi, BaYei, and others to hunt elephant and other game, extracted tribute from them in the form of ivory and furs, and prohibited their *batlhanka* from trading. By 1844 the BaNgwato were coercing the BaSarwa into hunting elephant. Hunting labor in areas well north of their capital of Shoshong provided the BaNgwato ruler, Sekgoma I, with virtually all his trading profits.[43] And force, rather than any mutual bargaining, was the main element of the hunting equation. Arkwright, who visited the BaNgwato in 1845, wrote of their hunters

> [as] having been taken captive [and] made to work like slaves for their masters. They are frequently brutally treated, to say nothing of every article belonging to them being at the indiscriminate use of the [BaNgwato]. They are made to kill the most dangerous animals for the chief, provide him with food & make carosses for his benefit. In short every article belonging to them, even to the hair on their heads, is at his disposal.[44]

Hunting was strenuous and dangerous work usually carried out on foot. The general pattern for hunting elephants involved BaTswana leaders organizing a hunting expedition. Horses and guns were assembled, along with *batlhanka* and hunting dogs. With the dogs, *batlhanka* were expected to track and corner the elephants, and BaTswana horsemen would then deliver the coups de grace with their guns. Many *batlhanka* were maimed or injured in this work. Big game hunting also involved extensive porterage, since elephants yielded tusks and a large amount of meat. The exercise was exacerbated by the fact that porters were already weakened by strenuous hunting and having to cut and dry the meat prior to carrying it and the ivory the long distance back to the capital or an outlying village. The Kalahari sandveld, hot and dry, was also the prowling grounds of lions, making the slaves' task of hunting as dangerous as it was debilitating. According to the descendants of BaYei who hunted for the BaTawana, carrying the heavy loads to the *kgosi*'s town was itself the cause of high mortality. BaNgwato masters admitted to beating their porters severely for getting tired. *Batlhanka* unlucky enough to be part of an unsuccessful expedition were beaten for "bringing bad luck" with them![45] As was observed in 1844 by Gordon-Cumming, a well-known ivory hunter, "so great was the fatigue endured by these poor creatures while so employed [as porters] that many of them continually died on the way."[46] Other tasks associated with the hunt, such as that performed by the BaTswana's grooms, also entailed risk. When Letsholathebe I's horse died in a quagmire while in the care of two BaSarwa:

> The chief ordered the halter of the dead horse to be loosened, and the hands and feet of the Bushmen to be secured with it. This being done, they were thrown into the mud alongside the dead quadruped, where of course, they soon miserably perished, Lecholatebe coolly exclaiming "There, now mind the horse!'[47]

Batlhanka villages were also a source of tribute in marketable goods. As of 1843 the BaKwena had forced the BaKgalagadi back into hunting for them and rendering up tribute in game trophies.[48] Khama III of the BaNgwato recalled in his twilight years that in the precolonial era his living and that of other *dikgosi* "depended upon [tribute]."[49] Khama also hired out what Parsons refers to as his "serf" hunters to European hunters.[50] In Ngamiland in 1850 Livingstone observed that the BaKgalagadi under the BaTawana were "much oppressed by the Bechuanas who visit them annually in order to collect skins."[51] As a result hunter-traveler William Baldwin commented in 1858 that Letsholathebe I, the MoTawana *kgosi*, had "ivory, [ostrich] feathers, and karosses brought to him from all quarters, which he can barter with the traders for every article of luxury."[52] Until the 1870s substantial hunting revenues enabled rulers with monopolies such as Sekgoma I, Sechele I, Letsholathebe I, and Gaseitsiwe to enlarge their states by attracting immigrants with their new wealth. They also purchased guns and horses and consequently were able to dominate large areas with relative ease.[53]

BaSarwa, BaKgalagadi, BaYei, and other *batlhanka* were prevented from engaging in trade and acquiring wealth. They were also expected annually to pay tribute in the form a certain number of animal skins, ostrich feathers, and the *biltong* (dried meat) of the animals they killed. Together with the proceeds of hunting expeditions, tribute from *batlhanka* enabled *dikgosi*, along with their headmen, to sell these goods to passing traders for money or goods ranging from guns to tea and coffee. They were also prohibited from moving about freely. As a result, their areas declined precipitously in the nineteenth century in terms of trade. For example, the BaKgalagadi of the western Kalahari, who had formerly traded south into the northern Cape area, lost their trade autonomy to the BaNgwaketse and BaKwena.

BaNgwato hegemony over the eastern Kalahari likewise ended BaSarwa trade with the BaKalanga and AmaNdebele of present day eastern Botswana and western Zimbabwe. The tribute system deprived these people of the means of acquiring grain, cattle, and metal and forced them to suffer increasing impoverishment. Noncompliance invited severe penalties. Villagers who failed to provide the desired number of skins faced severe whippings and other forms of retribution, such as having their homes and possessions burned.[54] "They are cruelly punished by those who claim them," remarked E. Solomon, "and their death under punishment is no very unusual occurrence, and excites but little attention."[55] Missionary J.D. Hepburn related the story told to him by a trader who had

> had the terrible ordeal inflicted upon him of seeing twenty-nine Masarwa shot down close to his waggons, and with all his efforts he could not save one. What fault had they committed? They had gone to get the meat which the trader had killed, and their masters shot them down without mercy.[56]

Hepburn, who evangelized among the BaTawana in the late 1870s, was himself interrupted during a prayer meeting in the capital by the whipping of what he termed a "slave":

> Our hearts were lacerated by hearing the heavy blows of a rhinoceros-hide whip, and the screams and earnest cries for mercy of the victim, unheeded by the cruel oppressor. Every space for breathing time, we could hear the trembling, quivering voice piteously, vainly pleading, followed by the rapid strokes of the merciless whip, which rained down blows, until the master who wielded it had to stop again for another brief breathing time. This he repeated furiously until so exhausted that his arm had no longer power to strike.[57]

Batlhanka were subject as well to all sorts of restrictions and humiliations. They were forbidden to enter the main village during the daytime, which was the right only of free persons.[58] The beating Hepburn witnessed appears to have been administered for this reason. Disobedience was punishable by other methods, as well. LMS missionary John Mackenzie stated that:

> The punishments were *corporal punishment* for youths or people of low rank, or slaves... *maiming the body*, as cutting off an ear or burning a hand in boiling fat in the case of slaves who were inveterate thieves....[59]

BaSarwa *batlhanka* were depicted as sub-humans and were given various negative stereotypes.[60] The BaNgwato were said by one experienced traveler to "hold the Bushmen as beasts, term them bulls and cows, heifers and calves. In speaking of a female they say she has calved."[61] A common

SeTswana expression of the nineteenth century maintained that *Masarwa ki linoga fela* ("BaSarwa are perfect snakes").[62] The *kgosi* of the BaTawana, Letsholathebe I (1847-74) referred to *batlhanka* as "his dogs and he would do as he liked with them."[63]

The extremes to which violence and dehumanization were employed to maintain this system of extraction and the extent to which slave trading itself might be used to secure the *kgosi*'s position can be illustrated with the example of the rebuilding of the BaTawana state under Letsholathebe. The BaTawana are one of the five groups to have migrated into Ngamiland in the late eighteenth century. They were led by a small BaTswana group that had seceded from the BaNgwato of eastern Botswana ca. 1795. They had sufficient military power, nevertheless, to subjugate the BaSarwa and BaKgalagadi of the lake Ngami area.[64] In the 1830s Ngamiland was invaded by Sebitwane's BaFokeng (BaKololo), who divested the BaTawana of their cattle and held many of these people captive for several years as they moved northeast. Around 1840 the BaTawana were able to return to Ngamiland, where they re-established themselves by incorporating various non-BaTswana, particularly the BaYei of the Okavango delta, and raiding cattle.[65]

When Letsholathebe ascended the throne in 1847, BaTawana expansion— based on tribute extraction—gained momentum. That year he was visited by Sechele I, the MoKwena *kgosi* and host of David Livingstone. Letsholathebe asked Sechele to pass on his invitation to Livingstone to come to Ngamiland and trade for ivory. Livingstone traveled to Ngamiland in 1849 but disappointed Letsholathebe, who wanted guns rather than the gospel. Livingstone nevertheless helped to publicize the area among British, Griqua, and Boer traders connected to the Transvaal and the Cape, with the result that Letsholathebe's capital was visited with increasing frequency by traders in search of ivory. The BaTawana entered the ivory trade with alacrity and strived to gain a monopoly. They obtained guns and horses, which were used to drive the BaKololo out of northeast Ngamiland and conquer most of the western sandvelt areas including Ghanzi and Nyae Nyae. Plumbing these areas for additional ivory, the BaTawana increased their stock in guns and horses. Political power in the region quickly passed to the new BaTawana elite.[66]

As Livingstone later discovered on his travels north into BaKololo territory, Letsholathebe was engaged in a fierce rivalry with the BaKololo of Sebitwane (and his successor, Sekeletu) over control of the *balala* villages situated between these two kingdoms. Both monarchs raided and extracted ivory from these subject peoples and used the proceeds to trade externally and to enhance their internal powers.[67] Following Sebitwane's death in July 1851, Letsholathebe's forces invaded the *balala* areas under BaKololo control and "not only carried off tusks, but whole villages who [sic] had always acknowledged the Makololo as their masters. Many such acts enraged the Makololo...."[68] After defeating the BaKololo in 1854, Letsholathebe's regiments turned their attention southwest and invaded the Ghanzi area. Letsholathebe's conquest and treatment of these newly subjugated people was ruthless. When a BaSarwa leader in Ghanzi opposed BaTawana rule, Letsholathebe dealt with his followers in the following manner:

> He sent a man with tobacco to buy skins of them, and having by a long course of deceitfulness lulled their suspicions, he proclaimed a *grand battue*. Of course the quarry were the Bushmen themselves, who were surprised, disarmed, and brought before [Letsholathebe] when sitting on his stool. He superintended the deliberate cutting of their throats, embittering their last moments by every taunt and sarcasm his imagination could supply.[69]

After this event, which occurred ca. 1856, the BaTawana collected tribute in the form of hunting trophies, agricultural labor, and children, and instituted a general reign of terror through local BaTawana headmen detailed from the capital. Raiding *balala* villages and tribute collecting within Ngamiland also yielded children who could be exchanged for a range of goods with visiting traders.

As early as 1850 or 1852 Letsholathebe received the attention of OviMbundu slavers, who sent him "handsome presents" and promised to visit his capital at Toteng.[70] More than likely the OviMbundu had learned of the BaTawana through the HaMbukushu, who had in recent years been trading slaves with the OviMbundu in exchange for guns. According to one contemporary source:

> The [Ovimbundu] carry on a flourishing trade [in the Okavango region] with the natives for slaves and ivory. In exchange for these they give guns, capitally manufactured, the barrels being far superior to our common musket. They also supply the natives with gunpowder, red and blue cloths, beads, and other minor articles or trade.[71]

The OviMbundu canceled their trip to Letsholathebe's, however, after hearing that European traders from the south had penetrated the area.[72]

In 1850 Kgosientsho (lit.: "the black king"), likely a MoTswana resident of the Griqua settlement at Philippolis, had reached Letsholathebe, and in April 1851 Kgosientsho's party passed through Livingstone's Kolobeng mission escorting the Marico district field-cornet, Jan W. "Fellew" Viljoen, and two other Boers, north on their way to Ngamiland.[73] The "road to the north" or "missionary road," as the passageway between the northern Cape and interior was to become known, was being pioneered by slave, as well as ivory, traders.

In 1851, I was in the Bahorotse [BaHurutshe] country [in Marico district], and the natives brought me a boy for sale, asking a sheep or a goat for him. The lad was taken from the Baqueans [BaKwena], a tribe a little to the north of the Sovereignty. Shortly after this, three men were brought to our party for sale, when we told the natives the horror that our countrymen were against slavery. They told us 'other white men buy them, and we thought you would.'[74]

Somewhere between Marico and the BaKwena country, Viljoen had encountered Kgosientsho's party and bought a "Bushboy" (BaSarwa boy) for a horse from the Griquas.[75] Once in Ngamiland, Viljoen and his partners, Lucas Marthinus Swartz and Petrus Jacobs, were observed by the hunter-traveler, John Leyland, who was visiting Toteng at the time.

[Viljoen and the others] exchanged several Cows, brought with them, for Slaves: and a Griqua exchanged a Slave for a dog....They were principally boys, nine or ten years of age; their countenances were sad, melancholy, and miserable. The chief [Letsholathebe] treats them as dogs; they are not permitted to associate with the tribe they are under. I remonstrated with the Boers and Griquas, for trafficking in human flesh; the only reply I received was, that their condition would be improved, and better cared for, than they would be with their own tribes.[76]

Another source maintains that Viljoen's party bought ten slaves on this expedition.[77] A guest at Viljoen's farm later in 1852 wrote in his diary that he:

...saw several children sold or bartered away. Some were offered to me. One man came to my friend Cornelius Botha's house and offered a little girl for 4 wagon tyres.... Another woman was sold for 6 heifers and £6.[78]

The following year Viljoen returned to Ngamiland accompanied by the trader, John Chapman, who kept a journal.[79] Viljoen almost bought a boy from a "Bushman" in BaNgwato territory but backed out when reminded that outsiders were obliged to trade directly with the MoNgwato *kgosi*, Sekgoma I.[80] Chapman recorded no other slave dealings on that trip, but he did say years later that in 1852 he had seen Boers coming south from Ngamiland with "a number of children" of BaYei origin, some of whom may have been given to Letsholathebe by Sekeletu.[81] At the time, Livingstone later learned at Linyanti, Sekeletu's capital, that Letsholathebe was threatening Sekeletu and boasting of his gun trade with the Boers,

while stealing ivory [from Sekeletu's territory] with which alone guns can be bought; [and Letsholathebe] begs servants from Sekeletu while it is known he sells them to the Boers, and takes every opportunity of enticing servants away from the Makololo.[82]

Livingstone was told by BaTawena visiting there that the Boers were troubling Sechele of the BaKwena. Livingstone then remonstrated with the BaTawana about Letsholathebe's selling children to the Boers. "He may now perceive his folly," Livingstone entered in his journal, "in *inviting* Boers into his country by that traffic."[83] In 1855 the Smithfield correspondent of the *Graham's town Journal* stated that a regular, small-scale trade between Ngamiland and Transvaal was underway.

> I also know that a party that was absent some six months, and indeed at or in the vicinity of the Great Lake [Ngami], on an elephant expedition, who brought with them three fine boys, whom they said they had bartered from the natives—the youngest about 8 and the eldest 13 years of age. I saw these children well-fed and clothed, and kindly treated.[84]

The reporter, probably OFS landdrost J. M. Orpen, said that two of these boys later escaped and were never recaptured. Though other references to slave trading in the early 1850s have yet to surface, it is noteworthy that by 1854 a fairly large number of "apprentices" obtained from "distant regions" were in the western Transvaal. The Volksraad issued a directive to the Rustenburg landdrost to ensure that these children had been obtained legally.[85]

Viljoen was a prominent ZAR figure who among other things had acted as ZAR representative to the BaKwena, BaNgwato, AmaNdebele, and other African polities.[86] He began to conduct ivory and slave expeditions into Botswana and Zimbabwe after 1850 and continued to trade in these areas for the next thirty years. Viljoen and such cohorts as Swartz and Jacobs violated the Sand River Convention often, selling large numbers of guns inland.[87] As a Marico field-cornet, responsible for law and order, Viljoen violated ZAR laws regarding gun selling and slave dealing with impunity. He made no attempt to disguise these operations, transporting his and others' purchases back openly through Shoshong, at the time the second-largest town in southern Africa.[88] After the attack on the BaKwena at Dimawe in 1852, he and the other Marico Boers proved too weak to mount slave raids as the Rustenburgers had done.[89] Apparently, the only BaTswana willing to deal steadily with the Marico Boers were the Letsholathebe's BaTawana. The distances involved in the Ngamiland trade were compensated by the difficulties these children faced in trying to flee home from distant Marico.[90]

In 1857 and 1859 Viljoen was accompanied to Ngamiland by William Baldwin, who also published his travels. Baldwin stayed with Viljoen and Jacobs in the Marico district prior to both journeys. On these trips, Baldwin bought five BaSarwa boys—four from the BaTawana and another from some BaNgwato hunters.[91] Baldwin also claimed that his Griqua hunting companion was "given" three "bushmen" by the BaTawana.[92] At the time Baldwin was accused by Cape newspapers of slave dealing, which he denied, claiming instead that he was saving these children from death by starvation and inhumane treatment. Baldwin does not record what became of the eight slaves, though he left two in the care of the resident Lutheran missionary of Marico in between his trips.[93]

Other reports of Boer slave dealing in BaTswana areas surfaced at the time. Kistner notes that the BaSeleka (AmaNdebele subjects of the BaNgwato) either bartered thirteen "Vaalpens" [BaKgalagadi] to, or were raided by, Transvaal Boers in 1855. A ZAR commission investigating the affair found no evidence that the "Vaalpens" were kidnapped. A "legitimate sale," it was declared, had taken place.[94] BaNgwato *kgosi*, Sekgoma I, may have had a role in the affair, which involved a minor BaSeleka revolt prior to the involvement of the Boers. Four years later, two hundred "Vaalpens" from BaNgwato and BaKwena territories "applied" to live in the ZAR purportedly to escape the depredations of BaTswana regiments. Some of them were apprenticed.[95]

The slave expedition recorded in the most detail was that taken by Viljoen, Swartz, and Hendrick Van Zyl in 1869 (see Plate 4).[96] Their caravan traded all the way into OvaHerero territory, though it was likely to have been at least the second to reach that destination via the Kalahari. One traveler tells of a "Damara" slave belonging to one of Viljoen's neighbors in 1864.[97] On the way back Viljoen and his partners brought about seventy samples of what the Boers called "black wool," fifteen of whom had been bought from Letsholathebe for a single, "salted" horse. These slaves were all children taken from *batlhanka* unable to deliver sufficient tribute to Letsholathebe.[98] An anonymous observer who saw Viljoen's caravan reported that "we have a visit of Trans-Vaal Boers. We...believe them to be...slave-traders. They have bought many children at Ngamisca[sic] and elsewhere whereof they make no secret."[99] Van Zyl's profits from this journey helped him buy political influence, and he eventually became a Volksraad member.[100] Van Zyl later migrated permanently to Ngamiland and lived in the Ghanzi area, where he served as a headman for Moremi II (1876-1891) and gained notoriety for his cruelty toward local BaSarwa.[101]

By the 1870s, the exporting of slaves from Ngamiland appears to have subsided perhaps because the only route to the Transvaal (i.e., through Shoshong) was gradually obstructed by the BaNgwato *kgosi*, Khama III (1875–1923). Though responsible for expanding *botlhanka* among the

BaNgwato, Khama opposed the external trade, because it induced Boers to tread on his territory. Khama, who was new to the throne, was charting a regional policy based on alliances with the Cape British, who he had learned from his LMS missionary allies had since 1868 adopted an anti-slavery position. In 1875 Khama reported to governor Henry Barkly that Boers were trading slaves in his area. He had noted Boers with "two waggons full of people, whom they bought at the River Tanane (near the Lake)."[102] That year Khama "prohibited the sale of Sarwa children."[103] And, in 1877, Khama refused to allow Boers into BaNgwato territory, partly to prevent slave dealing. He also confiscated five slaves that a party of Boers had "purloined" in Ngamiland and had tried to take through his area.[104] Events in Ngamiland and the region also undermined the trade. Moremi, Letsholathebe's successor, turned to the export of exotic cattle to finance his breechloader purchases. Increasing wage labor in Griqualand West and eventually within the ZAR itself also reduced interest in slave trading in the Transvaal.

Cattle and Botlhanka

The ivory trade in the Kalahari declined in the 1870s, and by the 1880s it had largely disappeared along with much of the elephant population in the entire Zambezia region.[105] The BaNgwato and BaTawana, who had used their ivory proceeds to build up substantial cattle herds in the northern Kalahari following the severe losses earlier in the century, adapted *botlhanka* increasingly to cattle production.[106] Extensive areas were converted to herding. Khama, who had long coveted Nata as a private grazing area, sent his regiments to conquer its BaSarwa residents in ruthless fashion ca. 1890. Khama's cattle were then driven in and turned over to the local BaSarwa population for caretaking. Those who refused to herd were executed. For the next three generations, *botlhanka* was maintained in the Nata area by violence, according to local inhabitants.[107]

In the southern Kalahari and the northern Cape, *botlhanka* tended to decline in the 1870s. Such groups as the BaRolong, BaTlhaping, BaKwena, and BaNgwaketse did not rebuild their herds to the extent as the BaNgwato and BaTawana were able. Slow revival in this respect was due partly to wars with the Boers and British and subsequent land alienation but also to high levels of immigration into what is now eastern Botswana from the Transvaal following the intrusion of the Voortrekkers. Beginning in the 1840s and continuing into the 1880s, such peoples as the BaKgatla bagaKgafela, BaLete, BaTlokwa, and BaRolong migrated into BaKwena and BaNgwaketse territory and encroached on established grazing lands. As inter-BaTswana clashes erupted, unarmed *batlhanka* herders were often victimized by opposing regiments, who retaliated against one another by raiding cattle and killing herders.[108] The BaKwena lost a great deal of stock to the BaKgatla in struggle for territory in the 1870s, and they and BaNgwaketse withdrew their cattle, along with their BaSarwa and BaKgalagadi herders, into the desert.[109] In the southwest Kalahari, *batlhanka* paid tribute in skins, and their children were used by the BaKwena and BaNgwaketse as domestic servants.[110] After the diamond fields opened, BaSarwa and BaKgalagadi men under BaKwena and BaNgwaketse control found it easier to escape these forms of exploitation and find wage employment.[111] By the turn of the century, therefore, *botlhanka* was largely restricted to major cattle-producing areas of the northern Kalahari, though small numbers of *batlhanka* continued to live among the BaKgatla bagaKgafela, BaKwena, and BaNgwaketse as herders and domestics.

British colonial rule in Botswana, which began tentatively with the proclamation of the Bechuanaland protectorate in 1885, had little, if any, impact on *botlhanka*. If anything, colonial rule strengthened the hand of the ruling elite which had a vested interest in keeping *botlhanka* intact. Ngamiland was itself not placed under effective British rule until 1906 following the intervention of an armed British force and the deposition of the *kgosi*. Formal administration in all parts of the Protectorate was lightly staffed and left to its own devices until the reforms of the 1930s. Until then, and in some parts of the protectorate even after, the administration depended on *dikgosi* ("chiefs" to the British) and their *dikgosana* ("headmen") to manage affairs within their respective "reserves." With a few exceptions, *dikgosi* held supreme authority over their own African subjects at least until the 1930s and even more so in remote areas of the Kalahari far from colonial assistant commissioners or magistrates.[112] Colonial officials nevertheless were aware of the manner in which BaTswana treated their *batlhanka*, whether BaSarwa, BaKgalagadi, or BaYei, and their reports constitute an excellent source on BaTswana-*batlhanka* relations, particularly in the northern Kalahari. Officials, however, turned a blind eye to the widespread abuses that came to their attention, because in most cases the culprits were members of the elites governing the reserves.[113] Official recognition that *botlhanka* was viewed as slavery, if not something close to it, was evident in the official pronouncements made inside the Protectorate. The governor of South Africa and high commissioner of Basutoland, the Bechuanaland Protectorate and Swaziland, himself the highest ranking British official resident in the region, proclaimed in 1926 in Serowe, capital of the BaNgwato, that:

> It has been stated that the Masarwa are the slaves of the Mangwato. The Government does not regard them as slaves, but realizes that they are a backward people who serve the Mangwato in return for the food and shelter they receive. I understand that for the most part they are contented and that

they do not wish to change. But the Government will not allow any tribe to demand compulsory service from another, and wants to encourage the Masarwa to support themselves. Any Masarwa who wish to leave their masters and live independently of them should understand that they are at liberty to do so, and that if the Mangwato attempt to retain them against their will the Government will not allow it. It is the duty of the Chiefs and Headmen to help these people to stand on their own feet....

As a young ethnographer surveying the BaSarwa commented four years later, "What effect this pronouncement has had upon the status of the Bushmen it is still too early to determine."[114] The first official investigation of *botlhanka*, in fact, was not undertaken until 1935 and even then it was slanted in favor of chiefs and large cattle owners.[115]

During the colonial period, *batlhanka* were subject to the arbitrary rule of cattle owners and to the compulsory and uncompensated rigors of herding. BaTswana cattle-herding techniques are often described by Europeans as requiring little mental or physical effort, yet nothing could be further from the truth. Cattle required daily supervision and long walks in all types of weather. Herders had no days of rest. In the Kalahari, cattle had to be watered for five months a year at the period when milk and food are at low levels. Wells, the digging and maintaining of which entailed arduous effort, were then essential to the survival of the herd.[116] Herders were responsible in all respects for the lives of all cattle in their care. Even in years of good rain, cattle could be killed by vermin, from eating sour grass, or from a host of other causes. Wild predators, especially lions, were a constant concern. Yet, masters punished, and occasionally killed, *batlhanka* for losing a single animal. *Batlhanka* who otherwise displeased their masters also suffered severe reprisals. In one instance a MoNgwato immigrant was given a boy to use as a goat herder by the *kgosi*. When the boy lost some goats entrusted to his care, the master attempted to burn him severely and eventually killed him.[117] In another case a boy of twelve, having committed an offense, "...was killed by torture, having been tied to stakes with thongs by his neck and arms....He eventually died from exhaustion and strangulation."[118] To ensure that herders did not drink too much of the milk produced by the cows they were herding, masters punished herders if calves were thin.[119] In the early colonial period, *batlhanka* herders were observed to live "in an indescribable state of general squalor, filth, and dirt." They suffered severely from such diseases as whooping cough, syphilis, and especially scurvy. Death from malnutrition was not uncommon.[120] Further examples of such cruelty could be given, both from BaTswana and colonial reports. The BaTawana elite was unashamed. As *kgosi* Moremi II asserted before the *kgotla*, "we have always killed Bakoba [BaYei], and taken their children, and we shall go on doing it... we shall still go on killing Masarwa and Bakoba—for ever and for ever."[121]

Batlhanka were commonly shifted among different masters in BaTswana societies and could be borrowed, inherited, bought, or acquired as gifts. Perhaps the most insidious feature of the internal market was the abduction of children from their parents. Abduction was said to happen "constantly" in parts of the Kalahari. Examples have already been cited from the nineteenth century of this practice, and it continued into the colonial period.[122]

[Children] were caught like wild game by unscrupulous recruiters (Bamangwato) and brought together from the different posts tied together and being driven by the recruiters to the posts where they would be distributed like things without life.... [Children were] given away as presents or sold to friends....They became the children of devilish circumstances.... They were utter savages, joyless soulless animals hoping nothing, but fearing much for they were surely oppressed by their Bamangwato masters.[123]

Ngamiland's first colonial magistrate discovered that:

the slaves are fearfully ill-treated and often killed.... I hear that a good many Bushmen have been killed around the Ghansi veldt by the Tawanas, because they objected to giving up their women and children as slaves, I hear the Tawanas frequently kill their slaves, both with and without [the *kgosi's*] knowledge.[124]

In Ngamiland in the 1890s, raiding for women and children led to the virtual extinction of two Namibian ethnic groups, the BaGceriku and BaSambiu, and is evidence of the extreme brutality with which the BaTawana elite was prepared to enslave others. On a major excursion, BaTawana regiments defeated the BaGceriku and BaSambiu, killed all men who surrendered, and hauled hundreds of women and children by canoe through the Okavango swamps back to Toteng, their capital.[125]

For all *batlhanka* a sexual division of labor tended to apply. Herding cattle along with hunting wild game for meat and skins was a major function of men.[126] Others were used in agriculture, particularly at harvest time. Female *batlhanka* were employed in two capacities. First, they worked as domestic servants inside their masters' households. Second, they performed agricultural labor both for the *kgosi* and their respective masters. Female *batlhanka* are difficult to find in the sources and as yet have received no attention from researchers. They were taken from their parents at a young age and then trained in the household. Women attached to *batlhanka* were routinely seized by owners or by their sons, and in other cases attractive young women were abducted.[127] In this condition, they were kept out of contact with their families and placed under strict supervision within the household.[128] In other cases they lived independently for part of the year, but during the harvest they were forced to work at their masters' fields as agricultural laborers and scarecrows.[129] They performed all manner of daily chores, such as preparing food, cooking, cleaning, fetching water and wood, and looking after infants. BaTswana men had open sexual access to *batlhanka* women, whom they raped and impregnated without penalty. In some cases male slaves were prevented from sleeping with their own wives.[130] Many were raped or used as concubines by their masters.[131] Such was the frequency of concubinage with these women that a proverb arose throughout the Kalahari region, varying slightly by locale: "The male servant is a serf, the female servant is your countrywoman."[132] Apparently, they were prevented from marrying. Their children were liable to become *batlhanka* as well, though some became free persons. As for conditions of their service, they were given little food in many cases and were ill-clad. As a reminder of their low status, they were forced to sleep outside and to eat separately from the family.[133] One early colonial official described *batlhanka* women as being "in an emaciated state evidently caused by starvation...[and being] made to do all the hard work at the lands."[134] Women were not killed as often as male *batlhanka*, but they too were liable to corporal punishment.[135]

Batlhanka worked for little, if any, compensation. All were liable to till the *kgosi*'s fields as communal laborers. In addition, most worked for their masters in the fields at harvest time. Agriculture remained the domain of free women, though *batlhanka* were a vital component of agriculture.[136] One MoNgwato believed that BaNgwato women had become so dependent on *batlhanka* that they "can never do good work by themselves without being assisted by Massarwas and MaKhalangas [BaKalanga]."[137] They seldom received remuneration, owners insisting that *batlhanka* were "children."[138] Hunters did not get to keep any of the salable parts of the animals they killed. At most they received a little meat and the offal. Female domestics got nothing but food and clothing, and little of either.[139] Herders received perhaps the most remuneration for their services, in that they had access to cows' milk, which nevertheless had to be shared to the advantage of calves and which was available only half the year.[140] Herders commonly received a beast every two to three years if they performed satisfactorily, particularly if they belonged to a BaSarwa land-owning family. Nevertheless, herders were liable at any time to have their property expropriated. Many *batlhanka* were routinely robbed of their possessions and livestock by their masters, often just after they died.[141] Masters also were known to discard *batlhanka* who lived to old age, providing them no support.[142]

Batlhanka changed masters fairly often. Newly married daughters of masters, for instance, were given domestic slaves to take with them to their new residence.[143] In certain cases selling *batlhanka* was legally proscribed by *dikgosi*, as it had been by Khama III in 1875, but exchanges among owners in the BaNgwato, BaTawana, and BaKwena areas continued to take place nevertheless.[144] According to their own 1913 testimony, BaYei had been bought and sold extensively by the BaTawana prior to 1906.[145] One case that has been preserved in the Botswana National archives indicates that in 1894 a BaTawana man sold his uncle's only slave, a young MoYei woman, Ngwanalolwapa, to an English policeman for £10. She was sold without the uncle's permission, and so the sale was annulled.[146] Evidence from another case suggests that healers demanded payment in slaves, rather than the customary cattle. An LMS evangelist moonlighting as a doctor demanded a girl as payment for medicine, "saying that since he was a poor man and had no servants or children, and the [patient] was rich and had many slaves, that it would be more to his liking if the said man gave him one of his slaves in payment, which he did."[147] In other cases young BaYei girls were abducted and sold for a rifle each. Prices for *batlhanka* were said to be an ox for a young man, while a roll of tobacco would purchase a girl.[148] In the southwest Kalahari, BaTswana traded *batlhanka* as a matter of routine. BaRolong men sold "Bushmen" children to the BaKwena for goats, while BaNgwaketse purchased children with cows.[149]

Batlhanka were accorded the lowliest status in BaTswana societies. According to a MoNgwato headman, "it was difficult to control [*batlhanka*]— animals are easier." Another stated that they "are lawless and disobedient.... Animals can be collected but not Masarwa."[150] As a MoNgwato remarked with regard to the *batlhanka* caring for his cattle:

> Once you see a masarwa leave the cattle and go away he has something on his mind. He is going to steal or murder. He becomes a danger to the community.... Catch them and make them live like people.[151]

Allowing groups perceived as subhuman such as the BaSarwa to live free of *botlhanka* was seen as a threat to law and order. The BaNgwato regent, Tshekedi Khama, asserted that the "Bushman has always been a nomad, a thief, primitive in his habits and ideas and perhaps more savage than any other Bantu man."[152]

Botlhanka was defended as benefiting the downtrodden and helpless and reflecting the beneficence of the BaTswana elite. As Tshekedi Khama said of his father, Khama III, whose regiments had ruthlessly colonized the Nata area in the 1890s:

> My father noticing the game was getting scarce, ordered his people to give their cattle to be herded by Masarwa, so that they might benefit by the milk....It will be observed that the Bushmen were brought into their present state not

in any spirit of enriching their masters but in a determined effort at uplifting them.[153]

BaTswana owners asserted their magnanimity by claiming that many *batlhanka* were orphans. The BaNgwato "looked after" these children, Tshekedi explained, because "masarwa will seldom if ever at all, care for the orphans."[154] For some BaTswana, even the advent of nationalism and two decades of independence based on a democratic, nonracial constitution failed to erase the mentality associated with the domination of their former subjects. *Botlhanka*, said a MoNgwato man to a university student in 1983, "was the only way that Masarwa could be ruled or controlled.... He cannot do anything for himself."[155]

Though apparently unchallenged violently by their subjects, the BaTawana did have to contend with the problem of runaway slaves. The anarchic Caprivi Strip, an area for which few published sources are available, appears to have attracted such fugitives. Schulz and Hammar twice mentioned individual runaways after passing through there in 1884, and in 1908 another German traveler, F. Seiner, came away convinced that the majority of Caprivi BaSarwa were runaways from the BaNgwato and BaTawana.[156] BaTawana regiments were used to track them down, though how successfully is unclear. The runaway problem was serious enough in the 1880s to persuade the BaTawana to include runaway clauses in all mineral concessions. One, signed by Moremi II in 1889, reads:

> My servants or mesaros [MaSarwa] shall not be taken into service or work without the permission of their masters. All fugitive servants must be delivered up forthwith on demand made by their respective masters or myself. And I must be in no way interfered with in my treatment or punishment of them.[157]

During the colonial period, when apprehending BaSarwa "runaways" was prohibited by law, cases came before resident magistrates in which BaTswana claimed ownership of even the children of BaSarwa who had left their service. In Molepolole, one man admitted to seizing the children of one of his BaSarwa "servants," Mmamonashele, who had moved away and lived with a man "without my permission."

> Mmamonashele and her parents were my Masarwa servants. Charlie [with whom Mmamonashele was living] was the Mosarwa servant of my uncle....I eventually located them, and took three of their children from them....I did not ask for these children to be given to me, because they were the children of my servant, and therefore belonged to me.[158]

Botlhanka Redux

The type of servitude that emerged in the Kalahari sandveld in the nineteenth century denied *batlhanka* adult status and the right to arbitration. In each BaTswana polity, the dominant royal family claimed descent from the original founder of the society, and kinship was indeed important in defining relations within this group. Royal family members dominated affairs at large through inheritance of cattle, marriage alliances, and filial ties to the *kgosi*. The rest of BaTswana households were divided up into neighborhood commoner wards, each BaTswana polity having large numbers of them.[159] Every ward had its own leader and court and controlled its internal affairs. Wards, importantly, also apportioned to their families the land designated to them by the *kgosi*. Many, if not most, of the nonroyal wards were made up of peoples of foreign or non-BaTswana descent, who had joined the *morafe* (polity) for one reason or another. Each adult male ward member had access to the *kgotla*, or court, system, and was initiated at puberty into a *mophato* (age-regiment, pl. *mephato*), to which he belonged for his remaining life. Age-regiments were cross-cutting institutions in that they created ties between the royal members of the regiment (who led them) and their commoner age-mates. As Tlou has asserted with regard to the BaTawana of the nineteenth century, *batlhanka* did not enjoy membership in a ward.[160] Thus, they lacked the ability to become members of BaTswana societies. Nor were *batlhanka* allowed to undergo initiation and join *mephato*.[161] In this way, as Tlou has emphasized, they were prevented from growing up with their commoner counterparts.[162] Lacking, therefore, ward and *mophato* membership, *batlhanka* remained the voiceless "children" of their master and thus lived in a state which denied them status as BaTswana. This was especially true of the servants who lived within the villages as domestic servants.

BaTswana are among the few African societies so far studied historically to have reduced their immediate neighbors to bondage. Generally, persons elsewhere in Africa were rarely kept in slavery close to their places of birth, because such captives were the most likely to escape and return to their relatives. Partly for this reason, their value increased the further away from home they were taken. Yet in the Kalahari, many *batlhanka*, and in particular the BaSarwa who herded and hunted, were allowed by their BaTswana masters to continue living on the very land where they had been subjugated. The probable reason for this development lays in a contradiction recognized by Comaroff, who noted that *dikgosi* were able to maintain strong political control over large numbers of people only by requiring adult males to remain in the central village for most of the year, even though BaTswana societies needed to exploit grazing and hunting resources over large areas.[163] Keeping large numbers of cattle close to the capital was suicidal ecologically; big herds would eat and drink up available resources at a rapid rate. In southern Africa, even in the modern borehole era, conserving beasts and resources requires dispersing cattle over a large area.[164] Thus, the *dikgosi* and other cattle owners needed to keep their herds at distant grazing areas away from the largest source of labor (i.e., men). Expanding BaTswana cattle-owning communities thus entailed preventing a labor shortage. The shortfall was met through conquest and subjugation of the BaSarwa, or other BaTswana, such as the BaKgalagadi. Such *batlhanka* far away from the capital were also able to provide hunting tribute and work as porters when needed.

What probably doomed the BaSarwa of the Kalahari sandveld was their own system of land tenure. Wilmsen's detailed research in the northern Kalahari indicates that "the basis of entitlement [among BaSarwa] to land is membership in a kinship group whose history is associated with a specific parcel of geographic space.... For only persons who can claim participation in the social polity are admitted...."[165] BaSarwa kin groups who owned unconquered land were reluctant to share their resources with outsiders, as attested by the many recorded instances of groups killing trespassers. Most BaSarwa simply had nowhere to go if their land was conquered, which BaTswana appear to have understood clearly. Consequently, BaTswana rulers were able to force BaSarwa to herd their cattle confident that they would not escape because they could not reestablish themselves elsewhere.[166] Though subjugated, BaSarwa could at least forage and hunt in their original territory and could thus feed and clothe themselves. The penalty they paid was having to provide labor and tribute to their BaTswana masters, without compensation, and to suffer the indignity of competing for resources with the animals forced into their care. These *batlhanka* also retained their land rights vis-a-vis other BaSarwa and therefore were able to reproduce their own families. While BaTswana masters used the BaSarwa land tenure system to their advantage, they did not respect it legally as BaSarwa land fell under the jurisdiction of BaTswana wards. And while *batlhanka* could marry and raise families on their land, these families were not legally recognized. Wives could be sexually violated, children taken away to the capital, and family property alienated at any time.

BaTswana used *batlhanka* almost entirely for economic purposes, in contrast to other African societies in which slaves also performed political, social, and military functions. BaTswana rulers who worked to counter the influence of brothers and other relatives rarely, if ever, resorted to the use of *batlhanka* as advisors, officials, or producers of legitimate offspring. Instead, they elevated individuals of commoner status from outside the royal wards who became known as *batlhanka ba ga Kgosi* ("the chief's servants").

Notes

1. The point was made a decade ago by Harries (1981), 309-12, and remains valid.

2. Miers and Kopytoff (1977), Miers and Roberts (1989), Robertson and Klein (1983), and Watson (1980). The brief discussion of indigenous slavery in Lovejoy (1983), 242, adheres to Tlou (1977). Only Lovejoy, however, has challenged prevailing assumptions about the assimilative and meritocratic nature of difaqane/mfecane states by arguing that the "elites" of the AmaZulu, AmaSwati, and AmaGaza kingdoms of the early nineteenth century used war captives as slave laborers "to maintain their political and economic power." (ibid, 243). See ch. 6 in this volume.

3. Isaacman and Isaacman (1977) and Tlou (1977). See also Isaacman (1972a) and (1972b) and Tlou (1985), as well as the introduction to Miers and Crowder (1989), which is derived from Tlou (1977).

4. With the exception of the Delagoa Bay hinterland. Smith (1969) and Harries (1981).

5. The institution of *botlhanka* (for persons, pl. *batlhanka*, sing. *motlhanka*) is the term used by central and northern SeTswana-speakers in Botswana, whereas *bolata* (*malata, lelata*) is more often heard in southern Botswana. The former derives from the SeTswana root, *go tlhanka* denoting subordination, the latter from *go lata* ("to go to" or "to follow"), Ramsay (1991), 45 & n.

6. Schapera and van der Merwe (1945), 2-6; Schapera (1977), 32, 250-1, and Schapera (1979), 28.

7. Livingstone (1857), 31. See Schapera (1960), 150n.

8. Schapera (1970b), 89, also 163-4. The David Livingstone correspondence and journals Schapera edited also contain evidence of the selling of children. For example, Livingstone wrote the LMS agent in Cape Town about Jan Viljoen, Boer commandant of the Marico district, "the individual...who bought several boys at the Lake in 1851." Livingstone to Thompson, 12 Oct. 1852, in Schapera (1961), 222; and in his journal entry of 4 Jul. 1853, Livingstone with reference to the MoTawana chief, Letsholathebe, "it is known he sells [servants] to the Boers." Schapera (1959), 2: 125. For similar references see also idem (1960), 150, 154. For Viljoen and Letsholathebe, see below. Of course, the argument can be made with regard to Livingstone's assertion, as cited in footnote 7 above, that a chief in selling subjugated persons was not selling "his people," but clearly such a leader trafficked in persons effectively under his authority.

9. Wilson (1969), 148-9.

10. Silberbauer and Kuper (1966), 172. With regard to "ownership," see note 24 below.

11. South Africa aside, the books and articles written mainly by anthropologists on Botswana's BaSarwa, who constitute less than 1 percent of the nation's population, is greater than all published anthropological and ethnographic work on the BaTswana, BaKalanga, BaYei, BaKgalagadi, BaPedi, BaSubiya, OvaHerero, and other linguistic groups combined. See the bibliography in Morton, Murray, and Ramsay (1989), 149-60.

12. Tlou (1977), 372, 379-80.

13. Ibid, 384.

14. Ibid, 372; Chirenje (1977), 261; Wilmsen (1989), 97; and Miers and Crowder

(1989), 175-6. For similar accounts and references to *malata* and *batlhanka* as "serf employees," "clients," and "vassals," see Parsons (1977), Hitchcock (1987), and Parsons (forthcoming).

15. Gadibolae (1984), 5-6.

16. Mautle (1986).

17. Mautle (1981), appended interviews.

18. Kebiditswe (1984), Richard (1980), Moeng (1986).

19. Notes of Tshekedi's address to the LMS South African District Committee and others, Serowe, 21 Mar. 1935, BT Admin 15/6, BNA, published in heavily edited form as London Missionary Society (1935) which features prominently in Tlou (1977), Wilmsen (1989), and particularly in Miers and Crowder (1989).

20. This article uses many BNA files examined by the author in May/June 1992 and Feb./May 1993.

21. For a survey of the pre-1820 BaTswana expansion into the Kalahari region, see Legassick (1969), Sillery (1974), 7-9, and Ngcongco (1979).

22. Brown (1876), cv. *Lelata*, Slave. This dictionary, compiled by an LMS missionary, is based on SeTswana primarily as spoken in the Kuruman area, then settled by the BaTlhaping.

23. Schapera (1938), 168, 170. Schapera translation with accompanying text of a statement in SeKgalagadi by Baoonwe Seloilwe, Jul. 1938: *Go jweng ho kgosi ya BaKgalagari ya laola go re go phutyhwê basalagari le batyhwana mbancuana ba BaSarwana, go re ba iswe gaa. Go simologa ho, k'a lobak'a lwa kgosi Seloilwe wa ntha, BaKgalagari a simolola go rua BaSarwa....Be ruiwa k'a phenyô a ba henyijwe k'a yô ke....* For similar testimonies, see references to BaLala in Schapera and V.D. Merwe (1945), 55-7, 150-2, 184 and Silberbaur and Kuper (1966). SeKgalagadi is a distinct language in the SeSotho group, with many affinities to SeTswana. The verb "go rua" is common to SeKgalagadi and SeTswana. According to Brown (1876) "go rua" means to inherit, possess, or own. Silberbaur and Kuper (1966), 177, point out that the BaLala BaSarwa were owned by the BaKgalagadi in an economic sense (as inheritable, exchangeable, and salable property), though in a social sense they were regarded as inferior members of the family to which they belonged and were "entitled to some of the consideration due to kinfolk." Among the BaKgalagadi, ownership (as in SeKg. m*unyi*, "owner") may also be assigned to the superior party in "asymmetrical kin relationships," such as father-son, chief-subject, based on control, clientage, or voluntary submission. It is clear, however, from the testimonies collected among the BaKgalagadi and their subjects in the 1930s and 1960s that ownership, insofar as the Balala were concerned, entailed rights over them as property. Unlike BaKgalagadi, Balala could be "acquired by inheritance, by purchase, or as part of dowry." Silberbauer and Kuper interviewed elderly Balala who could recall the owners of their parents and in some cases before that. "My mother lived with the Kgalagari from the time she was small," stated an elderly BaSarwa woman, "and her mother used to feed from them too. God knows how long the Bushmen have been with the Kgalagari and how they first started living together."

24. *Malala* (*balala*) was a term in circulation in the mid-nineteenth century. In 1835, when he passed through BaKwena country, Andrew Smith noted the existence of "BaLala" who "belonged" to the BaKwena and who paid them tribute in game. Kirby (1939-40), 199, 202. As of 1876, *balala* was understood to mean "poor, inferior people," a *molala* a "poor one, one who belongs to an inferior tribe." Brown (1876),

cv. Balala, Molala. Likely they represent original inhabitants who were subordinated by BaTswana in the seventeenth century. *Bolala* in nineteenth-century SeTswana meant "the desert side of the country, the northwest" carrying in other words the same meaning as "Kalahari," another toponym by which the persons inhabiting the area were known generically by their BaTswana conquerors. See also cv. Servant, with regard to the term *molalediwa* (literally, "an inferior who is detained," and translated as "a hired servant." See also references below to *balala* villages under the BaTawana and BaKololo in the 1840s and 1850s.

25. Testimony of Mokolbe and Khekheng, in Schapera and van der Merwe (1945), 105. Segotshane was the uncle of k*gosi* Gaseitsiwe and himself acting *kgosi* ca. 1830-1845. Schapera notes that Segotshane's grandson, Ramokae Makaba, was in 1943 "still [the] 'overseer' of very many BaKgalagadi in the Ngwaketse Reserve." Ibid.

26. Translation by D.F. van der Merwe of the testimony of Mogotsakgotla, Lebogang, and Rrakaisa in Schapera and V.D. Merwe (1945), 140-1. The original text, in the Boolongwe dialect of SeKgalagadi, reads: *Ha he ze go re he ruilwe zwang ke beTswana, ka bo-rraetsho ha be he bolelee sepê ka hoo beTswana be ruile ka hone....Borraetsho ha ba he bolelee sepê sa tyhulaganyô ya tyhuô e be ruilwe ke baNgwaketse.... He bôna he ruilwe hezi. Ba he ruile ka he le bana ba bathanka ba bô, ka nde be ruile bo-rara....* For similar references see ibid, 43-4, 105 and Schapera (1952), 72, 96-7.

27. Statement of Lekhome, in ibid, 43. Emphasis added.

28. Ramsay (1991), 45 and n. See also note 25 above.

29. Brown (1876), cv. Batlhanka, Botlhanka, Servant, Slave, Slavery.

30. The best source on this process is Schapera and van der Merwe (1945), 9-21.

31. Schapera (1942), 2.

32. Lemue (1847), 32, my translation.

33. Schapera (1970a), 3.

34. Schapera and van der Merwe (1945), 16-9.

35. S. Ratshosa, "Disclosing," 1-2. s. 43/7, BNA. On BaNgwato tradition and Kgari see Schapera (1970b), 80.

36. Evidence of headman Phethu in Discussion of Chief Tshekedi's Statement, 22 Mar. 1934, BT Admin 15/6, BNA. The BaNgwato settled in Shoshong in the late eighteenth century, abandoned it ca. 1817 and returned to the site in ca. 1840. Sillery (1952), 116-9.

37. Schapera (1952), 96-7, Schapera and van der Merwe (1945), 19.

38. Miller (1989), 19, 220, 226, 263-4.

39. On HaMbukushu trading, T. Tlou interview with Kangumbe of Maun (1970), BNA and IUATM; Nettelton (1934), 358.

40. Koelle (1854), 15.

41. Interview with T. Basekete of Gomare (20 Jul. 1983) in interviews appended to Kebiditswe (1984). In 1853 Livingstone was told by the BaYei that "their forefathers...were in the habit of taking the children of their younger brothers and selling them for food or for a hoe." Journal entry of 22 May 1853, in Schapera (1960), 135.

42. Campbell (1853), 140-1.

43. Gordon Cumming (1850), 1: 330-1.

44. Arkwright (1971), 54. A kaross is a stitched set of animal skins used as a rug or blanket.

45. Group interview, Boyei ward (10 Aug. 1983) in interviews appended to

Kebiditswe (1984); interview with J. Ntuane of Nata (2 Jul. 1983) in interviews appended to Gadibolae (1984). Twentieth century traditions with regard to ivory hunting and portering necessarily pertain to the period before 1880, by which time the elephant population in the Ngamiland area had been hunted out. For the decline of ivory in the Kalahari trade, see Parsons (1977), 121.

46. Gordon-Cumming (1904), 255. Cf. ibid, 435 with an eyewitness account of fifty porters sent with him on a hunting expedition. For another description of hunting expeditions and dead porters, Solomon (1855), 51. See also Lemue (1847),108.

47. Andersson (1856), 422. Corroborated by Chapman (1971), 1: 127 and Baines (1864), 175.

48. Livingstone to Tidman, 24 Jun. 1843, in Schapera (1961), 37.

49. Khama's speech before the High Commissioner, Serowe, 28 Mar. 1916, BT Admin 11/6, BNA. In the 1890s, Sebele I of the BaKwena had the same recollection. "Early Days," 37, in MSS British Empire, s. 1568 (i), Ellenberger Papers, RH. For examples of tribute collection in skins in BaNgwato territory, Gordon Cumming (1850), passim, and Holub (1880), 166-82.

50. Parsons (1977), 118. More recently Parsons prefers the term "vassal," for reasons that are not explained. Parsons (forthcoming).

51. Livingstone to Tidman, 24 Aug. 1850, in Schapera (1961), 160.

52. Baldwin (1967), 267.

53. Wilmsen (1989), 98-101 and passim; Parsons (1973), 22-5.

54. Lemue (1847), 31. See also Hodson to assistant commissioner Francistown, 9 Apr. 1908, AC 5/10, BNA; interview with S. Hake of Nata (16 Jun. 1983) in interviews appended to Gadibolae (1984). On tribute collection among batlhanka of the BaNgwato before Khama III abolished the practice in 1875, see "Government," n.d., File 761, WP.

55. Solomon (1855), 51. In 1858 in Ngamiland Baldwin purchased a young "bushman" boy who was skinny and underfed. The lad had been responsible for herding goats, and for losing one he had been beaten almost to the point of death. Baldwin (1863), 269-70.

56. Hepburn (1896), 189-90. The artist-explorer Thomas Baines himself witnessed the BaSarwa murdered for inattentive herding. Baines (1864), 419.

57. Ibid, 188-9.

58. Mackenzie (1871), 368.

59. Dachs (1975), 10. Cutting off ears by BaTawana was noted also by A.J. Wookey while in Ngamiland. Anon (1893), 290. The extremely cruel form of maiming hands continued in the twentieth century, as Simon Ratshosa asserted in 1935 that "there is another well known punishment made to these slaves—is to burn one of his hands that you will find fingers all clamped like a clenched fist." S. Ratshosa, "Disclosing Some Serious Facts...etc.," 6, s. 43/7, BNA. And its origin goes back at least to the mid-nineteenth century. Shomolokae, an LMS evangelist and Kuruman resident in the 1850s, later recalled "cruel punishments meted out to the children of slaves...how wisps of grass were put between their fingers, or hands and feet, which were put together, and set on fire so that the pain of the burning might fix on their memories the fact that for them theft was wrong.' Brown (1925), 75.

60. Lemue (1847), 32.

61. Chapman (1971), 1: 74. These lowly stereotypes were likely of early derivation. Stephen Kay, who traveled in Transorangia and the Transvaal, noted that "bushmen [are] regarded by all other tribes as the lowest cast, and are placed in general on a level with the brute creation." Kay (1823), 4.

62. Mackenzie (1871), 181.

63. Chapman (1971), 2: 127.

64. Kirby (1939-40), 2: 271; "Ngamiland, historical and anthropological notes," 1, in MSS British Empire, s. 1198 (i), Ellenberger Papers, RH.

65. Livingstone (1857), 74; Andersson (1856), 455, 476, 480. See also below. The BaYei in 1854 attributed their defeat to a lack of shields.

66. Morton (1990), which challenges the assertion in Tlou (1985) that most BaTawana expansion occurred between 1876 and 1890.

67. See especially Livingstone's journal entries for June 1853 in Schapera (1960), 151-4.

68. Livingstone to Moffat, 12 Sep. 1855, in Schapera (1959), 2: 264.

69. Baines (1864), 174-5.

70. Campbell (1853).

71. Ibid, 343. After the 1840s the HaMbukushu began to enslave small-scale societies around them. In the twentieth century, colonial administrators estimated that between 5 and 10 percent of the HaMbukushu were enslaved. Cited for the entire Okavango valley in Gibson, Larson & McGurk (1981), 32. Muslim traders connected to the east African coast reached the Okavango area in the 1850s, and some slave trading with the HaMbukushu probably resulted. One early colonial official was told that "Arab [sic] slave traders used to come to the headman and purchase slaves with guns, powder, lead, prints, beads, etc. , and....the headmen often sold whole villages to them." Nettelton (1934), 358.

72. Campbell (1853), 140-1. Nor did the OviMbundu appear later. Tlou (1985), 57, is surely correct about this. The BaTawana were nevertheless by then involved in slave dealing, a fact they openly admitted for years after. In 1906 Wetshootsile Dithapo, a prominent royal, stated publicly that "when the Batawana were at [Toteng], in the time of Letsholathebe and Moremi [1876–90], slaves were sold among them, but Moremi put a stop to this trade and the Batawana have not bought or sold people since." Dithapo's statement, enclosure no. 181, Resident Commissioner to High Commissioner, 10 Jul. 1906, COCP 879/802.

73. Livingstone to Moffat, 14 Apr. 1851, in Schapera (1959), 2: 125. Livingstone's other references to Kgosientsho, "an apostle of Satan," show that he was connected to Waterboer. See Livingstone to Moffat, 4 Mar., 8 Jul., and 2 Oct. 1850 in ibid, 2: 79, 86, 106, respectively. The late 1840s coincides with the time when Griqua of Philippolis and Griquatown were resuming their frontier hunting and trading activities. Legassick (1969b), 614-5. The role of nineteenth-century Griqua and Oorlam hunters and traders in the Kalahari remains almost entirely unresearched. Both groups were the BaTawana's main source of guns for a while, and they are known to have "captured" some BaSarwa to be used as slaves. Andersson (1854), 31; Bleek (1928), 25; Schapera (1959), 2: 125; Leyland (1852), 181; Baldwin (1967), 338-9. They were also particularly eager in the 1850s to trade with the HaMbukushu, who were known for their slave dealing. Chapman (1971), 2: 102. Further research is also needed regarding the great many Boers who hunted and traded in the Kalahari region between 1850 and 1877. A file noted by Wagner (1980), 323, indicates

that some Boers did leave behind accounts of their trips, and my own preliminary inventory in the Pretoria archives reveals at least 180 files on J.W. Viljoen alone.

74. "Nemo" of King William's Town, in *GJ*, 7 Sep. 1853.

75. Livingstone to Moffat, 14 Apr. 1851, in Schapera (1959), 2: 125.

76. Leyland (1852), 181.

77. *The Friend* (Bloemfontein), 20 Oct. 1851. The source is John McCabe, who had been in Ngamiland in 1850–51.

78. Chapman (1971), 1: 88. For other material describing slavery in the western Transvaal, Holden (1855), 288-91; *The Times* (London), 3 Aug. 1868; "Statement of August, a native of the Batlapin Tribe," enclosure 2 in No. 24, COCP 879/61; Morton (1988), passim; Wilson (1901), 198; Wallis (1945), 1: 154; *GJ*, 7 Sep. 1853.

79. Chapman (1971). Chapman, incidentally, learned how to speak SeTswana.

80. Ibid, 1: 54.

81. Ibid, 2: 164.

82. Livingstone journal, 9 Jun. 1853, in Schapera (1960), 154.

83. Emphasis added. Livingstone journal, 4 Jun. 1853, in ibid, 150.

84. *GJ*, 26 May 1855. For Orpen, see ch. 5 by Eldredge in this volume.

85. Kistner (1952), 233.

86. Theal (1969), 4: 450-1; DSAB, 1: 848-9. In the 1860–64 civil war in the Transvaal he commanded the rebel *Volksleger* army.

87. Tabler (1960), passim; idem (1955), passim; Le Roux (1939), 79-87, 116-7; Wallis (1945), 2: 4, 121. His activities expose the charade conducted by the Boers against David Livingstone and other missionaries, whom they claimed were violating the Sand River Convention by supplying the BaKwena and other Africans with arms. These charges were leveled against the LMS after the Boer attack on the BaKwena at Dimawe, near Livingstone's station at Kolobeng, in September 1852. The raid resulted in the seizure of hundreds of women and children captives. See also ch. 7 in this volume.

88. Dachs (1975), 24. On field-cornets in the ZAR, see van Jaarsveld (1950).

89. See ch. 7 in this volume.

90. See statement of "August (no. 2)," in enclosure 3 of 24, COCP 879/61. August was a fugitive *inboekeling*.

91. Baldwin (1967), 247-8, 269, 287, 337.

92. Ibid, 338-9.

93. Baldwin (1967), 338. Other British traders were possibly involved in slave dealing if only on a minor level. Elizabeth Lees Price, living in Molepolole in 1866, noted in her diary that a trader passing through, by the name of Hewitt, "...has a little boy from the Lake—a little pet of his—bought for a trifle I suppose." Long (1956), 240-1.

94. Kistner (1952), 238-9.

95. Ibid, 240.

96. Wallis (1946), 2: 486-8. The frontispiece of Baines' published diaries depicts this caravan; it is also the source of this volume's cover.

97. Wallis (1953), 11. See Gewald (1991) for the Namibian trade to the South.

98. *The Friend* (Bloemfontein), 22 Jul. 1869.

99. Extract of a letter [probably Mackenzie] enclosed in No. 9, C. 4161.

100. Trumpelmann (1948), 14.

101. Schulz and Hammar (1897). Van Zyl's history has been distorted in various

popular accounts.

102. Khama to Barkly, 22 Aug. 1876, Box no. 4, WP. For Khama and the British, Parsons (1973).

103. Schapera (1970b), 89.

104. Gillmore (1878), 212, 319.

105. Parsons (1973), 41 & n.21; Parsons (1977), 121. The East African ivory market was also becoming a popular alternative at the time.

106. "General Report on Khama's Country and People," 25 Feb. 1895, HC 129/2, BNA; Tshekedi Khama address, 21 Mar. 1935, 3, BT Admin 15/6, BNA. Even so, the payment of skins as tribute continued into the 1950s in some areas.

107. Gadibolae (1984) and appended interviews, passim.

108. Burchell, (1822), 2: 336, 377-8; Campbell, (1822), 2: 73, 128; Long (1956), 461; Mackenzie, (1871), 132, 285; Holub (1971), 2: 423; Ramoshaoana Montshogang's account of the 1872 BaNgwato civil war in *MAB*, Mar. 1880.

109. Morton (1991), 18-20, Ramsay (1991), 158-9.

110. "Correspondence re Slavery, etc.," passim, HC 153/1, BNA; Anderson (1874).

111. Mackenzie (1871), 132.

112. Morton, Murray, & Ramsay (1989), 1-3, 114-5.

113. For the administration's efforts to prevent knowledge of *botlhanka* from reaching the British public, See Tlou(1977), 383-4.

114. Schapera (1930), 149n (also for the governor's speech quoted above).

115. See comments above on "kgotla research."

116. Joyce to Serowe district commissioner, 3 Oct. 1935, DCS 5/13, BNA; Schapera (1940), 165; Mgadla (1985), 90.

117. Schulz and Hammar (1897), 352-3.

118. Walsh to Newton, 5 Dec. 1894, COCP 879/484, enclosure in 151.

119. Interviews with S. Hake of Nata (16 Jun. 1983)), S. Ketlhoilwe of Nata (16 Jun. 1983), D. Shabe of Nata (21 Jun. 1983), M. Sehube of Nata (22 Jun. 1983), S. Moseto of Manakanagore (6 Jul. 1983), and M. Ramorago of Tshwaane (21 Jun. 1983) in appended interviews of Gadibolae (1984); S. Ratshosa, "My Book etc." ch. on Masarwa, n.d. [ca. 1930], MSS. 3, BNA; Joyce to Tshekedi Khama, 3 Dec. 1935, BT Admin 15/6, BNA.

120. Apart from interviews, the best picture of *batlhanka* life at the cattle post can be gleaned from "Cattle Post Teacher," on the years 1936–40 in the Motloutse area. DCS 21/11, BNA. On malnutrition, see Joyce report, BT Admin 15/6, 19, BNA; Cf Death Notices, passim, AC 7/3, BNA; Joyce to asst. resident commissioner, 18 Sep. 1935, DCS 5/13, BNA.

121. Hepburn (1896), 262.

122. Long (1956), 464; Joyce to Tshekedi Khama, 11 Aug. 1936, BT Admin 15/6, BNA; Ratshosa, "Disclosing Some Serious Facts....," s. 43/7, BNA. It is rumored to continue to this day.

123. S. Ratshosa, "My Book...," ch. on Masarwa, MSS. 3, BNA.

124. Resident magistrate to colonial secretary, 18 Oct. 1894, in COCP 879/484, enclosure in 92. This source is confirmed in ibid, enclosure 220, and also by BaNharo traditions. Sekgoma was *kgosi* from 1891 to 1906.

125. Fisch (1983), 43-71. Corroborated by COCP 879/484, enclosure 3 in No. 314, statement by Lloyd, 6 Aug. 1894.

126. Resident commissioner to high commissioner, n.d.[Apr. 1899], HC 130/2, BNA.

127. See the testimony of Linchwe Pilane, 22 May 1897, Ellenberger diaries, EL 1/1/1/1, ZNA; interview with M. Sehube of Nata (22 Jun. 1983) in interviews appended to Gadibolae (1984); Joyce to Tshekedi Khama, 11 Aug. 1936, BT Admin 15/6, BNA; Joyce to Serowe resident magistrate, 10 Dec. 1935, DCS 5/13, BNA. A good source on women is s. 343/11, BNA. For an account by a participant in a woman-hunting expedition, see EL 1/1/1/1, 22 May 1897, ZNA. So far, the only precolonial reference to domestic slave women is Fredoux (1858), 23.

128. For one poignant case, see resident magistrate to government secretary, 22 Jan. 1930, s. 47/1, BNA.

129. Lemue (1847), 31.

130. Mautle (1984), 24-5 and appended interviews; interview with M. Ramorago of Tshwaane (21 Jul. 1983) in interviews appended to Gadibolae (1984).

131. Interviews with M. Sehube of Nata (22 Jun. 1983) and E. Tshabaesele of Nata (20 Jul. 1983) in interviews appended to Gadibolae (1984); Reilly to Tsau acting magistrate, n.d.[1907], s. 36/1, BNA; Joyce to Tshekedi Khama, 11 Aug. 1936, BT Admin 15/6, BNA.

132. *Molala ke eo motonyana, eo monomagadi Mokoena*, a "Kwena proverb" according to Plaatje (1916), 64. The BaNgwato equivalent, cited by most of Gadibolae's informants, is: "The real Mosarwa is the male one; the female one is a Mongwato."

133. S. Ratshosa, "Disclosing Some Serious Facts....," n.d. [ca. 1930], 4-5, s. 43/7, BNA; Mautle (1986), 26. This practice was noted among the BaHurutshe as early as 1821. Kay (1833), 229.

134. Hannay to government secretary, 30 Jun. 1907, s. 36/1, BNA.

135. Interview with M. Ramorago of Tshwaane (21 Jul. 1983) in interviews appended to Gadibolae (1984); Tsau acting magistrate to government secretary, 27 Jun. 1907, s. 36/1, BNA; "Proceedings of an Enquiry...10th June 1895," HC 143, BNA; Wookey to Shippard, 21 Jun. 1887, HC 153/1; Ratshosa, "Disclosing Some Serious Facts...," 6, 8, s. 43/7, BNA; Francistown district commissioner to high commissioner, 27 Jan. 1931, DCF 2/19, BNA.

136. Fox to Maun resident magistrate, 1 Jan. 1935, s. 343/11, BNA; interview with E. Tshabaesele of Nata (20 Jul. 1983) in interviews appended to Gadibolae (1984).

137. Ratshosa, "My Book...," ch. on taxation, MSS. 3, BNA.

138. Evidence of Leburu, Folio 3d, 32, s. 310/5/1, League of Nations: Slavery: Report of the Advisory Committee of Exports, 1935.

139. Fox to Maun resident magistrate, 1 Jan. 1935, s. 343/11, BNA; Motshabi Letsholathebe to Kasane resident magistrate, 3 Nov. 1928, s. 34/7, BNA; Ratshosa, "Disclosing Some Serious Facts....," 4, s. 43/7, BNA.

140. For various forms of payment, see Folio 3d, 32-3, s. 310/5/1, League of Nations: Slavery: Report of the Advisory Committee of Exports, 1935.

141. See evidence of Ngcau, 4 Nov. 1930, and Ratshosa, "Disclosing Some Serious Facts...," s. 43/7, BNA; Interviews with T. Shaba of Dzoroga (10 Jun. 1983), M. Mojaki of Dzoroga (11 Jun. 1983), B. Hake of Xamokwai (14 Jun. 1983), and K. Diesala of Nata (20 Jun. 1983) in interviews appended to Gadibolae (1984); Interview with M. Mosupkwa of Maun (16 & 19 Jul. 1983), in interviews appended to Kebiditswe (1984).

142. Fox to Maun resident magistrate, 13 Jul. 1935, s. 343/11, BNA.

143. Brown (1925), 75.

144. Schapera (1970b), 88; interview with M. Mopelwa of Nata (20 Jun. 1983) in interviews appended to Gadibolae(1984). For a MoSarwa girl exchanged between BaNgwato masters, statement of Impule, 10 Dec. 1891, letter 348, File 691, WP.

145. Maun resident magistrate to government secretary, 6 Mar. 1913, s. 1/8, BNA; Reilly to Tsau acting magistrate, n.d. [1907], s. 36/1, BNA.

146. "Proceedings of an Enquiry held at Nakalechwe, Ngamiland on...10th June 1895...," HC 143, BNA. The policeman was forced to resign his post. The name, Ngwanalolwapa ("house girl" is an appropriate translation), is very suggestive not only of her status but the uses to which she was put.

147. A.E. Jennings report, Apr.–Aug. 1905, folder 3, box 3, annual reports, Africa South, LMS.-SOAS. The evangelist in question happened to have more than ten children, apparently too few to herd all his cattle and small stock.

148. *BN*, 28 Apr. 1894.

149. Reilly to Tsau acting magistrate, n.d.[1907], s. 36/1, BNA; Statement of Sekhome, 4 Sep. 1894, HC 144, BNA; Wookey to Shippard, 21 Jun. 1887, HC 153/1, BNA.

150. "Notes at a Meeting at Mafeking on 11th October 1944 re Masarwa on Crown Lands," evidence of Tshilwane Batshogile and Pelotona Kuate, DCF 9/12, BNA.

151. "Notes of Meeting at Mafeking on 11 Oct. 1944...," DCF 9/12, BNA.

152. Tshekedi Khama to Kerr, 31 Jul. 1933, BT Admin 15/6, BNA.

153. *Cape Argus*, 29 May 1933.

154. Tshekedi Khama to Harris, 23 Jun. 1934, BT Admin 15/6, BNA. Cf. the Boer defense of their holding *inboekelinge* children, as noted elsewhere in this volume.

155. Interview with M. Seisa of Nata (18 June. 1983) in interviews appended to Gadibolae (1984). Another of Gadibolae's informants stated that: "Serfdom was good because it helped Basarwa to know how to look after cattle properly...." Interview with J. Ntuane of Nata (2 Jul. 1983), ibid.

156. Schulz and Hammar (1897), 243, 276; Seiner (1977), 36.

157. "Contract made between the Chief of the Twowana [sic] Moremi and John Strombom, James A. Nicholls, and Robert T. Hicks," Nokaneng, 28 Aug. 1889. MSS British Empire, s 55, Lugard Papers, RH.

158. Statement of Baitsadi Mokwakwaila, 22 Aug. 1927, DC Molepolole, 5/8, BNA. This file contains many other cases of BaKwena attempts to apprehend runaway *batlhanka*. See also resident commissioner to government secretary, 21 Nov. 1928, DC, Molepolole, 5/7, BNA.

159. For a description of BaTswana wards, Schapera (1952) and idem (1977), 19-24.

160. Tlou (1977), 132. In the 1930s BaKgalagadi were settled in wards in many BaTswana capitals. Schapera and van der Merwe (1945), 7-21. Wards created to accommodate other *batlhanka* persons, such as BaSarwa or BaYei (BaKoba) wards, however, were not in existence when Schapera made his comprehensive survey in the 1930s and 1940s. Schapera (1952).

161. Schapera and van der Merwe (1952), 3-4; Schapera (1977), 252.

162. Tlou (1977), 384-6. Meillassoux argues that in African slave-owning societies, becoming an adult is the sine qua non of "freedom." Meillassoux (1991), 23.

163. This point has often been made by John Comaroff [e.g., Comaroff (1979)].

164. For an example of the deleterious effects of animal concentrations near settled communities, see Germond (1967), 68.

165. Wilmsen (1989), 193. For suggestive testimony by nineteenth century BaSarwa, see Kirby (1939-40), 1: 285-6, and Stow (1905), 281-2.

166. BaSarwa did flee *botlhanka* but evidence suggests that only a small proportion of BaSarwa *batlhanka* became runaways. See Gadibolae (1984), passim, on the Molele clan.

10

Slavery in South Africa

Fred Morton

The caged and chained children depicted on this volume's cover and Plate 4 were purchased in 1869 in Ngamiland, almost 1,100 miles north of Cape Town.[1] In the same year in the Zoutpansberg 560 miles southwest of Ngamiland, hundreds of VhaVenda women and children were captured for sale in one raid alone.[2] In other words, since the 1730s, when apparently the first commando raids for captives were carried out in the western Cape, slavery had spread into a space resembling an obtuse triangle—its vertex in the Cape, its sides extending roughly north and northeast over fourteen decades and hundreds of miles, its ultimate base stretching between Ngamiland and Zoutpansberg, and its area eventually covering 4,000 square miles. This triangle of slavery was formed as Dutch-speaking stock keepers and hunters migrated inland by force.[3] For more than a century and a half, extant reports of raiding for captives and of trading and using captive laborers refer to places and persons located almost entirely inside this triangle. The victims seized were all indigenes, mostly children, and they were taken from a remarkable panorama of South Africa's Khoikhoi-, San-, SeTswana-, Nguni-, and SeSotho-speaking peoples.

The number of persons enslaved in the process of Dutch expansion is difficult to calculate at this preliminary stage of research. As Tables 10.1 and 10.2 indicate, references so far obtained for the period 1731 to 1869 identify thirty slave raids and twenty-two raiding periods, some of the latter lasting for years. Of the sixteen single raids for which the numbers of captives are specified, the total is 2,983 south Africans taken, or 186 per raid, an average which, if applied to the thirty known single raids would yield altogether 5,580 captives. As for the twenty-two raiding periods, if a minimum of two raids per each reported period is assumed, an estimate based on the above average of 186 captives per raid would be 7, 998, which, when combined with the estimated total for single raids, gives an estimated total number of captives at close to 14,000.

TABLE 10.1 Documented Raids. * = likely multiple raids; Bd = bonded; Cp = captured; Ki = killed; ab = and before; ‡ = also p. 198, n. 62.
Source: See page and end note references in table.

Year	Event	Quantity/Frequency	Men	Women	Children	Unspecified	Page(s), endnote(s)
1731	Commando raid	4		Cp	Cp		p. 32, n. 69
1767	Khoikhoi sell captives into Cape*	?				Cp	p. 32, n. 70
1774	Commando v. "Bosjesmans Hottentots"	?	Cp				p. 97, n. 9
1775	Commando v. "Bushmen"	503	Ki	Ki	Ki		p. 97, n.10
1775	Commando v. "Bushmen"	241	Cp		Cp		p. 97, n. 10
1779/80	Commandos v. "Bushmen"*	?			Cp		p. 97, n.11
1785	"Hottentot" captives * "[at] most houses in province"				Cp		p. 33, n. 72
1790s	Raids on San* unenumerated "occasions"					Cp/Ki	p. 33, n.75
1790s	Raids on Bosjemen"*	Ki: 2-3,000		Ki	Cp	Ki	p. 97, n. 13-7
1795+	Raids on "Bosjesmans"*	?				Cp/Ki	p. 97, n. 12
1797/8	Kora attack BaTlhaping*	?	Ki	Ki	Cp		p. 102, n. 37-41
1801	Attacks on Bastaards*	?					p. 98, n.18
1804/6	Kora sell war captives*	?			Cp		p. 103, n.42
1810s	Bergenaar attacks on "Bechuanas"*	?				Ki	p. 106-7, n. 61-3
1823	Raids on Khoikhoi & San on Cape frontier*	?	Cp	Cp			p. 34, n. 78
1824	Bergenaar attack BaSotho group	?	Cp	Cp		Ki	p. 107, n. 65-5
1820s	Griqua raids onBaTswana, San*	?		Cp			p. 109, n. 72-4
1825+	Kora attack BaSotho, BaKubung, BaTswana*	?		Cp			p. 109-10, n. 75-6
1820s+	Kora/Griqua attack BaTswana, BaSotho *	?		Cp			p. 110-1, n. 77-80
1831	Kora/Griqua attack AmaNdebele*	?	Cp	Cp			Legassick (1969), 429
1830sab	"Colonists"/Griqua attack San/BaSotho*	?		Cp			p. 112-3, n. 86-93
1830s	Voortrekker attack AmaZulu*	?		Cp			p. 114, n. 94
1830s	Boers attack AmaNdebele	?		Cp			p. 115, n. 95
1840	Boers/Mpande v. Dingane	400		Cp			p. 117, n. 102
1850	Potgieter commando v. Zoutpansberg Africans	200		Cp			p. 197, n. 56

Year	Event	Number				Reference
1851	Warden commando v. BaThembu	60		Cp		p. 120, n. 116
1851	BaTawana v. "balala" of BaKololo*	"whole villages"			Cp	p. 227-8, n. 86
1850s	Warden commando v. Bushmen	107	Cp	Cp		p. 120, n. 117
1850s	BaTawana v. Ghanzi BaSarwa	?		Cp		p. 228, n.69
1852	Scholtz commando v. BaKwena	600	Cp	Cp		p. 170, n.17-9
1852	Potgieter commando v. BaPedi	?		Cp		p. 170, n. 20
1853	Commando v. BaLanga/BaKekana	?		Cp		p. 170, n. 22
1853	Commando raids, Tvl.*	?		Cp		p. 170, n. 3
1855	Commando v. BaLetwaba	2,000/400	Ki	Cp	Ki	p. 197, n. 57
1856	Jacobs patrol v. Rasikhuthuma	13/25		Cp	Ki	p. 197, n.58
1856	Bronkhurst raid v. Ramabulana	5/11		Cp	Ki	p. 197, n.59
1857	Commandos v. BaLanga/BaTlhaping/Kora*	"hundreds"		Cp		p. 172, n. 27
1860	Du Plessis commando v. Mashau	?	Cp	Cp		p. 197, n. 60
1861	Commando v. BaLobedu	400		Cp		p. 172, n. 29‡
1861	Commando v. Makakabula	14/10		Cp		p. 198, n. 61
1863	Commando v. VhaVenda	77/?/?	Ki	Cp	Ki	p. 198, n. 63
1860s	Munene raids*	22		Cp		p. 198, n. 64
1865	Commando v. Magoro	300/?/60	Ki	Cp		p. 199, n. 68-9
1866	Commando v. BaKekana/Zoutpansberg	?		Cp		p. 172, n. 22
1867	Schoeman commando v. Mashau	?/5		Cp		p. 200, n. 70
1867	Schoeman commando v. Modjadji	?/74		Cp		p. 200, n. 70
1867	Schoeman commando v. Makgatho	?		Cp		p. 200, n. 70
1868	Buys patrol v. Serakalala	"a few"		Cp		p. 200, n. 70
1868	Commando v. BaLanga	?		Cp		p. 172, n. 34
1868	Commando v. BaRolong	"two whole villages"	Cp	Cp		p. 172, n. 35
1869	AmaSwati v. VhaVenda	400		Cp		p. 200-1, n. 68-71

Naturally, this figure is a crude estimate and one likely well below the actual sum. No attempt has been made to calculate for inclusion the trade in slaves into the eastern Transvaal from the AmaSwati, for example, which contemporaries estimated as reaching 1,000 p.a. in the 1860s, or the apparently much smaller trade from the BaTawana to the Marico district, or to estimate how many raids might have occurred in given areas within the triangle or within given periods. As Table 10.2 shows, references to raiding in the 1851–69 period nearly equal the number of references for the preceding 150 years, implying a sudden increase in the rate of raiding, but the higher rate of reporting after 1851 may be the result of greater availability of written and printed records relative to the areas affected. In other words, more literate witnesses were present in raiding areas in the highveld than had been present in the early Cape frontier. The 1851–69 data shows instead that the characteristics of raiding during this narrow period are in very close agreement with those of earlier period and the entire 1731–1869 period.

Any figure is unlikely to compensate for the dearth of detailed references to most known raids or satisfy those convinced that many raids were carried out for which no clear reference survives. Throughout the period, the enslavement of indigenous persons was legally prohibited by governments claiming jurisdiction over the territories involved. The acquisition of slaves was seldom reported by officials appointed or elected to enforce the laws; in many known cases, officials turned a blind eye to such raids, participated in them, or personally acquired slaves as a result. Thus, as a rule, few of the raids, and fewer instances still of any trade in slaves arising therefrom, were subject to open accounting procedures. Even more difficult to estimate is the number of persons killed during slave raids. Though the chapters in this volume make frequent reference to the killing of men and women when children and women were being removed, few references to numbers of persons killed in these raids appear to exist. It seems reasonable to think that at least one man died for every woman and child stolen; as Table 10.2 shows, men were rarely taken as captives. But as slave raids were often associated with stock raids, and as two children were taken for every woman, it is possible, too, that instances occurred in which boys were carried off with the stock they were herding and without interference to the raiders of more than a few adult men present.

The most unmistakable characteristic of the data is the extremely high rate of reported captive children. Of those raids in which captives are specified, children were taken in virtually all cases. Without question, the purpose of slave raids was the procurement of youngsters rather than adults, although women constitute a significant secondary captive category. Preference for children is not difficult to explain. In other slave societies, children were as a rule in greater demand than were adults once slave trading was prohibited by law.[4] Apart from the comparative ease of controlling them from the point of capture, children raided on the Dutch frontier were, as contraband, far easier to retain and exchange legally than were captive adults. Children could be held as slaves by removing them from their parents or kin and rendering them fully dependent on their masters, who were entitled to compensate themselves by legally binding the children's labor services, and transfer the same, over many years of *inboekstelsel*, or "apprenticeship." As long as the circumstances of their initial procurement remained officially unknown, captives remained the *inboekelinge* of registered owners until they reached full adulthood. No gender data for children captives are available, but it is tempting to accept some of the contemporary reports to the effect that girls were often preferred. Such youngsters held out the promise of growing up to have children themselves, who could be apprenticed by a master without his going to the trouble of joining a commando and who could be educated to the household without much assistance from the master or his wife. *Inboekstelsel* enabled the owners of children as well to retain control of mothers who had finished their own apprenticeship, because such women

TABLE 10.2 Estimated Captives Before 1840 and After.

	1731-1840	1851-69	(1731-1869)
A. All raids			
1. Total raids/raiding periods referred to	24	27	51
2. Raids, captives specified by gender/age	18	26	44
a. Raids, *children* captives specified	16	26	42
b. Raids, *women* captives specified	5	14	19
c. Raids, *men* captives specified	1	2	3
B. Single raids			
1. Raids referred to	7	23	30
2. Raids, captive numbers specified	3	13	16
3. Total of captive numbers specified	645	2,257	2,983
4. Average number when captives specified	215	180	186
5. Estimated number of captives (total single raids x 193)	1,302	4,278	5,580
C. Multiple raids (raiding periods)			
1. Raiding periods referred to	18	4	22
2. Total number of captives (193 x 2 raids per raiding period)	6,696	744	8,184
D. Total estimated captives	7,998	5,022	13,764

Source: Figures derived from Table 10.1.

FIGURE 10.1 Gender/Age Proportions Among Captives.

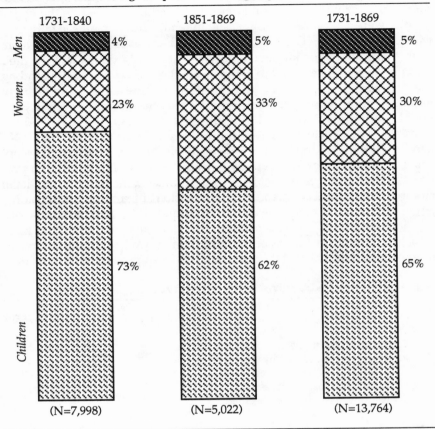

Source: Based on figures in Table 10.2.

were likely to remain with their children even if it meant working on the old terms. For these and other conveniences, legal apprenticeship (*inboekstelsel*) emerged in south Africa in areas where slave raiding and slave trading had occurred, whereas a system of legal slavery did not, except for slaves legally imported into the Cape by sea prior to 1808.

Inboekstelsel

So-called "apprentices," or *inboekelinge*, were slaves from the time the institution of apprenticeship was introduced. They could indeed be sold, even though sales appear to have been infrequent, and were sometimes disguised as the payment of fees for transference or for registration. The measures introduced by the British in the Caledon Proclamation of 1809 did not reduce the status of Khoikhoi laborers; rather these measures regularized their treatment legally to prevent the most severe abuses which had characterized a *de facto* system of slavery for the previous one hundred years. British laws dealing with Khoikhoi labor may be regarded as "protective" only in the sense that they amounted to an improvement over practices that had already reduced the status of Khoikhoi to one of slavery. Ordinance 50 of 1828, which ended compulsory Khoikhoi labor, implicitly recognized the slave status from which such labor had to be emancipated, just as the mobility of Khoikhoi laborers following the 1828 ordinance demonstrates the degree to which they had been previously immobilized by their masters. Evidence from this volume demonstrates that legal slavery in the Cape was not the only form of slavery practiced in this colony. Clearly, the form of servitude to which indigenous Africans in south Africa were subject, through the initial violence of raids and the ongoing threat of violence, was slavery. The illegal enslavement of indigenous Africans reinforced the rigidity of legal slavery within the Cape, since it prevented imported slaves from seeking refuge among a free local subordinate population, made indigenous slaves widely available to Europeans with limited means to purchase imported slaves, and reinforced the division of society along lines of race and class. As the distinction between imported slaves and enslaved Khoikhoi, San, and people of mixed descent became blurred, every person of color became subject to enslavement in South Africa.

The origins of *inboekstelsel* are closely related to the manner in which Cape settlement was expanded. In contrast to other plantation economies in the Atlantic world, the Cape's export economy lost steady ground to its internal economy. South Africa's Cape lacked the vitality of other Atlantic slave economies, because its climate and geographical location restricted planters to raising cash crops that were suitable only as part of a limited victualling trade, namely in wine and grain, on the India-European route. Without the means of expanding profitability through exports, the Cape received little investment or credit, and its growth depended increasingly on its internal economy, which was tied to household production and exchange.[5] Instead of being restricted to the plantation economy, slavery expanded in south Africa as part of the household economy, in which the demand for skilled labor was constant. Shell in chapter 2 shows that no later than the 1740s skilled domestic slaves were in far greater demand than unskilled field hands, and creolized children even more so. Women slaves, who in the Cape made up a much higher proportion of the slave population than in other Atlantic slave societies outside of Africa, were engaged almost entirely in domestic chores. In the better watered portions of the Cape, the household economy generated capital by producing import substitutes, such as cloth, woven and stitched clothing, furniture, tools, candles, and rugs, by growing truck, and by raising some stock, whereas in the drier districts and on the frontier, stock keeping and hunting predominated. With the expansion of the colony, the direction of the Cape's economy was influenced progressively less by the planters in settled areas near the coast and more by stock farmers in outlying districts. In the eighteenth century, cattle, sheep, and such stock by-products as tallow, butter, and hides made their way to the settled Cape in steadily increasing quantities, with the corresponding expansion of herds and flocks into ever larger territories.[6] In the nineteenth century, the frontier expanded even more rapidly as it supplied Cape ports with the means to develop a thriving export sector based on wool, hides, and game trophies, especially ivory.

Just as economic initiatives within the colony shifted inland, so household labor in the interior was drawn increasingly from indigenous sources. Mason in chapter 4 notes that slaves (by which he means legally owned, imported slaves) made up a smaller percentage of the labor force the farther they were located from the western Cape with correspondingly higher numbers in frontier areas of "legally free" blacks. To what degree this "legally free" element was made up of coerced or apprenticed persons obtained through slave raids has yet to be determined, but Newton-King and Penn have demonstrated that commandos were used on a number of occasions to procure otherwise independent people in this manner and to run down indigenous persons fleeing from the employ of farmers.[7] Also, the chapters by Shell, Penn, and Mason reveal the difficulties in differentiating between slave and free laborers in the Cape in the eighteenth and nineteenth centuries, in terms of their actual working conditions, treatment, property, families, gender, and even legal status in some cases. Such evidence, taken together with the many known slave raids in the Cape in the eighteenth century (see Table 10.1), means that as the eighteenth century unfolded the population of *de jure* free indigenous laborers in Cape households was likely to include an increasing proportion of *de facto* slaves.[8] Captive laborers were more important to the expansion of white settlement than were imported slave laborers. The presence of coerced labor in western Cape households likely means, too, that an internal market for slaves was being supplied from the frontier at an early stage.[9]

Household slavery, which best describes *inboekstelsel* in the Cape and among the Voortrekkers, was a highly incorporative form of labor exploitation. A farmer was apt to take into his labor force persons of considerable diversity, in terms of age, ethnic and linguistic background, and technical knowledge. Probably half of all household laborers were female. At the same time, persons in such a force worked in small groups or as individuals, often without direct supervision, occasionally at a great distance from their masters, at tasks that entailed considerable skill, intelligence, daring, and effort. The marked level of socialization among creolized slaves of various backgrounds is noted by Shell and reflected by way of the examples in this volume of the many tasks to which Dutch household laborers were assigned. "Apprenticeship" aptly describes the essential educational and social component of household slavery. The culture created by household slaves, who developed "kitchen Dutch" as a way of communicating among themselves and their masters, became the culture of the Dutch frontier. Without question, household slavery was a dynamic institution capable of rapid adaptation and mobility.

Inboekstelsel was suited best to mixed farming over large spaces, with a heavy emphasis on stock keeping on horseback and hunting with firearms. In most other slave societies, slavery tended to halt at the point where rainfall dwindled below levels suitable for agriculture.[10] In south Africa, slavery was adapted to expand into areas where large-scale agriculture was impractical. The Dutch frontier was expanded through the accretion of stock, the space needed to accommodate large flocks of sheep and herds of cattle, and the skilled labor to manage them. Dutch settlement was sustained through the export of stock, stock products, and the proceeds of the hunt. Throughout the slavery triangle, most slave owners were engaged in these activities, which alone generated capital in the years before diamonds and gold. In the western Transvaal, experiments in plantation agriculture appear to have been carried out briefly with slave labor, but for the most part male slaves were used as herders, hunters, and drivers who worked and traveled alongside or on behalf of their masters, whereas female slaves cooked, gardened, sewed, made butter, soap, and tallow, and raised and educated children. At the farmstead, slaves acquired skills in masonry, carpentry, building, thatching, plastering, gun and wagon repair, ox-training and driving, tannery, harness-making, and blacksmithery.

In Dutch farmsteads, hired labor was rare.[11] In addition to slaves, two categories of unpaid labor were present on the farms of at least the wealthier landowners: poor Boer clients (*bijwoners*) and African tribute laborers.[12] Little is known about either. The *bijwoner* was an impoverished Boer client, who maintained himself or his family as well by using the land and/or stock of his Boer patron. In return the farm owner received a portion of the *bijwoner's* crop, the care of some of his own stock, and assistance on commando.[13] African tribute labor (in Zoutpansberg referred to as *opgaaf*) appears at least on the highveld to have been supplied over short periods for specific tasks by African leaders to the more powerful land owners. The degree of control over subject African communities was relative to the ability of Africans to retain control over their own means of reproduction—cattle, lands, and the freedom to maintain and increase production. Africans living within Boer-controlled territory were dependent on land owners for access to land for farming and settlement, but not for grazing, hunting, or, for that matter, the privilege of migrating elsewhere. Africans could take it or leave it—and many did, as the refugee communities surrounding the Transvaal attest. As a rule Africans living under Boer rule were economically self-sufficient, retained their homes and families, accumulated capital, and retained support from and obligations to kinship groups into which they were born or married. In a real sense, these were the conditions under which Africans appear to have accepted Boer rule. The cost of the labor provided by *bijwoners* and African tribute laborers therefore included the costs of supporting the families and kin for which they were responsible.

A captive or *inboekeling* need cost the owner few if any of these expenses. His/her productive labor was greater, moreover, because it normally continued uninterrupted over many years, exceeded easily the cost of his/her subsistence, and could be expropriated at will by the owner. *Inboekelinge* were also mobile and most valuable to owners on the move, with or without families, who lacked the power to force *bijwoners* or groups of independent or quasi-independent Africans to migrate with them. Until the 1870s stock keeping and hunting remained the principal avocations of land owners, who needed a permanent, mobile labor force. The cost of raising captive children was insignificant, if not offset by useful chores they could be assigned in a pastoral setting; boys could be easily supervised and employed within a herding group and nourished from the milk and *veldkos*; girls fed from the gardens and *veldkos*, and put to work weeding fields, chasing birds, and tending infants.

Inboekelinge were held in service through intimidation and isolation. Resistance to slave owners in the form of disobedience, retaliation, or flight was met promptly with force. *Inboekstelsel* and slave raiding were merely two variations of a single form of frontier violence. Fugitive *inboekelinge* were hunted down by commandos or by African auxiliaries, just as ex-apprentices were often domiciled nearby with their families and periodically dragooned. Seized as they had been from surrounding African societies, *inboekelinge* were encouraged to socialize themselves within a Dutch, rather than an African, culture. Children captives were particularly suited for detaching from their parent African societies and educating in a paternalist Dutch milieu. *Inboekelinge* were socialized into the dominant culture as well to cultivate their sense of superiority over surrounding Africans, rather than treated as savage inferiors incapable of "civilization." Examples from this volume show that many *Oorlamse kaffers* ("civilized" or "sophisticated" blacks, as *inboekelinge* as a group were sometimes classified) were trained, educated, and Christianized. Some even read the Bible to their masters. They were used on commandos against other Africans. In certain ways they resemble military slaves in the western Sudan who constituted with their Muslim owners a dominant class over black Africans, whom they raided. Social isolation of *inboekelinge* from the surrounding African communities from which they had been taken required, in other words, that they be repersonalized and recruited into Dutch society. Among Dutch-speakers, however, race distinguished owners from those they owned, who constituted in social terms an inferior (i.e., black) caste. Offspring from sexual exploitation, about which little is known, apparently remained in the mother's racial caste.

Slave Raiding

Inboekstelsel was different than other forms of slavery in the Atlantic world, and different again than slavery in other parts of Africa connected to the slave trades of the Atlantic, Mediterranean, Indian ocean, and Red sea, in that it was neither tied to nor stimulated by an external slave market. It developed very much as an internal regional phenomenon, although its genesis was located near Cape Town, which imported slaves in the seventeenth and eighteenth centuries, and at its farthest extent as an institution reached almost to Delagoa bay, which exported slaves in the nineteenth century.[14] The closest approximations to any long-distance slave trading in south Africa were the AmaSwati and BaTawana supply routes, which delivered captives to Boer traders operating out of the Transvaal. Trading of slaves within the Dutch frontier was common, as were reports of a highveld-to-Cape traffic. But in all cases, the trading of captives took place within the slavery triangle and not beyond. No evidence has so far surfaced to indicate that slaves on the Dutch frontier were imported or exported by land or water.

Armed raids within the triangle, rather than importation, were the primary means by which slave owners acquired and regenerated their household slave populations, just as surplus labor was disposed of through internal exchange and trade, rather than exporting it from the region. The methods used were rather uniform—a commando, raised for the purpose and augmented by African auxiliaries, raided Africans and took children and women, together with stock. Throughout the period, the commando functioned as an instrument of enslavement, its members served or enabled allies to serve as slave traders, and the slaves were dispensed, exchanged, or traded to individuals who tied such persons to their households. Some *bijwoners* participated in commando raids as a means of acquiring their own stock and workers and increasing their chances of becoming independent Boers. Organized violence and slavery were closely intertwined on the Dutch frontier.

As the Dutch frontier advanced, the pattern and purposes of raiding changed depending on geography and climate, the densities of raided populations, and the cohesiveness of raiding groups. On the arid and rocky Cape frontier, which in the seventeenth and eighteenth centuries was occupied by scattered Khoikhoi and San, commandos were at times assembled on a large scale in order to divest whole territories of their populations and open them to advancing Dutch stock keepers. Such periods of conflict necessarily generated captives who were sold or exchanged. Transorangia, home to Kora and BaTswana pastoralists, was reached in the late eighteenth/early nineteenth centuries by small armed groups of assorted Dutch-speaking stock keepers and ivory hunters. They lacked the numbers to clear out or enslave this region's inhabitants but, amidst the disarray created by severe drought and food shortages, they had the arms and horses to raid at will. The consequence was extreme territorial instability in the early decades of the nineteenth century; during this time, when no dominant group emerged, raiders and raided often changed roles and defenseless refugees became particularly susceptible to seizure. The surviving, stronger groups, in particular the Griqua, took slave captives which were either sold to Boers in the Cape or added to their own bevy of herders and servants. With the Dutch out-migration from the Cape in the 1830s and 1840s into Transorangia and the Transvaal, slave raiding assumed a more varied and complex pattern related to Voortrekker territorial ambitions. The Voortrekkers encountered entrenched groups of varying strength, and they formed alliances with weaker groups for the purpose of attacking the stronger ones. Dislodging Mzilikazi's AmaNdebele enabled groups of Voortrekkers to demand labor tribute from many African groups who remained in the Transvaal and use their assistance to hunt for ivory and raid for stock and slaves on the borders of their newly claimed territory. Resistance from the BaTswana on the edge of the Kalahari and from VhaVenda and other groups of the Zoutpansberg determined the geographical limit of raiding but did not end its practice. Slaves and stock were captured most often on the Boer side of these informal boundaries, where no group held permanent sway. Raiding served, in other words, also as a weapon of terror to cow those who otherwise were too strong to be subjugated, and African auxiliaries were willing to participate in raids rather than contemplate themselves as victims. Though Boers raided often, their moving targets show that they lacked sufficient strength to return to the same victims time and again to "crop" their cattle and children.

African leaders who on their own initiative obtained captives and traded them to the Boers gained access thereby to useful European merchandise that was otherwise virtually unavailable. Mswati, Kgamanyane, Mokgatle, Letsholathebe, and other Africans from whom the Boers obtained slaves acquired guns, horses, tools, wagons, and other supplies that strengthened their economic and political positions and those of their followers. Demand for these supplies played its own part in encouraging slave raiding, just as access to them through traders operating independently of Boer-controlled territory were vitally important to leaders striving to repel slave raiders, as Sechele of the BaKwena was fully aware. The Sand River Convention of 1852, which prohibited Cape merchants from selling firearms to Africans, had the effect of encouraging some Africans to raid for slaves in order to obtain firearms and powder from the Boers.

Indigenous Servitude

The triangle into which slave raiding was introduced contained mainly pastoralist societies. Most of this territory has historically received too little rainfall to make agriculture reliable without irrigation. Sorghum and other drought-resistant crops merely supplemented diets built primarily on milk, stock and game meat, and wild, gathered foods, or *veldkos*. In the dry areas of eastern and central Africa, pastoralist societies are usually constructed in such a way as to distribute human and stock populations more or less evenly. Small groups of people move separately with their stock on a frequent or regular basis, and concentrate only temporarily. Yet in south Africa and in the sandveld of the Kalahari were located in the nineteenth century, and before, not only large concentrations of cattle and/or sheep, but permanent, large central settlements and small outlying settlements. From their homesteads in the capital and the satellite villages, stock owners ventured out periodically to oversee their herds, which were protected from predators and moved to available pasture and water by a subordinate labor force. Herders were obtained and held to their tasks in a variety of ways. Some were the owners' children or junior relatives, who grew up near the milk supply and learned the veterinary and herding skills they would need as adults overseeing their benefactors' herds. Others were non-kin clients of cattle-owning patrons, who in what was called in SeTswana a *mafisa* arrangement allowed their clients and their dependents the use of the cattle and a portion of stock progeny in return for their care. In such a way, cattle-poor members of society often began the process of developing their own herds, while cattle owners received the benefits of labor of these non-kin, along with their political support. *Mafisa*-holders resembled closely the *bijwoners* in Boer societies. In areas where regimental labor was highly developed for the purpose of obtaining, protecting, and deploying stock, as with the polities emanating from Natal at the turn of the nineteenth century, herders were often drawn from young captives or conquered subjects. Because they constituted a captive group of the state, rather than slaves held by individuals, the role of young captive herders in such states as the AmaZulu and AmaNdebele was temporary and transitional, leading generally to recruitment into regimental units.

Other, more permanent, forms of coerced herding labor were present in the Kalahari before the emergence of these militarized states and, with the arrival of the Dutch frontier, were in some cases adapted for the purpose of slave trading. Whole communities of BaSarwa and BaKgalagadi were divested of their stock and subordinated as a herding force in the wake of the piecemeal conquest of the Kalahari by BaTswana stock keepers from the late seventeenth through the mid-nineteenth centuries. *Batlhanka*, as these conquered persons were known, were distributed among individual BaTswana stock owners—most importantly the ranking royals—and used as personal, inheritable possessions. Individual *batlhanka*, and in many cases entire groups, were treated as inferior beings, permanent outsiders, and as servants liable to be transferred from one owner to another. The BaTawana in Ngamiland on the northern fringes of the Kalahari traded *batlhanka* children with Griqua and Boer traders in exchange for guns and horses, whereas BaTswana farther south apparently did not; they obtained these articles instead from British ivory traders using routes direct from the Cape. Throughout the Kalahari, the productive value of *batlhanka* was greater than their exchange value with Griqua and Boer traders, except when a surplus of *batlhanka* existed, as appears to have been the case when the BaTawana subjugated a number of agricultural *balala* communities in the 1850s. Until the 1880s, active trading in ivory and other game products enhanced the utility of male *batlhanka* as trackers, hunters, and porters, and investments in cattle from ivory profits increased demand for *batlhanka* herders. By the turn of the twentieth century, in areas where large cattle herds had been developed, enslavement of *batlhanka* was routine even after colonial rule was put in place.[15]

The *botlhanka* system represents, therefore, a variation of coerced pastoralist labor, as does *inboekstelsel*. Many obvious differences between the two exist, but perhaps the most fundamental arises from the purpose for which cattle were kept in each of the two societies. Cattle in *botlhanka* areas were accumulated as the principal repository of social and political, as well as economic, capital; whereas cattle held in areas where *inboekstelsel* was the law were exported for sale along with other stock and trade goods in demand in the Cape. *Botlhanka* enabled BaTswana cattle owners to strengthen their dominant positions within their respective territorial states; whereas *inboekstelsel* helped Dutch-speaking, horse-and-gun elites to advance their raiding and trading frontiers. BaSarwa in BaTswana societies were used for the most part in the care of cattle and in the case of female *batlhanka* in domestic and farming chores; whereas in Dutch-speaking societies *inboekelinge* were used in a wide variety of tasks, many of which required technical skills. *Inboekstelsel* evolved as a highly varied labor instrument useful to a plundering society that fanned out over diverse terrain, much of it suitable for stock keeping, whereas *botlhanka* was established as, and remained a method of, keeping a conquered labor force in specific grazing areas of the sandveld.

Additional types of servile categories surface in regard to other parts of nineteenth-century south Africa, but calling them slavery contradicts the circumstantial evidence. Kuper, for example, alludes to *titifunjwa* and *tigcili* categories of captive or orphaned youngsters used as servants among the AmaSwati. Her assertion that the AmaSwati did not regard either as property "to be bought or sold on the open market" has been somewhat qualified by Bonner's account of the AmaSwati-Boer slave trade, but no clear connection between *titifunjwa* or *tigcili* and the trade has been established. The AmaSwati sold captives of recent wars, rather than their own subjects, to the Boers.[16] As Eldredge shows, opportunities to trade in slaves at Delagoa bay were available to the AmaSwati in the 1820s and 1830s, but the AmaSwati appear not to have participated.[17] They and other Nguni-speaking peoples, such as the AmaZulu, clearly had the choice to do so. Large numbers of persons within these societies originated outside them. Their initial captive status, along with their primary functions as military and agricultural laborers, is regarded by Lovejoy as evidence of their enslavement, and certain parallels between *inboekelinge* and AmaZulu war captives may be drawn.[18] Both, for example, were incorporated socially as a means of creating an identity synonymous with the ruling group, but in the case of the AmaZulu such persons may hardly be termed permanent outsiders, the *sina qua non* for slavery, as black *inboekelinge* certainly were among their Dutch or Griqua owners and BaSarwa were among BaTswana.

Several Europeans traveling in the northern Cape in the early nineteenth century were offered children in exchange for goats and other items, but whether these represent attempts to sell persons or preserve lives is unclear.[19] As Eldredge notes in chapter 5, drought and famine were frequent visitors on the highveld, and survival of groups often required reducing their size through expulsion, pawning, or emigration. In other parts of Africa during famines, children were often exchanged for food as a means of preserving them and their parents.[20] Southern African societies studied in the twentieth century are noteworthy for their heterogeneity, attesting to major periodic shakeups that occurred during climatic, demographic, and political crises in the nineteenth century and before.[21] The *mfecane* paradigm is too simplistic, too narrow, and, on the basis of new evidence, too suspect to account for these phenomena. Before a more comprehensive and balanced view can come into focus, however, these societies, past and present, need to be studied and compared in considerable detail. Until then, the exchange or subjugation of peoples sometimes referred to in early travel literature will be difficult to explain, as will many other types of observed behavior. If at this stage any firm conclusion may be drawn with regard to African societies in the southern region during and before the nineteenth

century, it would be that in general there is little that is known and a great
deal that can be learned through further research.

Inboekstelsel and Other Forms of Coerced Labor

It is tempting to regard *inboekstelsel* as the "missing link" in the purview of
South African labor relations. As a form of indigenous slavery that originated in the Cape and was transferred inland in the nineteenth century,
inboekstelsel appears to serve for analytical purposes as a transitional form
of coerced labor the history of which begins with the plantations of
Stellenbosch and ends with the mining compounds of Witwatersrand.
Giliomee for one suggests as much, though he refrains from regarding
inboekelinge as slaves.[22] Such an interpretation dovetails nicely with the
spread into the interior of pass laws, land restrictions, disruption of family
life, and denial of rights associated with early forms of racial segregation.[23]
It fits as well into the standard sequence offered by neo-marxist historians
of South Africa's transformation during the same period from a mercantile
outpost to a periphery of capital. In one study of "inboekselings" in the
eastern Transvaal, it has been argued that ex-*inboekelinge* themselves experienced a transformation in harmony with the economic undercurrent, by
moving from the countryside into town.[24]

Understanding *inboekstelsel* within the larger context of south African
history, particularly following the mineral revolution, is likely to require
further study of labor practices on Afrikaner-owned ranches and farms.
Inboekstelsel originated and persisted as a form of skilled agricultural and
pastoral labor, the demand for which did not lapse with the discovery of
diamonds and gold. For purposes of future research, it would be a mistake
to assume that slavery disappeared with the rise of mining capital. As the
nineteenth century United States cotton and Cuban sugar industries demonstrate, slavery was capable of flourishing in the presence of industrial or
mining capitalism. Also undetermined is the degree to which twentieth
century commercial farmers coerced a permanent, resident labor force. To
date, studies of agriculture and stock keeping in modern South Africa have
revealed the many sorts of pressures exerted on African peasants, tenants,
and squatters for the benefit of white farmers and the South African state,
but little has been forthcoming regarding farm laborers employed by
Afrikaners on a continual, year-round basis.[25] In the 1940s Edith Rheinhallt-
Jones learned in the Transvaal that such a category of "labour-tenants"
existed.

> In some cases the labour-tenants work when required throughout the year
> and receive no cash wages at all. The farmer ploughs for them and provides

seed, and markets their crop. Food is provided on the days they work, not otherwise. Even church subscriptions and clothes are provided. The worker and his family are completely bound to the farm. The sons may, if the farmer does not need them, be given passes to look for work, and I gather that the younger people will not settle down to such conditions—it is probably a remnant of an older stage.[26]

One farm worker told Rheinhallt-Jones, "my grandfather woke one morning at his own kraal and found a white man who said 'You are living on my farm and you must work for me.'"[27]

Britain's achievements in the cause of abolition notwithstanding, evidence has yet to be provided that the British government in south Africa or British south Africans were determined to prevent slavery's survival. Considerable furor arose in parliament in the late 1860s over Boer slave raiding, but enthusiasm for the welfare of *inboekelinge* was not one of its by-products. Kistner argues that the Transvaal administration briefly established by Britain in the wake of these protests was itself guilty of using forced labor.[28] Watson has shown, too, that abolitionism failed to take root among Cape colonists.[29] Recent studies in other parts of Africa are demonstrating that Britain's record of stamping out slavery was less than exemplary.[30] Colonial officials tolerated slavery in Africa it seems wherever slave owners were needed to govern colonial subjects and generate capital to cover the costs of administration. Whether the British dominion of South Africa is an exception to this rule remains to be seen, but the signs are not encouraging. *Inboekstelsel* may have persisted in rural areas served by the labor recruiting industry. Gewald has noted that in 1906 the Cape government refused permission for the the indenturing of two Namibian lads, imported for a local farmer, only on the grounds that they were too young. Phillipus Albertus Briers claims to have acted in good faith:

I am a farmer and reside at Matjeskuil in this district. In consequence of information received I made application to the West Coast & Rand Native Labour agency, Cape Town, about April this year for two Damara boys. In October last...I went to Cape Town and got two Damara boys named Jacko and Hans from the above agency. I paid the sum of four pounds ten shillings sterling to the Agency for expenses incurred in bringing the boys to Cape Town from Walfish Bay. I paid this money to the agency by cheque on 30th October 1906 and hold a receipt for same. I was told at the offices of the Agency to take the boys to the Magistrate, Paarl, where proper contracts will be entered into. I was told by the man at the agency that the boys were not brothers and that they had no parents or relations here. The boys are now on my farm. [31]

Across the border in the Bechuanaland protectorate, itself under the authority of the British governor of the Union of South Africa, *botlhanka* thrived well into the twentieth century. When threatened by the possibility of a public outcry, the governor and Protectorate officials escaped censure by championing the view of *batlhanka* holders that *botlhanka* fell outside the legal definitions of slavery.[32]

Research into these and similar forms of coerced agricultural and pastoral labor originating before the twentieth century may prove useful in several respects. Apart from serving to increase knowledge about servitude itself, investigation will aid in recovering a past that in modern South Africa has been largely invisible, if not oddly mysterious. The nineteenth-century highveld in particular remains underexamined, the identities of its communities and persons having left barely a mark, if any at all, in the published literature. The study of slavery, among other topics, might contribute in restoring them and in illuminating how from place to place these communities competed for the highveld's limited resources and exploited them, it would seem, by sharing power, joining economic interests, and splicing cultures.

Notes

1. Or 1,750 km. Ngamiland is located in the northwest of present-day Botswana. See ch. 9 by Barry Morton in this volume.

2. They were, however, never delivered to the Boers. See ch. 7 by Fred Morton and ch. 8 by Jan Boeyens.

3. "Dutch" and "Dutch-speaking" include primarily the *trekboers*, Voortrekkers, Boers, and burghers of what later became the Afrikaner community, together with a much smaller number of Dutch- (and Afrikaans-) speaking groups of mixed origin such as the Griqua, Bastaard, Oorlam, and "Coloured."

4. E.g., demand for slave children in the Americas increased dramatically after the slave trade was prohibited because the long-term costs of raising them were calculated as lower than the current, skyrocketing prices for adult men. Manning (1990), 99. In the Cape, slave raiding was prohibited by the VOC from the onset of Dutch settlement.

5. By "household" is meant a nuclear family and its dependents, including slaves and other laborers, all of whom were engaged complementarily in production. Slaves augmented the labor force in the household rather than freed their masters from labor.

6. By the 1770s, the colonials' sheep population stood at one million, its cattle at 250,000. Ross (1989), 251-6.

7. Newton-King (1981a & 1981b), and Penn (1987), 475-6.

8. Cape historians have only recently begun to address the question of the forcible incorporation of indigenous laborers and continue to subsume them in a free, wage-earner category. See, for example, Crais (1992).

9. Comparatively better nineteenth century data show that slaves captured on the frontier were routinely traded into settled areas. See chs. 5, 7, 8, and 9 in this volume.

10. The Sahel of west Africa is another exception.

11. Until the matter of Khoisan labor on Cape farms prior to 1800 is reviewed, it will be difficult to accept Elphick's description of the Khoisan as a "class of wage labourers." (1989), 35. His many examples of "payment in kind" to Khoisan laborers, and of other of their conditions, reflect a status in important ways akin to slavery.

12. By the 1860s a fourth category had emerged in the Transvaal in the form of African squatters, who were limited by law to several families per farm.

13. Guelke (1989), 87; Ross (1986), 58; Marks and Atmore (1980), 35; Giliomee (181), 80, 88.

14. The maritime slave trade was an indirect factor in the early stages of slave raiding, however, in the sense that many farmers in the more remote parts of the Cape colony could not afford the cost of slaves imported via Cape Town.

15. See ch. 9 by Morton in this volume. In ch. 5, Eldredge's argument based on Tlou, that "harsher institutionalized forms of *botlhanka*" emerged only after factors related to white expansion emerged, is contradicted by BaSarwa and BaKgalagadi testimony cited in ch. 9.

16. Kuper (1947), 68; Bonner (1980), 90.

17. See ch. 5 by Eldredge in this volume.

18. Lovejoy (1983), 242-3.

19. BaTlhaping offered to exchange young captives with Lichtenstein and Burchell. Liechtenstein (1928), 2: 396-7; Burchell (1822), 2: 473. Two BaRolong offered Campbell two children in 1820. Campbell (1822), 1: 296. See also Broadbent (1865), 97; Kay (1833), 221, 229; Anon (1815-19), 335.

20. Lovejoy and Falola (1993).

21. Parsons (forthcoming).

22. Giliomee (1981), esp. 86-7 and 93. See also ch. 1 in this volume.

23. See, for example, the comments of Southey (1992), 13-4.

24. Delius and Trapido (1983).

25. Among the more recent studies of African agriculture in industrializing South Africa, see especially Bundy (1979); Bozzoli (1983), 1-150; and Beinart, Delius and Trapido (1986).

26. Rheinhallt-Jones (1945), 9.

27. Ibid, 7.

28. Kistner (1952).

29. Watson (1990).

30. Miers and Roberts (1989), *passim*; Morton (1990), 137-68; Lovejoy and Hogendorn(1993).

31. AG/1733, CAD, as cited in Gewald (1993), 3.

32. See ch. 9 by Barry Morton in this volume.

Bibliography*

ABORIGINES' PROTECTION SOCIETY (1881) *The Native Policy of the Dutch Boers in the Transvaal*. London.

ADHIKARI, M. (1992) "The Sons of Ham: Slavery and the Making of Coloured Identity." *South African Historical Journal* 27: 95–112.

AGAR-HAMILTON, J.A.I. (1928) *The Native Policy of the Voortrekkers: An Essay in the History of the Interior of South Africa—1836–1858*. Cape Town.

ALPERS, E.A. (1970) "The French Slave Trade in East Africa (1721–1810)." *Cahiers d' Etudes Africaines* 10: 80–124.

————— (1975) *Ivory and Slaves: Changing Pattern[s] of International Trade in East Central Africa to the Later Nineteenth Century*. Berkeley.

ANDERSON, A.A. (1967) *Twenty–Five Years in a Waggon: Sport and Travel in South Africa*. Reprint. Cape Town.

ANDERSON, E. (1985) *A History of the Xhosas of the Northern Cape 1795–1879*. Cape Town.

ANDERSSON, K.J. (1854) "A Journey to Lake Ngami." *South African Commercial Advertiser and Cape Town Mail* 22 May: 31.

————— (1856) *Lake Ngami, or Explorations and Discoveries in the Wilds of Southern Africa*. New York.

ANON. (1815–9) "Transactions at Lattakoo." *London Missionary Society Quarterly Transactions* 307–10, 331–6, 370–4, 409–12.

ANON. (1832) "Sale of Slaves at the Cape of Good Hope." *The Tourist, or Sketch Book of the Times* 1, 15: 122–3.

ANON. (1893) "Arrival of Messrs. Wookey and Reid at Lake Ngami." *London Missionary Society Chronicle* N.S. 2: 289–91.

ANON. (1953) "The Origin and Incidence of Miscegenation at the Cape during the Dutch East India Company's Regime, 1652–1795." *Race Relations Journal* 20: 23–7.

ANON. (1972) "Juwawa of the Magwamba." *Bantu Studies* 9, 8: 29–32.

ANON. (1985) *Mr. C. van Vollenhoven's Verspreide Geschriften*. 's-Gravenhage.

ARBOUSSET, T. (1992) *Missionary Excursion into the Blue Mountains, being an account of King Moshoeshoe's Expedition from Thaba-Bosiu to the Sources of the Malibamatso River in the year 1840*. D. Ambrose & A. Brutsch, ed., trans. Nairobi.

————— and DAUMAS, F. (1852) *Narrative of an Exploratory Tour to the North-East of the Colony of the Cape of Good Hope*. J. Croumbie Brown, trans. Paris (reprint: Cape Town, 1968).

---

* The titles listed consist of published primary and secondary sources and unpublished secondary sources either cited in this volume or included for their relevance to south African slavery. Useful bibliographies are indicated with an (*). The editors are grateful to Rob Shell for making available his extensive bibliography on Cape slavery.

ARKWRIGHT, R. (1971) *Sport and Service in South Africa*. E.C. Tabler, ed. Cape Town.

ARMSTRONG, J. C. (1979) "The Slaves, 1652–1795." in R. Elphick and H. Giliomee, ed. *The Shaping of South African Society, 1652–1820*. Pp. 75–115. Cape Town.

_____ (1981) Malagasy slave names in the seventeenth century. Paper presented at Université de Madagascar Colloque d' Histoire, Malgache.

_____ (1983–84) "Madagascar and the Slave Trade in the Seventeenth Century." *Omaly Sy Anio* 17–20: 211–32.

_____ (1988) Review of R. Ross, *The Economy of the Cape Colony in the Eighteenth Century*, Leiden, 1987. *The International Journal of African Historical Studies* 21, 4: 718–9.

_____ and WORDEN, N. A. (1989) "The Slaves, 1652–1834." in R. Elphick and H. Giliomee, ed., *The Shaping of South African Society, 1652–1840*. Pp. 109-183. Middletown.

ARNDT, E.H.D. (1928) *Banking and Currency Development in South Africa, 1652–1927*. Cape Town.

AYLWARD, A. (1881) *The Transvaal of To-day: War, Witchcraft, Sport, and Spoils in South Africa*. 2nd ed.: Edinburgh.

BACKHOUSE, J. (1844) *A Narrative of a Visit to the Mauritius and South Africa*. London.

BAINES, T. (1864) *Explorations in Southwest Africa*. London.

BALDWIN, W.C. (1967) *African Hunting from the Natal to the Zambesi from 1852 to 1860*. Reprint. Cape Town.

BANK, A. (1991) *The Decline of Urban Slavery at the Cape, 1806 to 1843*. Cape Town.

BARRINGTON, G. (1794) *A Voyage to Botany Bay, with a Description of the Country, Manners &c*. London.

BARROW, J. (1801) *An Account of Travels into the Interior of Southern Africa...with a Statistical Sketch of the Whole Colony*. Two vols. London (2nd vol. 1804) (reprint: New York, 1968).

_____ (1806) *A Voyage to Cochin China in the Years 1792 and 1793 to Which is Annexed an Account of a Journey Made in the Years 1801 and 1802 to the Residence of the Chief of the Booshuana Nation*. Two vols. London.

BEINART, W. (1980) "Production and the material basic [sic] of chieftainship:Pondoland, c. 1830–80." In S. Marks and A. Atmore, ed., *Economy and Society in Pre-Industrial South Africa*. Pp. 120–47. London.

_____.and DELIUS, P. (1986) "Introduction." In W. Beinart, P. Delius and S. Trapido, ed., *Putting a Plough to the Ground: Accumulation and Dispossession in Rural South Africa, 1850–1930*. Pp. 1–55. Johannesburg.

BERLIN, I. and MORGAN, P.D., ed. (1991) Special Issue of *Slavery and Abolition* 12, 1.

BEYERS, C. (1929) *Die Kaapse Patriotte, 1779–1791*. Cape Town.

BIRD, J., ed. (1888) *The Annals of Natal: 1495 to 1845*. Two vols. Pietermaritzburg.

BIRD, W.W. (1823) *State of the Cape of Good Hope in 1822*. London (reprint: Cape Town, 1966).

BLEEK, D. (1928) *The Naron*. Cambridge.

BLOMMAERT, W. (1938) "Het invoeren van de slavernij aan de kaap." *Archives Yearbook for South African History* 1, 1: 1–29.

BLUSSÉ, L. (1988) *Strange Company: Chinese Settlers, Mestizo Women and the Cutch in VOC Batavia*. Providence.

BÖESEKEN, A. J. (1964) *Simon van der Stel en sy Kinders, 1658–1700*. Cape Town.

BÖESEKEN, A. J. (1967) *Belangrike Kaapse Dokumente. Memoriën en Instructiën, 1657–1699.* Two vols. Cape Town.

——— (1970) "Die Verhouding tussen Blank en Nie-Blank in Suid Afrika aan de hand van de vroegste Dokumente." *South African Historical Journal* 2: 3–18.

——— (1977) *Slaves and Free Blacks at the Cape, 1658–1700.* Cape Town.

——— et al. (1957+) *Suid-Afrikaanse Argiefstukke: Resolusies van die Politieke Raad.* Eleven vols. Cape Town.

——— and CAIRNS, M. (1989) *The Secluded Valley: Tulbagh: 't Land van Waveren, 1700–1804.* Cape Town.

BOEYENS, J.C.A. (1987) "Nuwe Lig op die Uitleg van Schoemansdal." *South African Journal for Cultural and Art History* 1, 2: 182–6.

——— (1990) "Die Konflik tussen die Venda en die Blankes in Transvaal, 1864–1869," *Archives Year Book for South African History* 53, 2: 1–114.

BONNER, P. (1983) *Kings, Commoners and Concessionaires: The Evolution and Dissolution of the Nineteenth-Century Swazi State.* Cambridge.

BOSHOF, A. (1987) "Slawe-orkeste en musiekinstrumente aan de Kaap." *Bulletin of the South African Cultural History Museum* 8: 49–55.

BORCHERDS, P.B. (1861) *An Auto-Biographical Memoir.* Cape Town (reprint 1963).

BOUCHER, M. (1974) "The Cape and Foreign Shipping, 1714-1723." *South African Historical Journal* 6: 3–29.

——— (1979) "The Voyage of a Cape Slaver in 1742." *Historia* 24: 50–8.

BOUWS, J. (1976) "Slawemusiek in vergange se dae." *South African Musiekonderwyser* 90: 10–11.

BOXER, C.R. (1965)*The Dutch Seaborne Empire: 1600–1800.* New York.

BOZZOLI, B., ed. (1983) *Town and Countryside in the Transvaal: Capitalist Penetration and Popular Response.* Johannesburg.

——— (1991) *Women of Phokeng: Consciousness, Life Strategy, and Migrancy in South Africa, 1900–1983.* Portsmouth.

BRADLOW, E. and BRADLOW, F, ed. (1979) *William Somerville's Narrative of His Journeys to the Eastern Cape Frontier and to Lattakoe 1799–1802.* Cape Town.

——— (1983) "Emancipation and Race Relations at the Cape." *South African Historical Journal* 15: 10–33.

BRADLOW, F. and CAIRNS, M. (1978) *The Early Cape Muslims.* Cape Town, 1978.

BREUTZ, P.-L. (1953) *The Tribes of Rustenburg and Pilansberg Districts.* Pretoria.

——— (1956) *The Tribes of the Mafeking District.* Pretoria.

——— (1987) *A History of the Batswana and Origin of Bophuthatswana: a Handbook of a Survey of the Tribes of the Batswana, S.-Ndebele, QwaQwa and Botswana.* Ramsgate.

BROADBENT, S. (1865) *A Narrative of the First Introduction of Christianity among the Barolong Tribe of Bechuanas, South Africa.* London.

BROWN, J. (1876) *English & Secwana Vocabulary.* n.d.[c. 1876], London (3rd ed. 1925, reprinted 1982 as *Setswana-English Dictionary.* Gaborone).

BROWN, J.T. (1925) *The Apostle of the Marshes.* London.

BRUIJN, J.R. et al (1979) *Dutch-Asiatic Shipping in the 17th and 18th centuries.* Three vols. The Hague.

BUNDY, C. (1979) *The Rise and Fall of the South African Peasantry.* London.

BURCHELL, W.J. (1822) *Travels in the Interior of Southern Africa.* Two vols. London (2nd vol. 1824) (new ed., I. Schapera, ed., London, 1953).

BURKE, E.E., ed. (1969) *The Journals of Carl Mauch: His Travels in the Transvaal and Rhodesia, 1869–1872.* Salisbury.

BURROWS, E.H. (1988) *Overberg Outspan: a Chronicle of People and Places in the South Western Districts of the Cape.* Swellendam.

CAIRNS, M. (1980) "Goede Gift: its Early History." *Simon's Town Historical Society Bulletin* 11: 63–8.

_____ (1983) "Slave Transfers, 1658–1795: a preliminary survey." *Kronos* 6: 5–20.

_____ (1984) "The Murder of the Slave Joris at Simonsvlei." *Quarterly Bulletin of the South African Library* 38: 47–60.

_____ (1988) "The Weigt Slaves of Wagenmakers Vallei and their Emancipation." *Quarterly Bulletin of the South African Library* 42: 145–50.

CAMPBELL, D. (1853), "Interior-Africa: Progress of Discoveries," *African Repository and Colonization Herald* 140–1.

CAMPBELL, G. (1988) "Madagascar and Mozambique in the Slave Trade of the Western Indian Ocean, 1800–1861." *Slavery and Abolition* 9, 3: 165–92.

CAMPBELL, J. (1815) *Travels in South Africa.* London.

CAMPBELL, J. (1822) *Travels in the Interior of South Africa...being a Narrative of a Second Journey.* Two vols. London.

_____ and MADEIROS, E. (1987) *O trafico de excravox de Moçambique para as ilas do Indico 1720–1902.* Maputo.

CHAKRABARTY, D. (1989) *Rethinking Working-Class History: Bengal, 1890–1940.* Princeton.

CHAMBERLIN, D., ed. (1969) *Livingstone, Some Letters from 1840–1872.* Reprint. New York.

CHANGUION, L. (1987) "Dorpstigting, Goud en Oorloë: Haenertsburg se Eerste 20 Jaar." In L. Changuion, ed., *Haenertsburg 100, 1887–1987.* Pp. 14–41, Pietersburg.

CHAPMAN, J. (1971) *Travels in the Interior of South Africa. Comprising Fifteen Years' Hunting and Trading.* E.C. Tabler, ed. Two vols. Cape Town.

CHESSON, W.F. (1869) *The Dutch Boers and Slavery in the Transvaal Republic.* London.

CHILD, D. (1973) *Charles Smythe: Pioneer, Premier and Administrator of Natal.* Cape Town.

CHIRENJE, J.M. (1977) *A History of Northern Botswana, 1850–1910.* Cranbury, N.J.

CHURMS, B.V. (*) "The Early Anti-Slavery Movement: Pamphlets in the S.A. Library." *Quarterly Bulletin of the South African Library* 39 (1984): 21–5.

COBBING, J. (1988) "The Mfecane as Alibi: Thoughts on Dithakong and Mbolompo." *Journal of African History* 29: 487–519.

_____ (1990) Grasping the Nettle: the Slave Trade and the Early Zulu. Paper presented to the workshop on "Natal and Zululand in the Colonial and Precolonial Periods," University of Natal, Pietermaritzburg.

_____ (1991a) Rethinking the Roots of Violence in Southern Africa, ca. 1790–1840. Paper presented at a conference on The "Mfecane" Aftermath; Towards a New Paradigm, at the University of Witwatersrand, Johannesburg.

_____ (1991b) Ousting the Mfecane: Reply to Elizabeth Eldredge. Paper presented a conference on The "Mfecane" Aftermath; Towards a New Paradigm, at the University of Witwatersrand, Johannesburg.

COETZEE, C.G. (1948) "De Kompanjie se besetting van Delagoabaai." *Archives Year book for South African History* 11, 2: 167–276.

COLE, M. (1966) *South Africa.* 2nd ed. London.

COLLINS, W.W. (1965) *Free Statia: Reminiscences of a Lifetime in the Orange Free State*. Reprint. Cape Town.

COMAROFF, J.L. (1979) "Tswana Transformations, 1953–1975." In I. Schapera, *The Tswana*. Pp. 67–76. New ed. reprint. London.

COOLEY, D. (1833) "A Memoir on the Civilization of the Tribes inhabiting the Highlands near Delagoa Bay." *Journal of the Royal Geographical Society* 3: 316–23.

COOLHAAS, W.P.(*) *A Critical Survey of Studies on Dutch Colonial History*. The Hague. 1960.

COOPER, F. (1979). "The Problem of Slavery in African Studies." *Journal of African History* 20, 1: 103–25.

CORY, G.E. (1940) *The Rise of South Africa*. Cape Town.

CRAIS, C, (1990) "Slavery and Freedom Along a Frontier. The Eastern Cape, South Africa: 1770-1838." *Slavery and Abolition* 11: 190–215.

_____ (1992) *White Supremacy and Black Resistance in Pre-Industrial South Africa: The Making of the Colonial Order in the Eastern Cape, 1770–1865*. Cambridge.

CRUSE, H.P. (1947) *Die Opheffing van die Kleurlingevolking*. Stellenbosch.

CURTIN, P.D. (1969) *The Atlantic Slave Trade: a Census*. Madison.

_____ (1990) *The Rise and Fall of the Plantation Complex: Essays in Atlantic History*. Cambridge.

CUTHBERTSON, G. (1980) "The Impact of the Emancipation of Slaves on St. Andrews Scottish Church, 1838–1879." *Studies in the History of Cape Town* 3: 49–63.

_____ (1992) "Cape Slave Historiography and the Question of Intellectual Dependence." *South African Historical Journal* 27: 26–49.

DACHS, A., ed. (1975) *Papers of John Mackenzie*. Johannesburg.

DAS NEVES, D.F. (1879) *A Hunting Expedition to the Transvaal*, M. Monteiro, trans. London.

DAVENPORT, T.R.H. (1981) *South Africa: a Modern History*. 2nd ed., Johannesburg.

DAVIDS, A. (1980) *The Mosques of the Bo-Kaap*. Athlone.

_____ (1985) *The History of the Tana Baru*. Cape Town.

_____ (1991) "The Afrikaans of the Cape Muslims from 1815 to 1915." M. A. thesis, University of Natal, Durban.

DE BEER, F.C. (1986) "Groepsgebondenheid in die Familie-, Opvolgings- en Efreg van die Noord-Ndebele." D.Phil thesis, University of Pretoria, Pretoria.

DE CASTILHO, A. (1881) *O Districto de Lourenço Marques no Presente e no Futuro*. Lisboa.

DEHERAIN, P.T.H. (1907) "L'esclavage au Cap de Bonne Esperance au XVIIe et XVIIIe Siecles." *Journal des Savants* 488–503.

DEHERAIN, P.T.H. (1909) *Le Cap de Bonne-Esperance au XVII siecle*. Paris.

DE KIEWIET, C.W. (1929) *British Colonial Policy and the South African Republics, 1848–1872*. London.

DE KOCK, V. (1950) *Those in Bondage: An Account of the Life of the Slave at the Cape in the Days of the Dutch East India Company*. London.

D'ELEGORGUE, A. (1847) *Voyage dans l'Afrique Australe...1838–1844*. Two vols. Paris. (Delegorgue, *Travels in Southern Africa*, vol. I, F. Webb, trans. Pietermaritzburg, 1990).

DELIUS, P. (1984) *The Land Belongs to Us: The Pedi Polity, the Boers and the British in the Nineteenth Century Transvaal*. Berkeley.

_____ and TRAPIDO, S. (1983) "Inboekselings and Oorlams: The Creation and Transformation of a Servile Class." In B. Bozzoli, ed., *Town and Countryside in the Transvaal: Capitalist Penetration and Populist Response*. Pp. 53–81. Johannesburg.

DE MIST, J.A. (1920) *Memorandum on the Cape*. Cape Town.

DE VAAL, J.B. (1953) "Die Rol van João Albasini in die Geskiedenis van die Transvaal." *Archives Year Book for South African History* 16, 1: 1–154.

DE VILLIERS, C.C. and PAMA, C. (1981) *Geslagsregisters van die Ou Kaapse Families*. Two vols. Cape Town.

DE VILLIERS, D.W. (*) *Reisebeskrywings as Bronne vir die Kerkgeskiedskrywing van die Nederduitse Gereformeerde Kerk in Suid Afrika tot 1853*. Vrije Universiteit te Amsterdam. 1959.

DE WET, G.C. (1981) *Die Vryliede en Vryswartes in die Kaapse Nedersetting, 1657–1707*. Cape Town.

DOMINICUS, F.C. (1919) *Het Huiselik en Maatschappelik Leven van de Zuid-Afrikaner*. 's-Gravenhage.

DOOLING, W. (1992) "Slavery and Amelioration in the Graaff-Reinet District, 1823–1830." *South African Historical Journal* 27: 75–94.

DORNAN, S.S. (1925) *Pygmies and Bushmen of the Kalahari*. London.

DU BRUYN, J. (1981) The Oorlams Afrikaners: from Dependence to Dominance, c. 1760–1823. Paper presented to the South African Historical Society Conference, Durban.

DUFF-GORDON, L. (1927) *Letters from the Cape*. Oxford.

DU PLESSIS, I.D. (1972) *The Cape Malays: History, Religion, Traditions, Folk Tales, the Malay Quarter*. Cape Town.

_____ and LÜCKHOFF, C.A. (1983) *The Malay Quarter and its People*. Cape Town.

DU PLESSIS, J. (1911) *A History of Christian Missions in South Africa*. London (reprint 1961).

DU TOIT, A. (1983) "No Chosen People: The Myth of the Calvinist Origins of Afrikaner Nationalism and Racial Ideology." *American Historical Review* 88, 4: 920–52.

_____ and GILIOMEE, H. (1983) *Afrikaner Political Thought: Analysis and Documents. Volume One: 1780–1850*. Berkeley.

EDWARDS, I. (1942) *Towards Emancipation: A Study of South African Slavery*. Cardiff.

ELDREDGE, E. (1991a) The Delagoa Bay Slave Trade, ca. 1729–1830. Paper presented at the Canadian Association of African Studies Annual Meeting, York University.

_____ (1991b) Slave-raiding beyond the Cape Frontier, ca. 1800–1860. Paper presented at the African Studies Association Annual Meeting, St. Louis.

_____ (1992) "Sources of Conflict in Southern Africa, c. 1800-1830: The 'Mfecane' Reconsidered." *Journal of African History* 33, 1: 1–35.

_____ (1993) *A South African Kingdom: The Pursuit of Security in Nineteenth-Century Lesotho*. Cambridge.

ELLENBERGER, D.F. (1912) *History of the Basuto Ancient and Modern*. J. C.. Macgregor, ed. and trans. London.

ELLENBERGER, V. (1939) "History of the Batlokwa of Gaberones (Bechuanaland Protectorate)." *Bantu Studies* 13: 166–198 and supp.

ELPHICK, R. (1979) "The Khoisan to c. 1770." In R. Elphick and H. Giliomee, ed., *The Shaping of South African Society, 1652–1820*. Pp. 3–40. Cape Town.

_____ (1985) *Kkoikhoi and the Founding of White South Africa*. Johannesburg.

_____ and GILIOMEE, H., ed. (1979) *The Shaping of South African Society, 1652–1820*. Cape Town.

ELPHICK, R. and GILIOMEE, H. (1989) "The Origins and Entrenchment of European Dominance at the Cape, 1652–c. 1840." In R. Elphick and H. Giliomee, ed., *The Shaping of South African Society, 1652–1840*. Pp. 521–66. Middletown.

_____ and MALHERBE, V.C. (1989) "The Khoisan to 1828." In R. Elphick and H. Giliomee, ed., *The Shaping of South African Society, 1652–1840*. Pp. : 3–65. Middletown.

_____ and Shell, R. (1989) "Intergroup Relations: Khoikhoi, settlers, slaves and free blacks, 1652–1795." In R. Elphick and H. Giliomee, ed., *The Shaping of South African Society, 1652–1840*. Pp. 184–239. Middletown.

ETHERINGTON, N. (1991) "The Great Trek in Relation to the Mfecane: A Reassessment." *South African Historical Journal* 25: 3–21.

EWART, J. (1970) *James Ewart's Journal*. Cape Town.

EYBERS, G.W., ed. (1969) *Select Constitutional Documents Illustrating South African History, 1795–1910*. Reprint. New York.

FAIRBAIRN, J. (1831) *Five Papers on the Slave Question from the South African Commercial Advertiser*. Cape Town.

FERREIRA, O.J.O. (1978) *Stormvoël van die Noorde: Stephanus Schoeman in Transvaal*. Pretoria.

FILLIOT, J.M. (1974) *La Traite des Esclaves vers les Mascareignes au XVIIIe Siecle*. Paris.

FINLEY, M.I. (1983) *Economy and Society in Ancient Greece*. New York.

FISCH, M. (1983) "Die Kriegszug Der Tawana Zum Kavango." *Namibiana* 4, 2: 43–71.

FRANKEN, J.L.M. (1926) "Die Franse Vlugtelinge." *Die Huisgenoot*, 16 July, pp. 35–41.

_____ (1930) "Vertolking aan de Kaap in Maleis en Portugees," *Die Huisgenoot*, 23 May, pp. 41–69; 27 June, pp. 43–69; and 18 July, pp. 41–69.

_____, ed. (1933) *Duminy Diaries*. Cape Town.

_____ (1940) "'n Kaapse Huishoue in die 18de Eeu uit Von Dessin se Briefboek en Memorial." *Archives Yearbook for South African History*. 3, 1: 1–88.

FREDERICKSON, G.M. (1981) *White Supremacy: A Comparative Study in American and South African History*. New York.

FREDOUX, J. (1858) "Station de Motito: Lettre de M. Fredoux, en date du 8 Août 1857." *Journal des Missions Évangéliques de Paris* 33: 4–26.

FREEMAN, J.J. (1851) *A Tour in South Africa, with Notices of Natal, Mauritius, Madagascar, Ceylon, Egypt, and Palestine*. London.

FREUND, W. (1971) "Society and Government in Dutch South Africa: The Cape and the Batavians, 1803–1806." Ph.D. thesis, Yale University, New Haven.

FREYRE, G. (1971) *The Masters and the Slaves: A Study in the Development of Brazilian Civilization*. New York.

GADIBOLAE, M. (1984) "Serfdom (Bolata) in the Nata Area 1926–1960." B.A. dissertation with appended interviews, University of Botswana, Gaborone.

GAILEY, H. (1962) "John Philip's Role in Hottentot Emancipation." *Journal of African History* 3: 419–33.

GARDINER, A.F. (1836) *Narrative of a Journey to the Zoolu Country in South Africa*. London.

GERMOND, R.C. (1967) *Chronicles of Basutoland*. Morija.

GEWALD, J.B. (1991) Untapped Sources: Slave exports from southern and central Namibia up to the mid-nineteenth century. Paper presented at the University of Leiden, Leiden.

GEWALD, J.B. (1993) The Road of the Man called Love and the Sack of Sero: The Export of Herero Labour to the South African Rand, 1890–1914. Paper presented at the African Studies Association Annual Meeting, Boston.

GIBSON, G.D., LARSON, T.J. and McGURK, C.R. (1981) *The Kavango Peoples*. Wiesbaden.

GILIOMEE, H. (1981) "Processes in the Development of the Southern African Frontier." In H. Lamar and L. Thompson, ed., *The Frontier in History: North America and Southern Africa Compared*. Pp. 76–119. New Haven.

_____ (1989) "The Eastern Frontier, 1770–1812." In H. Giliomee and R. Elphick, ed., *The Shaping of South African Society, 1652–1840*. Pp. 421–71. Middletown.

GILLMORE, P. (1878) *The Great Thirst Land*. London.

GLAMAN, K. (1981) *Dutch-Asiatic Trade: 1620 to 1740*. 's-Gravenhage.

GODÉE-MOLSBERGEN, E.C. (1912–13) "Hottentotten, slaven en blanke in compagniestijd in Zuid-Afrika." *Handeling en Medelingen van de Maatscappij der Nederlandsche Letterkunde te Leiden*. Pp.102–118.

_____ (1916) *Reizen in Zuid-Afrika in de Hollandse Tijd*. Four vols. 's-Gravenhage.

GORDON CUMMING, R. (1850) *The Lion Hunter of South Africa*. Two vols. London.

GRAY, S. (1978) "Our Forgotten Drama." *Speak*, March/April, pp. 14–5.

GREAT BRITAIN, PARLIAMENTARY PAPERS (1835) *Papers Relative to the Condition and Treatment of the Native Inhabitants of Southern Africa within the Colony of the Cape of Good Hope or Beyond the Frontier of that Colony, Part I: Hottentots and Bosjesmen; Caffres; Griquas*. 50, 34.

GREENSTEIN, L. (1973) "Slave and Citizen: The South African Case." *Race* 15: 25–45.

GREYLING, J.C. (1943) "Die Vraagstuk van Slawehandel en Slawerny in die Suid-Afrikaanse Republiek tot 1877." M.A. thesis, University of South Africa, Pretoria.

GROBLER, H.J. (1919) "Storie van 'n Vergane Voortrekkerdorp." *Die Brandwag*, 24 December, pp. 217–22.

GUELKE, L. (1976) "Frontier Settlement in Early Dutch South Africa." *Annals of the Association of American Geographers* 66, 1: 25–42.

_____ (1983) "A Computer Approach to Mapping the 'Opgaff': The Population of the Cape in 1731." *South African Journal of Photogrammetry, Remote Sensing and Cartography* 13, 4: 227–37.

_____ (1989) "Freehold farmers and frontier settlers, 1657–1780." In R. Elphick and H. Giliomee, ed., *The Shaping of South African Society, 1652–1840*. Pp. 66–108. Middletown.

_____ and SHELL, R.C. (1983) "An Early Colonial Landed Gentry: Land and Wealth in the Cape Colony, 1682–1731." *Journal of Historical Geography* 9, 3: 265–86.

HAMILTON, C. (1992) "'The Character and Objects of Chaka': A Reconsideration of the Making of Shaka as 'Mfecane' Motor." *Journal of African History* 33, 1: 37–63.

_____, ed. (forthcoming) *The Mfecane Aftermath: Reconstructive debates in southern African history*. Johannesburg and Pietermaritzburg.

HAMPSON, R.M.(*) "Islam in South Africa: A Bibliography." School of Librarianship, University of Cape Town. 1964.

HARRIES, P. (1981) "Slavery, Social Incorporation and Surplus Extraction: the Nature of Free and Unfree Labour in South-East Africa." *Journal of African History* 22: 309–30.

_____ (1984) "Mozbiekers: The Immigration of an African Community to the Western Cape, 1876–1882." *Studies in the History of Cape Town* 1: 153–64.

HARRIES, P. (1988) "The Roots of Ethnicity: Discourse and the Politics of Language Construction in South-East Africa." *African Affairs* 346: 25–52.

_____ (1991) "Exclusion, Classification and Internal Colonialism: The Emergence of Ethnicity Among the Tsonga-Speakers of South Africa." In L. Vail, ed., *The Creation of Tribalism in Southern Africa*. Pp. 82–117. Berkeley.

HATTERSLEY, A.F. (1923) "The Emancipation of Slaves at the Cape." *History* 8: 180–66.

HATTINGH, J.L. (1981) "Slawevrystellings aan die Kaap, 1700–1720." *Kronos* 4: 24–37.

_____ (1982) "Beleid en praktyk: die doop van slawekinders en die sluit van gemengde verhoudings aan die Kaap voor 1720." *Kronos* 5: 25–42.

_____ (1983a) "Naamgewing aan Slawe, Vryswartes en ander Gekleurdes." *Kronos* 6: 5–20.

_____ (1983b) "Die Klagte oor goewerneur W.A. van der Stel se slawebesit -'n Beoordeling met behup van kwantitatiewe data." *Kronos* 7: 5–20.

_____ (1984) "A.J. Böeseken se addendum van Kaapse slawe-verkooptransaksies: Foute en Regstellings." *Kronos* 9: 3–12.

_____ (1985) "Grondbesit in die Tafelvallei. Deel 1: Die Eksperiment: Vryswartes as Grondeienaars, 1652–1710." *Kronos* 10: 32–48.

_____ (1989) "Kaapse Notariële stukke waarin slawe van Vryburgers en Amptenare vermeld word — II — Die Tweede Dekade 1671–1680." *Kronos* 15: 3–48.

HEDGES, D.W. (1979) "Trade and Politics in Southern Mozambique and Zululand in the Eighteenth and Nineteenth Centuries." Ph.D. thesis, University of London, London.

HEESE, H.F. (1981) "Slawegesinne in die W. Kaap, 1665–1795." *Kronos* 4: 38–48.

_____ (1986) "'n Huigelaar en sy slavin: Tryntjie se glas koringbier." *In De Kat* 10: 50–3.

_____ (1986) "Mortaliteit onder VOC Slawe, 1720–1782." *Kronos* 11: 7–14.

HEIDER, F. (1958) *The Psychology of Interpersonal Relations*. New York.

HEMMY, G. (1959) *De Promontorio Bonae Spei, the Cape of Hope: A Latin Oration Delivered in the Hamburg Academy 10 April, 1767*. Cape Town.

HENGHERR, E.C.W. (1953) "Emancipation—and after: A study of Cape slavery and the issues arising from it, 1830–1843." M.A. thesis, University of Cape Town, Cape Town.

HEPBURN, J.D. (1896) *Twenty Years in Khama's Country*. London.

HITCHCOCK, R.K. (1987) "Socioeconomic Change among the Basarwa in Botswana: an Ethnohistorical Analysis." *Ethnohistory* 34, 3: 219–55.

HOFMEYER, S. (1890) *Twintig Jaren in Zoutpansberg*. Cape Town.

HOLDEN, W.C., ed. (1855) *History of the Colony of Natal, South Africa*. London.

HOLUB, E. (1880) "Journey through South Central Africa." *Proceedings of the Royal Geographical Society* N.Ser 2: 166–82.

_____ (1971) *Seven Years in South Africa*. Two vols. Reprint. Johannesburg.

HOPPER, M.J.(*) *Slavery at the Cape*. Cape Town. 1964.

HUET, P. (1869) *Het Lot der Zwarten in Transvaal: Mededeelingen omtrent de Slavernij en Wreedheden in de Zuid-Afrikaansche Republiek*. Utrecht.

HUTTON, C.W., ed. (1887) *The Autobiography of the Late Sir Andries Stockenstrom*. Two vols. Cape Town.

ILIFFE, J. (1987) *The African Poor*. Cambridge.

ISAACMAN, A. (1972a) *Mozambique: The Africanization of a European Institution: the Zambezi Prazos*. Madison.

ISAACMAN, A. (1972b) "The Origins, Formation and Early History of the Chikunda of South Central Africa." *Journal of African History* 13, 4: 443–62.

ISAACMAN, B. and ISAACMAN, A. (1977) "Slavery and Social Stratification among the Sena of Mozambique: A Study of the Kaporo System." In S. Miers and I. Kopytoff, ed., *Slavery in Africa: Historical and Anthropological Perspectives*. Pp. 105–20. Madison.

ISAACS, N. (1836) *Travels and Adventures in Eastern Africa*. Two vols. London. (Reprint: Cape Town, 1936).

JACKSON, A.O. (1982). *The Ndebele of Langa*. Pretoria [NB: year of publication uncertain].

JACKSON HAIGHT, M.V. (1967) *European Powers and South-East Africa: A Study of International Relations on the South-East Coast of Africa, 1796–1856*. rev. ed. New York.

JEFFREYS, K. and NAUDE, S.D., ed. (1944–1949) *Kaapse Plakkaatboek, 1652–1806*. Six vols. Cape Town.

JEPPE, J. and KOTZÉ, J.G. (1887) *De Locale Wetten der Zuid Afrikaansche Republiek, 1849–1885*. Pretoria.

JORDAAN, K. (1974) "The Origins of the Afrikaners and Their Language, 1652–1720: A Study in Miscegenation and Creole." *Race* 15, 4: 461–95.

JOUSSE, T. (1853) "Station de Motito." *Journal des Missions Évangéliques de Paris* 28: 15–9.

JUNOD, H.A. (1905) "The Ba-Thonga of the Transvaal." *British Association for the Advancement of Science* 3: 222–62.

KALLAWAY, P. (1982) "Danster and the Xhosa of the Gariep: Towards a Political Economy of the Cape Frontier 1790–1820." *African Studies* 41, 1: 143–60.

KAY, S. (1823) "Boschuana Country." (*Wesleyan*) *Missionary Notices* (London): 4.

_____ (1833) *Travels and Researches in Caffraria*. London.

KEBIDITSWE, K. (1984) "Subordination and Conflict in Ngamiland: The Bayei Protest of 1948." B.A. dissertation with appended interviews, University of Botswana, Gaborone.

KENNEDY, R.F., ed. (1964) *Thomas Baines: Journal of Residence in Africa, vol. 2, 1850–1853*. Cape Town.

KINDERSLEY, Mrs. (1777) *Letters from the Island of Teneriffe, Brazil, the Cape of Good Hope, and the East Indies*. London.

KINSMAN, M. (1989) "Populists and Patriarchs: The Transformation of the Captaincy at Griqua Town, 1804–1822." In A. Mabin, ed., *Organisation and Economic Change. Southern African Studies. Volume 5*. Pp. 1–20. Johannesburg.

KIRBY, P.R., ed. (1939-40) *The Diary of Dr. Andrew Smith, director of the 'Expedition for Exploring Central Africa' 1834–1836*. Two vols. Cape Town.

_____ ed. (1955) *Andrew Smith and Natal: Documents Relating to the Early History of that Province*. Cape Town.

KISTNER, W. (1945) "Beweerde Slawerny en Slawehandel in Transvaal (1852–1868)." M.A. thesis, University of Pretoria, Pretoria.

_____ (1952) "The Anti-Slavery Agitation Against the Transvaal Republic, 1852–1868." *Archives Yearbook for South African History* 15, 2: 197–278.

KLEIN, H.S. (1978) *The Middle Passage: Comparative Studies in the Atlantic Slave Trade*. Princeton.

KNOBEL, L. (1969) "The History of Sechele." *Botswana Notes and Records* 1: 51–64.

KOELLE, S.W. (1854) *Polyglotta Africana; or a Comparative Vocabulary of Nearly Three Hundred Words and Phrases in More than One Hundred Distinct African Languages.* London (Reprint, Graz, 1963).

KOLBE, P. (1968) *The Present State of the Cape of Good Hope: Containing, the Natural History of the Cape....* Two vols. Reprint. London.

KOTLIKOFF, L. (1975) Towards a Quantitative Description of the New Orleans Slave Market. Paper presented at the Workshop in History, University of Chicago, Chicago.

KRUGER, P. (1925) *Paul Kruger's Amptelike Briewe, 1851–1877.* S.P. Engelbrecht, ed. Pretoria.

——— (1969) *The Memoirs of Paul Kruger.* Reprint. New York.

KUPER, H. (1947) *An African Aristocracy: Rank among the Swazi.* London.

LATSKY, M. "Slawewetgewing aan die Kaap (1806–1834)." M.A. thesis, University of Stellenbosch, Stellenbosch.

LEGASSICK, M (1969a) "The Sotho-Tswana Peoples before 1800." In L. Thompson, ed. *African Societies in Southern Africa.* Pp. 86–125. London.

——— (1969b) "The Griqua, the Sotho-Tswana, and the Missionaries, 1780–1840: the Politics of a Frontier Zone." Ph.D. dissertation, University of California, Los Angeles.

——— (1977) "Gold, Agriculture, and Secondary Industry in South Africa, 1885–1970: from Periphery to Sub-Metropole as a Forced Labour System." In R. Palmer and N. Parsons, ed., *The Roots of Rural Poverty in Central and Southern Africa.* Pp. 175–200. Berkeley.

——— (1980), "The Frontier Tradition in South African Historiography." In S. Marks and A. Atmore, ed. *Economy and Society in Pre-Industrial South Africa.* Pp. 44–79. Harlow.

——— (1989) "The Northern Frontier to c. 1840: The Rise and Decline of the Griqua People." In R. Elphick and H. Giliomee, ed., *The Shaping of South African Society, 1652-1840.* Pp. 358–420. Middeltown.

LEIBBRANDT, H.C.V. (1896a) *Journal, 1699–1732.* In *Precis of the Archives of the Cape of Good Hope.* Cape Town.

——— (1896b) *Letters Despatched.* In *Precis of the Archives of the Cape of Good Hope.* Cape Town.

——— (1897) *Precis of the Archives of the Cape of Good Hope: the Defense of Willem Adriaan van der Stel.* Cape Town.

——— (1905, 1989 [sic]) *Requesten (Memorials) 1715-1806.* Five vols. Cape Town. [N.B.: in 1989 the South African Library printed Leibbrandt's unfinished manuscripts vols. 3–4, indexed these, and produced further addenda in vol. 5].

LEIPOLDT, C.L. (1976) *Leipoldt's Cape Cookery.* Cape Town.

LEMUE, P. (1831) "Détails sur les moeurs des Bechuanas." *Journal des Missions Évangéliques de Paris* 6.

——— (1834) "Voyage de M. Mellen...." *Journal des Missions Évangéliques de Paris.* 9: 266–76.

——— (1847) "Coup d'oeil sur les Kalagaris." *Journal des Missions Évangéliques de Paris* 22: 24–40, 67–80, 106–19, 143–58.

LE ROUX, S.D. (1939) *Pioneers and Sportsmen of South Africa, 1760–1890.* Salisbury.

LEYLAND, J. (1972) *Adventures in the Far Interior of South Africa including a Journey to Lake Ngami and Rambles in Honduras.* Reprint. Cape Town.

LICHTENSTEIN, H., (1928) *Travels in Southern Africa in the Years 1803, 1804, 1805 and 1806.* A. Plumptre, trans. Two vols. Cape Town (2nd vol. 1930)

LIEBENBERG, B.J. (1959) "Die Vrystelling van die Slawe in die Kaapkolonie en die Implikasies Daarvan." M.A. thesis, University of the Orange Free State, Bloemfontein.

_____ (1977) *Andries Pretorius in Natal.* Pretoria.

LIESEGANG, G. (1969) "Dingane's Attack on Lourenço Marques in 1833." *Journal of African History* 10, 4: 565–79.

_____ (1970) "Nguni Migrations between Delagoa Bay and the Zambezi, 1821–1839." *African Historical Studies* 3, 2: 317-37.

LISTER, M.H., ed. (1949) *Journals of Andrew Geddes Bain.* Cape Town.

LITTLEFIELD, D.C. (1981) *Rice and Slaves: Ethnicity and the Slave Trade in Colonial South Carolina.* Baton Rouge.

LIVINGSTONE, D. (1857) *Missionary Researches and Travels in South Africa.* London.

LOBATO (1949) *História do Presîdio de Lourenço Marques. Vol. I, 1782–1786.* Lisboa.

LOCKYER, C. (1711) *An Account of the Trade in India: Containing Rules for good government in Trade, Price Courants, and Table: With descriptions of...the Cape of Good Hope, and St. Helena....* London.

LONDON MISSIONARY SOCIETY (1935) *The Masarwa (Bushmen): Report of an Inquiry by the South Africa District Committee of the London Missionary Society.* Alice.

LONG, U. ed. (1956) *The Journals of Elizabeth Lees Price.* London.

LOVEJOY, P.E. (1991) *Transformations in Slavery: A History of Slavery in Africa.* New ed. Cambridge.

_____ and FALOLA, T., ed. (1993) *Pawnship in Africa.* Boulder.

_____ and HOGENDORN, J.S. (1993) *Slow Death for Slavery: The Course of Abolition in Northern Nigeria, 1897–1936.* Cambridge.

LYE, W.F., ed. (1975) *Andrew Smith's Journal of his Expedition into the Interior of South Africa 1834–1836.* Cape Town.

MACGREGOR, J.C. (1905) *Basuto Traditions.* Cape Town.

MACKENZIE, J. (1871) *Ten Years North of the Orange River.* Edinburgh.

MACKENZIE, N. (*) "South African Travel Literature in the Seventeenth Century." *Archives Yearbook for South African History* 18, 2(1955): 1–112.

MACLEAN, C.R. (1992) *The Natal Papers of 'John Ross': Loss of the Brig Mary at Natal with Early Recollections of that Settlement, and Among the Caffres.* S. Gray, ed. Durban.

MACMILLAN, W. M. (1923) *Bantu, Boer, and Briton: the Making of the South African Native Problem.* London (reprint: Oxford, 1963).

_____ (1927) *The Cape Colour Question: a Historical Survey.* London (reprint: London, New York, 1968).

MALHERBE, V.C. (1981) "The Khoi Captains in the Third Frontier War." In S. Newton-King and V.C. Malherbe, *The Khoikhoi Rebellion in the Eastern Cape (1799–1803).* Pp. 66–135. Cape Town.

_____ (1991) "Indentured and Unfree Labour in South Africa: Towards an Understanding." *South African Historical Journal* 24: 3–30.

MANNING, P. (1990) *Slavery and African Life: Occidental, Oriental, and African Slave Trades.* Cambridge.

MANSO, V. deP. (1870) *Memoria sobre Lourenço Marques (Delagoa Bay).* Lisboa.

MARAIS, J.S. (1939) *The Cape Coloured People.* London.

MAREE, W.L. (1962) *Lig in Soutpansberg.* Johannesburg.

MARKS, S. (1972) "Khoisan Resistance to the Dutch in the Seventeenth and Eigh teenth Centuries." *Journal of African History* 13, 1: 55–80.

———— and Atmore, A. (1980) "Introduction." In S. Marks and A. Atmore, ed., *Economy and Society in Pre-Industrial South Africa*. Pp. 1–43. Harlow.

———— and Gray, R. (1975) "Southern Africa and Madagascar." In R. Gray, ed., *The Cambridge History of Africa, Vol. 4 from c. 1600 to c. 1790*. Pp. 384–468. Cambridge.

MARTINS, F. (1957) *João Albasini e a Colonia de S. Luis*. Lisbon.

MARX, K. (1977) *Capital*, vol. 1. Reprint. New York.

MASON, J. (1990) "Hendrick Albertus and His Ex-Slave Mey: a Drama in Three Acts." *Journal of African History* 31: 423–45.

———— (1991a) "The Slaves and their Protectors: Reforming Resistance in a Slave Society, the Cape Colony, 1826–1834." *Journal of Southern African Studies* 17, 1: 104–128.

———— (1991b) The Fortunate Slave: Slaves as Labor Tenants in the Nineteenth Century Cape Colony. Paper presented at the African Studies Association Annual Meeting, St. Louis.

———— (1992) "'Fit for Freedom': The Slaves, Slavery and Emancipation in the Cape Colony, South Africa, 1806 to 1842." Two vols. Ph.D. dissertation, Yale University, New Haven.

MASON, R.J. (1968) "Transvaal and the Natal Iron Age Settlements Revealed by Aerial Photography and Excavation." *African Studies* 29, 3: 167–80.

MATTHEWS, Z.K. (1945) "A Short History of the Tshidi Barolong." *Fort Hare Papers* 1, 1: 9–28.

MAUTLE, G. (1981) "Bakgalagadi-Bakwena Relationship: A Case of Slavery, c. 1840– c.1930." B.A. dissertation with appended interviews, University of Botswana, Gaborone.

———— (1986) "Bakgalagadi-Bakwena Relationship: A Case of Slavery, c. 1840– c.1930." *Botswana Notes and Records* 18: 19-31.

MAYSON, J.S. (1861) *The Malays of Cape Town*. Manchester. (reprint 1963).

MEILLASSOUX, C. (1991) *The Anthropology of Slavery: the Womb of Iron and Gold*. A. Dasnois, trans. Chicago.

MELVILL, J. (1829) "Missionary Tour Through the Country of the Bashutoos." *Transactions of the Missionary Society* 52 (October): 123–8.

MENDELSSOHN, S. (*) *South African Bibliography*. Two vols. London, 1910.

MENTZEL, O.F. (1919) *Life at the Cape in Mid-Eighteenth Century being the Biography of Rudolf Siegfried Alleman, Captain of the Military Forces and Commander of the Castle In the Services of the Dutch East India Company At the Cape of Good Hope*. M. Greenlees, trans. Cape Town.

———— (1921–1944) *A Complete and Authentic Geographical and Topographical Description of the Famous and (all things considered) Remarkable African Cape of Good Hope....* G.V. Marais and J. Hoge, trans. H. J. Mandelbrote, rev. and ed. Three vols. Cape Town.

MGADLA, P.T. R. (1985) "Missionary and Colonial Education among the Bangwato, 1862 to 1948." Ph. D. dissertation, Boston University, Boston.

MIERS, S. and Crowder, M. (1989) "The Politics of Slavery in Bechuanaland: Power Struggles and the Plight of the Basarwa in the Bamangwato Reserve, 1926–1940." In S. Miers and R. Roberts, ed. *The End of Slavery in Africa*. Pp. 172–200. Madison.

Miers, S. and Kopytoff, I., ed. (1977) *Slavery in Africa: Historical and Anthropological Perspectives.* Madison.

———— and Roberts, R., ed. (1989) *The End of Slavery in Africa.* Madison.

Miller, J. (1988) *The Way of Death: Merchant Capitalism and the Angolan Slave Trade 1730–1830.* Madison.

Miller, S.M. and Tempelhoff, J.W.N. (1990) "Die Romantiek van 'n Grensterrrein." *Fauna and Flora* 47: 32–9.

Mirza Abu Talib Ibn Muhammed Khan (1810) *The Voyages of Mirza Abu Taleb Khan in Asia, Africa and Europe in the Years 1799, 1800, 1801, 1802 and 1803, written by himself...and translated by Charles Stewart.* Two vols. London.

Moeng, M. (1986) "The Root Cause of Poverty among the Bakgalagadi of Kweneng West." B.A. dissertation with appended interviews, University of Botswana, Gaborone.

Moffat, R. (1842) *Missionary Labours and Scenes in Southern Africa.* London (reprint: New York, 1969).

Mokgatle, N. (1971) *The Autobiography of an Unknown South African.* Berkeley.

Molema, S.M. ((1920) *The Bantu, Past and Present.* Edinburgh.

Moodie, D. (1842) *The Record, or a Series of Official Papers Relative to the Condition and Treatment of the Native Tribes of South Africa 1838–42.* Three vols. Cape Town (Reprint: Amsterdam, 1960).

Moolman, J.P.F. (1975) "Die Boer se Siening van en Houding teenoor die Bantoe in Transvaal tot 1860." M.A. thesis, University of Pretoria, Pretoria.

Morgan, E.S. (1975) *American Slavery, American Fredom.* New York.

Morton, B. (1990) "Marapo Fela": BaTawana Expansion in Ngamiland, 1847-93. Paper presented at Department of History seminar, Indiana University, Bloomington.

———— (1991) Constraints on Cattle Production and Patterns of Ownership among the Nineteenth Century Tswana. Paper presented at Department of History seminar, Indiana University, Bloomington.

Morton, F. (1985) "Chiefs and Ethnic Unity in Two Colonial Worlds: The Bakgatla baga Kgafela of the Bechuanaland Protectorate and the Transvaal, 1872–1966." In A.I. Asiwaju, ed., *Partitioned Africans: Ethnic Relations across Africa's International Boundaries, 1884–1984.* Pp. 127-54. London.

———— (1988) Manumitted Slaves and the Dutch Reformed Church Mission in the Western Transvaal and Eastern Bechuanaland at the time of the Colonization of Southern Africa, 1864 to 1914. Paper tabled at the 12th International Congress of Anthropological and Ethnological Sciences, Zagreb, 28 July.

———— (1990) *Children of Ham: Freed Slaves and Fugitive Slaves on the Kenya Coast, 1873 to 1907.* Boulder.

———— (1991a) Slave-raiding and Slavery in the Western Transvaal after the Sand River Convention of 1852. Paper presented at the Canadian Association of African Studies Annual Meeting, York University.

———— (1991b) Slave-raiding and Slavery in the Western Transvaal after the Sand River Convention of 1852. Paper presented at the African Studies Association Annual Meeting, St. Louis.

———— (1992) "Slave-Raiding and Slavery in the Western Transvaal after the Sand River Convention." *African Economic History* 20: 99–118.

MORTON, F., MURRAY, A., and RAMSAY, J. (1989) *Historical Dictionary of Botswana. New Edition.* Metuchen, NJ.

MOTENDA, M.M. (1940) "History of the Western Venda and of the Lemba" In N.J. van Warmelo, ed. *The Copper Miners of Musina and the Early History of the Zoutpansberg.* Pp. 51–70. Pretoria.

MÜLLER, A.L. (1981a) "The Economics of Slave Labour at the Cape of Good Hope." *The South African Journal of Economics* 49, 1: 46–58.

———— (1981b) "Slavery and the Development of South Africa." *The South African Journal of Economics* 49, 2: 153–65.

MULLIN, G.W. (1972) *Flight and Rebellion: Slave Resistance in Eighteenth-Century Virginia.* London.

NASSON, W.R. (1983) "Black Society in the Cape Colony and the South African War of 1899–1902: A Social History." D. Phil. dissertation, University of Cambridge, Cambridge.

NETTELTON, G.E. (1934) "History of the Ngamiland Tribes up to 1926." *Bantu Studies* 8: 343–60.

NEUMARK, S.D. (1957) *Economic Influences on the South African Frontier.* Stanford.

NEWITT, M.D.D. (1988) "Drought in Mozambique, 1823–1831." *Journal of Southern African Studies* 15: 14–35.

NEWTON-KING, S. (1980) "The labour market of the Cape Colony, 1807–28." In S. Marks and A. Atmore, ed., *Economy and Society in Pre-Industrial South Africa.* Pp. 171–207. London.

———— (1981a) "Background to the Khoikhoi Rebellion of 1799–1803." University of London Institute of Commonwealth Studies, *Collected Seminar Papers on the Societies of Southern Africa in the 19th and 20th Centuries* 10: 1–12.

———— (1981b) "The Rebellion of the Khoi in Graaff-Reinet: 1799 to 1803." In S. Newton-King and V.C. Malherbe, *The Khoikhoi Rebellion in the Eastern Cape (1799–1803).* Pp. 12-65. Cape Town.

NGCONGCO, L.D. (1979) "Origins of the Tswana." *Pula: Botswana Journal of African Studies* 2, 1: 21–46.

NICHOLLS, C.S. (1971) *The Swahili Coast: Politics, Diplomacy and Trade on the East African Littoral, 1798–1856.* London.

NIENABER, G.S. (1963) *Hottentots.* Pretoria.

NIXON, J. (1885) *The Complete Story of the Transvaal.* London.

OMER-COOPER, J.D. (1988) *History of Southern Africa.* London.

ORPEN, J.M. (1964) *Reminiscences of a Life in South Africa from 1846 to the Present Day.* Reprint. Cape Town (originally published 1908. Two vols. Durban).

Orpen, J.M. (1979) *History of the Basutus of South Africa.* Reprint: Mazenod, Lesotho.

Owen, W.F.W. (1833) *Narrative of Voyages to Explore the Shores of Africa, Arabia, and Madagascar.* Two vols. London (Reprint: London, 1968).

PARISH, P.J. (1989) *Slavery: History and Historians.* New York.

PARSONS, N. (1973) "Khama III, the Bamangwato, and the British, with Special Reference to 1895–1923." Ph.D. thesis, University of Edinburgh, Edinburgh.

———— (1977) "The Economic History of Khama's Country in Botswana, 1844–1930." In R. Palmer and N. Parsons, ed., *The Roots of Rural Poverty in Central and Southern Africa.* Pp. 113–143. Berkeley.

———— (1982) *A New History of Southern Africa.* London.

PARSONS, N. (forthcoming) "Prelude to Difaqane in the Interior of South Africa, c. 1600–c.1822." In C. Hamilton, ed. *The Mfecane Aftermath: Reconstructive debates in in southern African history*. Johannesburg and Pietermaritzburg.

PATTERSON, O. (1982) *Slavery and Social Death*. Cambridge, Mass.

PEDRO, K.J. (1984) "Die Doopbediening aan slawe en vryswartes in die Kaapse Kerk, 1802–1812." *Kronos* 9: 22–35.

PEIRES, J.B. (1981) *The House of Phalo: a History of the Xhosa People in the Days of Their Independence*. Johannesburg.

PENN, N. (1985) "Anarchy and Authority in the Koue Bokkeveld, 1739–1799: The Banishing of Carel Buijtendag." *Kleio* 17: 24–43.

———— (1986) "Pastoralists and Pastoralism in the Northern Cape Frontier Zone During the Eighteenth Century." In M. Hall and A. Smith, ed. *Prehistoric Pastoralism in Southern Africa*. Pp. 62–8. Cape Town.

———— (1987) "The Frontier in the Western Cape." In J. Parkington and M. Hall, ed. *Papers in the Prehistory of the Western Cape*. Pp. 462–503. Oxford.

———— (1989) "Labour, Land and Livestock in the Western Cape during the Eighteenth Century: The Khoisan and the Colonists." In W. James and M. Simons, ed., *The Angry Divide: Social and Economic History of the Western Cape*. Pp. 1–29. Cape Town.

———— (1993) "The Orange River Frontier Zone, c. 1700–1805." In A.B. Smith, ed. *Eiriqualand: The People of the Orange River Frontier*. Pp. 20–119. Cape Town.

———— (forthcoming) "The Northern Cape Frontier Zone, 1700–1815." Ph.D. thesis, University of Cape Town, Cape Town.

PENNY, J. (1815) *The Life and Adventures of Joshua Penny*. Cape Town (reprint 1982).

PERCIVAL, R. (1969) *An Account of the Cape of Good Hope*. Reprint. New York.

PHILIP, J. (1828) *Researches in South Africa*. Two vols. London.

PIETERSE, D.J. (1936) "Beweerde Slawehandel deur Boere: stelselmatige propaganda om [die] Republiek te ondermyn." *Die Huisgenoot*, 2 October: 27, 87, 89, 91, 93; 9 October: 53, 81, 83.

PLAATJE, S. (1916) *Sechuana Proverbs*. London.

POSTMA, J.M. (1990) *The Dutch in the Atlantic Slave Trade, 1600–1815*. Cambridge.

POTGIETER, F.J. (1958) "Die Vestiging van die Blanke in Transvaal (1837–1886) met Spesiale Verwysing na die Verhouding tussen die Mens en die Omgewing." *Archives Year Book for South African History* 21, 2: 1–208.

PRESTON, A. ed. (1973) *The South African Journal of Sir Garnet Wolseley, 1879–1880*. Cape Town.

PRETORIUS, C. (1979) "Verhaal van Anna Marais en die slaaf Claas van Bengalen." *Historia* 24: 42–9.

PRETORIUS, F. (1988) "Kommandolewe Tydens Die Anglo-Boereoorlog, 1899–1902." Ph.D. thesis, University of South Africa, Pretoria.

RAMSAY, F.J. (1991) "The Rise and Fall of the Bakwena Dynasty of South-Central Botswana, 1820–1940." Two vols.Ph.D. dissertation, Boston University, Boston.

RAVEN-HART, R., comp. & ed. (*) *Cape Good Hope, 1652–1702*. Two vols. Cape Town, 1971.

RAYNER, M.I. (1986) "Wine and Slaves: The Failure of an Export Economy and the Ending of Slavery in the Cape Colony, South Africa, 1806–1834." Ph.D. dissertation, Duke University, Durham.

RHEINHALLT-JONES, E. (1945) "Farm Labour in the Transvaal." *Race Relations* 12: 5–14.

RICHARD, P. (1980) "Basarwa Subordination among the Bakgatla: The Case of the Kgakole." B.A. dissertation with appended interviews,University of Botswana, Gaborone.

ROBERTSON, C.C. and Klein, M.A. (1983) *Women and Slavery in Africa.* Madison.

ROSS, R. (1976) *Adam Kok's Griqua: a Study in the Development of Stratification in South Africa.* Cambridge.

———— (1979) "The changing legal position of the Khoisan in the Cape Colony." *African Perspectives* 2: 67–87.

———— (1980) "The Occupations of Slaves in Eighteenth Century Cape Town." *Studies in the History of Cape Town* 2: 1–14.

———— (1983) *Cape of Torments: Slavery and Resistance in South Africa.* London.

———— (1986) "The Origins of Capitalist Agriculture in the Cape Colony: A Survey." In W. Beinart, P. Delius, and S. Trapido, ed., *Putting a Plough to the Ground: Accumulation and Dispossession in Rural South Africa, 1850–1930.* Pp. 56–100. Johannesburg.

———— (1988) "The Last Years of the Slave Trade to the Cape Colony." *Slavery and Abolition* 9, 3: 209–19.

———— (1989) "Oppression, sexuality and slavery at the Cape of Good Hope." *Historical Reflections* 6: 421–33.

SANDERSON, J. (1860) "Memoranda of a Trading Trip into the Orange River (Sovereignty) Free State, and the Country of the Transvaal Boers, 1851–1852." *Journal of the Royal Geographical Society* 30: 233–55.

SAUNDERS, C. (1984) "Between Slavery and Freedom: The Importation of Prize Negroes to the Cape in the Aftermath of Emancipation." *Kronos* 9: 36–43.

———— (1985) "Liberated Africans in the Cape Colony in the first half of the nineteenth century."*International Journal of African Historical Studies* 18: 223–39.

————, ed. (1988) *Illustrated History of South Africa: The Real Story.* Pleasantville.

————, ed. with Straus, T., comp. (*) *Cape Town and the Cape Peninsula post 1806.* University of Cape Town Center for African Studies occasional Papers 5, 1989, Cape Town.

SCHAPERA, I. (1938) "Ethnographical Texts in the Boloongwe Dialect of Sekgalagadi." *Bantu Studies* 12, 3: 157–87

———— (1940) *Married Life in an African Tribe.* London.

———— (1942) "A Short History of the Bakgatla-bagaKgafela of Bechuanaland Protectorate." Communications from the School of African Studies, New Series, no. 3. Cape Town.

———— (1945) "Notes on the History of the Kaa." *African Studies* 4, 3: 109–21.

————, ed. (1951a) *Apprenticeship at Kuruman: Journals and Letters of Robert and Mary Moffat, 1820–1828.* London.

———— (1951b) *The Khoisan Peoples of South Africa.* New York.

———— (1952) *The Ethnic Composition of Tswana Tribes.* London.

————, ed. (1959) *David Livingstone: Family Letters, 1841–1856.* Two vols. London.

————, ed. (1960) *Livingstone's Private Journals, 1851–1853.* Berkeley.

————, ed. (1961) *Livingstone's Missionary Correspondence.* London.

————, ed. (1963) *Livingstone's African Journal, 1853–1856.* Two vols. Berkeley.

———— (1965) *Praise Poems of Tswana Chiefs.* Oxford.

SCHAPERA, I. (1970a) "The Early History of the Khurutshe." *Botswana Notes and Records* 2: 1–5.

_____ (1970b) *Tribal Innovators: Tswana Chiefs and Social Change 1795–1940.* London.

_____, ed. (1974) *David Livingstone: South African Papers, 1849–1853.* Cape Town.

_____ (1977) *A Handbook of Tswana Law and Custom.* 2nd ed. London.

_____ (1979) *The Tswana.* New ed. Reprint. London.

_____ and VAN DER MERWE, D.F. (1945) "Notes on the Tribal groupings, History, and Customs of the Bakgalagadi." Communications from the School of African Studies, New Series, no. 13. Cape Town.

SCHMIDT, K.L.M. (*) "Bibliography of Personal Accounts of the Cape of Good Hope in Printed Books, 1715–1850." University of Cape Town School of Librarianship, 1955, Cape Town.

SCHOEMAN, K. (1984) "Slawe van die Kaap: 'n paar aantekinge." *Quarterly Bulletin of the South African Library* 39: 6–7.

SCHOLTZ, P.L. et al (*) *Race Relations at the Cape of Good Hope, 1652-1795: A Select Bibliography.* Boston, n.d. [ca. 1981]

SCHÖTTLER, P. (1989) "Historians and Discourse Analysis." *History Workshop Journal* 27: 37–65.

SCHULZ, A. and HAMMAR, A. (1897) *The New Africa: A Journey up the Chobe and down the Okavango Rivers.* New York.

SCHUTTE, G.J. (*) *Nederlandse Publicaties Betreffende Zuid-Afrika, 1800–1899.* Cape Town, 1989.

SEINER, F. (1977) "Die Buschmanner des Okavango and [sic] Sambesigebietes der Nord-Kalahari." *Botswana Notes and Records* 9: 31–6. [H. Vierich, trans, from *Globus* 97, 22 (1910)]

SEMPLE, R. (1968) *Walks and Sketches at the Cape of Good Hope.* Reprint. 2nd ed. Cape Town.

SHELL, R.C.-H. (1974) "The Establishment and Spread of Islam at the Cape from the beginning of Company Rule to 1838." Honors thesis, University of Cape Town, Cape Town.

_____ (1978) "Historical Background." In S. Ross, *Fish Cook Book for South Africa.* Pp. 12–6. Cape Town.

_____ (1984) "Introduction to S.E. Hudson's 'slaves'." *Kronos* 9: 44–70.

_____ (1986) "Slavery at the Cape of Good Hope." Two vols. Ph.D. dissertation, Yale University, New Haven.

_____ (1988) "A Note on Authochthonous Slavery." *Quarterly Bulletin of the South African Library* 43: 92–3.

_____ (1989) "The Family and Slavery: The Cape Slave Society, 1680-1838." In M. Simons and W. James, ed. *The Angry Divide: Social and Economic History of the Western Cape.* Pp. 20–39. Cape Town.

_____ (1991) "The Cape Slave Trade (1658–1808): Geographic Origins and Cultural Consequences with the Household." Paper presented at the African Studies Association Annual Meeting, St. Louis.

_____ (1992a) "Tender Ties: The Women of the Cape Slave Society." University of London Institute of Commonwealth Studies, *Collected Seminar Papers, the Societies of Southern Africa* 17, 2: 1–33.

SHELL, R.C.-H. (1992b) "The Changing Functions and Effects of the Domestic Slave Market at the Cape, 1652–1833." *International Journal of African Historical Studies* 25, 1: 285–336.

SHILLINGTON, K. (1985) *The Colonisation of the Southern Tswana, 1870–1900.* Johannesburg.

SILBERBAUER, G. and Kuper, A. (1966) "Kgalagari Masters and Bushman Serfs: Some Observations." *African Studies* 25, 4: 171–9.

SILLERY, A. (1952) *Bechuanaland Protectorate.* London.

———— (1974) *Botswana: A Short Political History.* London.

SILVER, S.W. & COMPANY (1877) *Handbook to the Transvaal British South Africa: Its Natural Features, Industries, Population and Gold Fields.* London.

SIMONSZ, C.J. (1924) "Opstel van Eenige Poincten, en ordres, getrocken (19 Apr. 1708)." In C.G. Botha, ed. *Collecteana* (first series). Pp. 25–48. Cape Town.

SMITH, A.K. (1969) "The Trade of Delagoa Bay as a factor in Nguni politics 1750–1835." In L. Thompson, ed., *African Societies in Southern Africa: Historical Studies.* Pp. 171–89. London.

———— (1970a) "The Struggle for Control of Southern Moçambique, 1720–1835." Ph.D. thesis, University of California, Los Angeles.

———— (1970b) "Delagoa Bay and the Trade of South-Eastern Africa." In R. Gray and D. Birmingham, ed. *Pre-Colonial African Trade: Essays on Trade in Central and Eastern Africa before 1900.* Pp. 265–89. London.

———— (1983) "The Indian Ocean Zone." In D. Birmingham and P.M. Martin, ed., *History of Central Africa. Volume One.* Pp. 205–44. London.

———— (1988) *The Changing Past: Trends in South African Historical Writing.* Athens.

SOLOMON, E. (1855) *Two Lectures on the Native Tribes of the Interior.* Cape Town.

SOREMEKUN, F. (1977) "Trade and Dependency in Central Angola: The Ovimbundu in the Nineteenth Century." In R. Palmer and N. Parsons, ed., *Roots of Rural Poverty in Southern and Central Africa.* Pp. 82–95. Berkeley.

SOUTHEY, N. (1992) "From Periphery to Core: The Treatment of Cape Slavery in South African Historiography." *Historia* 37, 2: 13–25.

SPARRMAN, A. (1977) *A Voyage to the Cape of Good Hope towards the Antarctic Polar Circle around the World and to the Country of the Hottentots and the Caffres from the year 1772-1776.* V.S. Forbes, ed. Two vols. VRS Second Series, No. 7. Cape Town.

SPOHR, O.H., ed. (1973) *Heinrich Lichtenstein: The Foundation of the Cape and About the Bechuanas.* Cape Town.

STOW, G.W. (1905) *The Native Races of South Africa.* G.M. Theal, ed., London. (reprint 1964).

STRUBEN, H.W. (1920) *Recollections of Adventures: Pioneering and Development in South Africa, 1850–1911.* Cape Town.

STRUBEN, R. (1968) *Taken at the Flood: The Story of Harry Struben.* Cape Town.

STUART, J. and MALCOLM, D.M., ed. (1969) *The Diary of Henry Francis Fynn.* Pietermaritzburg.

TABLER, E.C. (1955) *The Far Interior.* Cape Town.

———— (1960) *Zambesia and Matabeleland in the Seventies.* London.

TAS, A. (1969–70) *The Diary of Adam Tas.* L. Fouché et al, ed., J. Smuts, trans. Cape Town.

TEMPELHOFF, J.W.N. (1988) "Blanke Vestiging in die Distrik Soutpansberg gedurende die Negentiende Eeu, met Besondere Verwysing na die Tydperk 1886–99." *South African Journal for Cultural and Art History* 2, 4: 268–76.

THEAL, G.M. (1897–1905) *Records of the Cape Colony*. Thirty-six vols. London.
_____ (1903) *Records of South-Eastern Africa*. Nine vols. London (Reprint: Cape Town, 1964).
_____ (1919) *History of South Africa, from 1878 to 1884*. London.
_____ (1964) *Basutoland Records*. Two vols. Reprint. Cape Town.
_____ (1969) *The History of South Africa from 1795 to 1872*. Five vols. Reprint. Cape Town.
_____ (*) *Catalogue of Books and Pamphlets....* Cape Town, 1912.
THOMPSON, G. (1827) *Travels and Adventures in Southern Africa*. Two vols. London (Reprint: Cape Town, 1967, V.S. Forbes, ed.).
THOMPSON, L. (1969) "Co-Operation and Conflict: The High Veld." In M. Wilson and L. Thompson, ed., *The Oxford History of South Africa, I, South Africa to 1870*. Pp. 424–46. Oxford.
_____ (1990) *A History of South Africa*. New Haven.
TLOU, T. (1977) "Servility and Political Control: Botlhanka among the BaTawana of Northwestern Botswana, ca. 1750–1906." In S. Miers and I. Kopytoff, ed., *Slavery in Africa: Historical and Anthropological Perspectives*. Pp. 367–90. Madison.
_____ (1985) *A History of Ngamiland, 1750 to 1906; The Formation of an African State*. Gaborone.
TORRANCE, H. (1909) *Cape Town in 1823*. Glasgow.
TRAPIDO, S. (1976) "Aspects in the Transition from Slavery to Serfdom: The South African Republic, 1842–1902." University of London Institute of Commonwealth Studies, *Collected Seminar Papers on the Societies of Southern Africa in the 19th and 20th Centuries* 6: 24–31.
_____ (1980) "Reflections on land, office and wealth in the South African Republic, 1850–1900." In S. Marks and A. Atmore, ed., *Economy and Society in Pre-Industrial South Africa*. Pp. 350–68. London.
TRUMPELMANN, G.P.J. (1948) "Die Boer in Sudwes-Afrika." *Archives Year Book for South African History* 11, 2: 1–167.
UYS, C.J. (1933) *In the Era of Shepstone: Being a Study of British Expansion (1842–1877)*. Lovedale.
VALENTIJN, F. (1973) *Description of the Cape of Good Hope...* E.H. Raidt, ed. R. Raven-Hart, transl. Reprint. Two vols. Cape Town.
VALKHOFF, M. (1966) *Studies in Portuguese and Creole, with special reference to South Africa*. Johannesburg.
_____ (1972) *New Light on Afrikaans and "Malayo-Portuguese."* Louvain.
VAN ALPHEN, J.G. (1934) "Slaverny aan die Kaap: algemene afskaffing honderd jaar gelede." *Huisgenoot* 19: 17f.
VAN ASWEGEN, H.J. (1971) "Die Verhouding tussen Blank en Nie-Blank in die Oranje-Vrystaat, 1854–1902." *Archives Year Book for South African History* 34, 1: 1–393.
VAN DER CHIJS, J.A., comp. (1885) *Nederlandsch-Indisch Plakkaatboek, 1602–1811*. Sixteen vols. 's-Gravenhage.
VAN DER MERWE, P.J. (1945) *Trek: Studies oor die Mobiliteit van die Pioniersbevolking aan die Kaap*. Cape Town.
VAN DER SPUY, P. (1991) "Gender and Slavery: Towards a Feminist Revision." *South African Historical Journal* 25: 184–95.
_____ (1992) "Slave Women and the Family in Nineteenth-Century Cape Town." *South African Historical Journal* 27: 50–74.

VAN JAARSVELD, F.A. (1950) "Die Veldkornet en sy Aandeel in die Opbou van die Suid-Afrikaanse Republiek tot 1870." *Archives Yearbook for South African History* 13, 2: 187-354.

VAN RENSBURG, A.J. (1935) "Die Toestand van die Slawe aan die Kaap, 1806–1834." M.A. thesis, University of Cape Town, Cape Town.

VAN SELMS (1952) "Die Oudste Boek in Afrikaans: Isjmoeni se 'Bertroubare Woord'." *Hertzog Annale*: 61–102.

VAN WARMELO, N.J. and PHOPHI, W.M.D. (1949) *Venda Law, Part 4, Inheritance*. Pretoria.

VAN ZYL, D.J. (1978) "Slaaf in die ekonomiese lewe van die Westlike distrikte van die Kaapkolonie, 1795-1834." *South African Historical Journal* 10: 3–25.

VENTER, C.F. (1991) "Die Voortrekkers en die Ingeboekte Slawe wat die Groot Trek Meegemaak het, 1835–1838." *Historia* 36, 1: 14–29.

VENTER, P.J. (1934) "Die Inboek-Stelsel: 'n Uitvloeisel van Slawerny in die Ou Dae." *Die Huisgenoot*, 1 June, pp. 25, 59, 61.

_____ (1940) "Landdros en Heemrade (1682–1827)." *Archives Year Book for South African History* 3, 2: 1–242.

VOS, M.C. (1867) *Merkwardige Verhaal*. Amsterdam.

WAGNER, R. (1974) "Coenraad de Buys in Transorangia." University of London Institute of Commonwealth Studies, *Collected Seminar Papers on the Societies of Southern Africa in the 19th and 20th Centuries* 4: 1–7.

_____ (1980) "Zoutpansberg: The Dynamics of a Hunting Frontier, 1848-67." In S. Marks and A. Atmore, ed., *Economy and Society in Pre-Industrial South Africa*. Pp. 313–49. London.

WALKER, E.A. (1934) *The Great Trek*. London.

WALLIS, J.P.R., ed. (1945) *The Matabele Journals of Robert Moffat, 1829–1860*. Two vols. London.

_____, ed. (1946) *The Northern Goldfields Diaries of Thomas Baines: First Journey, 1870–1871*. Two vols. London.

_____, ed. (1953) *The Diaries of Thomas Leask*. London.

WALTON, J. (1952) *Homesteads and Villages of South Africa*. Pretoria.

WAR OFFICE (1881) *Precis of Information concerning the Transvaal Territory*. London.

WATSON, J.L., ed. (1980) *Asian and African Systems of Slavery*. Berkeley.

WATSON, R.L. (1987a) "Religion and Antislavery at the Cape of Good Hope." In N.R. Bennet, ed., *Discovering the African Past*. Pp. 95–107. Boston.

_____ (1987b) "Slavery and Ideology: The South African Case." *International Journal of African Historical Studies* 20, 1: 27–43.

_____ (1990) *The Slave Question: Liberty and Property in South Africa*. Hanover.

WESTRA, P.E. (*) "The Abolition of Slavery at the Cape of Good Hope: Contemporary Publications and Manuscripts in the S.A. Library." *Quarterly Bulletin of the South African Library* 39, 2 (1984): 58–66.

WILMSEN, E. (1989) *Land Filled with Flies: A Political Economy of the Kalahari*. Chicago.

WILSON, D.M. (1901) *Behind the Scenes in the Transvaal*. London.

WILSON, F. and PERROT, D., eds. (1973) *Outlook on a Century: South Africa 1870–1970*. Alice.

WILSON, M. (1969) "The Sotho, Venda, and the Tsonga." In M. Wilson and L. Thompson, ed. *The Oxford History of South Africa, Vol. I South Africa to 1870*. Pp. 131–182. Oxford.

WILSON, M. and THOMPSON, L., ed. (1969) *The Oxford History of South Africa, Vol. I. South Africa to 1870*. Oxford.

WOOD, P. (1975) "More like a Negro country: Demographic Patterns in Colonial South Carolina, 1700–1740." In S. L. Engerman and E. Genovese, ed. *Race and Slavery in the Western Hemisphere: Quantitative Studies*. Pp. 131–72. Princeton.

WORDEN, N. (1982a) "Violence, crime and slavery on Cape farmsteads in the eighteenth century." *Kronos* 5: 43–60.

WORDEN, N. (1992) "Diverging Histories: Slavery and its Aftermath in the Cape Colony and Mauritius." *South African Historical Journal* 27: 3–25.

_____ (1982b) "Rural Slavery in the Western Districts of [the] Cape Colony during the Eighteenth Century." Ph.D. thesis, University of Cambridge, Cambridge.

_____ (1985) *Slavery in Dutch South Africa*. Cambridge.

_____ (1992) "Diverging Histories: Slavery and its Aftermath in the Cape Colony and Mauritius." *South African Historical Journal* 27: 3–25.

WRIGHT, J. and HAMILTON, C. (1989) "Traditions and transformations: the Phongolo-Mzimkhulu region in the late eighteenth and early nineteenth centuries." In A. Duminy and B. Guest, ed. *Natal and Zululand From Earliest Times to 1910*. Pp. 49–82. Pietermaritzburg.

WRIGHT, W. (1831) *Slavery at the Cape of Good Hope*. London (reprint: New York, 1969).

Zimmerman, M. (1967) "The French Slave trade at Moçambique, 1770–1794." M.A. thesis, University of Wisconsin, Madison.

Index

About the Book and Editors

South African slavery differs from slavery practiced in other frontier zones of European settlement in that the settlers enslaved *indigenes* as a supplement to and eventually as a replacement for imported slave labor. On the expanding frontier, Dutch-speaking farmers increasingly met their labor needs by conducting slave raids, arming African slave raiders, and fomenting conflict among African communities. Captives were used as domestics, herders, hunters, agricultural laborers, porters, drivers, personal servants, and artisans. Slavery was legalized as *inboekstelsel* and portrayed by authorities as a form of "apprenticeship," in which abandoned and orphaned youths were bonded as unpaid laborers until their mid-twenties. In practice, they were captured as children and held for most of their lives. At least 60 percent were female. Adults who escaped or were released from bondage became tenant farmers, settled on mission stations and abandoned Boer farms, or entered African communities.

Elizabeth A. Eldredge is associate professor of history at Michigan State University. **Fred Morton** is professor of history at Loras College.